T0374531

"Dawn rises to set in Dusk and Dusk sets in to rise in Dawn".
AN OCEAN OF INFINITE OPPORTUNITIES

D 2 D

"A drop of learning today will be an ocean of wisdom tomorrow".

DAWN to DUSK

An Essay on Humanity

Dr SHREE RAMAN DUBEY

PARTRIDGE

A Penguin Random House Company

To order additional copies of this book, contact
Partridge India
000 800 10062 62
orders.india@partridgepublishing.com

www.partridgepublishing.com/india

Contents

PART I
Dawn

PART II
Today is Mine

Dawn to Dusk
is a gift to my son
Dr Shreeyam Dubey to further
continue my works on humanity.

"Ye who love and serve society for humanity,
Without an ounce of thought of self"

To

You this is inscribed with my unreserved devotion and love.

"Till you pursue your right goal people will say you were foolishly chasing the wrong dreams".

<u>Dr Shree Raman Dubey</u>

Congratulations!

To The Team

DAWN To DUSK

Project Id 637832

Blessed is humanity that a new dawn will witness, "An Essay on Humanity" from the Project Team.

Congratulations to the entire publishing, distribution and marketing team working on Project Id 637832.

I wish to begin with my unending gratitude for all of them directly or indirectly associated with this project of humanity, "DAWN TO DUSK" putting their hearty efforts in making it available in reality by translating the dreams of millions and millions of humans on this lovely planet earth.

It is through this project that I could make new friends Amanda Dayham, Gemma Ramos, Karen Hamilton, Nancy Acevedo, Carla Alvarico, Mario Nielsen, Rey Flores and other dedicated team members of the elegant project, from Partridge Publishers, A Penguin Company.

I will ever remain faithful to you all for making me author of humanity at a time when the World Humans are looking for great teachers on humanity. It is a worthwhile journey with you all to voice the message of regenerating humanity across the globe.

I wish the project team best wishes in the endeavors of understanding humanity.

With Cheers & Happiness

Dr Shree Raman Dubey

Preface

My Dear Cheerful Readers,
Good Dawn to All,

Morning is too late in the day after dawn's twilight.

At the dawn of this New Year I am reaching you all with hopes of resolution for reinventing ourselves to revolutionize the mankind.

In my words, "Man standing at the horizon owns nothing, neither the sea nor the sky. You have to decide either to dive deeper into the sea or to fly higher into the sky to own something in life".

The brightest of the brightest dawn is here today. I wish you all have a wonderful, meaningful, peaceful and valuable day today from dawn to dusk.

Dawn to Dusk is the factual distance between dreams to reality. I pray that my voice for humanity will equally be resonating with you towards the peace of this world from this golden dawn.

I am with great hopes selling only priceless promising dream of humanity today at dawn, but one day, trust me, you all will go beyond the dusk in fulfilling your dreams. I may be addressing more learned readers than me to further magnify my idea of humanity through your intellect to the whole world.

I am writing to more powerful readers than me to voice my idea of humanity through your connectivity and supremacy all over the world. I am confident of my reader's faculty that they will surely ignite the world with their wisdom of humanity.

In short "Dawn to Dusk" can be addressed as "D2D", the nick name the readers may love it easier to spell. This sweet title may be easier to make a place in the preoccupied space of the doubtful mind. I would be happy not much by the name this seed of humanity is going to gain readers but by the fulfillment of purpose it would meet as conceived. Weeks are passing like days. Months are rolling down as days. Years are slipping away as moments. Man is withering away the precious time of existence. Time is running into history. Centuries and centuries have been underutilized to study the real worlds of humans.

I have a dream of humanity for my readers at every dawn this existence will unfold. Will you join this campaign of D2D? I have great faith that all my readers are the future leaders of humanity. I have my strong desires that my courageous readers will become Champions of Humanity.

They shall teach the whole world lessons of humanity. I know my trust shall not be broken by my readers as they are the prime cause for me in reaching them to fulfill the expectations of existence. I have only an idea of humanity to give to you. There may not be any other better wealth than this that humans might have received in this world. Love was not meant to be hidden within the walls of homes.

We all are children of the Universal Home. We have only one culture and religion. We have only ideal, the ideal of humanity and only humanity.

Remind yourself often, "It's better to wear out than rust out". Finally every man has a choice of life. Why we should not be humanitarians? Human mind can be only cleaned by spirituality.

Life reveals truth in phases from dawn to dusk. Without hardships we might never get to this awareness. This may be one of the prime reasons of innocence and ignorance at birth.

In my understanding,

"A drop of learning today will be an ocean of wisdom tomorrow".

All we need is the divine grace as we invariably witness the sun of the old year set in dusk with all the negatives of 2014 and the New Year rises with the dawn of new opportunities for 2015 and beyond and beyond.

"You want to change 9 billion people in world. Have you ever thought that one is immediately available and it is you? If we all change by ourselves it may take only one billionth of a second to transform the entire world."

I believe that the Year 2015 is the dawn of an unprecedented and advantageous period for all of us.

I wish you all well in all respects.
Have a fruitful day of humanity today.
With Faith, Hope & Love
Dr Shree Raman Dubey
Well Wisher of Humanity

Dedication

PRAYER TO HUMANS

"I shall consider myself eternally absolved from a debt of obligation when I have sincerely contributed in serving this divine Earth, which nurtured me to what I could learn today".-Dr Shree Raman Dubey

My dear respected friends let us start by rearranging the words of "EARTH", and see its valuable gift the "HEART".

EARTH is HEART to millions and millions of life in this Universe. Let our heart beat for the mother earth with feeling, kindness, affection, sympathy, compassion, mind, spirit, empathy, gratitude, ideals, morals, wisdom, love, hope, faith and thanks.

Dawn to Dusk is the maiden essay by me reflecting the vision & mission of millions and millions of humans. This will be again a new beginning in reforming ourselves towards uplifting the humanity in the world.

With the believe, faith, hope and trust, that dawn to dusk shall become an indelible voice indispensable in transforming society in times to come, I dedicate this "Dawn to Dusk" as the prime lesson towards the learning of humanity at the feet of society.

I pray to humans with an earnest appeal to interrogate, intervene, analyze, study, introspect, diagnose, explore, the causes of degrading humanity all over the world.

Every man on this earth has a chapter of humanity with him. Every dawn on this earth has a opportunity of humanity with it. Every dusk on this earth has a lesson on humanity for humans to add to their wisdom of living.

What is Humanity?

Of course no doubt you will have as many definitions and conclusions as there are humans on this earth. The power of perceiving is not unique and universal in all of us. We begin with an individual idea on the subject. Both our inner and outer worlds are responsible for defining it.

Why do not you ought first to pause and consider what humanity is? Do not you feel that Humanity is something more than Homo sapiens?

Humanity is, a vast subject of course, many things - most of which I won't be able to mention or illustrate everything here, but living examples of which can be found by everybody throughout from dawn to dusk. It seeks to celebrate humanity's intrinsic nature, potential and creativity in the spirituality, arts, the sciences, genius, meditation, healing, caring, helping, trusting and love.

Why civilization collapses? What is the purpose of all the worldly glory of humans? How to create a more ideal world? How to build a moral world? Don't you think ethnicity should dissolve completely in globalization now?

We are lacking in humanitarian aspirations? We have been equally sharing good and bad both for the sake of humanity.

All is within the man, with the man, between the man, among the man and without the man. The core summary for mankind is continually moving from worldliness to saintliness, from ingenuousness to virtuousness, from blamelessness to sacredness, from negativism to positivism, from evilness to holiness in regenerating humanity.

Finally committing with the dedicated appeal and prayer to all my promising readers, please accept my heartfelt eternal gratitude for your kind willingness towards sincerely joining in rekindling the cause of humanity through dawn to dusk.

Friends, the existence has been sustaining even today despite the evil doers, crime, terrorism, destructions, invasions, imperialism, capitalism, all over the world. What else would you like to review as evidence for the existence of goodness being witnessed from dawn to dusk all over the world?

One and only one good man holds the power to demolish the entire evil of the world. The question is how to become that good from dawn to dusk. And who will do that. Why not you? Why not me? Why not we? Why not us?

Ever yours with happiness
5th August, 2014.
Dr Shree Raman Dubey.
Mahuaon, Bhojpur, Bihar, India.

Acknowledgement

TO
REFORMERS OF HUMANITY

I pray with folded hands to all the reformers of society since the existence of civilization and evolution of humans, to all the scriptures, epics, books, periodicals, articles, journals, lectures, seminars, sermons, gatherings, discourses, contributing to the learning of humanity, and to all the institutions, organizations, committees, groups, nations in upholding the spirit of humanity.

I am thankful to this world, an open book to learn from all walks of life and my heartfelt gratitude to nature and the earth for unfolding new lessons daily for humans.

Dawn to Dusk is an ocean of infinite opportunities.

Think big to achieve big. Live clean to grace divine. Break the prison of ego to design the future of man. The purpose of penning down will be realized even if mere handful of readers takes oath to revolutionize our society to the pursuit of humanity.

"My ideologies may not be in same line as perfectly perceived by you, moreover it is not intended to question your strong belief and culture, and neither have I wished to dominate your valued thinking, nor to impose my infant philosophy, however faithfully I believe that somewhere around the globe the flame of our dedicated work will light the hearts of seekers of humanity".

Dawn to Dusk is a universal idea of humanity. The day in between these ends is looking for ideal means to reestablish the glory of humanity. Dawn to Dusk is an inspiring tool to craft the new face of humanity. Let us all join this race. The earth is a playfield for humans. We all are universal players of humanity. Every player is human and part of humanity. The golden dawn has come to fight the War of Humanity.

With my own realization to share

"When I knew nothing I was challenging the whole world, on knowing something I am learning to understand my world".

Right knowledge can only lead to right realization. Right wisdom can only lead to right living.

The every dusk that has passed is a lesson preparing, developing, training, coaching, leading, guiding and mentoring to capitalize the opportunities and challenges of new dawn and finally with my prayer to life the very existence, an indelible opportunity for realizing the living and the self.

Dr Shree Raman Dubey

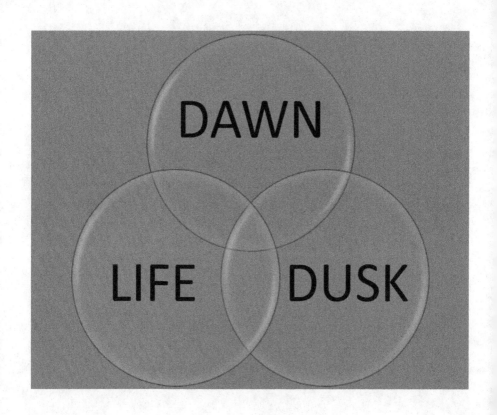

Introduction

DAWN TO DUSK

Dawn to Dusk is saga of life every day.

I faithfully begin this dawn with the promising hopes to my anxious readers that,

"Every dawn to dusk every man in the whole world has finally two chances either to unproductively continue his hypnotized sleep with prolonged dreaming or to promisingly wake up early to chase his inspiring dreams in illuminating humanity".

"Let us impartially commit ourselves to the unfailing resolution for regenerating humanity in the world and consider 2015 to be the "Year of Great Change for Humanity in the history of mankind". It should be the year of learn, teach and practice humanity".

In the words of Benjamin Franklin,

"Tell me and I forget. Teach me and I remember. Involve me and I learn".

Life evolves and dissolves between dawn to dusk involving various faces of humans. Man lives and dies with success and failures between dawn to dusk. The world constructs and destructs itself between dawn to dusk. Man smiles and tears between dawn to dusk. Man feels and peels between dawn to dusk. Man loves and lusts between dawn to dusk.

Dawn to Dusk is indispensable to all.

None can escape this journey between dawn to dusk. The involvement with innovation can bring miracle powers of change. The novelty in humans is as eternal as existence. The infinity is the grace to humans to understand the eternity of humanity.

At the dawn of learning only man can transform his ignorance into wisdom of existence. At the dawn of leading only man can become Champions of Humanity.

Today again is a new promising sunshine with great hopes of better tomorrow. The passing dusk leaves us lessons of reconciliation for improvised understanding of today, passively elapsing into tomorrow. The darkness of dusk is lightened by the brightness of silent moon though it keeps sleeping between crescents to full moon. The pleasantly shinning moon is the beauty of night to be seen in the tranquility of floating dusk.

The life swings like pendulum between dawn and dusk without any fulcrum of equilibrium. All the way journey of realization is between beginning and the end. Every moment is infinitesimally new, by the time we wish to hold, it collapses into the subsequently following, series of new minute capsules of definite time into infinite.

Dawn to Dusk is the saga of all activities with different perspectives in this universe and undoubtedly may be of any other similar galaxies known to mankind. I bow to goddess of learning who has been with me from dawn to dusk in inspiring, mentoring and guiding out this summary of thoughts far and near to the daily living of us. It is her blessings which has manifested into a book for society urging the readers to spread the message of humanity.

Let us give love a chance to bring smile to one and all. If you love a person daily, help a person daily, teach a person daily, bring happiness to a person daily, share with a person daily, play with a person daily, guide a person daily, listen to a person daily, then we can see that we all are being loved, taught, cared, shared, helped, regarded, respected, thus lifting one and all.

The whole day is yours. The complete time can be sliced equally into different areas, people, community, works, thoughts, actions, deeds, and so on.

I positively admit to say, before my readers take the reading of this book **"Dawn to Dusk"**, that it is nothing new which the chapters may reveal but a glance into it may question your intuition as it is written with great hope, unconditional trust, ever ending faith and indelible love for humanity that the intended purpose of sharing will definitely be a beginning to the novelty in living as invariably dusk descends awaiting the promising rising dawn.

Today is the grace of destiny that readers are holding "Dawn to Dusk" in their godly hands. A divine force within me was inspiring to pen down the thoughts which had made their impressions in my mind over the years. It is now that I am trying to assimilate them with my prospective readers, who will pick up this "Dawn to Dusk", only to gain forever in their life.

> **I strongly believe that**
>
> **"A drop of learning today will be an ocean of wisdom tomorrow".**

It began nearly five years ago, when I wrote very exhaustively but was afraid to present it lucidly in compact and comprehendible form, so that the time taken to glance it must not take more than couple of dawn to dusk. Hence, decided to compress it without scarifying the beneficial aspects for the readers.

My objective to methodologically compile and introduce this is to reinvent, rediscover, redefine, retransform, realign and rekindle ourselves. This is an essay with bit of art, science, management, natural lessons, developed strategies, proven principles, rejected postulates, trusted practices, cultural virtues, civilizations findings, and finally from the legacy of wisdom from the kingdom of humans.

It had taken over a year to edit my own writing. I confess to say that some valuable thoughts on the subject might have been lost control of my sight to get it produced here as the content of appreciation by the readers.

Every dawn was giving me new visualization to the subject of this essay. The substance of the subject was getting redefined and refined on every attempt of edition for the welfare of my prospective readers.

15

The more I was visiting this essay the more my attitude and appetite was increasing towards affection for the readers. My inner world strengthened my conscience to work towards justifying the readers once they hold "Dawn to Dusk".

It is hoped that D2D will be at least useful if not instructive to the reader. Therefore with an eye to the public good for universal humanity this is being exported to the world of humans.

I am still not convinced that the essay has been released to the readers. The fever of writing D2D is one thing which I would like to relapse again and again. In fact I was learning humanity by writing on life and trying to understand man on behalf of my lovely humans all over the world.

This writing has inspired me to further personally probe into the subject of humanity. I hope this will equally incite my readers to learn about ourselves in regenerating humanity. We all are inherited stakeholders of humanity. Let us work for the dividends it pays to be human on this earth.

Dawn to Dusk is the result of our deeper interrogation of man on war of humanity. For no fault of us we are humans which every human should realize at the end.

By the time I thought to again have a quick review for bettering D2D it had been released to reach your hands. Unwillingly I had to compromise with time and unhappily with marginal containment because there was more to pour down from my heart, mind, body and soul to all of you, could not hold the separation of D2D from my desk of humanity.

At the last perfection was not my objective and I am happy to see that the main idea of humanity would reach you all.

"Dawn to Dusk" is a seed of humanity.

I believe one day every house will have a tree of humanity in this world.

As we all know perfection is infinite. There is no end to improving anything in this world. This is how we have to work for humanity. There is much and so much to share. Unless the pebble is rubbed for years together you do not discover the diamond it holds.

Human is to be rubbed with realization till the self is enlightened with the light of humanity. All is within us waiting for the golden dawn.

A single essay cannot empty my mind for the love I continue to write for humanity. Time of the readers is also a partial constraint to keep the essay not lengthy. It pains to understand that human in us is dying. We together have to save ourselves, before the Homo Sapiens are lost from this universe forever.

I have neither scientifically nor emotionally anticipated how "Dawn to Dusk" will contribute, but have a deep faith that it might revoke our unwillingness towards betterment of mankind. It hopefully will rekindle the spark of humanity.

The world presently needs more and more teachers of humanity. I stand nowhere near to the great philosophers, researchers, scientists, artists, writers, reformists, philanthropists and humanists this earth has gifted to change the dynamics of existence.

This is as a prime token of acknowledgement to those divine souls who kept contributing towards transforming the dimensions of human life in sustaining the challenges of nature from dawn to dusk. All the happening from dawn to dusk is to renew the man in you. Let us relight the man in us.

Who will revive humanity?

Who will fight the war of humanity?

I truly confess to say from the bottom of my heart, cannot proudly own the content to be solely mine, as they represent the findings in one form or other from observations, lessons, realizations, discourses, and conversations, lectures, witnessed in society from time to time, though at the out most it has attempted to develop a rocketry force to boost the intermittent uninterrupted missions into a vision of man to realize the importance of time in the life of humans.

I firmly believe that had any of my readers taken up the similar subject of humanity they would have written a better book than this. The society needs more and more preachers of humanity primarily than the fancy story telling. There are even better writers than me but this is no where an impediment to voice the pains of humanity. Preaching is to be manifold supported by the practices of humanity.

The problems of humanity are daily new from dawn to dusk. By the time you have resolved one the other one creep in. In fact addressing them all at a time is impossible for anyone from any part of the world.

Life is a weighing balance of problems and solution. The state of equilibrium keeps the fulcrum of life balanced with the pans of problems and solutions. When can man be free of problems? Actually what we see them as problems may not be problem in the real sense. A proper definition on problems and categorization is essential by every individual.

My memories were the inks to the pen which journeyed the essay "Dawn to Dusk". I was writing the ideas of my friends, families, colleagues, strangers, acquaintances, teachers, priests, relatives, whatnot, whenever I paused to read through my lines, I found missed out something more valuable than what I had already scribbled. For the fear of erasing and losing time I continued with the content and style which I feel could have been better in perfection had I gained some time in writing. Nevertheless it is not inferior in driving the essentialities of humanity from dawn to dusk.

My teachers were sources of inspiration right from the day one of my consciousness in school. I would feel school was a better place than home. May be here we are formally tuned to be coming to attain knowledge. Home remains in our memories as place of love, caring and discipline. The innocence is eroded by the time you are likely to graduate. And finally the purity of mind starts depleting with the first employment. There is no career in the world with bit of human politics. Is there any human in the world without a bit of political ethics? The art of people management has its own limitations.

Survival, success, situation, strategy, synergy, solitude, solace, secret, sacrifice, surrender, settlement, scenario, salvation, search, surface, society are the ingredients man is surrounded by for sweet or sour results from dawn to dusk.

My friends Kamesh, Zakir, Nagraj, Meghraj, Joseph, Thomas, Anwar, Roshan, Jain, Abdullah, Tom, Antony, Imran, Zaved, Rao, Murthy, David, Pandey, Dubey, Banerjee, Reddy, Patnayak, Ganga, Siamhachalam, Venkatesh, Manish, Upadhyay, Vikas may not be surprised to read these again which I have been rehearsing in day to day living with them again and again to be branded as philosopher of humanity prior to penning down this memorable thesis.

My family, to start with my son Master Dr Shreeyam who's coming to the world conferred me with the award of Degree of Doctor of Philosophy in Commerce and Management Studies for my research work on, "Energy Crisis in India's Power System Undergoing Reforms and Restructuring". The area of research was promisingly with the bent of mind to contribute in social and national reforms by the power sector in India.

My wife Smt Shobha Dubey (Ph.D) ; courageously stood by me. Her research in Labour Welfare in coalfields regarding the welfare activities is always a source of inspiration to uplift the humanity. Her love for labor is a never ending source for dignity of humanity to me and all our family members. All that I credited myself above would not have been possible without her sacrifices and unconditional support because of my extended occupancy at project sites, research work and this essay.

I was unfortunate to share my completion of this essay with my father-in-law Late Sri Tarak Nath Mishra because of his sudden demise. I am fortunate to have learnt the lessons of honesty and simplicity from his living. His separation during this time was difficult to accommodate but his teachings were strength to rise again to the forefront to face the challenges from dawn to dusk. His divine nature continues to grace all of us.

Time was not in our favor to rest in peace. It was not even a year that my elder mother passed away bringing the pains of memories embedded with nectar of love. She was personification of hospitality. No one ever returned without having a sweet and glass of water from our home. I learnt the sacrifices of mothers from her. Either it was summer or winter she would be the last one to go to bed after all had slept.

No doubt separation is a natural process in the cycle of life. But it really cannot be separated from the minds of humans. It is a perennial weakness which gives emotional strength to understand the love of humans to each other.

"Dubey Tolla", our divine living place, as we are identified at Mahuaon Village, probably the name from the sweet fruit it is surrounded with, has witnessed in its history many celebrations with huge gatherings of families, friends, relatives, cousins, nears and dears, reflecting the love and affection among the undivided spirits of family members even today in recession of true relationships. I wish this legacy brands us all over the existence.

I was blessed to have played with my cousins in the orchids of mango groves in hot summers cherishing the sweetness of brotherhood.

My cousins Lalitha, Chibu, Anita, Munny, Savita, Alok, Kamal, Ruby and many more continue to share with our new generations for understanding the humanity in family relationship.

An individual's value is built up from the family only. In this there is no second opinion on my endless gains from the unified members of the family.

My brother-in-law, Dr Amar Nath Mishra being a Professor who voluntarily takes responsibility to educate the whole society, a dedicated patriot of the nation, and the bit of social welfare which I picked into my daily livings from his grand arena of reformists. Irrespective of the expectations of returns he gives whatever he can to uplift the needy.

If you want to know the effective utilization of resources and time, nursing and knowledge sharing then Dr Asutosh Upadhyay stands next to none. He is a doctor prescribing smiles by his touch of humanity. He is husband to Dr Nishi, my young sister has become bold pathologist today to test the bloods of patients seeking medication. The feeblest of the feeble love to visit her diagnostic centre to hear her sweet advises and experience hearty reception and spiritual counseling.

My sister's father-in-law Sri V.N.Upadhyay who served the Indian Power Sector never misses an opportunity to help the near and dears associated with him. His philanthropist ideologies for the community and society keeps inspiring me to follow the humanitarian Leadership style he implements with enthusiasm from dawn to dusk.

Ms Vibha Mishra my sister-in-law blessed with a divine soul spreads love and humanity with all she is associated. My sister's sweet daughters Ayushi and Misthi inspired me with their regular follow ups on importance of family relationship, parents and relatives were at their patience to see it has been completed at the earliest so that I could give more time again to the mainstream of life.

The task was difficult but not impossible. A little pain to family for the world gain is sweeter taste not to be denied by anyone.

My focus was to write with values for the readers. They should be the real beneficiary of the values represented here again for the reinstatement of humanity. May be I am one of the manifestations to build a huge team of reformers all over the world. The incarnation is needed very badly to realign our thoughts and outlook of society from dawn to dusk.

Let me introduce Sri Ram Bachan Dubey, my respected elder father who would teach us without a classroom in the holidays of summer and winter with the twinkling light of the lantern in the darkness of the village and before the twilight of the dawn would break out from the night, we would awake having our lessons again with him. This became over the years our deeply rooted culture for learning, education and time of concentration. The tranquility of these moments still vibrates in all of us.

I owe my spiritual inclination to my grandfather Late Sri Baidyanath Dubey who made me accompany him to pray the goddess of existence right from the days of infancy. His art of living was filled with generosity. He would leave his eating meals to serve the people from nearby villages and towns who visited him. I learnt to love animals from him. He was so caring that the pets would refuse to eat if he was out of station and food was not served by him. It was a great experience to realize that animals also cry wetting their eyes with tears for their lovers. Above all his simplicity reminds me of the style of pious living even in scarcity of times and before I could miss him in life his sense of telepathy about our wellness, healthiness, happiness and living in those days of almost poor communication infrastructure. He was an unbeatable leader of the united joint family meeting the needs of one and all which the society is longing today. He showers his love to one and all from dawn to dusk.

What else could have been a better title than "DAWN to DUSK ", in the above background?

These lessons learnt at dusk have become the fundamental principles of one and all in our family today. Every evening we waited his arrival as the sun was setting down. We were prepared to receive his lessons right from English grammar, history, science, Sanskrit, mathematics to geography. I hope we were graced to have him as our natural teacher without books and blackboards. His style of teaching I still could not see elsewhere even till the award of my Doctorate in Philosophy. This once more emphasizes the recalling of old saying leaders are born not made.

Can we cultivate charisma?

He had equally taken the responsibility and struggled to make my father Sri Kashi Nath Dubey, a very good Civil Engineer, who went on building great projects of national importance in India, before his retirement at the position of Chief Vigilance Officer of a public sector undertaking. I regard his loyalty which has become our legacy. This was not an end there were my cousins Dwarika an equally good Civil Engineer, Dr Akhilesh Dubey took up medicine to become a Doctor, Bimal in Projects, Nawal a successful C.A,

Varun an Electrical Engineer, and many others ended up well established in life.

My mother Smt S.P.Dubey accompanied me during my kindergarten to primary schooling enjoying daily commutation through local trains in the busy hustle of Howrah Railway Station, Calcutta. This place at the bank of holy river Ganga gave the royal look of The British Empire Rule with its buildings standing along, in and around the main markets of Badabazzar despite the flurrying of Indian flag signifying the freedom of humanity.

This is a city of world heritage which was once the seat of Royals. It speaks of the freedom of Hindustan from the foreign rule. Calcutta besides being the trading centre had been the centre of many revolutionary activities in the history of India. The land has its own fortune to shape your life from dawn to dusk. There was lot for me to pick from this busy life. The daily movement and struggle for survival in all walks of life was a good learning platform for me in early years.

The cosmopolitan culture with literary influence of Noble Laureate Sri Rabindranath Tagore charms the city with his poems from the collection "Gitanjali". It brings great life to it dignifying the dignity of labour in the background of eastern philosophy. Perhaps this is the land which tried to race with the western philosophy.

Not far from the main city of Calcutta, the Dakhineswar Temple of Maa Kali, at the bank of Ganga brings alive the life of very recent saint Sri Rama Krishna Paramahansa, who built a strong disciple Sri Swami Vivekananda to storm the World Parliament of Religions at Chicago. He made known to the world that eastern philosophy is unique in its pursuit of humanity comparing it to the western philosophy.

Children love their maternal uncle the most is universal truth anywhere in the world. In Hindi language mother is much known as "MAA" and the maternal uncle is called by the relationship "MAAMAA". Most of my Indian readers are familiar with this. However, the readers can understand the importance of MAAMAA in their lives that has been a very important part of our family relationships since we jumped in his laps to enjoy our freedom of childhood.

I too have a story of childhood with my respected maamaa Sri Jaykant Pandey who would without tiredness keep commuting me from my father's home to his home number of times in a day connected by a road which people say was built by the great Indian Emperor Asoka The Great. . It never mattered to him the time at dawn and dusk. No sooner I would reach one of the homes my longing could not be more than an hour to rush to the other home to know their wellness. This is the natural mischief of my infancy to embrace the love, affection, hospitality, caring, blessing and grace of both the members of the homes.

Such was my love for both the homes. I learnt the lessons of hospitality, service, sacrifices and caring from my mother's mother and still from my maamaa. I bring here another elder maamaa, a great teacher Sri Rama Kant Pandey who has contributed by his simple teachings and living wisdom in developing great leaders in society. A man of humanity the society likes to witness their celebrations, joys, sorrows and crisis at any point of time from dawn to dusk with him. A humanist the village and the society are proud to be blessed by his unselfish contribution from dawn to dusk.

Villages even today remain the seat of cultures, virtues, values, patriotism, sacrifices, ideals, trust, faith, love and affection for any civilization in the world. The fundamentals of family are very deeply rooted in the bliss of existence in villages of humans. Villages reflect the inner innocence of humans. Towns and cities somehow are trying to maintain their ego of development and smartness with an identity of advancement and modern living from dawn to dusk.

There are many more in relations and acquaintances who are champions of their destiny obeying the laws of humanity despite the formal recognitions and applauses. What matters to them is that there is nothing above humanity?

There are millions and millions of such homes in the world holding the spirit of humanity. Dawn to Dusk is a project to integrate such homes to build a world of mammoth humanity.

We are blessed to be son of this land. He taught us the true meaning of secularism and way to liberation through humanity. They were born leaders of humanity. Their purpose in life was to learn, teach, preach, act, voice, share, spread, built, only humanity and humanity. They wanted seeds of humanity to be sown in the barren fields of man's life.

A mango tree gives mango not grapes. Good cultures will give good humans. A good idea will nurture good dream. A good thought will go into good action. Good faiths are bearing divine humans. Because you can see the moon and sun you speak of only sun and moon. This is human's limitations. We have practiced certain rituals so we doubt the others which are in vogue somewhere else. They are in existence for the same universal purpose. Unless you know the truth of truthfulness the learning of yourself has not reached perfection of existence. The existence is infinite and hence is the learning and perfection.

The world is moving so is the universe and over all the existence. The new findings, the new postulates, the new beliefs, the new faiths, the new wisdoms, the new purposes, the new ideas, the new concepts, the new minds, the new brains, the new livings, all new order will be coming and going in this existence.

What remains to all of us is the present. The present is the seat of man. The present is the seat of wisdom. The present is the seat of human. Seeing is like believing has been man's legacy of weakness.

Knowledge is the tool which dissolves the doubts of existence.

Why Man is a doubter of his own existence? There are many things which man does not witness in his life time. We learn from the past. Had I been born in Mecca I would have known Prophet Mohammad more, his teachings deeper from Koran, his ideas better, his emotions and love internally intensified, for the humans? Had I been born in Jerusalem I would have learnt more from the Bible of Jesus, "Father be in heaven, holy be your name, thy kingdom comes, thy shall be done, forgive us for our sins since we forgive them who sin against us".

My birth was not in my hands. God decided to send me to learn the teachings of Lord Krishna and Lord Rama. He had his purpose to be fulfilled through me. So being here I have been chanting their verses. And again the teachings of Koran and Bible which overlap here and there are equally being practiced to the tune of Gita, Vedanta, Upanishads and Ramayana. All have the central message of humanity. When all are born from the same source how they can be different to each other? When all lands are born from the same mother earth and same universe how they can be different to each other? Similarly take the sea, oceans, rivers, ponds, lakes all are from the same source.

Is the color of water orange? Is not the grass of the world green? Do the leaves of trees in America are blue? Does the grass in Egypt is red? Does the water in Arabia is pink? Does the tomato in New Zealand is black? Why the color of milk all over the world is white? Does the cat in Greece barks? Which part of the world the blood of man is not red? The more nearer you are to pure basics of life from dawn to dusk the clarity in life is revealed.

We all are one. The world is one. The vision is one. The mission is one. The religion is one. The culture is one. The perception is one. The mind is one. The body is one. The heart is one. The thought is one. The life is one. The man is one. The human is one. The universe is one.

Oneness is universality.

Love is universality. Man is universality. Human is universality. History interferes in our beliefs, faiths, trust, perception, and understanding of theories, philosophies, theology, practices, thus creating the urge to doubt all and then work on the individual hypothesis with individual reasoning.

Man examines his intellect in the background of his wisdom. The inner world struggles with the outer world from dawn to dusk.

Every new dawn is a challenge and opportunity for man. My readers too have to throw light on the following, "Is humanity for life?" Or "Life is for humanity?" A similar conceptualism like the chicken or the eggs, the seed or the fruit, the heart or the mind, the life or the death, the earth or the sun, the world or the man, the nature or the universe. Which is first and which is second? And still no answers to the world.

Hindustan has been home for many cultures from the world. It might have been God's destiny to unit all through secularism. God is working with his mission. Man is working with his intellect. Nature is working with its love. Universe has the power to unify the globe. There are similar cities in India and World with various cultures being practiced for years and years. They all are towards unification of humans towards universal humanity.

I have described the above to understand that once you become learned you have to take up the leadership to shape others. It does not matter the resources you own provided you have the main aim, zeal and spirit to do something for mankind. And what can be a better place than your home, your own village, your own town, your own city, your own nation, and your own earth.

I have heard from my distant relatives and neighbors from far and near villages that as Head Post Master, he would find time to pen down letters of joys, happiness, sorrows, news, invitations, who ever approached him with proper dictation and even read the telegraph/telegram messages and letters to them. There is much to learn from him. It is rightly said that the busiest man has all the time in the world.

I believe there are such great heroes in every family throughout the world. Those days I was studying at St. Thomas Church School, Howrah, in Calcutta, and was sometimes worried to understand that my elder father with his simple wisdom and intellect would cover all the assignments of English grammar with ease where as the teachers at school stumbled to get them right in one go. He never looked for resources. His lessons were his learning's. His learning's were his teachings. He knew actually what we needed today. He believed to benefit from today's dawn.

The knowledge is open to all. Man has to incite himself to gain it. The point what I wish to drive here is that learning does not essentially need an infrastructure, it requires quality teachers who can fill the mind of students. An academic degree is not what is meant by education. A digital classroom in modern times speaks of the advancement of technology only rather than in reality about the evolution of human wisdom in humanity. Is technology unable to enrich the human mind with humanity? The sophistication of our brains is unanswerable to the queries of humanity.

From the lanes of my memory a very remarkable and pleasurable moment without which I may not be justifying the youth of the world. My brother in law Dr Amar Nath Mishra, who is presently Asst. Professor at Department of Polymer Engineering in Birla Institute of Technology, Ranchi, and my wife Smt Shobha Dubey, associated with the Department of Management, happened to invite me to witness the convocation ceremony of the Institute. My happiness had no bounds when I came to know that it will be presided over by the Ex-President of India, Sri A PJ Abdul Kalam.

To me he appeared as the Professor of Inspiration rather than the Chief Guest of the celebrations. The vibrating gallery of students welcomed him as a friend as if he was known to all of them. He is admirably the personification of simplicity, greatest reformer of society and above all a sincere teacher of the youths, the mother India has produced. This is very much evident from the rising responses of youths of India.

He has galvanized them to stay strong against corrosive forces of society. The recent book "Forge Your Future" written by him goes beyond admiration to the cause he has penned and published. It is not a mere collection of enquiries and replies but is the dreams of millions of youth in India and the

World. Sir is working more after relinquishing the post of State Head and the title of first citizen of India.

Many have contributed with their resources, family and learning. This is how the whole process of learning and living is simultaneously being experienced all over the world. Either it is Grand Pa, or Granny, your Aunt, Uncle, Parents, Teachers, Friends, Relatives, Colleagues; there is something for all of us among, and in between us and the nature. The society has taken years and years to evolve.

Was evolution to see this face of humanity today? Why humans are allowing themselves to diligently become undignified? Mankind has lost all its legacy of kindness. Compassion and harmony are rarely been seen in societies of today. We have created a world of chaos with our intellectuality and wisdom. The brains are draining their ideas in uprooting humanity from dawn to dusk.

Are we living to cherish all these inhumanity? Who will end these atrocities? How to transform cruelness into kindness? How to move from mistakes to maturity of morality? Man has to consistently work and work till he becomes human of heart fullness.

I believe as Rome was not built in a day so is, "Humanity is a legacy of existence, civilizations and generations".

The truth is no man can blame a single man for loss of humanity. The good men should question the reason for badness of the remaining. Why we are losing our worthiness as humans?

Humanity is dying is being witnessed by all.

I worked with British, French, Germans, Japanese, Chinese, Russians, Arabians, Americans, Iranians, and many more in this list during execution of projects in India. I had the grace to be associated with few of the giant Corporate like IBM, Hitachi, Mitsubishi, Alstom, Siemens, Armco, Rolls-Royce, Bechtel, Shell, for the technological coloration, consultancy services and supplies needed for the projects. We would work as a team with no barriers of race, caste, culture, habits, religion, traditions, languages, without sacrificing the dignity of labor.

Thus daily I would cultivate a deep concern for the team members, staff, our workmen and all who ever were associated in the construction project. This is what I saw my other fellow beings also doing. We were a community living for humanity. I had been heading the HSE (Health, Safety and Environment) at some of the project sites in addition to my functional assignments. It was a great opportunity to understand the various organizational cultures and values. Our engineering fraternity reflects the importance of dignity of humanity.

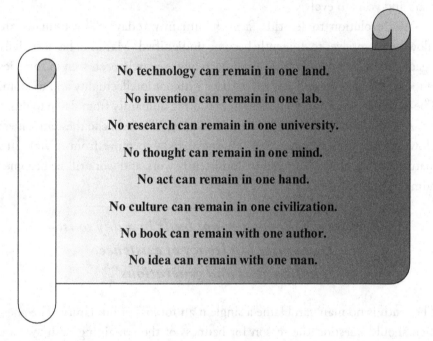

No technology can remain in one land.

No invention can remain in one lab.

No research can remain in one university.

No thought can remain in one mind.

No act can remain in one hand.

No culture can remain in one civilization.

No book can remain with one author.

No idea can remain with one man.

It has to flood the whole world. It will fill the air of the world. This is the law of nature. Nothing is yours. It is for the mankind of the world.

Industrialization has brought in scientific revolution in humanity across the world. Though it is hard on the efficiency and effectiveness it is soft on the welfare of humanity. In addition to the central and state organizations there are private organizations in India like TATA, Birla, Jindal, Reliance, Hinduja, Adani, Infosys, who are giants with philanthropy values for society and the country. They have separate foundations serving the humanity.

Industrialization after the green revolution has changed the face of humanity all over the world. Humanity was linked to the scientific principles of labor management and human resources. It was a new definition to the outlook of humanity. A complete cultural transformation took place revolutionizing the entire society from 1850 to 1950. The impact in the underdeveloped nations was felt till the recent last decades of the setting century.

The above was one part related to the standards of living, comforts, luxuries, entertainment, clubs, social welfares, well being, parties, groups, and communities, all reflecting some signs of innovation in humans.

People start to compete with machines from dawn to dusk. The virgin lands of nature with the green landscapes were ravaged to smoke the environment where humans were breathing fresh air. The beauty of the sunset is dulled by the smokes of the chimneys rising high to demonstrate the human feat of industrialization. The modernization brought their cousins power and politics in society.

Man became machine and the emotions of love, affection, admiration, kindness, compassion; gratification slowly was lost in the shadow of performance and professionalism. The impact of emerging cultures cannot be taken lightly in the background of studying humanity.

The other part has remained till today. That is the bifurcation of "LABOURS and OFFICERS" in the industrial sector. This division continues to disturb the society even today from dawn to dusk. This is a subject to be mastered far beyond industrial relations and management of human capital.

Is human only a resource in this world? Welfare is only for the sake of business. I need my readers to participate at the global platform to enrich your learning on humanity from dawn to dusk. A continual approach is only the way to understand the mantra of humanity. Only by reading a book now and then may not be sufficient unless you are working with the ideas and philosophies of the author.

Organizations are reflection of humans. Organization is power. Organization is a culture. The professional Man spends more than fifty percent of his time from dawn to dusk in organizational homes. Its impact on humans cannot be neglected in the emerging economies of the world.

All giant Corporate are examples of excellent leadership with philosophy of humanity. They have proved to the world that business does not only mean profit but it up lifts the humanity in totality. The above is to address the point that either it is home, school, business, government, institution, organizations, corporate, society or any other establishment of people all over the world the ultimate purpose of any activity is to look towards the betterment of mankind from dawn to dusk.

My dear readers it was not only for the sake of writing that I wrote it, a greater force and regret was springing in me for not coming forward to share these valuable lessons of life learnt, experienced, heard, narrated, observed, discussed, analyzed, for the betterment of society.

I strongly say that you all have equally great experiences from dawn to dusk either small or big. Take some time to share it, pen down, narrate it, voice it, debate it, by doing so the concern for all of us is regenerated, rekindled, realigned, reminded, and the relationships gets better and better. Utilize such inspiring moments, moments of motivation, institutional awareness, awakening of the mind, intellect, to transform the humanity.

The presentation of the chapters has followed a style to facilitate freedom to the readers for their analysis. The literature specifically covered is for their usefulness in enriching their process of understanding the importance of dawn to dusk. They can apply the best mathematical tools to empirically derive at the submission of their suggestions.

However, it may be, by any means or form, my present concern that the issue is alive to transform the living from dawn to dusk keeps moving every dawn, that it invades the existence day by day. This is the core purpose of this published thesis.

Dreams, desires, demands, are to be mapped to supply, search, research, findings, explorations, inventions, discoveries, innovations, queries, quests, doubts, and so on from dawn to dusk. Man at earth is trying to explore existence at mars. May be mars will be our next destination and home to millions and millions of future humans. Humans of the past who were heroes for the brief history of time one fine dawn may not be surprised or shocked to know a planet has been discovered to sustain life.

Finally, I take the opportunity to translate my views to you through this essay, near to a book "Dawn to Dusk". The principle idea behind it is to apprise while questioning, to visualize beyond by retrospections, marching ahead by retrograding, implementation by retroacting to have perspectives in unearthing the uncanny of life, which we take for granted today. The mystery of the self is mysterious than the anonymous journey of life. It is what each of us has been bothered to solve from dawn to dusk. Most of us have become the pots calling the kettle back.

Today we have hardly few salt of the earth. Let us be not the scum of the earth. We all know there is no royal road to learning. There is more than one way to skin a cat.

I shall never stop dreaming till my last breath to see that, "Dawn to Dusk shall remain as one of the promising tools of times initiated to bring in transformation of lives through the short essay on humanity on this earth".

It will keep floating now and then in the hands of young, old, weak, strong, leaders, followers, preachers, teachers, students, and many more as optimist readers becoming dynamic leaders of humanity.

Any man holding Dawn to Dusk should at least once feel the necessity of mankind in society. Society is unexpectedly getting the blows of man's duality. It should raise your motivation to work consistently for saving humanity. It is with a heart full of love, gratitude, hope, faith and trust that I take up my body, soul and mind to write to you.

Friends you have a combination of feelings, knowledge, potentials, energy and willingness to bring ideas into realized forms from dawn to dusk.

Wake up, wake up, wake up, this is the first step to be taken and huge things grow out of small undertakings. Our society has been doing well but now is the time to do better, better and better. Unity is before creation, diversity is creation. Now if this diversity stops, creation will be destroyed. When it ceases or is stopped from breeding varieties, it dies.

Human is bound to produce immense variety or else it must die. Varity does not mean inequality or any special privilege. The practice of solitude is to allow the germination of divine thoughts which is necessary to harvest humanity all over the world. Do you think only by absolutions can man become free from his sins?

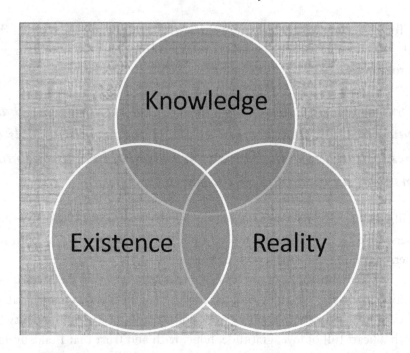

What is the use of the penance when there is no time left with you? Whatever you could know through existence sooner or later will be withdrawn from you? Reality to will not be with you. You will have no real existence. Your living will only be a history. The remains of you if you have worked, performed, voiced, inspired, shared, given, taught, sacrificed, may be recollected to remember you.

It may sound unpleasant but this is reality. Please try to understand the overlapping of knowledge, reality and existence. Only by the study of the skeleton and bone you cannot comprehend man in totality. Osteology has its own limitations. The fraternity of medicine is struggling to make man immortal. The undying hopes are fueled now and then by the department of astrology and palmistry. God gave man his hands and the lines on them to decide his destiny. When the sphere of man joins the knowledge, reality and existence he is bound to be under the influence of mystery.

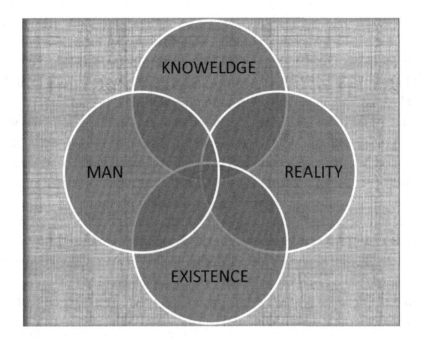

Every man has a unique current of life. Find your mission and vision to move towards your aim and goals from dawn to dusk. Compete with your potential within not compare with the other man. Monitor your betterment not waste time on analyzing the trend of another man.

Always remember true sacrifice cannot be seen. It only works in the hearts of humans. Heartless humans do not understand the rhythm of existence and love of nature. The bliss is in all of us.

Human shall work incessantly until they die, and ever after death they shall work for the good of the world. Truth is more infinitely weightier than untruth, so is goodness. If man possesses these, they will make their way by sheer gravity.

Dawn will give you a deeper and deeper insight everyday into character, purity and truth. Life is too short to be spent in talking. Work, work, work beyond the dusk. There is too much talk, talk, talk only talk in the world. In this short life there is no time for the exchange of compliments and getting the admiration of the world when the real work has not been finished.

Man is yet battling out the man in him. There is nothing in the name; it is ideas that are to be realized. Each is an individual, yet all are one at the axis of existence. Nature, body, matter, moves on creating the illusion that the soul is moving. Is misery natural? Or Man has created it? Can man remove it?

As mud cannot wash away mud, misery cannot wash away misery. No great work can be achieved by humbug. Manifest your manhood. Give up the desire for name, fame, power and the ego in you will get demolished forever and forever. Hold on to purity, patience and perseverance from dawn to dusk.

Happiness is something which cannot be borrowed, begged, robbed and bought. It has to be created in your mind and this can happen if you only understand your mind. Why it is that because of the stick of chastisement that our society remains within bounds? The freedom of mind is to be controlled by wisdom of life. What use is of education if at the end it fails to build character in humans? What use is of literacy if it cannot address the inequality in society?

Man in society is working against the ideals of society. What are the ideals of society? Why the man in society is unable to sacrifice his individuality? Who will arrest the drift between ideology of individual man and the philosophy of grouped society? Are you waiting for the idea to be born? Why I cannot go beyond the bondage of society? It is these steps which are always difficult in one's life. After that all is history of the man.

Unwillingness is a mania in all of us to take the first few steps of change.

Society is a battle ground of evils not the breeding place of devils.

Unification of ideas should centralize the wisdom of humanity. Why Man is disorganizing his way of living to support the chaos in the world? And in addition to it the fruits of leveraging being shamelessly enjoyed by the politics of power from dawn to dusk. Defaming the divinity of humans for the mere marginal unethical gains of few speaks of the inhumanity in us.

What do you know about your own mind? What do you know about any other mind? We have been bed ridden for years and years together in our mind unable to see the light of the self within us from dawn to dusk. We remain there to experience poverty, failure, misery, unhappiness, worries, anxieties, sorrows, grief, pain, disquiet, arrogance, insanity and so on a very infinite list of unwanted worldly pleasures. Is the way to god directed opposite to that of the world? How to remain same under all circumstances?

Can man unravel his own mystery?

God and Man are no two separate destinations. They are neither two journeys apart. A sincere thought on this should provoke mankind to work towards regenerating humanity of that excellence.

Man should inflame himself to burn all the jungle of evils in the world. The society is lacking the aggressiveness to eradicate the thought of terror in mind. Fear of terror should be buried forever. The root of all miseries is the human mind. Mind at dawn should be filled with the vigor of happiness. The mind at dusk should be satisfied with the fulfillment of the day's activities.

Either it is Hong Kong of China, Tokyo of Japan, London of England, New York of America, Perth of Australia, Rome of Greece, Paris of France, Berlin of Germany, Moscow of Russia, Kuwait of Saudi Arabia, Seoul of Korea, Calcutta of India, Colombo of Sri Lanka, Islamabad of Pakistan, every where the philosophy of necessity is more or less the same for humans as they are fighting the prime cause of humanity through means right or wrong. The core issue is universal from dawn to dusk.

What are the evils of the world from dawn to dusk? Man has to become harbinger of peace globally. Man has to work his best. If there is any seed of truth for regeneration of humanity in it, it will come to life. So man should not have any anxiety about anything. The greatest work is purification of the soul to make it fit for the true knowledge. Will the soul find its freedom?

Man is a born idealist.

He should owe everything what he has in this world to the existence. The whole life is a succession of dreams, thoughts, ideas, innovations, inventions, discoveries, explorations, manifestations, believes, findings, so on and so forth. World is now very much informative than earlier world of Stone Age. The Stone Age to Cyber Age has seen man transform from survival to luxury standards of living. Though the outer world looks extremely luxurious yet it reflects a big void. This voidness, emptiness, hollowness, restlessness, points towards the man's inner world.

HUMAN

HEALTHY

HARMONY

HAPPY

HUMANITY

Man has not learnt farming of his life.

He is unable to get the desired yields. The crop of knowledge is to be successfully harvested. Knowledge has the power to absorb you. All is in you. Just as the tree shades away its leaves during the season so is the man's ego in cycle of life. It drops and sprouts to be dropped again and again, it goes on till the end. The man is as eternal as nature.

My readers before I sum up the introduction have a thorough look at the 5 H's. The sphere of humanity can only enlarge to the outer orbit from the central nucleus of human if man is in healthiness, harmony and happiness.

I understand from dawn to dusk that human is certainly part of humanity and it is eternal in existence.

Time is the greatest wealth for all humans anywhere in the world. No human can purchase time. The wealthiest, the powerful, the dynamic, the emperor, the king, the ministers, all at the helm of power cannot buy time and create time. Can you buy time? Can any human fix a price for time? It is an impossible proposition all together. No we cannot manipulate time at any level.

What can be important than time to human? With this background and awareness human should value time from dawn to dusk. What percentage of it will be utilized in developing humanity? Every activity you do should be linked to the welfare of mankind.

How many of us know the following days and why the celebrations are made as stated in the table below?

Day	Celebration	Purpose
14th February	Valentine's Day	Understand the feeling of love
20th March	International Day of Happiness	Happiness in World
8th March	International Women's Day	Importance of Women
7th April	World Health Day	Healthy World
22nd April	Earth Day	Energy on Earth
10th May	Mother's Day	Recognizing Mother
15th May	International Day of Families	Importance of Family
21st June	Father's Day	Importance of Father
17th July	World Day for International Justice	Justice for Humans
19th August	World Humanitarian Day	World Humanity
12th August	International Youth Day	Youth's of the World
21st September	International Day of Peace	World Peace
5th October	World Teacher's Day	Importance of Teacher
9th October	National Student Day	Student

12th October	Thanks Giving Day	To recognize for thanking the person who has helped in need
15th November	National Philanthropy Day	Love for mankind
20th November	Universal Children's Day	Love for children
16th November	International Day of Tolerance	Importance of Non-violence
25th November	International Day for the elimination of violence against women	Protecting rights of women/ security
5th December	International Volunteer Day	To do by SELF
10th December	Human Rights Day	To protect rights of humans
6th February	International Day against Female Genital Mutilation	Regard to Female

Every dawn is a celebrating day. Humans have to pick it up. If you pick the seeds of happiness you shall get the fruits of happiness forever in your life. If you pick up the seeds of cruelty you shall get the fruits of inhumanity forever in your life.

Human is as the seed he sows.

There is nothing like true reconciliation gain in life when you have selected the wrong seed in the beginning of your life's dawn. It is always wisdom to persist with the sweet pain of destiny initially if you're determined to reach a destination of purpose from dawn to dusk.

The days should not be useless dots in your life. The secret of knowing the life is in the exploration of the days.

Every month there may be days marked for one or the other celebrations. Just as we celebrate our personal days of birth, death, graduated, married, anniversaries, and so on the above days are important in developing a society and the individuals.

I feel our basic problem is, "We have the concern but not the commitment". This is what the prime-facie is for the unbecoming of society rapidly in the second half of the last century.

I wish my readers were busy throughout the 365 days celebrating all the days either this way or that way, directly or indirectly associated with the core of humanity.

The need of the hour ever in the history of humanity is to reestablish the touch of humans. A harmonious culture of humanity should be the reflection of the human world.

With great faith in my optimistic readers I wish to share that, "Perfection can only come to humans if humans are sincerely willing to work selflessly in this world".

Every human can be an idealist of humanity. Humanity is human product. It is how humans manufacture it from dawn to dusk. It is outcome of the actions and reactions of the life process from dawn to dusk.

We live in a world penny wise pound foolish.

Before I conclude my introduction please make a note that, "Dawn to Dusk is like the bow and arrow. Dawn is the bow from which infinite opportunities as living arrows is sent forth for the humans to understand humanity in existence."

Will the Dawn of Humanity reach all humans before the Dusk?

PART I
DAWN

Chapter I

DAWN IS LIFE

"Dawn is Life for the entire existence."

The Bhagavad Gita says,

"Verily none can remain, even for a moment without performing action."

It is universally accepted that activity is the sign of life.

The moment action ceases existence becomes still.

Existence awakes with the freshness of life at dawn. Every dawn is a new life. It undergoes regeneration after dusk daily to bloom with the tenderness touch of evolution. Once more the day begins to justify our lives. It brings in desired turbulence to the tranquility of your dreams which you were holding till the dawn.

The mind awakes to feel the vibration in you. The hands are ready to take the day. The feet are opening up to run the day. It is time, time for action all around the world. The world is becoming alive at the stroke of dawn.

As dawn befalls life begins into action. The sunshine graces the existence. Nature springs into action. Man waits to be blessed with the unfolding of the nature. Are you looking for a golden dawn? If yes, then this dawn of change is yours. Grab it before the thought of changing loses the intensity of humanity.

Every day man is new. Man in me does not remain same at all dawns. The dawn brings different thoughts to the same existence in the same man. An idea evaporates before it is tasted. It diffuses without the fragrance of harmony.

Man struggles between his beliefs of uncertainties. Man fails to capitalize dawn due to lack of openness towards other man. The dawn in ideal perception is yet striving to rise above the horizon. Ignorance at every moment is dusking the opportunities at dawn.

Dawn is the time to live your nest of edginess. Man should thank SUN for burning himself to save us. Man should thank MOON for beautifying the darkness of night. Man should thank plants and trees for sacrificing their life for us. Trees live to support man and animal existence in nature. Man should thank all the living creatures helping us to live and sustain our lives in this world for some time.

Can we imagine Man's Life without plant and animal? Can we imagine life without nature? We get all from the Mother Nature and finally Man's Life without Man? Every dawn is an opportunity to go inner layer by layer into our understanding of the universal humanity.

We should not be surprised to know that hardly we give anything to the nature in the true sense? In fact all our activities right from dawn to dusk are supported by the nature. Means and ends are very well from the nature. The Creator has sufficiently arranged it for all the living beings.

Principally man does nothing for another man. Can man grace another man? Man can only serve another man. So do not frown with the useless tail of ego which you are not shading it away thinking that it will crown you one day. We live in a world not owned by any single man. It is my narrowness to live in garbage of inhumanity. I am unable to educate, tame, train, learn and earn the values of human at dawns.

Man is unable to differentiate between sunrise and sunset. Daily the sun in us is setting away without the glow of sunshine. Man should absorb the warmth of rays of humanity from dawn to dusk. Who would not like to be a Golden Man?

Nature is the greatest dawn that existence has witnessed followed by man. World is a toy for man to play from dawn to dusk. Man has been chained by the creature to understand the very mystery of existence.

Daily start at the dawn to demolish your doubts, discrepancies, dependencies, difficulties, disturbances, distractions, destructions, evils, ego, cruelty, enmity, hastiness, jealousy, sadness, weakness, fear, etc. Anything which occupies your mind with negativity is to be transformed into positivity. This just cannot happen with passivity in living.

What use is all the transformation towards goodness when you would have lived your entire life in badness? Hence timely action now leaves you at the end to remain with memoirs of humanity. It finally becomes your inertia for the rest of your life.

Life begins at dawn.
Dawn is window to the world.

Why you are worrying when today is in your hands? Man still is at the dawn of history. Has the evolution lost its momentum? Why human is struggling with the origin of human race? This is the golden dawn. Do not think when to act.

Come in action now. It is instantly happening. The mind and body cannot be at rest for long time. Action is to be performed. It is secondary to categorize either right or wrong. But be in the existence to experience it moment by moment. By the time you decide, the valuable time in the process of deciding has been lost forever. Half of the early hours of the day are lost in deciding what to do.

Every moment has a golden touch.

The astrologers have survived by victimizing humans with the fear of superstition beliefs. How a destiny can be slave of astrology? Astrology to the best might be a forecast supplementing the vision of humans. The more you fall in this web the greater chances of losing your positive energy towards existence. Is it not that you doubt your own existence surrendering to astrological sciences? Whatever astrology has to do with us or not, we should be clear that the life is of existence. If astrology had all the powers no man would have been mortal. Is it not the universal truth of life? Why then the hesitation in mind to accept graceful death? Humanity is also to know the limitations of humans.

Right now start your work towards your dreams. This instant is a gold mine of opportunities. The first steps are the initial rungs of ladders taking you to the heights of your achievements. Your thoughts run your life. You are the only person who can make changes in your life. Start raising your voice for change.

Every dawn can bring a golden change. It has the potential as infinite as the energy of sun. The golden sunshine is for everyone from dawn to dusk. Trust yourself to deliver excellence. The only perennial disability in life is a bad attitude. Attitude is an attribute of the self.

Why any person should be held responsible for your attitude? It comes from within the individual. It is the reflection of an overall development of the individual. The attitude is independent of the laws of living. Our attitude can make enormous differences in people's lives. Without the obsession for excellence you cannot become extraordinary.

Life is an episode made of dawn to dusk.

This dawn an inner thought vigorously started shooting me to share with society what was bubbling in my turbulent mind. It was time to leave aside everything and sincerely start working on the reader's project being undertaken as "Dawn to Dusk".

The mind was vividly vitalized and I was voiceless and reluctant no more. This was a new beginning with an entirely new golden dawn with the blessings of all. In front of me this was a very huge task to be accomplished without the actual choice of readers and opinion of the respondents. I knew I am not writing for the taste of readers. I would be lucky if few would have been dreaming the same prior to reading my manuscript.

There is a vast difference between orators and writers. Orators believe the audiences are big fools. They gain strength and confidence to deliver their lectures melodiously without breaking their rhythm of voice and speech. And finally at the end they finish up delivering the message to the whole community of intellectuals. Similarly the ideas of humanists may look to be foolish in the pursuit of humanity.

Good orators and their revolutionary speeches have transformed the world from time to time. The induction to the listening followers is immediate. The impact of the speech on mind is instantly felt. By the time you walk out of the auditorium you are already a transformed human. Such is the power of speech.

Nevertheless I wrote not to see that how well I could write but to sincerely witness the revolutionary feelings of my heart through the community of my readers in reestablishing humanity in the world. Converting my voices to speechless writing on paper was a tough task against the fear that it should not lose the power of speech.

I wanted to drive my purpose that every reader is an owner of dawn to dusk. I wanted to realize that every reader is an orator of humanity from dawn to dusk. I wanted my readers become an idealist and keep going to the masses with their hearts of love. How could I bring this inspiration filled drive in my readers?

The present society mix is not limited to few tastes and philosophies. Under these circumstances it becomes really difficult to address this subject. I had to take up this assignment, was my earnest resolution from dawn to dusk till the last word written.

When I had finished writing Dawn to Dusk, I was passively regretting for the time lost and delay in sharing with my readers. I honestly confess to say, had I started early both the purpose might have been bearing fruits by now. However the time lost in preparing the seed of humanity will have all its goodness unfolded in times to come.

I convinced myself to stop worrying about what can go wrong, and got excited about what can go right from dawn to dusk. Life invariably is to search the right things. Men at times have to walk away from the moods impeding his true living.

I would have joined the battalion of warriors of humanity early to work for peace with my readers. Nevertheless I believe nothing much has been lost if we all realize even at the earliest dusk to start by the immediate dawn.

Never anticipate shrinking your expectations. I begin with my humble prayer bowing down to that divine dawn which with its enormous force of inspiration could grace me to scribe the first alphabets on blank paper before it has been realized in the form, which we are pleasantly holding as Dawn to Dusk.

Man is the beginning point in the ocean of miracles. We are probably experiencing the infant stage of manifestations of the existence. Man is not endeavoring sincerely. Man himself is encumbering his dreams. Man's every attempt should be towards emulation. Man is emperor of his dreams. Make the mind reach the highest elevation. Man is not enterprising in the right direction of aims. Just by elocution services are not rendered in the true sense.

Man is an envoy to this earth.

Why we are seeing exasperation everywhere? Why man's expediency is being questioned again and again? All noble men are exhorting to exhilarate the society. Gladness should envelope the whole world from dawn to dusk.

Man should make his life an exquisite one. Philosophy of extenuation has become the rule of living all over the world. How do we exterminate it? Fill the day with exuberance. We have been hearing so many fables right from our childhood only to extenuate ourselves at the end.

Is Man fallible by nature? That is why he is seeking perfection? Dreams, fantasy and reality have their own perceptions. Why fatigue from life? Is life miserable from dawn to dusk? Is flora and fauna are not part of your existence? Man may not be receiving you but doors to fauna and flora is always open. Think for them. They too need you. Nature is to be maintained by man. All plants, animals and humans integrate to sustain the universal life.

Humans alone would have been worse than the stones. Do not allow fear to fester you? Never allow fear to make home in your mind. This may kill all the units of bravery in you. Always have a fervor feeling for life? The negatives of the mind are insidious to the complete living. Fill your life with noble aims, thoughts, feelings, creative power. Man should have carnival not carnage. Can man resolve the problems of society by homicide alone? Why do not we give chance to homily?

Dawn to dusk is a daily hymn by creator of life for humans.

What else is going to remain when the human race will become extinct? You have to decide to be idol or idle? The haziness of life is only going to harm the opportunity of existence.

Life is inscrutable. Is it really unreadable by man? How do you feel about it? What can you make out of it? Dawn to Dusk is the real tale of society, nothing invented or imagined. It is far away from the fiction. Life is impenetrable till ignorance. Wisdom is the tool to work with it. Man has to yet decode the enigmatic life.

Life is a journey from unknown to known.

During this it gives you choices, chances, and changes to overcome circumstances. A bit by bit boldness from dawn to dusk moves you towards confidence of living.

Man's fidelity has remained a universal concern ever since civilization. Lessons of prosperity, spirituality, intellectuality, wisdom, living and humanity all are existing in nature. Man as student is not willing to receive it. The teachers and students are present without the effective interaction. The learning should begin. Do not delay to lose the opportunities at dawn. Focus on minimizing the regrets at dusk.

Life is to ride not die. Do not tie it with adversity. They are not on your roads to success. A cascade of positive events will impact all areas of your life. I agree saying is the easiest thing on this earth. But do not run the risk of missing out on such an opportunity.

Everyone is replaceable. The cycle of learn, unlearn and relearn is the ball of real development and growth. It leads towards the infinite perception. Keep riding the bicycle of life. The movement is important. Let it not stagnate till the last energy to paddle it. You should always be on board at dawn.

Make today amazing, happy, cheerful, serving, nursing, wealthy, prosperous, exciting, inspiring, enjoying, blessing, gracing, living, riding, thriving, whatever you wish towards betterment of humanity, make it, do it today. The day is to do. Go for it. Get it. Today is the day of the fullest action, the best in you to come out, pull it out, a little more, endure a little, a bit patiently, and finally you see, you have done it today.

Keep the passion alive to achieve before the dusk. Keep moving with the light of sun in day to hold the light of success at dusk. The evening is the moment of cherishment. Be an enthusiastic encourager. The world has plenty of critics already. The world needs reformers, inspirers, encouragers, go-getters, helpers, to balance the virtue of existence. Love what you are doing. Success is not the key to happiness. Happiness is the key to success.

<u>Ocean of Infinite Opportunities</u>

I always wished that,

"Man was unfortunate to have fins and wings so that he could swim all the oceans of the world and fly to the highest zenith of the Universe".

It was no sooner that man reached moon he has started to conquer mars. Hopefully may be this journey one day lead to sun, and the other galaxies of the existence.

Primarily Opportunity is in the mind. It is not in the world. It is there. It is only to be perceived. The existence is in fact is a dream rolling down rapidly into past and future. The present is just a moment of witness. Man at dawn should become god at dusk. Such should be the grace on one and all. The pursuit of man from imperfection to perfection can be realized through dawn to dusk.

Dawn to dusk is the battle field where man has to fight out his dreams. Voluntarism should be the pen for rewriting the destinies. What is the root cause of anxiety and worry? Is it wealth? Is it poverty? Is it death? What exactly it is?

Are humans born to solve their own mysteries? Are humans born to solve the mysteries of the world? The dawn inspires to look towards the solutions of survival. It is a daily fight with the existence at individual levels and grouped levels as society, community and nation in the world. Helplessness is becoming man's style of living. Is it not a sorry state of affairs for the man in us?

Every person is beset with anxiety of one kind or another. Anxiety in one form or another is present everywhere from dawn to dusk. How can we be released from the fetters of anxiety? Opportunity is to be explored to tame the anxiety in man.

Knowledge is that medicine which perhaps cures all diseases. This is the area mind regularly strives to master it. Man had been foolish to look for opportunities in the material culture rather than in the spiritual culture. Otherwise the world would not swim in ocean of chaos today. Every good idea need not be nipped in the bud at the dawn of development. It needs to be explored with the probable opportunities from dawn to dusk.

Man's uncertainty is an unavoidable shadow with him. It is again followed by the fear. He is bounded by the chains of fate. He is unwontedly tagged with the pleasure of misfortunes and adversities. All is part and parcel of the life from dawn to dusk. Let us understand it very clearly that no man truly wishes to bring pain to another man.

Never conceive anything which is not moral in mind. Evaluate the ideal of the idea at the dawn of exploration itself. Reconciliation of life is like the spilt milk which you never drink. By dying the hair black grayness cannot be ceased. Life is to be seen in its true sense.

Aging is an opportunity to take up liberation gracefully. The old should give chance to young ones. Let us not deprive them from opportunity of living. We had enough trails for perfection till the time of retirement. Matured men should leave and generate place for the upcoming youths to experience the dawn of experience in all walks of life. Thus man can create opportunities for another man. This is where the seed of humanity lies with us.

Discrepancy is said to be the mother of discovery.

Unless you face it you do not race towards novelty. Who would search the master if man had ruled the world? Ultimately man is at the feet of existence to realize the truth of life from dawn to dusk. Let not these sheets of paper remain blank. Write and rewrite till you get a meaningful writing of life. Opportunities are abundant in existence for man to unearth.

Man should understand the overlapping relationships of needs, desires, dreams, aim, self, idea and thought which create infinite opportunities in existence. A thought leads to millions of ideas and equally an idea brings in millions of thoughts. The self influences the idea. The idea also in turn has impact on the living of self. All are very well embedded in the sphere of opportunity. None can be considered for analysis in isolation. All of it together keeps propelling the abilities, potentials, capacities, vision and mission of man. No one can deny the infiniteness of opportunities in humans as well as the world of existence from dawn to dusk.

Opportunities are infinite in man.

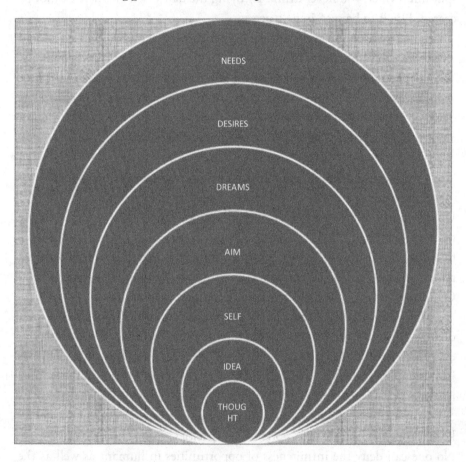

Lao Tzu said,

"If you correct your mind, the rest of your life will fall into place".

Today's world community is not from any single idea, thought, origin, civilization, philosophy, religion, culture, perception, values, morale and way of living. The emerging global village is rewriting the definition of society, colonization, communism, socialism, capitalism, democracy, and imperialism. All the convergence from diversities is to realize the oneness of existence.

Man should germinate the seed of humanity for universal harmony from dawn to dusk. Everyone can be awesome but it takes extra ordinary to make a universal difference.

A goal with no plan is just a wish.
Perception of Opportunity is the beginning of transformation.

It should be applicable to all of us. The Universal Life is itself transforming. Hence its accessories and other related philosophies are likely to be further enriched. One important point to debate is that will the competition cease to universality conquering the diversity of existence? Why individuality is not dissolving? Why Man is maintaining the latent ego in him?

The sphere of dreams, sphere of desires and sphere of needs are having metabolism of excelling in humans. It is because of this self motive force the individual is at unrest with his containment from dawn to dusk.

The sphere of goal, sphere of success, sphere of achievement, sphere of sacrifices, sphere of happiness, are products and by products of the entire process of perception.

One is the infiniteness of opportunity for humans and other is the infiniteness of the success for humans which need a correlation in the world. And all depends on the human you are. The personality of human speaks about his opportunities, success, sacrifices, perceptions, values, ideals, morals, ethics, and principles and at the end his inclination towards humanity.

Human hence is categorized as leader, follower and scavenger based on the sphere of existence.

Perception of Opportunity

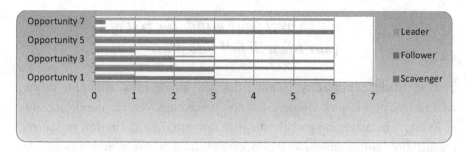

The above graph reflects some of the combinations of leader, follower and scavenger in an individual man as perception of opportunity from dawn to dusk. It will vary with respect to the qualities of the individual. The leader is born to explore opportunities alone, while the followers and scavengers cannot explore without the support of each other. The life of scavenger looking into opportunity is as good as the parasite. Neither ownership nor own ideas.

The question is to the individual as to how to avail the opportunity. The time rolls out in this decision. Again followers should have substantially good leaders. When leaders topple then followers derail. Scavengers have to do nothing. They are dependent on the followers and leaders. At times followers are leaders to them. While scavenging they cultivate the attributes of followers too. A good scavenger may be at par with the follower.

Thus the discussion is near to the inference that there can be innumerable categories of opportunities to the individuals based on the advantages, situations, capabilities, potentials, skills, smartness, talent, and so on but the prime factor is attitude to do so.

A leader does not wait for opportunity. He finds out opportunity. He sees opportunity. He breathes opportunity.

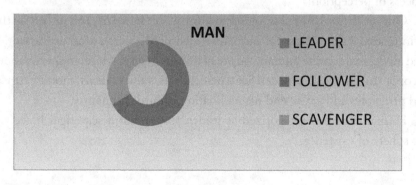

Leaders create opportunity.
Opportunity creates opportunities.

Not only for themselves. It is for the whole lot with them. They multiply opportunities from dawn to dusk. They invent opportunities.

Leaders discover opportunities. They are obsessed with their inheritance of opportunities. Their legacy finds opportunities for one and all. This is the charisma of leaders. In all walks of life we have legacy of leaders. They are humans with power of unearthing the impossible. They create dawns of their destinies. They know to slice the day out for their followers. Followers are equally benefiting with great leaders vision and mission.

What are you a leader, follower or scavenger?

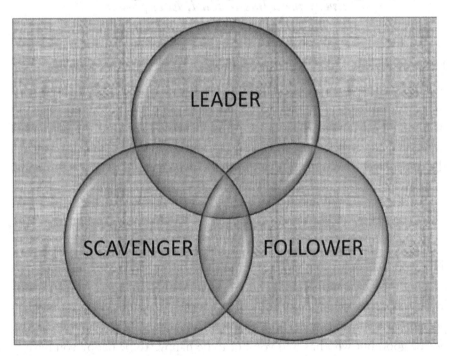

Leadership is the inertia of opportunities transforming the huge population of followers. It is again manifested through them from dawn to dusk. The world needs more and more leaders of humanity. Leaders with potential of universal change are to be looked for. Leaders with the dedicated and committed drive are the need of the hour.

The relationship between leader, follower and scavenger is not free from the overlap of characteristics, roles and responsibilities in regenerating humanity in the world. Humans are to have all the three proportionate to their dynamics of living. If man is going to be the influencer in the team definitely he is leading the battalion of followers and scavengers. It is a very interesting subject for the readers to comprehend from the dimensions of humanity.

A complete renaissance of mankind rests with them. Opportunity of success, career, wealth, happiness, achievements, betterment, effectiveness, optimization, togetherness, love, kindness, sacrifices, serving, mentoring, rearing, nurturing, preaching, teaching, helping, guiding, leading, directing, planning, monitoring, controlling, implementing, socializing, humanizing, civilizing, improving, counseling, awareness, volunteering, and so on are in front of us.

Every man has to lead. Every man has to make the best of him.

How to classify man? How to categorize man? How to identify man? Whatever you do to prioritize ultimately this evaluation cannot meet the inherited attributes of human beings. All theory of evaluations is at crossroads of humanity. Man's satisfaction to bring in peace is beyond the sciences of humanity. Nevertheless the struggle is on from dawn to dusk to at least scratch the upper layer of man. It is only spirituality which can dig out the humanity in man.

Let us become man of opportunity.

The world needs us today. They forge their future. There are again leaders holding their base supported by huge followers and scavengers. The integrity, loyalty, sincerity, punctuality and ethics are the factors on which individual's perception, living and opportunities can be categorized. The whole world may not be good but who has told you not to be happy. To be happy you have to find out how to be happy.

Rearrange the word "EVIL" and it becomes "LIVE". Rearrange the word "CHEATER" and it becomes "TEACHER". Rearrange the word "FILE" and it becomes "LIFE". Rearrange the word "CARE" and it becomes "RACE" .See the game of alphabets in life. A little rearrangement can change the entire life.

*Every man can rearrange himself. A bit by bit
can bring big by big changes in mankind.*

Our aims are not to just die.

It has to be of purpose. Let us have a very clear purpose for living. No diplomacy with the self. Ultimately you are owner of your life. Would you not like your life to be crafted well? Why to live a redundant life? The worst may be for fun. Let us be the clowns of existence for some time. It is far better than the ghost of enmity.

Good are born in every generation since civilization to continue the goodness of existence. The truth that I will be ashes tomorrow cannot be challenged by any school of thought. But before I perish, my daily existence from dawn to dusk should have a meaningful living. Great lives have been lived without recognitions and applauses.

May my last remains be untraced, if an ounce of difference I have made in my living in the pursuit of existence. The more you do the less satisfaction comes because of the realization that some more could have been done. It is very much true with the time of life. The time of life will never return back at the dawn of existence once past in history of memories.

I know not my form even today; perhaps it is just the beginning in me to understand what I am from dawn to dusk. I keep hanging on to one or the other manifestations of the same being never finitely known to man since the very first civilizations inhibited on this struggling earth and invariably evolving in trying to define its universe.

My heartfelt prayer to Thee for inspiring me to recall the learning's from dawn to dusk finally shaping it into an entity, comprehensible to the readers to further debate from dawn to dusk in redefining its perspectives till ultimately perfection may be achieved.

Life is the point of no return.

The journey is always ahead. Past are lessons of existence for future. Day is the time to do all you can. Create till the best of your will. Again no time is going to be yours though you may have the strongest of wills later on in your life. Every creation of today is studied as miracle of tomorrow.

The world is one's oyster.

Daily feel the world is your oyster today. Why wait for tomorrow which never turns up? Today is what actually all of us have in the real sense.

Past and future are only the virtual worlds.

Man only speaks more about the past and future. Everything happens in today only from dawn to dusk.

Today's Dawn to Dusk is the definite time for action. Avail this to the fullest. It is destined to be yours. The time never repeats its fortune. Everything is yours and you for everything now. You never know the time of disappearance; hence experience it to the state of self- actualization.

My objective of writing is to build the objectives of readers to live and die for humanity. The fear in us should exist that we all will have to face the viva-voce examination at heaven and hell accordingly to give the statement of days lived from dawn to dusk.

This book "DAWN to DUSK" is a mode of universal appeal to all the respected human beings on this earth to do their best to protect man from man and man for man.

Dawn to Dusk is an infinite opportunity for all to deliver their best in all walks of life.

Despite our efforts results do not seem to satisfy us. It needs betterment daily. This is imperative for humans and inevitably the secret behind development and growth of life. Our struggle for survival towards abundance makes us to face the challenges of life. Everyone is involved to maximize the utilization of time. We may be at more mistakes seeing them remain idle. Is it not our responsibility to see our other friends to work along with us?

Laziness is no exception to craziness of life. All want something to the satisfaction of self. However, in reality the picture is not rosy as thought of. The attributing factors are enormous. Ranking them may be next to impossible. Action does not cease. Madness to succeed is the instinct of man. No one wishes to be left behind. Every good action is bound to give better result.

Day and night, right and wrong, won and lost, good and bad, fair and black, cold and hot, short and long, healthy and weak, rich and poor, kind and cruel, clean and dirty, ugly and beauty, love and hate, truth and lies, big and small, literate and fool, reward and abuse, marriage and divorce, failure and success, give and take, teach and preach, war and peace, death and life, fight and perish, heaven and hell, pass and fail, young and old, there are infinite combinations of quadrants, and equally all are in the race from dawn to dusk. Any activity irrespective of identification, preparedness, prior to implementation, has the consequences of the action. The time is competing with time such that you cannot be on the nets to watch the game of life just as a referee.

Man is more bothered to evaluate another man. Man has to examine himself.

We are swimming in the sea of ignorance. Man is trying to identify his position. No sooner than one attains, the other reclaims. Is the real reel of life from dawn to dusk is running with the projector of purpose? The painter of life is hardly waiting for the canvas to unfold. Though drums of life are beating from dawn to dusk, man is unable to hear the music of life. The senses are running away from the beauty of life.

Complexity is overruling the simplicity of life. Manipulations are clouding the ethics of man. Is survival at the risk and cost of another man ethical? Let us live a life of great order, values, ethics, morals, dignity and humanity.

Let me question the nations, what control mechanisms they have to check the trespassing of light, air, wind, clouds, rains, snow, water, rivers, seas, oceans, heat and cold over and beneath the land from dawn to dusk. Can man make any physical barriers for these? If no, then why did we establish boundaries on lands as line of control to discriminate man? No land is man's true property. The land on earth belongs to nature, the universe. Who are we to possess it? It was never ours and it will be never ours. Is man an intruder in nature? We are invariably at any point of time are sure that the nature was not created by us.

Who is the custodian of nature? Is it that we have evolved to housekeep and maintain the nature from dawn to dusk? To what extent our interference is causing latent changes in nature? You will not be surprised to be appraised that many species are becoming extinct and on the other hand numerous new ones are coming into existence. The beauty of existence perceived, felt, explored, experienced through the life in many forms as nature wishes.

Why not make a difference today?
Begin to live for the cause and the
cause will show you the way.

Tomorrow's uncertainty can be encountered by completing the task today. That which can be achieved today, should not be left incomplete for the next day. Cultivate this theory of endurance and you shall never regret in future. I will tell you, practice it; it will stretch your success beyond imagination and anticipation. All what you see are only personifications of hope from dawn to dusk in various uninterruptable forms of diversity and manifestations.

Rise beyond all limitations as no one is above you. Your sheltered self is the one enemy you have been protecting again and again ever since the civilizations of our own race as human beings. Man is uniquely one of the mysterious manifestations of the almighty conflicting and competing with its own self. You are no more frog in the well with introspect to the several years of journey on this exploring earth in brainstorming from dawn to dusk.

Let the whole Universe be your swimming pool. Don't be the Sphinx-like. There is nothing like unsolvable problems. Life has hidden lessons to be unearthed from existence. Faith, trust, hope, love, inspiration and realization are attributes in which the life is played and ranked from dawn to dusk. Let us be grateful for having a life in this form to experience the Universe outside and inside the self. Say, we had no life, never came into existence, then there itself the whole process of experience, learning and realization ceases.

Are all our worries due to the life? And the most mysterious part of query, we are here not by our choice. When in reality nothing seems to be ours then why to cry for something which later or sooner will not be yours.

Earth is a temporary place for all of us.

It had been home for billions and billions of species. It is a laboratory where evolution of life is being explored and witnessed. Many experiments are being conducted, observed, analyzed, summarized, concluded and comprehended.

But ultimately the life operation and maintenance manual could not be accessed so far. A control centre yet to be discovered.

True knowledge is to understand our own limitations.

Let us not ride the same bicycle again and again, unfruitful paddling the same wheels of ignorance from dawn to dusk. The emphasis should not be on governing the nature. The life has its own path of flow. Break all your chains of bondages to enjoy the float. Be like ants swarming towards the sweetness of life. Keep reminding yourself, it is grace that you are living to see more, more of the world.

Balloon of Billion Thought

To quote Emerson,

"The Universe does not jest with us, but is in earnest".

Man is a balloon of billion thought. The whole life is a balloon of thought. Let it not burst. The more you will hold with the air of life the greater it will float.

My readers continually keep inflating your ideas of balloon at dawn to be at the top of dusk. Raise it higher, and higher to be praised by the kingdom of god. Every thought has the power to demolish the indecipherable life from dawn to dusk. The obscurity is in the mind only.

Thoughts are prime movers of man. A good thought propels you to a good destiny. A bad thought ends up in giving you all the miseries with worries and unhappiness of life. Have you ever thought why in the same world happiness and sadness exists parallel? Is it that happiness of one is at the cost of other man?

Will thinking good bring goodness? Is not thinking bad bringing badness? What are you willing to do with your thoughts? Will your balloon of billion and billion of thoughts float the entire mankind in tranquility of space? Why the land has lost its peace as the sky? A great transformation is to be done by the inhabitants of land in order to make the land peaceful than the heaven. Why differences in land, sky and heaven? Man should be same everywhere.

Deeper lies the humanity within man. Unless there is intellectual crusades all over the world humanity cannot be uniformly reestablished. I am speaking for Unified Humanity. A Universal Humanity across the Universe is Human Goal. A Universal goal for mankind is to be implemented. This can only happen with the beginning of Universal Thought. A bigger and bigger balloon of dreams of humanity should inflate the entire Universe.

The genesis of the problem lies with the humans only. There is no use in blaming the past humanitarians. They sacrificed themselves to make the seeds of humanity. Now is the time to launch the new struggle in all walks of life formally and informally to uphold the spirits of human sovereignty.

Actions of today will be reactions of tomorrow. The delay is in preparing the seed of humanity only. Once it is sown the plants of humanity are to be protected from dying. Man needs to pass on to another man and it will go on from one generation to another reaping the benefits of existence.

Legislation of man is like the milk and the cat. It appears that god has given the secrets to cat to steal milk from the kitchens however protected it is to enter without the notice of the owner of homes. The point of discussion is related to similar activities of man in the world playing hide and sick like the cat. He pretends to be invariably innocent in the outer world very well under the suffocation of realization in the inner world. Thus the thoughts are divided in reality. Some balloon of thoughts keep bursting without flying in the outer world of existence.

Humanity is not a balloon of duality.

It cannot float with two halves. The impurity restricts its flight of divinity. Man is unable to merge with god because of duality in thoughts. How one balloon of dream can burst and float at the same time? We require our minds to be pure first.

My dear readers you believe it or not it works. At the dawn of liberation you will realize if not today. At the dawn of learning it is imperative to be doubtful as you have not traversed the truth of existence. You are beginning to learn the truth. The infancy and your ignorance are only a matter of time.

The Life has its own way to take you to the bank of realization.

The thirst for the truth predominates only when the water of learning recedes from your reservoir of life. Hence before you become feebler physically let the mind generate thoughts randomly, spontaneously, consciously, sub-consciously to explore the meaning of existence. Man's rise is meaningless if he has failed to understand thyself. Before you fall at the feet of existence weigh yourself with the wisdom of existence.

Dawns are the initial seeds of changes, renovations, reinventions, revolutions, reformations, reestablishments and awareness towards giving a new dimension towards humanity. The Society always experiences the mix of young, matured and old humans at any point of existence. A good coordination and cooperation among these populations of people speaks the vision, mission, growth, development, maturity, ideals and morals of any society all over the world from dawn to dusk.

The subject of humanities is concern of one and all.

Ever human should have balloons floating in their hands filled with thoughts of humanity. Let the color of balloons be red, blue, green, yellow, violet, blue, white, pink, orange, purple, grey, black, silver, whatever mix it may be, representing the different faces of man across the world, the importance is to the content of air of humanity. Let the purity of air soar the humanity into the space of existence throughout the universe.

Let us keep Humanity flying as high as the sky. Think to float it beyond the blueness of the space as seen to the man with limitations from the land of existence. Hearts are to mingle in space of humanity. Let these hearts be nearer to heaven from dawn to dusk.

Man is lacking the inspiration to integrate the definitions of life. The proper beading of values, ideals, morals, ethics, virtues, wisdom, thoughts, principles, attitudes, concerns, disciplines, services, behaviors, wills, ways etc are very essential to summarize the overall personality of man. Living brings in learning at all levels. The process of thinking changes with the transformation in the self. It is to the individual man to be a big or small balloon of humanity.

***In my opinion every human should be like the
"KITE", an indispensable acronym
I think can be better understood as
"Kindness in the Existence".***

This no doubt would take all of us to revisit our childhood where we had been literally mad to raise these kites higher and higher furling swiftly to soar into the sky against all odds of wind, altitudes, pressures, rains, clouds, heights, colours, sizes, shapes and attachments taking out most care in maneuvering it to the extreme space of existence. Today is again the time to unconditionally keep hoisting these kites of kindness to make a new umbrella of humanity. The world needs it to protect itself from the unwanted acidic rains of inhumanity.

I will be extremely happy to learn that this book has been torn apart by majority of the readers in reading again and again, trying to examine, reexamine as many times as it can be. I will be glad to know that the exercises recommended here have been religiously worked weighing tons and tons of papers at your homes. Then only it can bring some solace to the author who wrote to potential readers to rewrite destiny of humanity.

This would be the right use of the text before it is sold to the hawkers to be distributed as packets for sweets at beaches and parks and there is every possibility it holds the cigar to be blown into smoke mercilessly at bars and clubs. In this way I would be fortunate to touch their hearts at least through the refusal of some. Even pieces of it will have assurances of reformation.

I will be sad to know that "Dawn to Dusk" is lying decoratively in shelves with the dust of reader's unlikeness. It is meant to be raged with the anger of curiosity. It is to be redefined with the perceptions of readers. It is a workbook to be exercised again and again till you have mastered some ideas, thoughts, views, opinions, perceptions, philosophies, strategies, principles from this essay. Be sincere in practicing the recommendations and certainly you will be transforming yourself from dawn to dusk. Both the ways are available here for you to pick up. You can reform yourself as suitable by art, science and measurement techniques discussed here in this promising essay on humanity.

Readers are to give wings to dawn to dusk to fly all over the world. Your thoughts and ideas on humanity should become the extension of this essay. A drop by drop addition will create the ocean of opportunities for one and all.

Always remember limitation is in the state of mind.

Let us have a philosophy that live and let live. All are to be accepted as the idea of heaven. Why things are not clear on the grass of earth? Definitely it will help the readers to see the light of day. The reading of this book is the process of reinventing yourself. The more you do, the more you are changing yourself. Believe me you will win to ink one day a more inspiring thesis than this one.

You will certainly bring many dawns of love to touch the hearts of humanity. At the click of a mouse you can send cheers, hope, prayers, blessings, thanks, appreciations, inspirations, gratitude, to millions and millions of people all over the world.

Man's advancement in living with the revolution in communication technology is a great resource of recent times to share our minds. This is a tool to demolish all the viruses crushing humanity. In millionth of a second you can communicate your mind to billions and billions of your fellow beings humans on this earth. What else can be better thought of to voice your message of humanity into this integrated network of the world from dawn to dusk? The human network on humanity should go live.

Let each one of us browse the mind with humanity. Communicate, communicate to the entire world, we will live and die for humanity. Each one of us needs the grace and strength of the existence to survive and excel.

Change is part of existence.

It's, even its foundation, since everything is in perpetual transformation. Nothing is fixed. Everything is permanently transforming. Time passes. Years succeed one another in each person's life, automatically bringing their share of mental, physical and spiritual transformations. It's impossible to freeze things and hold on to the past. The past never returns.

Time is life. Time lost is life lost. You were, you are, and you will be someone different in future. The path of austerity is not for others, it disciplines our own living. The process of becoming never ceases. You mustn't be afraid of change, but instead be capable of adapting to the changes and transformations inherent in life. If humanity hadn't changed, we'd still be living in caves and warming ourselves huddled around wood fires.

Change is life. Life is for change.

Both the world and man are interchanging. So don't be afraid to change, but rather be afraid of not changing, in other words of not being able to adapt to the changes taking place around you. Changing does not mean succumbing to all the latest fashions, and thoughtlessly adopting all kinds of new ideas as they are, without discriminating. On the other hand, it is very possible to adapt your ideas and behaviors to the changes in life that are unfolding around you. Resisting change is like trying to hold water in your hand. You can never hold air, water, earth, time and life in hands.

The best wisdom is to work with them towards existence. I advise you, instead of trying to retain the water in your hands, to follow the current with your hand. Do the same thing with your life. Follow its current without resisting, but without letting you get carried away by it either.

Every truth cannot be wisdom.
Every wisdom cannot be truth.

It is a difficult axiom to understand. All realism cannot be truism. Today is again a new dawn. Day is likely to begin. I have to do my best today. I have to work for my dreams. I should not wait any more.

Waking up early is like grabbing the major bunch of time from dawn to dusk. I have to put my body, mind, soul, and self all to work for life. My life is the prime subject of concentration every day. I have to meditate on it to nourish it in the right direction. I will enterprise it to do the maximum business with time.

Time utilized is life capitalized.

Let us not live life like a scavenger. The success is within me. I have to achieve it out. I have huge potentials; today I will deliver it to the last time till dusk. I should beat my all previous day's target of achievements.

I have to rewrite my story of success. I should equally encourage my peers, team members, colleagues, and neighbors, fellow beings, to do or die in the endeavor of excellence. The day should be completely eaten away ambitiously. I am questioning the "I" within me. I am energy of thought, bank of ideas, ocean of dreams, and mountain of hopes, moreover with promising support of nature, earth, and abundant resources to battle the day of opportunities. I am confident to smile the dawn today.

This dawn I will make it the most amazing one. Life is no more unfathomable to me. I will persuade beyond my dreams. The power of persuasion can bring wonders to our lives. Persuasion teaches you not to quit. It strengthens you gradually to win progressively. It is like hatching your eggs of ideas. The embryo of thought is to be visited again and again, till you see that shell is now going to protect your dreams. Finally a day comes exploding the dreams into reality.

Learn to persuade your own thinking.

The garden of life is for flowery plants not greenery of weeds. Unless you keep taming the "I" in you towards the path of productivity, desired efficiency may not be obtained. You have to be CEO (Chief Executive Officer)/COO(Chief Operating Officer) of your organization that is your life. You have to own it. You have to supervise it from dawn to dusk. You have to operate it resolving the issues and problems. You have to lead it. You have to drive it. You have to finally see you have done your best in regenerating humanity.

You have to apply the principles of management to increase the stakes of your life. The environment of organization is always challenging from dawn to dusk. You have to compete to excel. Start analyzing yourself with respect to time and the state you are sailing in today from dawn to dusk.

Human evaluation is a necessity today. The management approach is not to be neglected if it helps in measuring your attributes in humanity. Our deeds are to be accounted by us. Moreover if you are analyzing yourself daily then it is true that you are reforming regularly. The implementation of the plans, schemes, resolutions, promises, assurances, commitments, learning's, are equally important in the overall process of integrated restructuring of the humanity in the world.

How can we extricate ourselves from the daily woes from dawn to dusk? Cannot we think of making one more person happy today? Dawn to Dusk may definitely bring in some sensible sharing that will help you to look towards life with a very new perspective again. I will tell you let us not be fork in the road.

Everyone should pledge right now, "I will sincerely do my utmost to make it succeed against all odds." Above all do not delay; times will not wait for you? Who will change the culture? It is only we. Let us understand the depth, breadth, width, height and length of "we".

Where are leaders of humanity? Who is imparting the lessons on humanity? Humanity is being humiliated from dawn to dusk. Never blame anyone in your life.

Man has to first look within and then the world.

The discussion of small minds is restricted to people only, whereas great minds discuss ideas. Debate and conflicts is tool of brainstorming. It kindles totally a new ray of light into the whole process of evolution. The most important stage, question yourself what you truly want to become? Something is really bothering us? It is as exhaustive as individual brains.

Brain exploration offers powerful possibilities. Eyes are windows to the soul. Please start opening as many tabs as possible to enrich yourself. Let the vision be cleared and flushed of suspended impediments of humanity. Though books are effective tools for transforming society,

I am sad to disclose against the statistical data's that nearly fifty per cent of our population on earth cannot read and write. This nowhere makes them inferior than us as they have their own way of learning, understanding and expressing their self. And at the same time some sections despite this know how are unable to propagate the message of humanity. Moreover reading book as hobby may not rightly reflect the approach of the individual towards the perception of the subject seriously.

Every reader cannot be a leader of change. Every leader may not be a reader. Only on reading no one has become leader. Leader has the face of many followers. Leader has the grace of fortune, faith, truth, hope and love. Above all leader is blessed with attitude to do the right things. Common people have been showing their mediocrity by just doing things rightly. Awareness of humans in humanity is to be campaigned endlessly from dawn to dusk.

Man is a leader. The slavery is in the mind. Why are we becoming slaves? Why our own ideals have remained idle? Author's are on mercy of readers to flood their idea into society. Authors and readers are the rear and front wheels of the bicycle in journeying the idea of transformation from Dawn to Dusk.

What is the language of humanity? Is it Sanskrit, Hindi, English, French, German, Persian, Spanish, Chinese, Russian, Arabic etc? Which started earlier than the other? What language is followed in the animal kingdom? Animals do not have schools as humans need them.

When everything fails, why we pray to god?

Why prayer to god is through the folded hands? Atheism to the outmost can be stretched to the limits of realism but not to truism. This is the universal language of love. Wiping out the tears is the intrinsic concern for sharing the sorrows. Holding hands in despair speaks of the intuition within to help .Much time is lost in deciding to do what we really intend to do.

Every moment is an auspicious time as per the astral. Do not wait till your hairs have turned white. Think of completing your assignment in life before the final call. How can you expect your work to be done by others? Your sense of achievement may not bring happiness to the observer.

I am an Asian, American, European, Arabian, African, Russian, Korean, Japanese, Australian, and so on, is a classification respect to the land of inhabitants. But do we really possess the legacy seeing the globalization and rapid migration taking place in recent times. Why you are fighting for the land and not the sky?

Do you have different departments of humans in the sky? Do the heavens have separate palaces for humans of different faiths? Why the World is full of discriminating humans? Why all humans unite at the heavens?

All the civilizations are of humans only. Our focus is on humans not the man in me, you, us, yours, theirs, mine, hers, and his. I am speaking of the Universal Man. The real, ideal, practical Universal Human. With great love we pet kittens and puppies. With great love we plant our gardens and orchids. A similar love man needs to pet another man.

Let us work towards developing Universal Homes. All of us are workers of the project humanity. It should not be defeated by the barriers of land. Humanity is a Universal Project.

Human is one.

Man is also one. Man is different faces of the same human. The papers of anthropologists of different regions infers that the more we know about human origin the more confusing the concept and the theory of human evolution becomes unpredictable. The primitive man was lack of modern tools of exploration into human science. Flower is also one. But if you want to realize its vastness, fragrances, colors, tenderness, then look at the variety of them through the different plants and trees being produced by nature from dawn to dusk.

Either it is Homo sapiens from Africa, Neanderthals or Homo erectus; we are ultimately humans of today. Human origin dates back to 150,000 years, 100,000 years or beyond it, with doubts or conclusions, the point to be understood is that the exactness of dates and existence are not that critical to stubbornly discriminate ourselves reflecting our stupidity of life.

The Ultimate truth is we all have origin. The time temporarily holds the exploring truth. It is nothing definite but always infinite. The basic question of philosophy is formulated as the relationship between being and thinking. What is primary in between matter and thinking? The world can be broadly distributed in two major thoughts one is Materialists and the other is Idealists.

Now it is up to each individual to decide where they want to align. The object of interest is the very process by which the end results of thought activity come into being. Can the world be cognized through thinking? Can man's thinking be reproduced? Motives are not simply conditions under which thought activity unfolds but factors affecting its productivity.

Materialists as well as the Idealists both will remain as part and parcel of the existence from dawn to dusk.

You cannot have only one stream of this flowing in the society. Man is with freedom of choice to sail in it. Is man's existence the act of thinking? Is it that difficult to classify the types of thinking?

Does the type of thinking have impact on the style of living? I hope you will agree to it without any hesitation and second thought on it. Certainly thinking basically denotes differing processes. Can man interpret the psychology of thinking? Thought is the reflection of man. It develops inside to explode outside. The lava of it should be filled with happiness, kindness, humbleness and humanity. It should flood the plains of human existence from dawn to dusk.

Thinking as action, behavior, motivator, self-awareness, individual, motives, goals, gains, concepts, compassion, winner, intruder, invader, conqueror, emperor, inventor, developer, cheater, teacher, researcher, worker, admirer, lover, trusted, sinner, realize, nobler, reformer, player, younger, older, inspirer, there is no end it.

Thinking reveals Man's view of himself.
Everything then follows the thought.

Thought is the cause for the unfolding we see in life. All the different becoming is because of the respective thought. Good thought good becoming of man. Bad thought bad becoming of man. Thought leads to action. Action leads to the type of becoming. A spiritual thought leads you to temples, churches, mosques, sermons, monasteries, holy places, pilgrimages, etc. A scientific thought leads you to invent. A curious thought leads you to do research. Finally you become what you think. This is the power of thinking. It manifests to see that you are the result of your own thinking. Never have shallow thoughts. Deep within you is the vastness of the life.

Idea is Life

I have one bright idea for my dear friends,

"Let no idea slip away from you leaving
behind no way for you".

Idea is Life. Idea is the seed of life. How an "Idea" can bring revolution in man's life? Let us look at the word "Idea" from the core of the existence. It itself is the core of all the existence you are witnessing today.

Idea is a gateway to millions and millions of postulates of life. It brings in a chain of linkages from dawn to dusk.

Sir Charles Robert Darwin was an English naturalist and geologist best known for his contribution to evolution theory. Darwin has been described as one of the most influential figures in human history till date.

What made him to study humans? Why he wanted to know the origin of species? What made him share The Voyage of the Beagle?

Darwin was a great Scientist who had revolutionized ideas for the evolutionism of humans. His great works The Origin of Species and The Descent of Man were all because of the idea of searching the root of origin. He gave birth to evolutionism through Darwinism.

Thus Darwinism became a movement covering a wide range of evolutionary ideas. And then there were followed ideas, ideas of criticism, ideas of acknowledgement, ideas advocating the concept, ideas challenging this idea.

Thus an idea could multiply in millions and millions for the betterment of humanity.

The evolution of human psychology is the child of that parent idea Darwin introduced to the word. To further continue learning from his works, "A man who dares to waste one hour of time has not discovered the value of life".

Why Darwin questioned his own existence?

This was the beginning in him to explore the origin of humans.

My readers may not be new to know about Darwin. The central idea "Dawn to Dusk" is willing to share is that how many of us are questioning the value of humanity. How many of us understand the core purpose of life? This is a seed of humanity.

DAWN to DUSK is a seed of Humanity.

I firmly believe that,

"The Value of Life can be only through the Value of Humans".

Darwin was an idea. Darwin is a seed. His seed has germinated all over the world. Restrictions are in the mind only. Let the mind open up with hidden seeds of universality. His ideas continued to be in discussion, debate, conflicts, arguments, and is also being done today. It does not matter what the idea has concluded, what it matters is, is the idea alive. Is the seed sprouting? Is the plant growing? Are the branches spreading? Is the tree developing and growing?

Yes the idea of Darwin is alive today and will remain alive forever. So, Darwin was an idea can be corrected to Darwin is an idea. This is the power of idea.

Idea never dies.

A seed gives birth to billions and billions of seeds. A leading idea is followed by billions and billions of ideas. The chain reaction is infinite. My dear readers such should be the seed of humanity in the world.

Are not we similarly living with the ideas of Newton, Aristotle, Buddha, Jesus, Krishna, Mohammad, Confucius, Shakespeare, Churchill, Lincoln, Nehru, Gandhi, Vivekananda, Mother Teresa, Plato, Pasture and many more?

Is it not in fact with all the humans with their own ideas of existence? Any idea of any human is for the humans only. This way or that way, up or down, right and left it comes back to the feet of humanity.

Every man is a powerhouse of ideas.

Humans are banks of ideas. It has the potential to create miracles. It has the strength to resolve the mysteries. Man is the greatest idea of existence in existence. It is continuing to evolve from dawn to dusk. It reflects, refracts, radiates, transmits, receives and translates its own understanding towards the central idea of existence. The core of humanity is in fact the central idea and goal of all humans.

Is Man questioning his own existence?

Is man questioning the existence of other man? Is man thinking of another man? Is man worried about another man? Is there quest to protect life? Is there concern to add value to life? The answers of humanity are within us. Man has to remove dust to see his own true face.

Idea is way forward to life.

Realization is again a way forward to life for betterment through looking backward and learning lessons from the past. An idea brings with it millions, millions, and billions of ideas. Idea multiplies just like the division of cells in organisms. In fact human is an organism of ideas. Mind is the central control room of the entire evolution being programmed, implemented and commissioned.

Be it be home, institute, market, organizations, fields, corporate, corporations, governments, societies, hospitals, care centers, schools, monasteries, committees, everywhere all activities are being redefined only through better ideas. The art of betterment should be both through science and spirituality. Science can increase the material efficiency and spirituality can heal the humanity. No man denies the existence of god. He doubts it. He argues it. He suspects it. Time has different definition of god. As the mind never dies so the idea never dies.

Man floats in ocean of ideas. Man is swimming in ideas. Let man get dissolved into it.

Life is filled with galaxies of ideas.

The human in man has to pick it up for the self. Harbor it to the port of humanity. The human ships are daily going through the ups and downs of humanity waves.

What is your prime aim in life? What really differentiates between ancient and modern living? Is it the standard of living with amenities and mechanized facilities? Let us remove the materialistic world from the evaluation, and then what remains is the spiritual world. Is there meaning to life without the spiritual realm?

Is evolution the evaluation of humans? Meaning of life changes from person to person. Naturalism, subjectivism, objectivism, humanism, materialism, and many more have their own definitions of life as per their principles. What exactly the life is searching from dawn to dusk? The unbeatable idea of creating Man will ever remain unchallenged in the annals of history till the existence of life.

Every Man irrespective of region, race, caste, religion, culture, is a power house of ideas. Billions and billions of Man is thinking from dawn to dusk. Man is trying to create beyond the Universal Creator.

An idea of today may become the principle of tomorrow.

Why an idea springs from thinking? Do all humans think the same? Ideas can trigger revolution in all walks of life.

Life is an idea. Live it to the fullest. Imagine ourselves as Apes wandering in the darkness of existence. The present advancement cannot be credited to any one human. Human has taken billions and billions of years to attain the sophisticated attributes it owns today. Isn't it true that people can be individualists, unfeeling and selfish, they are also capable of social engagement, compassion, kindness and generosity of spirit.

Dawn to Dusk is yet to reveal the perfect definition of life.

Is life immeasurable? Do you have an idea on it? Philosophy of life has many chapters for man to be read and understood. We all are philosophies of our own existence. The perception of the respondent's on philosophy of life from dawn to dusk keeps floating from the conscious to subconscious levels of the individuals. But somewhere the central idea is more or less the same.

Man's quest of this central idea is through his own ways of understanding himself, nature, soul, god earth, and universe and so on. Is life only a format of 24 hours in a day and 365 days in a year? How many of us everyday do an activity which was not done before? Why be like a deadpan? Man needs to be a trend setter. He has to be go getter. The times of life are not always with your tide. It rifts and drifts to the tune of existence. Before the list of regrets enters your life you should have done with the time of humanity.

Idea is to arrive at liberation without bondage from dawn to dusk. Do not dwell in the orphanage of mediocrity? How long would you like to fool yourselves staying in the charitable world? Rise above the mercy of nature. Truly speaking you are the part of nature. I am speaking of the Universal Nature in Man. I am emphasizing the Idea of Universal Humanity.

Have you sincerely asked yourself? The whole of our life is lost in specialization of the same trade and services. The barber ends up chopping the hairs, the cobbler plays with the leather, the tailor with the needle and thread, the farmer toiling the soil, the teacher with the blackboards, the doctors and nurses nursing the illness, the engineer building the nation, the politicians holding the ministry and governance, the economist striving to sustain the livelihood, the preachers to bring awareness in society, the traders to exchange commodities, etc.

Why you live your whole life with one idea of work? Why with one idea of service? You have lost the opportunity of ideas life gives you to explore? Did you ever have an idea for humanity? How many times you have thanked the barber, the cobbler, tailor, farmer, the teacher, the doctor, the nurses, the engineer, the minister for their services to you? It is really surprising to note that, we hardly peep into the other activities which might have been of interest and a knowhow could be attained. It is just like knowing only one single color white.

How can you paint a colorful picture of life? To understand unity in diversity the mind has to wander the world. The debate is not to defend but to explore coloring your life. Blessed are those who have acquired multi dimensions in their vision, mission and objectives.

Restrictions are in mind.

The nature is an open school. It welcomes students from all sectors. Recreation should not be the only reason to visit the hills. Do not take a pilgrimage tour for pass time. Nature is not to be seen only for amusement. It should have the purpose with your idea of existence. Moreover Man in order to modernize his living has brutally murdered the environment. Global warming and climatic changes are being reengineered to compensate the challenges of survivals. The conventional living is close to nature. Unadventurous living would not have allowed man to open other windows of the world.

Life cannot be a play all time. That which is of prime concern to me, may not be a concern for other. Sometimes, incredible strokes of luck befall in an unexpected fashion in life. Can luck transform your destiny? Man can only pity on his folly. How to avoid this idiocy?

Ego is a silent killer.

Are you living with it? Who will evaluate humanity? How to impact humanity from Dawn to Dusk? Every man is trying to establish something. Where to get moment of happiness?

Dawn or Dusk any time, can be a time for deep reflection. Man should look to connect with his inner self. Thoughts arise and pass without influencing you. This is probably coined as meditation. How to obtain the moments of stillness? Can it be cultivated? We should be little more prepared to encounter the ups and downs in daily life from dawn to dusk. Man is trapped towards things which are not going well. For the good which is happening rarely we are grateful.

The human experience from dawn to dusk leaves no stone unturned. How to practice mindfulness? Why do we unnecessarily carry forward cobwebs of the setting Dusk to the rising Dawn? Any right or wrong which has been executed holds no intrinsic purpose to be stretched for coming days without comprehension and assimilation. When I can stay in light, why to sit in darkness? Darkness alone cannot bring light.

Let us build the air of optimism around the sphere of humanity. While many factors may be contributing to this sentiment, the positivity should be our tool to work for betterment of ourselves. Do it now and just now. If you cannot do now, you can never do ever in your life. Neither day nor night will wait for you. Try to accomplish before the dusk otherwise darkness is waiting to swallow you.

This is the time for action. Do not live in ifs, buts, perhaps, not lucky, no fate, no blessings, busy, tomorrow, not prepared, want little more time to think, let me evaluate, give me time to discuss with friends and family, and so on.; for postponing your action and finally you end up without even attempting in your life time. This is the worst part of our existence. Your opinion is supreme.

Nature also adheres to the strict discipline of time. The distribution of day and night, the coming of the season's summer, winter, spring, autumn all are so meticulously organized to facilitate the different faces of life on earth. The seasons too, influence the thinking process. Moods are the tuning of life. I am also one among all trying to contribute from dawn to dusk. Dawn tests you with report card at dusk.

Idea is the atom of dream.

Let us all salute this prime idea which has potential to create infinite ideas. All what we see is outcome of some or other ideas. Universe is the central idea where the different independent ideas are embedded just like the sectional appearance in water melon.

Is Universe created for Man to invade? Our Universe is a University of Life. Life is a University of Ideas. Ideas have kept transforming humans. Ideas have become inventions, discoveries, researches, innovations, advancements, and revolutions, all towards the pursuit of humanity.

It has many schools of species. The most sought for is the school of humans. The contemporary civilizations flourished distant apart to explore the various philosophies of life. The act of worshipping by performing rituals would have been the beginning of acknowledging the supreme creator. This truth need not be reestablished with the fact that the world is not created by humans. Is it exclusively meant for humans? It is ridiculous to say human is unable to convince another human.

Promising Writers are pouring down heavily to bring awareness in the society but all to dismay, as how many of them are really benefiting from a good book. The interest of society is another prime reason for the downfall of human conditions. Cultivate ideas to increase the rate of fertility in innovation. Novelty is human instinct. It writes new chapters of miracles. To unlock is to open the book of life.

Question yourself from dawn to dusk?

Why you are expressionless? Why humanity is not smiling? Life is bottomless? Opportunities are limitless. Restriction is in the mind. Attitude is to be reformed. There are endless ways from dawn to dusk. Firmly hold your idea of ideals. Have the idea to become human first.

Every moment a new idea is born.

Nurture it to reward the Universe with its fruits. It is here where Man can look to see his own traces of the past. Light the darkness of life. Plant the seeds of humanity wherever and whenever you can. A wider and denser forest of humanity should cover the society.

Man is light to the Universe.

Every idea is a bulb of twinkling lightness. It has the energy to glow the world. The star within you can explode the galaxy of ignorance. How can all have the same philosophy of life? Is it the reflection of existence?

Everybody may not pick only roses. Then where will the daffodil and lily go? The freedom of thinking is as big as the Universe. Collective ideas might have converged with consensus to have a well defined code of living as culture. And in order to adhere to it the instrument of fear protected by definition of god as religion. And another group of thinkers, braver never felt the necessity of culture and religion.

Ultimately above all, rules the faith of life.

Without your will what is going to happen. I could not pen down till the will interfered to do the needful for humanity. Once the will made the footing all the obstacles were uprooted. Will defined the way for writing and at the end with lots of understanding on the criticality and sensitivity of the subject I could share only the cream of the writing with you all due to the limitations of time and restrictions on volume of this book. The process was meant to bring justice to our lives and living. I am only reproducing the school of thoughts of many reformists, the works of humanists and the findings of researchers on humanity.

A dog cannot become a cat and a cat cannot become a rat. A mango tree cannot give grapes. An elephant cannot climb tree. A fish cannot fly. The sea water cannot become sweet. Ideas are seeds. A good seed only germinates into a healthy plant and fruitful tree. Cultivate good ideas from dawn to dusk. Give an idea of life to all connected with you. Let the mind work insistently towards humanity. Every idea should have traces of humanity.

One generation has to be the effective seed for the other generation to germinate into good plant and successfully into a fruitful generation of humanity. Is man being born to kill man from dawn to dusk? Who gave this dirty idea of killing to man? No research is as important as trying to explore humanity. A line can only be drawn with a series of uninterrupted continuity of dots.

Dawn to Dusk is every single dot of existence to draw the line of humanity.

Man's ashes should rise and fall in the universe to touch humans to remove the dust of ignorance towards humanity. The offspring's should be better than the parents. The son should strive and excel to beat the man of origin. This is what life needs again and again to strive for excellence till perfection is beaten.

A new thought should beat the old one. Idea of today should be better than idea of yesterday. The process of thinking should be directed towards the refinement of life. A new postulate should defeat the previous school of thoughts.

Aim towards it from dawn to dusk. It shall bring the victory to you without your sense of acknowledgement one fine dawn. Develop the idea of humanity. Enforce the idea of humanity. Share the idea of humanity. Let this chain of ideas make the universal garland of humanity.

Every dawn is a package of gift for you. You never know what it will fetch you. Break the barriers of vision, demolish the obstacles of mission, aim beyond the dreams, draft the goal of life and fight the hindrances in growth from dawn to dusk.

The dawn of humanity should be the dream of all humans at any point of existence. Let humanity over rule barbarism forever. If human has no idea for humanity then who will pursue it? Without questions where is idea going to sprout in man's life?

Finally in the words of Sir Albert Einstein, "Learn from yesterday, live for today, hope for tomorrow. The important thing is not to stop questioning".

Voice of Inspiration

This "Dawn to Dusk" is an opportunity for all of us to once more hear his voice of humanity roar stronger, stronger, louder and louder than the voices of all the great ideals in the world.

To quote the divine Saint Swami Vivekananda from his inspiration:

"Man stands on the glory of his own soul, the infinite, the eternal, the deathless- that soul which no instruments can pierce, which no air can dry, nor fire can burn, no water can melt, the infinite, the birthless, the deathless, without beginning and without end, before whose glory space melts away into nothingness and time vanishes into non-existence. This glorious soul we must believe in. Out of that will come power".

I have a point to voice that,

"We only live once, and so let us do it".

Do it to the best of your ability, loyalty and integrity. What remains is the deed of the doer but not the doer. Your deed in many forms should vibrate the world now and then to raise the spirits of humanity. The sounds should be heard at every corner of the world.

Never sell yourself short. Where is the chance to have such a huge market of humanity? This is an opportunity to share with millions and millions of humans about the philosophy, concept, idea, thought and action on humanity.

Let us become professors of humanity. The whole world is our classroom waiting to hear the lectures on humanity. No subject on this earth is as important as this. May be at home, office, public places, schools, hospitals, prayer halls, research centers, recreation resorts, and parliaments, so on, all are places of learning humanity.

Where to learn humanity from? It is like asking the fool have you seen a fool. Let your inner voices also be stronger and louder to raise the soul in you. The sleeping spirits are as good as dead men. Man livingly should not die. Livingly dying is no good wisdom of the man.

I recall a meeting at one of the Project Sites, where I was heading the Department of Quality Assurance & Control. The responsibility as Head-Quality Control is always a matter of human concerns rather than the technical aspects when sensitivity of the organization is concerned. I had to address a forum of seniors who would never let their ego sink. The discussion was drifting from the main issues to individuals.

I was praying within for a solution, and instantly the mind responded. Sirs, I beg to intervene with a discussion if the forum kindly permits. I was granted the liberty and there was no fear of address. I was now confident to put my point amidst these gentlemen, to convey them that they were fools discussing foolishly on the subject of fools.

This was possible through this dialogue by me, "I happen to pass through the streets of university one fine evening, saw two well learned scholars sitting close to each other, sharing a joke on fools, that fools are peculiar said the one, what is your comment on this, the other replied with great look of wisdom, not much to say it is the perception of the fool to consider the fool in the environment of fools." This I solely leave for the interpretation of my readers.

Resolution of the issue is important,
not the elimination of the person.

Everything has an exception too. And it is applicable to "Quitters are not Winners". I would like people to quit the battle grounds of evils. Stop participating in evil acts. Quit them as quick as you can. Quit all such association of criminal men voicing the enmity among humans. Here we can win the war of humanity only by quitting the arena of devils. Let them fight with themselves to win among themselves. This is not a competition for the learned man. Please abstain from filing your nominations to these events. And in doing so one fine dawn they will be the minority of minorities. Let them kill their ideas of enmity. We should remove ourselves from being their targets of immaturity.

ABC Analysis can be applied to any issue. That is to say Analyze, Balance and Control any issue influencing you. Though the scientific approach may have limitations, it can prime fascia assist in finding the immediate causes of disturbance or turbulence. The perennial solution is always with patience and perseverance.

Man's root causes may not be independent from the society's causes. Legacy of man cannot escape the realism of life. Is humanity the real voice of society? The society is not living with a unique idea of life. The world is blind and dumb to the universal idea of life. Then who will voice humanity?

Dawn to Dusk is a humble prayer to all humans for change of outlook of life. It is truism that material life is always secondary to the moral life. The diminishing candle too never stops giving light; in fact it perishes giving light. Live like a candle without traces meeting the purpose of life journeying from darkness to enlightenment.

Candles which do not burn to give light have no justification hence let us not be unlit candles with the regret of not illuminating the society. If you do not know your own worth and value, then do not expect someone else to calculate it for you.

Listen to the inner voice which regularly calls you.

At times the noise of the world fades away its intensity. This voice is one of the prime manifestations of power in you. Let it speak, interact, guide, question, criticize, inspire, energize you from within. The inner voice diffuses into your outside personality. If the voice is bold, you are bold, if it is feeble, you too become weak. If the voice is sweet your speeches are melody. If the voice is filled with vengeance, all your goodness is lost into anger and enmity. The workshop of renovation and modernization is within us. All refining takes place here. The inside lab holds all the secrets of chemistry of life.

Man has to microscopically examine himself for a better diagnosis. Man himself is the doctor of his own evils. He has to prescribe medicines with regulated doses to cure the diseases of evils.

Evils should be uprooted from within the inner system. Mind should be programmed as computers which by default may not accept any thought of evil inside as input. Awareness, communication, interaction, interfacings, workshops, workbooks, practices, discussions, classes, debates, brainstorming, daily, everyday from dawn to dusk on eliminating the evils of society should be part and parcel of living.

We are not curbing the evils but have been criticizing and penalizing the evil doer. The evil doer is to be seriously with sincerity examined, analyzed, and assisted by society in giving up the bad act he was performing. More and more such centers are to be established to regenerate humanity catering to all the age groups of society. The sub-lanes, lanes, streets, main roads, highways, all leading to homes of society should vibrate with the voice of eliminating evils.

Evils quit us, we do not want to associate with bad things, go away, leave us, and we are not for evils and evils are not for us. Chant it daily and one day the dawn of man will see the world free of evils.

Do you have any other paradise like earth? It is single home to all of us. Let us conserve it. Man is gift of god to nature. Faith is the breath from dawn to dusk. Why not make a difference this dawn? Dive deeper into the dusk to see the depth of dawn. Inspire to excel.

Learning is the process through realization.

Where to find educators of humanity? Aimlessness can only bring wilderness in life. Just look at the changes of celebrations, friendship day, mother's day, father's day, earth day, environment day, aids day, women's day, children day, teachers day, all these are reflections of the concern the society has initiated.

Harness the power of smiling.

A smiling face is a very positive source of energy. It radiates the positivity from one man to another. Much more is to be done from dawn to dusk. The progress at all levels and different walks of life is to be sustained continually.

Is man a good explorer? Can he become an equally good negotiator? What about our capabilities and capacities as resolvers? Why we are looking to each other? Is there need to beg another man? Man should voluntarily serve man. What loss you are going to incur by volunteerism? Does your inner conscience dead? Are you not listening to the call of the spirit? When will you awake?

Life is not to sleep. Sleeplessness is unwanted restlessness. Worry and sorry are unnecessarily becoming our vocabularies from dawn to dusk. Forgiveness and sacredness is the virtue of man. A day will come you will sleep for ever but before that get the best out of you. The world waits to see your miracles of manifestations. You are your prime resource.

Your life is your project.

You have to make a proper schedule, fix your goals, milestones, program, implement, apply and monitor your project from dawn to dusk. The field is yours. You have to make the ground. Do not throw away the life time opportunity to satisfy your queries of existence. Start exploring and you shall evolve with new findings again and again. The worst it may happen to you is that you might be nearer to attaining humanity.

The result at the end is always secondary to the process of transformation. It is like the titration of unknown salt to disclose its chemistry at the end.

The wheel of opportunity, thought, idea and inspiration integrated together brings out the best of the dawn, day, man and dusk towards the goal of humanity.

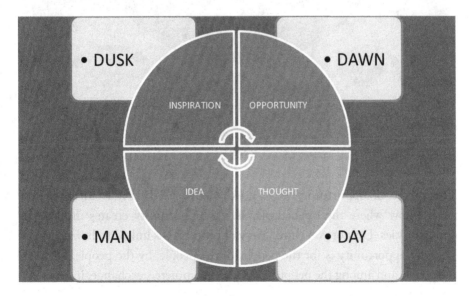

From dawn to dusk there is opportunity for all the departments of human to build the project life.

The environment of opportunity as shown below is one of the possible outcomes. Man can design with his freedom the environment of opportunity in accordance with his living and requirement.

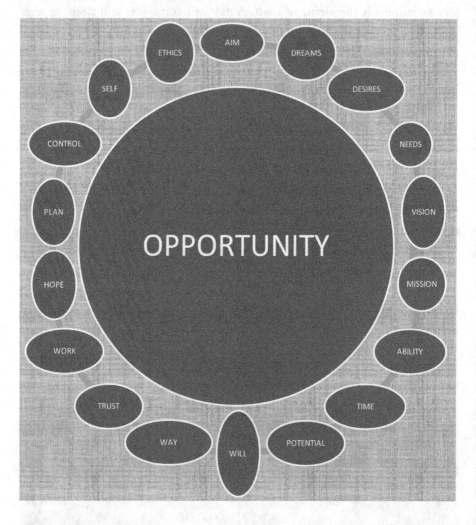

The sphere of opportunity is very exhaustive. In fact it is infinite. You never know where the opportunity is. An opportunity creates millions of opportunities. Do not you think every opportunity is linked to humanity?

Any opportunity is for the people, of the people, by the people, between the people and among the people. Any trade, commerce, exchange, interaction, economic or non-economic activity cannot be performed without the involvement of humans.

Every where there is voice of humans and let every voice be voice of inspiration for humanity.

Before we put somebody through the painful mill;
Drill & grill yourself in the journey of humanity.

Fundamentally it is no destination as an end product to be possessed. How can love be a destination? It is a feeling for sharing. It is an understanding of the hearts. It is a truth of realization. It is experience of existence. This is where the humanity breeds from dawn to dusk against all differences and discriminations. The voice of inspiration echoes throughout the Universe from dawn to dusk.

It is morality that maintains man's morale. Virtue strengthens, vice weakens. Why there is difficulty in practicing virtue? Is it not that we have been deviating from our moral course? No great deed is achieved by sagacity alone. No decent life is possible where dishonesty, arrogance and mistrust prevail. By dishonest means one may gain opulence but not happiness. How can you find joy with mental disquiet? Do you think excess of sense enjoyment can bring happiness? Where is the true happiness?

What are the essential needs of life?

Man wants to live and be happy? What can make man happy? Why the people of modern times have failed to preserve the universal harmony? Can we not reach the root of all miseries? Today, who will improve the mankind is a big question? Every man thinks he is right. All wants to be leaders. Then where will be the followers. Every man believes he knows more than the other man. Man does not want to compromise with man.

Basic needs of human beings will remain unchanged like food, shelter and clothing. Seeing the priority man can live without shelter and clothing for more time but without food which is the source for sustaining life it is difficult to survive long. The reality of the world for human survival is food not wine for merry making. The food security keeping in view the rising rate of human population is always a threat in time ahead's.

Is not human ashamed to snatch food of survival from another human? A concern for food is the prime beginning for humanity. A closer analysis on living may infer to us that many of the consumables do not come under the basic needs of humans from dawn to dusk. So it is an individual perception on needs that really matters rather than the status falsely attached and tagged with luxury.

A shelter protecting you from the heat, dust, rain, cold, wind is an essentiality not a palace with hundreds of rooms depriving the needy. Holding essentialities which may be supporting the life of other humans is not less than an act of crime. It indirectly harms the economy of the state. All is about the attitude you are living with. An open roof may also bring you all the happiness of the world instead of owning a palace without a night's blissful sleep.

Is Man becoming big by making other small? The competition is in between man, not within man.

As Man has many faces so life has as many ways. As living has many paths so nature has as many lessons. Integration and disintegration among these are being witnessed from dawn to dusk. Where is the complete man? Who will make it perfect? Is it evolving?

The becoming of man is the next revolution in the process of evolution to be seen at its best by the existence of Universe. Where to find the Lord among the people? A few good men are required to chip in from dawn to dusk to spread the goodness of mankind. No work is marathon. It is only the beginning which is being delayed. Why to have a dark future? One who laughs at all adversities and is happy when extremely upset is nearing to know the good within him. Do you think, you still have time to let your organization become sick and finally collapse?

Man rise, rise, awake, run as you have achieved nothing still. Restructure yourself to bring the impacts of reforms within you. Stop the deceleration of life. The momentum is not to be lost.

Have you ever asked what you have done with your time today? Most of us unconvincingly chat away the gracious time. We would have made people smile, laugh, cheer, earn, run, play, study, love, celebrate, nurse, serve, pray, think, peaceful, happy, energetic, dynamic, lively, knowledgeable, intellectual, spiritual, good, win, dream, and in doing so we could experience all the passion and gains of these activities.

Activities are window to learning. It brings in space and time together. It binds trust, faith, hope and goal with the individual man. To become what you want, you have to go with the activity of your choice.

Our focus is towards the goals of humanity.

Dawn to Dusk welcomes your synopsis of life. Let your hypothesis of resolution be accepted towards the new becoming of you. Let us run to hold the light of life. Every man has fundamental right by nature to become what he wants to become. Believe me you are the miracle of life. There is no mystery outside. You have to journey from illusion to reality within from dawn to dusk.

Dawn to Dusk is a model of its kind to introspect ourselves.

We are living among millions of variables. The attributing factors keep changing from time to time within you as well as society and equally from one to one. Your question paper will reflect the understanding you have for life. No need to search here and there. I trust, let us all try this.

Every day an analysis on self will unearth valuable findings, suggestions and conclusions for the betterment of the individual. We all are authors of our own lives. Let us be sincere research scholars in shaping our purpose of life. Some responsibilities are not liabilities. All faculties may not understand the realities. Search the purity of the snow at the hills. Bring the god in you out and whatever you have to do for it please do it at the earliest.

Our foundations of life are not to be weaker.

Become stronger than the teacher who taught you. Become stronger than the coach who coached you. Become stronger than the mother who cared you. Become stronger than the father who guided you. Become stronger than the existence which brought you in existence. Be bold to voice strongly than the voice of truth.

The uprooting takes place just by a light wind of ego. The society at large appears to be a battlefield of unwanted school of thoughts. The concept of life is not penetrating to the roots of society. Primarily all the samplings are blessed with the energy of life.

Let us dive deeper and deeper into ourselves, as all the answers to the questions are here, right now within the self. Are not we whiling away our precious time from dawn to dusk for nothing to be gained inherently? No resolution is required for the naturally dissolving issues. The ways of adversities are true paths of guiding the nascent life. To fight is to tame you in the journey of struggle.

An inspiration gives a ray of hope to all that can begin. It is in us to paint the blankness of time. The attainment of perfection can be unfulfilled without the waves of doubts and curiosities. Never fall behind till you are exhausted with the last breath of anxiousness with the highest spirit of enthusiasm.

Keep meditating to spear the self.

A controlled mind has more energy than the cosmic light. Without wounds the caring lags behind the initiation to recover. This regeneration from dawn to dusk keeps transforming you from time to time. The individual goals have to converge towards universal goal of existence.

Life is music. Music is voice of nature. Music expresses the gamut of human and divine emotions. The most sublime music uplifts and soothes the mind, bringing joy to the listener. The composer needs to follow his or her highest instincts in order to create music that is uplifting and healing.

Music has successfully been used in therapy to help the physically ill, the mental ill and severely retarded children. When one is feeling low or depressed, listening to music can help change the mood when nothing else helps.

Nature cures through music. Music is nature. It has the power of healing. When we are feeling dull, lethargic, restless music of a lively, vibrant nature can pull us out of that mood.

<u>Dream beyond Destiny</u>

Neil Armstrong the first man to walk on the moon. In his words after landing, "That's one small step for a man, one giant leap for mankind".

Does destiny has limitations by law of existence? What about dreams? They are far beyond destiny. Destiny is predefined. Dreams can redefine. They can rewrite destinies. Dreams are powerful than destiny. You are owner of your dreams. Would you like to be tenant throughout your life in the house of destiny?

Every man was a dream before he became man. Dreams expand to embrace the Universe. Destiny is at the outmost confined to you only. Your destiny cannot do any favor to your fellow being, whereas your dreams can bring millions of cheers.

Here is a question for my readers to answer, *"Can man challenge his own legacy?"*

Why not when he never fears life and death? He is here and there by the law of nature. Believe me dream is the best friend. It keeps holding you one after the other. It never leaves you alone. It need not be borrowed. It is you and only you. Dream is like your shadow. At no cost you can separate yourself from it. Dream is the bundle of opportunities. You never know what you will become tomorrow with these dreams. Nothing is wrong to have them as much as you can from dawn to dusk.

Dreaming is our inherent right. Human is created to dream. It is only through the power of dream that man can see the various branches of existence. Destiny is the subject from the divine world. Dream is the subject from the Man's World. It is the virtue of the dreams that the destinies are channelized into reality.

Man need not blink at the horizon of destiny and dreams. Man is the beneficiary of both the worlds. Neither the dream should wait for the destiny nor the destiny for the dreams. In fact the dreams are to go beyond destiny.

Destiny strikes once in a blue moon. *Dreams keep riding you from dawn to dusk.*

Human is stronger than the fate of the fortune. Man never waits for the rains to sow the seeds. His belief and faith melts the iceberg of misfortune. Dreams can reach any cloud of uncertainty. Destiny is specific to the cause. Dreams have no limitations and reservations in the world of existence. The mind generates the dreams. The divine disposes the destiny. Both are gifts to man. Destiny is only a limited package. Dream is an open field from dawn to dusk.

Neither dreams nor destiny are destinations.

Do you wait at the post offices to collect your parcels and packages? We receive them at homes. This is how you will receive what is thought to be yours. It is decided at the beginning and allocated to the respective whereas the dreams are in motion always. Dreamers are givers rather than takers.

The greater the dream the greater is the destiny. Dreams have heat to expand your thought beyond the universe. You might be satisfied with what you are today. This does not mean you have stopped dreaming.

Dreaming is like breathing.

Breathing stops only once so should be your dreams. If you have stopped dreaming for yourself, start dreaming for others. Do not be partial to uplift only the self. The society as a single unit should be elevated.

Dusk prepares you for the dawn. The realization at dusk strengthens your dreams with a forecast to be implemented at dawn. Let dreams flow into your existence. Develop wings, wings of dreams to fly high and high in your ambitions, aims, goals, desires, thoughts, ideas, life, living, go beyond the sky, horizon is to be beaten.

Dream can trigger any great idea you never know.

Let us not be like the frogs that are seen to explore the world only during the rains.

Rains of inspiration are pouring down continuously from dawn to dusk. It is up to us to wet ourselves permanently to rewrite the old destinies .Do not you like new dresses, new house, new garden, new books, new cycle, new car, new dishes, new thinking, new passion, something new should visit you daily. Welcome it and shall follow your home of inspiration.

We are visitors to this world. So your expedition should explore as much as you can. This life is a onetime golden opportunity for all of us. We have many tasks with us, many dreams, many desires, hopes, thoughts, ideas, put them into action, let them disperse into the nature, seek for your mind, experience the existence, do for the man in you, bring out the human in you, try to reach as many men as you can, share it, dare to tame, have urge to chase it, bring cheer, happiness, go do it, do not think to idle yourself, time is calling all of us.

Sir Newton changed the face of physics by the falling apple, Archimedes had the idea of floatation while bathing in a tub, the Wright Brothers were mad to fly to touch the sky, Thomas Elva Edison hated darkness to such an extent that he invented the electric bulb to illuminate the whole world, Hitler was bold and determined to conquer the world, Graham Bell wanted men to communicate, share though distant apart and to do it gave communication the telephone, Henry Ford thought to do something with the wheel to save time by venturing into manufacturing automobile the car.

Dheeru Bhai Ambani dreamt to put India on the business global map setting examples by beating the dead lines of projects thus bringing new dimensions to the entrepreneurship management, The Story of My Experiments with Truth, his influential autobiography, Mohandas Karamchand Gandhi persisted patiently to reinstate the freedom of India, The Social Reformer Mother Teresa volunteered the Missionaries of Charity for helpless and homeless people, will remain a hero with unparalleled personal and spiritual appeal.

Whatever they became was only with an idea which was giving them momentum daily. Their idea was their prime mover from dawn to dusk. Idea and inspiration are essentialities to man's ambitions and destinations.

Idea is the prime mover of life.

There are thousands and thousands of noble people without any public identity in society preaching and meeting their best ideals and values. They may not be heroes of stage drama but they are real warriors of humanity. I salute those men of destiny who passively have delivered without name and fame. It is remarkably good to understand these great contributors of humanity. Our pursuit is to rise above the average. The one who are successful give us the path of achievement.

It is unto us to capitalize?

Today the world needs more man of action in all fields. An overall development of the world is essential in all dimensions from dawn to dusk. Man has to form team to win the game of humanity. We all are contestants to a universal goal of reinstating humanity. There is infinite work to be taken up by man. There is absolutely no scarcity. We all can take up work from dawn to dusk.

Choice is yours to decide, but do something to add to this world. The greatest one being service to man. It is your birthright. Avail it to justify the heritage of man. Thinking is the process of shaping your dreams. Ideas are points of supports holding the dreams from falling down. Do not allow them to be dissolved. Primarily hold them at any cost, with great pains, trouble and sufferings. Let them float with you for some time and then finally you can see your ideas floating it into reality.

A dream to reality is journey from dawn to dusk.

The moment is with you. Capitalize it before it evaporates. As beauty is in the eyes of the beholder the dream is in the hands of the doer. You have to trim it to translate it into reality. Look on it, does not lose sight of this, and meditate on it with thorough concentration, hold the light of dream and you shall see it enlightening you to bliss.

Dream can galvanize the whole world.

Man should dream, dream, dream, dream if he wants the real cream of life. Why do not you rise, rise, rise above the sky? It might have been years you have seen the purity of sky. Help yourself to paint the blueness of divinity.

Most of us are like parrots in life pronouncing the same thing again and again. When will the children recite something better than "twinkle twinkle little star and rain rain come again"? Why not recite the poetry of life with the rhythm of existence. Why not fill your new poems with the love of humans. Why not abuses be replaced by applauses of humans?

We start our education in a monotonous fashion trying to replicate the history? It appears generations have been only advanced imitations of their own civilizations in recent past.

Human literacy is lacking true innovation.

Hardly one or two men, here and there around the globe have come out with their novelty or have attempted to bring new dawn to everybody.

Life at dawn should have the vision beyond imagination. Imagining has the tremendous power to overrule its subsequent imaginations. Throw yourselves to the gusty winds of dreams to sparkle the stormy darkness of dusk.

Let the wheel of day have the dynamic spokes of idea, dream, desire and need propelling your living from dawn to dusk in making you explorer, negotiator, follower and leader of humanity. The more you work with this wheel the experience of containment will breed happiness, worthiness, healthiness in society. By this way human reaches near destiny and finally with faith, hope, trust and love one fine dawn is seen to go beyond own destiny.

A lifeless journey in humanity is not the purpose of humans.

A need generates an idea. An idea generates a need. A desire generates an idea. A dream generates an idea. Idea, need, dream and desire work within you integrated from dawn to dusk utilizing the opportunities the day gives and facing the challenges the day brings.

A life is tamed, nurtured, nourished, experienced, and capitalized under the truth of reality and destiny from dawn to dusk.

Humans inner and outer spheres are orbits controlled from the one and only one nucleus of life. A difficult proposition only till the enlightenment of the mind's of humans. Once all barriers of true vision have been removed you can witness the divine human in you and existence.

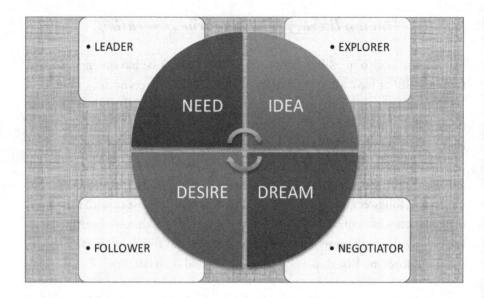

What we will be passing on to the invading generations? They should not be given the freedom to criticize that the people of this time were under-visionaries, unproductive and inhuman towards living. In fact, we should proudly strive to give them an indelible legacy of its kind, to be written in golden words bigger than the China Wall.

Dawn with the constructive attitude will certainly fulfill all the promises of man. Don't you think what use is of your life if you remained scavenger merely to manage your survival? Are you so weak to live crawling? Uphold yourself to know the energy of life. Without the fruitful experience and witness, will you be doing justice to the whole process of existence? Aimlessness can only bring wilderness in life.

Understanding your self is like becoming indispensable to very purpose of living and existence. Be your own boss of life. Autonomy nowhere dilutes the principality of living. Can any flower plant bloom roses and lily through the same bud? Let the dawn of today be one of the greatest dawns of your living.

Live daily like the lily loving the whole earth. The aroma of your life should reach one and all. There is lot to be unlocked within us to benefit from the power of selfless collaboration of humans. Imagine if the whole world was blessed with even hundreds to thousands of perfectionists.

Our limitation to understand life imperatively triggers the inner institution at dawn. The daily lessons from the natural teacher dawn to dusk should not be lost.

Leaders have affinity to problems as they are destined resolvers. Managers have a total different approach towards the troubles. Troubles always flow towards leaders.

Leaders live the day. Managers pass the day.

The professionalism however fails to attain the perfectionism. The learning comprehended is to act from dawn to dusk irrespective of the results. No activity is without cause. Cause springs from thought. Thought is the living force.

Life is designed to be in motion. The inertia cannot be controlled by man. The war between Life and Man will remain forever. How long you can wait for the rub of the green? There are plenty more fish in the sea. Wherever you go, be not surprised to see that thereby hangs a tale.

Every matter has its own saga of pros and cons. It seems the writing is on the wall for humanity in the world. Why, can anyone not research it out?

Who is in control of Life? We need the impetus to hunt and chase. Man is progressing from ignorance and suffering to enlightenment and freedom from dawn to dusk. Virtues are vanishing faster than the speed of light. Instantly a man behaves with duality forging all the morale of humanity. Is it like man is no more considering himself as human? Right and wrong both are in you.

Life is nothing if not inevitable.

Where is the paradise of life? Life is our latent instinct to know ourselves. Who wishes to be in graveyard with full of regrets? Life is not to just roll the days allotted to you. What is foreseeable without commitment?

Every dawn to dusk should leave behind indelible reminiscences in your life. The final recollections should help in liberating you .Thus you would have made an inspirational history for others to maintain the inertia of valuable living. Is every individual in search of his existence from dawn to dusk? Are we not the wandering souls? We all have to journey this. The enormity of life is such that hardly one can, ever in the life time experience and sail through all the facts.

Complete perfection is infinite.

The day it is attained the whole process of evolution will collapse. The seed of thought is always fertile but inordinate abeyance of fruitful cultivation has withered away our inherent ability to sow in time.

Let us peep in our ignorance to see the bright glowing light enveloped by the darkness in man. Life is never senile. Can the impact dwindling of life be forgone without regrets by us? This swindling act will be unpardonable by the self in life. Life will wear out whether we sit still or go about from dawn to dusk. Twinkling of life is the natural existence. It should jump, play, smile, thrill, rise, act, voice, to manifest in all forms.

Why Life is shrinking?

The advantage of being a human being is that we have the virgin power to engineer our evolution. If you are wondering why your life isn't turning out the way you planned, then you are probably on the right path of living.

Life is about innovation.

It has to change. Change is inevitable. People around the globe are having more or less similar challenges from dawn to dusk. A true insight into it simplifies the severity of existence. Contentment of individuals is a matter of personal choice. Religion is life not mere thought. It has to be lived. The secret of life is education through experience. Let it be any religion it should satisfy your soul and fill your whole being.

Dawn to Dusk will help millions and millions over the world to become what they were trying to become. It is not that the world presently has no great reformers from dawn to dusk. It is not that things are not happening towards humanity. It is not that nations are not concerned to globalize humanity. There are in fact millions of people having greater understanding of the subject than me. I am unfortunate to understand, learn and resolve from them my own queries of life just as the readers. I pray more of the readers become authors. It is one of the ways to reach all.

A voice can magnify to millions and millions voices. An idea can multiply to billions and billions of ideas. Brains can share to the whole brains of the world.

Books are always alive. It is read today, will be read in the years to come, again down and down carried over to centuries and so on. The idea lived through it. It never perishes with the civilization.

Idea is eternal.
&
Voice is immortal.

Today I am chanting with you, tomorrow the existence will chant with nature. Till the dreams are breeding the supply chain of thoughts, ideas, voices, concepts, philosophies, cultures, values, will continue to invade the existence. Nothing is of mine; it is through me to the existence, just in and out, the individual being a media of transmission and one life energy into other, another and so on, it goes on.

What I am emphasizing is that I am a sample in this population struggling to voice the reinstatement of humanity? I am trying to integrate through the available resources the effectiveness of the concern for humanity. I am sharing with the world to drive the awareness more rapidly before it is plumbed. I wish to join all the faculty of the world in penetrating the minds of society.

I am faithfully putting forward "Dawn to Dusk" with hopefulness not helplessness that this universal appeal finds all men of the world to think about humanity and equally work towards it.

My unending desire to be a party to it is irresistible. I will tell you, it is only due to the fruit of blessing that I am pouring down the possibilities of reformation through these chapters on humanity. I am joining the reformist faculty with this piece of small work believing it to be of substantial assistance in the journey of reformation, restructuring and regenerating humanity.

Why do we regret? This process somewhere again connects you to your desires, dreams, ambitions, aims, success, failures, achievements, containment, satisfaction, happiness, and so on; which keeps haunting your inner world daily.

Can man live without desires? Dreams are the metabolism of living. Do not give regret chances to drown you before swimming the ocean of life. Man is changing his mask as per situational adaptability. Originality suffers the flow to balance the purity of relationships.

Dawn to Dusk has something or other for everyone. You have to do deeds despite different needs. Nothing new is being advocated from dawn to dusk. All are studying their limitations to reach the ultimate ideals.

The day begins to help you. It is your attitude which converts into enthusiasm, inspiration, optimism, vigor, ability, action, admiration, accomplishments, affection, love, friendship, success, happy, satisfied, sad, aggressiveness, agony, misery, conflict, hatred, violence, enmity, etc, at the end of the dusk.

Few are creating racism, colonialism, violence, terrorism, imperialism, capitalism, aristocratism, negativism, tribalism, towards destruction for nothing to be glorified with their egoism. The other few are working towards peace, harmony, secularism, positivism, brotherhood, optimism, to lift the mankind.

Why man should work with duality in mind? Life is intrinsically single without predefined amendments and annexure to it. How to fundamentally organize it? How to positively benefit from this life time inherent opportunity?

Grapes were meant to be essentially eaten fresh and not to be drunk as wine after decaying for years. World likes to swim in wine. It has yet to understand the taste of freshness, neatness, cleanliness, truthfulness, and meaning of life. Our world today enjoys the decomposed taste rather than the naturally gifted fruits. This is what is becoming of man. As water is made sweeter by adding sugar so life is to be enriched with sweetness of humanity.

A day lost from this bundle of opportunities equally robs you from the grace of experiencing new things.

How to remove the dust on us? Let us awake into lightness of life. Universe is an open window to look for the secrets of justifying life from dawn to dusk. The Almighty can be seen through the love of heart, mind perceives the kingdom of universe and service is to be done through the physical body of existence.

A happy man can only give happiness to other man. A smiling man can only bring smile to the other man. A crying man can only bring tears to other man. An angry man can only make other man cruel. An inspired man can send vibrations of enormous energy to the depressed man. A spiritual man can kindle the light to vanish the evil in another man. A learned man can only teach the other man wisdom of life. It is up to us to decide from dawn to dusk, which category of man you would like to be.

It is always good not to know many negative things as their perception and reasons are also negative. If you search something in the garbage, finally you end up getting garbage.

Do not start the day with this idiotic tonic?

It has the power to dissolve all the goodness in you. Keep yourself away as much as you can. It very quickly pollutes your thinking. Never allow it to make home in your existence. We have been hearing that the world is not good, neighbors not nice, boss is bad, wife is not supportive, husband is exploiting, children are not listening, colleagues are criticizing, servants are not loyal, bills are soaring, inflation is rising, government policies are uncertain, and so forth.

Tell me, why we are in this type of predicament?

Did it happen in a blue moons day? All the happenings are truth. What we have done to cope with this truth? All may not be primarily influencing your living. If it is so also, the sky never falls. Why do not you become good to make the world good? Why do not you be nice to your neighbors, so that in turn they will be nice? How many times you have helped your neighbors voluntarily?

Man is born to volunteer services. Imagine a world without man? No man in existence. Only it is for the animals and plants. Now even eliminate the animals from it and again when all are withdrawn from the existence, i.e., world without animals, without plants, and world without man. A new world has evolved? How do you feel now? This perhaps was the state prior to our existence. Is it not an ambiguous question for all of us? When we are no more our issues are also no more? Where do the issues go?

Humanity needs voluntarism.

Voluntarism should be the new culture. Make voluntarism your religion. Do you have to ask someone to help the sick? Do you have to question your race to give blood for humanity? Voluntary is the true nature of man. Wherever there exists opportunity to volunteer yourself for mankind from dawn to dusk, do it blindly. This is the faith of righteousness. Faith in god is always a pure blind faith.

God does not require justification for faith. Voluntarily associate with him without any reason. That Man is man who stands against all uncertainties. Uncertainties shall certainly lead you to realistic destinations with the process of refinement through the phases of unwanted destinations. Let the world speak the language of voluntarism. Strengthen its foundations to become the Universal Secularism demolishing the conventionalism.

Can I witness a dawn of destiny?

Will my journey of life meet the destination of existence? There are Men without questions too. Think about their perception. It is not that they are lack of perceptions. For them the best perception is to follow the perception of destiny.

Perception is mightier than the sword of literacy.

It has the potential to cut all your miseries from dawn to dusk. It holds the courage and strength to sail against the wind. Ultimately it is perception that matters at the end. It is fuelled by the heat of inspiration. The energy of perception should be reaped by one and all. It is magnet to the whole purpose of existence. This is a treasure not to be lost.

Man's greatest wealth is to realize the abundance of life. It is inherent to your existence. What is that which you do not have? What is that which you cannot give? Is there beggar in you to weaken your kingdom of affluences?

Man is always rich by nature. Leaving the orchids we are running back of bushes of thorns.

All buds do not bloom to flower. Pray to be graced so. Gratify the other buds blooming. One day the reward of gratification will be at your feet. Nature is never partial. Man is not impartial to other man.

Prejudices are bringing discrimination in society.

How to get rid of your negative influences? The thought to live overcomes the fear of death. When the last ball of an over can win a cricket match, a penalty kick of football can give you a winning goal, kingdom with a move to checkmate the opposite king in chess, a millionth of a second in a sprint race, then why cannot you win the life. Have you thought to do so? If not done, start doing it from today. Say to yourself, you are here to only win, win, and win the humanity.

Life is to be won.

It is never too late, till the very moment you determine to win. Light the torch of Olympic to raise your spirits of life. Learn to win and you shall keep winning. Play life as sports. It is a great game of existence. The arena is the world you are in. It has its own rule of law from dawn to dusk. Without the zeal the passion is midway. Do it. Pull your shocks and you shall never regret. Sometimes you might have done it. You may be at the verge of the deserving success. An additional millionth of a second of patience might have been your destiny. So never quit.

Quitters are never winners. Sinners are never givers. Misers are never wealthy. Givers are never liars. Richness is an unwanted sickness in society. Lunch and dinner is what is required daily from dawn to dusk. You cannot be a fool to have the fields of grains in your homes?

Homes are not built to push the world in. In fact homes come out to build the world. We are living like the owl. Our darkness is the drawback to experience the life in vastness from dawn to dusk. Can you win over your opponents?

Many times your opponents win not because they are better in credentials than yours, but for the only reason, that you made the way for them by quitting. The positive competition elevates the level of performance. The mind struggles to beat the opponent, and in doing so the learning begins again. This continues to bring the best in both.

Every man is blessed with a specific talent. Right things happen at the right time. And our concern is right things should happen to one and all.

Summing Up & Exercise for Readers -Chapter-I

- I hope the literature might have started rekindling your innovations.
- Make sure from today that you do not lose witnessing the hidden opportunities in the twilight of the dawns daily henceforth.
- Try to work out a plan for yourself with dawn, ideas, opportunities, thoughts, voice, inspiration, and dreams to reestablish humanity.
- Construct pyramids of opportunities, ideas and actions for everyday.
- Utilize the power of pyramid to know yourself better.
- Monitor and direct your activities in line with the pyramid of humanity.

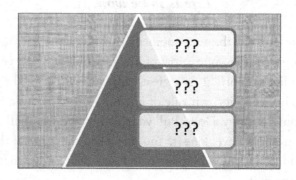

- Go out in nature to chase your dreams.
- Meet people whom you have never met earlier in your life.
- Try to change the faces with whom you had enough of time drained pushing your ideologies and philosophies.
- Become new by joining new people.
- Become good by associating with good people.
- Look for change and you shall change.
- Live by action.
- Reason out your time.
- Analyze your contribution from dawn to dusk.
- Make a daily appraisal report of your targets achieved.
- You need to operate your resources effectively and in direction of humanity.
- Every one of us should do these exercises regularly even after skills have become habit.
- Play like the child with these work books.

- Dawn to Dusk is a living work book. Repeat the exercises as many times as you can
- The more is practiced the more is perfection.
- Do not live in a theoretical world.
- Give chance to your ideas, thoughts, dreams to be seen physical moving with, in, around, beside, above, below people.
- If you are not a writer, or a writer, attempt to pen down a better essay on "Dawn is Life" which you have just read.
- Try to find out something which I might have not come across and is certainly going to be useful in our life pertaining to the cause of humanity.
- There is no limit to learning, teaching, preaching and sharing from dawn to dusk.
- Work and work on this chapter till you have excelled in understanding "Dawn is Life".
- There has been an underlying purpose to title the chapter so. There has been lot of research into it before it is has been finalized to reach out to readers. Can you say why?
- Bring dawn to your way of thinking and living.
- Rearrange, realign, reform, restore, and redefine all that were not working in the interest of humanity.
- Everything can be new. It is only your will at the dawn which can decide your way from dawn to dusk.
- Write your wills every day.
- Review your results every day.
- Make yourself accountable for your life.
- Maintain your daily life achievement journal.
- Jot down all you have experienced.
- Summarize the findings from dawn to dusk.
- Work on the lessons you have received today.
- All the above is exercise for one and all.
- By practicing so we will be certainly welcoming the dawn of humanity in us.

Chapter II
OWNERSHIP OF LIFE

"This idea of oneness is the greatest lesson India has to give,"
said Swami Vivekananda.

Looking back the indispensable contribution of India in uplifting the spirituality in World, the global expectations have never died down even today. This has been a land of interest to many across all the civilizations. The traces can be found everywhere imparting the lessons of nonviolence and tolerance in the world.

Life between philosophy and ownership is like the widest gap between land and sky. It can fly between these ends dimensionless never meeting in reality. The horizon has been waiting for ages and ages to witness the land meeting the sky. The horizon has been waiting for ages and ages to witness the ocean meeting the sky. The human has been waiting for ages and ages to witness the spirit meeting the body. The human has been waiting for ages and ages to witness the life meeting the death. The human has been waiting for ages and ages to witness the dawn meeting the dusk.

Will the land ever meet the sky? Will the ocean ever meet the sky? Will the life ever meet the death? Will the human ever meet the spirit? Will the dawn ever meet the dusk?

In my perception of life,

"Man standing at the horizon owns nothing, neither the sea nor the sky. You have to decide either to dive deeper into the sea or to fly higher into the sky to own something in life".

Your life belongs to whom? Are you the real owner? What is the percentage of your share in it? You are always at conflict? It appears that internal conflict in the human mind is the beginning of all evolutions. Is Man born to live and die without ownership of life? Can we own our lives? How and to what extent? Can you define the ownership of life? What man should own? Why he should own?

Life is to be owned.

Probably there will be as many answers as humans on this earth. Are we suffering because we do not own our life? Will ownership make the difference? Why do not you try? What you will lose by owning your life? Do you have to become more accountable? Will the responsibility increase?

Life is being considered as an organization, enterprise, unit, establishment, which has predefined mission, vision, objectives, goals, and is to be lead, managed and administered till it exists. The purpose continues to exist till the end of existence. The recent blending of man with bit of art, math, science, technology, social, economics, commerce, and management to redefine humans of modern times is being witnessed as the evolution of today.

Were earlier men not sophisticated as todays? Hopefully they perished trying to meet their survival needs at that time. There were fewer faculties to upgrade the standard of living. Agreed, but do you mean to say that modernization is the only marginally seen external development of humans.

What about the inner human?

Where is he? Leaving the inside can you own the outside? Man should not have a culture to beg. Did I come to this earth to fight, take revenge, cheat, molest, steal, flirt, lust, etc? Was I here really to enact all this? How good it would have been, if I would have been retained in heaven only?

Man is always at confusion to understand the objective of the self, nature, world, god, people, universe, destiny, life, existence, soul, mind, conscience, illusion, reality, oneness, duality, physical body, mortal, immortal, happiness, love, salvation, liberation, bondage, ethics, theology, philosophy, genesis, ownership, and so many in and around him, may probably be the question running in everyone's mind. The point of discussion is say there are no answers to the above queries, what worst is going to happen.

Man in me is a poor owner of life.

The institution in man is to be organized accordingly. The question gets unanswered despite the intellectual development of man in me. Is there any other supreme power in man, continuously invading his inner existence? Is it late to start owning our lives?

Let us be leaders, managers, administrators, teachers and mentors to our own lives first. Different departments are needed to streamline the derailing enterprise of life. Are you going to gain anything with inventory of days? It is good to utilize all of them before they are exhausted. Time is debiting them from your fixed deposit of days. Whether you act or not, live or not, do or not, think or not, realize or not, learn or not, they will never be credited and reversed.

Your stocks of days are limited. Once issued cannot be reconciled. I hope you understand what I am meaning to put to all through dawn to dusk. You are going to be product of your own engineering. Your quality as finished product will reflect and reveal the plan of manufacturing your life. Would you not like the market of society to appreciate this good product? Let society accredit you with all product standard certifications and acknowledgements.

Be a Man of Man.

What price can society pay for such a man? Society will remain indebted to you forever. Why mind is not at peace from dawn to dusk? Peace is not a commodity which can be purchased as and when you want. It is built drop by drop in you. The basics of all influencing factors need to be absolutely free from ambiguities.

The greatest wealth for any man is peace.

A peaceful mind can make better decisions, right interpretations; sincerely shoulder responsibility with ownership of life and subsequently harmony in society. A stick in hand does not mean you have to cane everybody. The assimilation by realization is the best process of understanding life. We need to cultivate adaptation to the reality but not at the cost of moral. Moral keeps intervening during the modes of survival. Is it not shame that for the sake of mere survival our intrinsic morals of man are being sintered mercilessly?

Man has to work towards integrating himself to the society. The society too has been unwontedly absorbing immoral attitudes and objectives leading to the disintegration of the primary principles of raising divine culture. When you have worked exhaustively, you will like to relax with the taste of sweat being sweeter than as it is. When you have written down exhaustively burning the midnight lamp, you will like to review and read to enjoy the views of the author, for further aligning it with the needs and objectives of the readers. Unless you put in sincere time and effort, the attachment with the outcome is superficial. It should rock the mountain in reality.

Ownership of Life

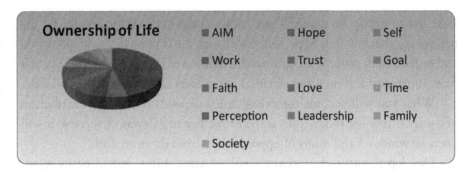

It is not necessary that the coach of the cricket team should be a cricketer. What is wrong if a football player is made the coach of a cricket team? I will put this principally to understand as what is the real role of the coach here. Is the coach going to do the batting and balling for the team.

I hope you all agree that he will not be at the field as one of the players playing the match. His role is to work out the strength, weaknesses, mental balances, physical fitness, and strategies of the game, understand the competitors, mentor the team, and work for overall integration of the team. He is responsible for the moral spirit of the players, their motivation level, dedication, commitment and the passion with which they play the game. They are to be regularly guided, mentored, and spirits elevated to win and only win.

This is how man has to understand the prime things of life. The idea should be backed up with clarity. When you are selecting or looking for a player to be inducted in cricket team, of course he is the one to bat or ball at the field not the coach.

I want to say through the above illustration that mapping of responsibilities either it is owned or entrusted should be properly justified. It is not that a chair is to be filled the person is nominated and appointed. Many areas of our public offices, governments, institutions, enterprises, are more or less suffering from this syndrome.

The Pie-Chart above reflects a sample of ownership of life. How you can distribute to have a good living? The variation is linked to the perception of an individual.

Own your life.
Then life too will own you.

First habits are to be made. Then habits make man. What should be the percentage share of aim, hope, self, trust, goal, etc is to be properly calculated and organized to arrive at an optimal distribution of ownership of life . Say you have 100% aim and no other essential parameters then where will you land.

What you will become tomorrow much depends upon your distribution of ownership of life today. This is the prime key to gateway of success. It will open all windows and doors of opportunities from dawn to dusk.

Develop the attitude and you shall see your ability unfolding its wings to zenith of life. Do and see, it has happened for many and you are not the exception to it.

Believe me friends no one, extremely no one, I repeat is exception to this.

Perception of Universal Living

In my opinion,

"A mole of misunderstanding should not
become a mountain of conflict".

What is your thought on life?

What is your idea in life? How to examine these? How to compare it? How to analyze it? Where to look for? Can a perception be established in a day? It is unimaginable to comprehend the world in a fraction of second. If all is known at the stroke of the beat then life should not have the chapters undisclosed in progressive phases.

My perception of life cannot be a benchmark to completely photocopy it. Perceptions will defer from place to place, time to time, man to man, society to society, humanity to humanity.

Life is attitude.
&
How to get attitude?

Darkness vanishes in the presence of light. Evil falls down in the presence of god. What is Wholeness of god? What is fullness of existence? Have you experienced it? Why to have careless attitude? What is the law of life?

Do you work with ideals? Is there any laboratory to test god? What can be better than humans? Say we all could not reach to the finding of our source; will it be catalyzing our existence? Humanity has a long way to go? Sometimes there may not be clarity in the direction of progress but continuity of progress is towards the final goal.

Life is perception.

The way you see the life looks. For me it is opportunity to work for humanity. For some it is grace to succeed intrinsically. Fundamentally many enjoy the joy of nature. Smile on your face is within you. It is reflection of your happiness, containment, satisfaction, peace, bliss and other things holding it. Anger on your face is also within you. It is reflection of your unhappiness, dissatisfaction, disquiet, jealousy, sorrow, sadness and other things holding it. It imperatively is due to the state of perception towards living.

Human needs fulfillment either at the physical plane or at the non-physical plane from dawn to dusk affects the other human behaviors. A satisfied man will not be angry. On the other hand an unsatisfied man will be arrogant.

Man quantifies his living. The limit is a question of morale in him. Man retires from activity but not from the mind. In fact is that man's suffering is more because of the mind? My sincere conscience admits that man's nature cannot be completely under the control of mind. This tool is with everyone.

And who can be the best master rather than the one operating it? How can I take control of your mind? And the other way too, where is the liberty for you to invade in my mind.

A perception perceived by me may not be in line with yours. Thus asking for a universal perception without the unification of minds is beyond the wisdom of man. What is actually attitude? Can it really make a difference from dawn to dusk?

If your approach today is to help as many as you can, you will not regret at dusk the contribution you have made since dawn. This feeling to do well gives you a positive outlook. The manner to assist, mentor, care, share, with the background mind-set speaks of the true attitude to bring harmony and peace in society. The thoughts are vibrating to serve mankind. The whole atmosphere inside and outside experiences the oneness of thought and goodness prevails. What is the single most quality a person should have? Why we fail to perceive as it would have been perceived?

Does time play an important role to arrive at a matured perception of life? It appears that once the major share of life has been drained, we start reconciling too late to hardly recover anything.

Society is equally divided into two major perceptions of living. Some are with the dawn of optimism. The other section sails silently with the theory of pessimism in the darkness of dusk but finally to the same goal of existence. Being merry on journey is like enjoying the grace of existence. With unhappiness and curses it is like burdening ourselves with the weight of existence. Feelings control the metabolism of life.

Do you feel for humanity?

Man appears to be helpless in front of circumstances. Always his perception, plans and wisdom are kept aside. Then he realizes that there is some unknown without whose assistance he cannot progress and prosper. There is some invisible power on whose silent permission and grace we live, survive, sustain, work, play, fight, enjoy, cry, laugh, help, no end to man's dramatic life on earth.

Nature's perception is the only universal perception.

All different perceptions in the world are towards this natural perception. Universal perception is the goal of all life.

Why we are missing the moral of living? If families are splitting off, how you expect the world to be unified. Nowadays the education on character, attitude, personality, mankind, spirituality and humanity needs sincere emphasis. We somehow tend to drift away from adding life values to ourselves despite the academic degrees awarded to us.

The gap between learning and values is diminishing exponentially without correction and inappreciably is being carried forward. The alarming point of transition is that will there be any legacy of values in the coming generations? It is hard to digest but this constipation will ruin the appetite of moral living. Whom to blame? The society is becoming so. The eccentricity is towards the downfall of humanity.

My dear respected readers, I wish to alarm you that "Will the Third World War be purely War of Humanity?"

To sadly quote to you through dawn to dusk from the daily newspapers, magazines, articles, television shows, documentaries, broadcastings, journalists, cinemas, stage drama, you will not be surprised to know that they do not have any better subject other than murdered, killed, accident, stabbed, robbed, shot dead, kidnapped, bombarded, retaliated, ceasefire, evacuated, jailed, gang raped, sexually harassed, hanged, brothel, divorced, bribed, and so on and forth.

This is our society today all over the world. Who made it? Why we are facing it? Why it is continuing? When will it end? Who will do it? It would not have happened overnight. Why did it go uncorrected? Did we take steps towards disciplining ourselves? Where to put the checks? Who is the culprit? Will man still continue with animalism?

This is story of all lands. No continent or country is exception to it.

Why Man is becoming immoral himself? Honestly we have been dishonest since times immemorial. There is abundant literature on man and society for review since the oldest civilizations. It had been a continual subject of understanding, enrichment, improvement, development and growth from dawn to dusk. But it nearly confirms that we are absolute fools who have failed to realize the basic purpose of man's societies across the globe.

Perception is energy of life. Let us not be traitors to our thoughts. Where to find the delight of senses? Is pleasure the only thing man is looking for in life? Think you will live, and you become lively.

Do not worry if a thorn pricks you to get a rose.

We unnecessarily ponder more murmuring about a time which has passed away. Most of the valuable present time is lost in analyzing and interpreting the past. The perception of individual leads to innumerable definitions of life from dawn to dusk.

It is very well known to Man that he is another piece in the puzzle of life.

Is there something innate which comes from our past life? This is a million dollar question with infinite unfeasible solutions. The empirical approach towards life invariably collides with the philosophical perception. The inherent abilities allow us to be distinguished from each other. How then an art of living customized so, may be a Universal law of existence for humans?

Why Man sins?

The scenario today is that sinners are winners. Man should not conclude as thinkers. Man has known Man since ages and ages. From dawn to dusk man is struggling with another Man. The process of self-purification both mentally and physically despite different modes by man converges to the central theme of oneness.

Distinctions are in thought though the substance being thought is same. The characteristics of life are being explored from dawn to dusk between the confined boundaries of respective cultures and religion.

Man is a social animal with instinct to perceive, compete, defend, fight, love, inspire and realize his own actions bearing result conducive to the society.

Thought, speech and action should be free of sins. One of the debatable understandings marginally throws light on the intellectuality of individuals though having the similar physical form all over the world.

Is it that mind is above body? There were great proponents of perception the Universe had produced fortunately to visualize the purpose of life. The research continues without concrete findings. Moreover everything gets assimilated to be electrified as the dense black clouds, unfortunately pouring down to wash the experience of reminisces.

Can Man perceive the Creator's perception? The throne of wisdom is in search of the kingdom of knowledge. Billions and billions of perception on life is unable to map with the Creator.

Let us not dwell in the past.

Call the present.
Work in the present.
Think in the present.
Serve in the present.
Look in the present.
Inspire in the present.
Act in the present.
Help in the present.
Nourish in the present.
Rise in the present.
Awake in the present.
Be present in the present.
Fight in the present.
Voice it in the present.
Do it in the present.
Live in the present.
Die in the present.
Sweat in the present.
Love in the present.
Learn in the present.
Play in the present.
Pray in the present.
Worship in the present.

Search in the present.
Teach in the present.
Preach in the present.
Meet in the present.
Breathe in the present.

Anxiety about future without planning is like murdering the present. Either small or big, being in activity is the essence of life.

Man should attempt to interact with the existence. Then only a true sharing of the basic substance may grace to uplift Man from the marshy lands of ignorance like the lotus. The process of blessing is being done by the nature from dawn to dusk.

Let the garden of humanity be flooded with butterflies of love.

Every human should be the flower in the garden of humanity. Why the life in me, is searching the perception of living? To vogue or to sacrifice are two extremes of the perception of living. What do I really want? Is it either to transform the world or the self?

Can I live without the world?
&
Where to go?

Do you want to be leader of your own destiny? Let our lives be not redundant ones. How to make it more productive from dawn to dusk? The taming of the self should be to attain the abundance of life before it is abandoned. Have I attained what I desired? Will my grievances be buried? Shall fate address all my worries? Who will live for me? Will my search for existence end?

Can I conquer the Dusk?

There is going to be more and more such questions arising in life to open avenues accordingly. Change is the only constant cannot be redefined. Do not stare at the sky, it will never fall? Do not fear yourself, the power is within you.

How to define the economics of life?

Does the science of today open the eyes of perception? Will the generations carry the established perceptions? Business and welfare both cannot go together. All the old doctrines are awaiting introspection of its beliefs. Hope and faith may have to prove their commitment.

Simply having a positive perception always may not be the right way of living. This may lead us to advocate the wrong things in the world. A positive experience is not that which sails you in comfort to ultimately worsen your sufferings at the end.

Love in Nature

My readers will agree with this thought that "Love is the lifeline of humans".

What nature is trying to give life from dawn to dusk?

At times it appears to be our home, where we retire to rest. And sometimes Man has to fight the uprooting facing the abnormal nature. It feeds like a brave mother to the hungry lovers. Man has fought battles to retain lands. Patriotism is the reflection of the true soldier's love for the nation. Wars have broken to uphold the spirit of love. Man is a desert without love.

Man and Nature are playing the game of hide and seek from dawn to dusk? Man aspires himself with inspiration from nature. The spirit in man is to hold the hearts of nature.

Love is universal.
&
Love is the nucleus which binds the life.

A flower blooms with fragrance to be offered at the feet's of god, without any such predetermined aim very early at dawn. Only the graced one makes it. The Almighty pretending unknowingly is fortunate to befall the heavenly fate to the bud to be honored gracefully at the service of Lord beginning with the dawn.

From it we can infer that from dawn to dusk it is our prime duty to unconditionally keep doing what we have been graced to do on. The fruits and rewards are like the dawn and dusk of the day.

Whom to love? This is a million dollar unanswered question. Do you need to justify anyone before loving? Hate the hatred. Repel the repellant. Warriors are to be replaced by lovers of humanity. Love the lovers. Loving has as many meaning as perception of understanding the life. Divinity in humans is to be explored. Purity of relationships should be honored. It need not be manipulated and exploited. The flirting of faith is like running your understanding of love. The limitations are blessings to be away from the lusting of love.

Love and lust needs to be differentiated.

It should bring out the best of every man on this earth. The innocence of love as child has to prevail in man.

Child is a man of his own thoughts.

Children are personification of love. Why man should manipulate other man? Let us just ask this to our true self. Lovers should rule the kingdom of humanity. Society can only be cheerful if flooded with true love from dawn to dusk.

Do you think of humanity? Can we stop crying? Why humanity is weeping? Just look into life and see how people are dying of love. Read their tired eyes. The tears are revealing the agony of attachment. Families are breaking like glasses. Irreparable damage is being done to see the dooms day.

Is this the definition of love?

Are we chasing the wrong dreams? It is never too late to clean ourselves. We have to modify our entities as we go through life. The change should keep coming into all of us. Try to find joy in everyday things from dawn to dusk. Let us become mad to reestablish the glory of humans.

Our understanding of a person may not be always right on all occasions.

There are people who lose to win to adhere to the wisdom of living. Living is itself an encyclopedia of feelings, emotions, fear, strength, happiness, sadness, moral, values, justice, etc. Living with right spirits is what dawn to dusk thinks about. Do not you agree that half of your time is lost in complaining and grumbling? Can we stop interacting with others?

Man has to speak to man. Leave this man, leave the next one, where are you going, in search of man of your like, keep jumping cities, towns, countries, continents, like a wild monkey, the end result is, you will end up alone.

Why no likeness, have you questioned yourself? Anger is like rotten apple, it helps you in losing all your friends. Likeness brings in sweetness. Soreness brings unhappiness. Who will take the responsibility of converting anger to love? Who will convert tears to cheers?

Dawn to Dusk has great task to convert anger to love.

We all have to join this workshop. Let there be more and more projects of revolutionizing the society. Simply sustaining the society economically should not be the only objective of all nations. A healthy society can only give a healthy nation. If nations are healthy, the world is the healthiest place to germinate the seeds of humanity.

Let the negative thoughts be dissolved forever and ever. Harmony has to spread through the landscape of the earth. Everyone visiting earth should proudly say there is no such wonderful place than our earth in the universe.

Man's greatest challenge is to rise above his own narrow limitations.

Man's heart has to expand million times to understand the love of nature. Why we are upset, unhappy, depressed, de-motivated, and sad? Aggression and violence takes away peace and happiness. Why violence? Why Man kills Man? Why fight for power? Is power to crusade with man? Do we really gain by paining life? Why cannot we daily kiss humanity?

Kiss the world.
&
Do not kill it.

Are we really giving importance to human life?

Till when man will deceive man. Leaders and followers, teachers and students, parents and children, wife and husband, brothers and sisters, friends and colleagues, schools and colleges, nations and societies, religions and cultures, books and publishers, young and old, research and findings, masters and slaves, rich and poor, good and bad, business and companies, family and marriages, saints and missionaries, monks and monasteries, soldiers and army, nursing and services, god and devotees, players and games, lectures and classes, labs and experiments, authors and readers, politics and governance, charters and citizens, philosophy and life, dreams and reality, man and humanity and so on are associations of living from dawn to dusk to excel in their respective departments of responsibilities.

Everywhere there is greater need to love the relationship. Help yourself to increase the concern for each other. There is no fun in only assuring. Live the relationship. Respect the association. It is due to the impact of relationship and association that the healthiness of society differs.

Contribute to enrich the existence. Kill the diplomacy to edify the relationship. Truthfulness is the right way to commit the living. Ask the son who has lost is father, the woman her husband, the mother her son, the nation the soldier for only reason being the war among humans. Are we not ashamed of this? Taking lives is not an optimal solution. Law of life is to be honored by one and all. It should not use the cane to tame the man. It is shame on society to survive with it.

Humanity is losing its eternal identity.

How many of them will be killed so to gain nothing in the end? If at all we want to kill, let us kill them by the love of humanity.

Kill as many as you like by love.

Encounter with love. Every man has a heart with love. Just by exchange of hearts you can love. There are abundant resources of love. Let the tsunami of love erode the society. The world should be stormed by super cyclones of love. Go anywhere the grains of love should feed you from dawn to dusk.

Poetry of life is a powerful feeling of man's heart. It expands and contracts with nature. As rightly described by the English Poet, William Wordsworth, "That best portion of a man's life, his little, nameless, unremembered acts of kindness and love".

His minute observation of nature, "The flower that smells the sweetest is shy and lowly".

And the lovable part of his expression, "The Child is father of the Man".

All hearts are centers of love.

Start magnetizing the society with love. The momentary space of time is mortally immortal in existence. The flowing streams at the hills descend to the lands breaking the tranquility of spring. The rising peaks of the mountains invariably inspire to touch the clouds. The sight of flying birds with unfolded wings encourages us to expand our ambitions. The breath in you wishes to explode the volcano of freedom. The true nature of life purely waits to embrace each and all through the love of existence.

Dawn to Dusk knows only the language of love.

The heart beats to the music of life either at dawn or at dusk. Life neither dies at dawn nor at dusk. Blessed are the ones who have done their work before the dusk has engulfed them. Deprived are the ones who despite grace of dawn could not liberate themselves from the ignorance of life. When nothing was yours before arriving here, what will be yours after departing from here?

All is ultimately not even a handful of ash of yours at the end. You were nothing and will again become nothing. You were only experiencing the transformation between dawn to dusk and dusk to dawn.

Love all beings.

Everyone has something to be appreciated. Can you roar like the lion? Do not look at the shortcomings as it is in all of us. Show me a perfect man says the self. Perfection alone cannot be the final destination. Look beyond it to merge the dawn into dusk. Perfection is infinite. It is no where a final destination for man. Be on the way to perfection.

Everyone has enough in the kingdom of world. The attribute of containment needs to be cultivated by all of us. Necessity should overrule the thirst of greediness.

Let the rain of love fall on all.

Love has no limitations. The true nature of existence is to explore love. The world is starving for love. There is huge crisis of love to be addressed between the roof and land of the world. Love has its own manifestations and perceptions. The un-attachment brings in liberty to love. It should have no bondage from dawn to dusk.

How to impact humanity? All our problems are with humans. Man is a typical robotic machine with an emotional drive. The world needs many happiness projects for humans. Our love can only help bringing smile to every face. Let us unlock our hearts into the insight of love. What use is of pilgrimage, if you have not discovered the God in you?

Every living being is happy with its own sense of understanding life. If all have similar opinions then where is the manifestation of comparing variations? An edification to elevate may be by virtue of the individual at times or sometimes the prime limiting factor is its own inherited nature of survival. Man appears to be enemy of man and again man is the greatest savior of man.

We all have the liberator within us to free ourselves from the chronic disease of hatred.

Man was never built in a day.

Relationships are also not built in a day. Why you like or hate man? Two human beings that come into conversation are committing an interaction between souls. God is a Universal soul. Life has infinite possibilities to be enacted.

Man is the result of his own thoughts.

Better thoughts better man. Bad thoughts will produce bad man. Evil thoughts will create devil man. Divine thoughts fabricate holy man. Foolish thoughts shape stupid man. Wisdom thoughts make learned man. A specific relation appears between thinking and becoming of us. Now the difficulty is to understand the controlling of thoughts in man. It is not that the people are not thinking today and were not thinking earlier, there are no concrete answers to many thoughts.

Parents are the first God to children is known to one and all. Parenting is the greatest definition of love. No land, no religion, no caste, no color, was my choice, before I came to see this world. I was above all discriminations. It was only when I descended from the heavens, could know of the fragile man dwelling in diversities of life. Today's rising of old age homes in society advocates the suffering relationship with diminishing love. New generation is nucleating themselves to redefine the emotional love into intellectual love.

Can love of parents be repaid by anyone of us?
&
Moreover we are forgetting to take care of them.

All battles were fought in the mind, to be lost truly at the end. Time was never gained to share but elapsed in confrontation. Wars of opinions could not melt the love of hearts. Unsightly things have been polluting the minds of insane humans. Man creates barriers to later fight it as stupid warriors. The mind is the battleground where all preparation takes place before it is physically executed.

All the wars are in minds.

Man is at war with mind from dawn to dusk. He is stressed by man. Why it is so? Try to work out on your own. There is always light at the end of the tunnel. Keep penetrating to see it and shall be submerged in the brightness of enlightenment. How anger can be an attribute of a peaceful soul which holds your life? Let us not germinate it, as the root of it is only going to erect the unwanted tree of unhappiness. We are living in darkness covered under the jungle of evils. There is no purpose in burning the candle at both ends. Look beyond the restricted visions of eyes, so that the limitations of the emotions can be overcome. The perfume of life cannot be locked in the bottle of self. It will find its way without demolishing the individual identity of all.

Love is universal.

It cannot be confined. It diffuses to reach all. Why cannot world be a single family? It is not only for the sake of philosophy. In fact the truth is that Man has made demographical barriers. Love without manipulation is the true way for living life. Predetermined thoughts and baseless ideologies from dawn to dusk keep polluting the intensity of love. Love is basically governed by the relationship among or between the individuals. Love should not be influenced by the man made barriers.

Nature is the greatest lover of all. It showers its love from dawn to dusk to the whole Universe. All the hills, mountains, rivers, streams, springs, lands, valleys, oceans, sky, trees, forests, gardens, villages, hamlets, cities, towns, nations, continents, what not everything are filled with atoms of love. There is great space to spread your love.

Love is the union of hearts. It reflects the oneness of existence. It is above all barriers. Try and try, and you shall embrace all, the rich, poor, needy, mighty, weak, unhealthy, cheerful, depressed, prosperous, helpless, unworthy, black, white, short, long, ugly, beautiful, handicapped, limping, struggling, all, one and all, as these attributes of life one takes to enact the drama of life. Let the waves of love rise to kiss the heart of heavens. Feel for the fellow living being, as nothing is more valuable than our existence. To exist is to live. Respect the existence. And only by living the gain and pain can be realized.

How can you have a tree without roots?

Similarly life without love is like the day without sun. Nature is the playground for love. There is exclusively an intrinsic quality with every individual to synchronize with love of life as per frequency of their own choice.

All humans should have great regard to the existence of life. A sound family is the basic need for a flourishing nation. These micro units are required to be integrated with the world agenda of love. Peace talks are hardly making way for togetherness.

Love is to be reinstated in humans for a universal brotherhood.

Let us look beyond the narrow limitations of the self. Preachers are more than performers. Evaluators are major in number than the actual doers. Right is always questioned by the wrong. Goodness is diminishing in the race of survival.

Man is transforming into machine. Emotions are dying down. Man is breaking. Man is sinking. Man is shrinking. Man is wearing out. Human is becoming unlovely. Why man is objectionable?

Is the World changing?

Under these conditions the sense of love is fading away. Children are playing in crèches rather than on mother's laps. Parentage is losing the truthfulness of love. Every land has been producing saints to spread the message of love. The permanent joy of sacrifice invariably supersedes all the instant pleasures of self-success. An individual gain no doubt is equally essential but may not be an answer to all promising beneficiaries waiting with a ray of hope to be graced by your humble touch.

Fly as high as you can to break the limits of the land. Go beyond your body to reach the hearts of millions and millions of species all over the galaxies known to man. This is the best time, right now, if not done today, and then it can never happen again.

Go leave your nest.

Now you do not need protection of the mother of existence. In fact you are the grown man to protect the world. We have been remaining in the nest for long despite the hatched eggs of existence. There is no insecurity to demolish the nest once the infancy has grown to the sunlight of dawn.

Silence is the best prayer of nature. Nature loves all. It reaches despite the barriers. The birds migrate from one part of the continent to another. The unique Sun shines to lighten the whole world. The inability of the land to hold clouds over it is very much imperative to the whole process of universality. The formation at one land and pouring out rain at another land speaks of the freedom of nature.

Is Man made to tame nature? Is nature threat to Man? Humans are not given liberty to divide the lands from dawn to dusk. We are inhabitants to this land but not owners. The animals keep obeying the nature. They occupy land to live and not to own. The earth has been fragmented into continents, countries and states. Wars are being fought to mast the flags of nationalism. Again communism faces the challenges of capitalism.

Democracy has its own saga of rule from dawn to dusk.

Man has started ruling Man. Amidst this humiliation the dying need emphasizes the reincarnation of love. Man should rise above this degradation. Man has to look inward with sincerity and dedicated commitment for overall refinement from dawn to dusk. Everyone has to be a researcher of his self. Then only a true synopsis of love can build the society of humans.

Cultures and Religions are the wheels of mankind.

How to differentiate between myth and reality? Fairy Tales are one of the tools of education. Where to learn the art of loving? It is not same for all. Love and hatred is the perception of the man. At one point of time the lovable person is the most hateful man. Why it so happens? Why the thought process takes a 360 degree turn? Why we do this way? What makes us vulnerable?

Dawn to Dusk awaits lessons from the life. The knife falling on banana or the banana falling on knife has no difference at all. It leads to same end result.

To prove or not to prove, may not be the secret of life, till you are willing to demarcate between existence and non-existence. Always the wind does not assist sailing in one direction. Do you really need the wind to sail? And at times may not be as per your will.

Will of God and Will of Man however it may be finally are nearer to the Will of Existence. Fortune never remains forever. It only lets your motivation to thrust the momentum. This in no way should be the reason to repel the destiny.

Live your life lovingly.

The love force in you is the latent energy from dawn to dusk. Expectancy hardly matches the requirement. Let us accept this truth. Love should not be conditional.

Humbleness and peace are great wisdom of life. Many people think lot, speak more but do less, when the actual time comes to deliver. If you have cultivated the habit of waiting for others, then you will definitely always be left behind. Containment, discipline and patience are golden values for prosperity and greatness. There always exists endless opportunities to change yourself, provided you are yielding to do so.

Smiling even at the time of worst chaos is a sign of true man.

The sanctity of marriage is getting lost. The piousness of the relationship is breaking down. Many couples are seeking the legal solutions. Is divorce the fruit of marriage? Why the times are changing? Equality in gender is a big question. Pairs are getting separated to form new pairs. People have their reasons to defend, but why it is happening? Why are we becoming disobedient in our relationship roles?

Why Homes are splitting off?

Homes are becoming unhealthy. The rate of deformation in humanity is escalating rapidly from dawn to dusk. The discussion is to prioritize the need of humanity today more than ever before. Way of life is to be periodically reviewed if we sincerely want to guide ourselves towards regenerating humanity in the world.

The meaning of love can be known better only if you have experienced the pain of separation. You will come to know about the dignity of labor only if you have experienced humiliation. You will understand hunger if you have starved for food.

Why do you see tears in lover's eyes?

This is the cry of one heart for the other. It is the inner sorrow of the humans. What was wrong with the lady who was divorced? It was nothing more than an unwanted happening because of literally a wrong decision and grossly misunderstanding of the relationship between husband and wife. At times couples may not have differences but the connected families' negative perception leads to the breakdown.

How many marriages will you do? The wives are finding faults with the husbands and husbands' unhappiness with the wives. Do you think polygamy is a solution to breaking up of love? The sanctity of the relationship is important to breed the love of life. There are couples and families at the same time reaping the benefits of love and harmony.

Children are the reflection of parents.
&
Are we not the children of god?

Cultured children have their lessons from learned, lovely and valued parents. Orphans are unfortunate but the society can shower their parenting love on them. This is where a life time opportunity waits to give your complete love to them. Widows are not to be blamed for their fate of love. The society should not allow them to feel the absence of home. Handicapped are not to be deprived of the opportunity of love. Every man has one or the other pain. The remedy of pain is love. Love manifests in many forms from mother, father, sister, brother, son, daughter, uncles, aunts, husband, wife, teachers, friends, colleagues, neighbors, society, and so forth.

Eyes are reflection of heart. Heart is the source for love, affection, kindness, sympathy, humbleness, gratitude, thanks in man. Purity of heart should be the mission of humanity on earth. Take up a child kiss him, go to the old to take blessings, be a vision to the blind, speak for the dumb, hear for the deaf, jump for the limping man, serve man as you can, but do it. This is the principle of love. It has no limitations of its own. You can love the entire world and move, move, towards man. The nearer you are to man, the closer you will be to yourself. Spread the voice of love aloud as much as you can.

Love is not based on attributes. It cannot be classified. Love is love. Heart is heart. Pour it on your fellow beings from dawn to dusk. The needy only know the necessity of help. All the cheers are useless, needless to say if it cannot bring smile to the crying heart. You can be god to millions and millions waiting for their hands to be touched. The current of love should electrify the humanity. Cannot each of us at least bring one cheer to man daily from dawn to dusk? Smile, smile, make people smile as many as you can, this is the language of love.

Love brings happiness. Happy people intensify love. Happiness promotes it to bliss.

Let all be blessed with bliss. Peace is the ultimate destination of love. The stillness is the position of oneness. Love has no boundaries to be restricted or discriminated. The basic element of nature is love. Love in nature can be seen wherever you go.

Nature is fountain of love.

Man is as lovely as nature. Look into the similarities of both. Eyes are to appreciate beauty and nose is to smell flowers. What else can be beautiful than the nature? Nature is itself the existence .The subject is difficult to understand but not impossible to learn. One form of nature into another, and again into another, and so on, the supply chain of nature is infinite. How can we be separate from this? We rise from this to fall into it. Everything which you see is your manifestation, and you being the broader manifestation of all.

The Almighty being the supreme nature of the nature's in existence. Watch the peaking mountains kissing the sky, feel the warmth of the rising sun, the pouring rain tempts you to dance, the calm night reflects the tranquility of the moon, the green carpet landscape excites you to roll on it, the flowing river waits to sail your boat of dreams, the lakes with lotus wishes to share the wisdom of life, the lovely resorts to freely relax, the dense jungle to explore the home of wildlife, the water to satisfy the thirst, wherever you go you feel you were invited by the nature. The destruction of nature by man to meet survival cannot be dispensed of. However, at the same time ecological and environmental balance cannot be sacrificed.

Love is the fulcrum to balance man and nature. The game of seesaw is only possible with equilibrium of the playing system. Worries are type of syringes which sucks the blood without your awareness. Keep yourself away from the deterrents of life.

Faith in Self

He who knows when he can fight and when he cannot will be victorious.

Life is a journey of faith.

The understanding of the self is beyond understanding of the mind. Dawn symbolizes freshness of lily in the garden of life, though short but purposefully lived is admired by all. It is pathetic to see that our vision always is at crossroads. Time itself is the greatest resource for dawn and dusk. Fixing them relatively cannot stop its permanent motion. It is passing away day by day. Inventory of time cannot be managed.

Production of time is also not in our hands. Your time cannot be transferred to another. Time scheduled to you may not be the same as yours to any other. Obviously in reality you neither can remain in past nor in future. The present also evidently, delicately departs with very marginal sense of thought of existence with the self.

Life is short of time despite availability from dawn to dusk for millions and millions of years best known to the existence itself.

Man is an intruder in one of the forms to redefine life.

The cycle of time is clocking dawn to dusk for the mankind to innovate from time to time. The explanation as well as the evaluation merges in and out to demerge at the end for beginning of the new emergence in totality. My own resolution fails to hold me longer. I always think to gain by the shortest route. But finally the time is longer than the realization. Nothing penetrates at the time of immaturity. The preparedness itself falls behind the prime requirement. The truth is covered behind the cloud of sincerity.

Life is meant to be lived. Life is to try something new. Life is little bit more than the usual. Sometimes look at it with a different perspective. Depression is a dark endless tunnel. Why people take their own lives? Is Life the property of any individual? Kissing and killing are being equally practiced as the art of living.

Why Man has no time to decide between wrong or right.? A feeling of change is the beginning of faith.

It is time to be patient and confident to see the good which definitely comes after the toughest moments have been fought.

Every human mother bears the pain of nearly nine months on average at any part of the world to bring a new life. Is this not imperative to understand the uniqueness of human beings towards oneness, despite the diversity of different races? It really questions our faith.

Ultimately we all are one. It is lack of faith which blurs our vision to realize our same source in spite of cultures, habits, demographics, tastes, likes, dislikes, etc, Unity in community .Faith is the breath from dawn to dusk. There is only one way, one way, to reach out the new, that is just stretch a little with faith in yourself keeping aside all the odds against you. Be bold to overrule the hindrances. All obstacles are new opportunities.

Adversities are unexplored avenues.

Dare to throw yourself to all challenges, as ultimately there is no defeat in any attempt to do the best. Let all your cells vibrate with the spirit of faith from dawn to dusk. Look for different ways to resolve issues holding you to fly.

Wings of adversities are not that wide to encompass the flying faith of life. An entire different look can make an indelible impact on life. Try building the foundations of faith and then you can see your castles of dreams spearing the sky.

Faith moves through different phases of life. The weakness of the faith reflects the retarding of spirit to march ahead. The maturity sublimes the beauty of life through the silence of faith. Time has its own way of building the faith. The innocence of it will wear out. The shrinking life strongly holds the invisible faith. Dwindling of faith questions the nearly diminishing life.

Is life only for performers? Is life only for reformers? Why some are under performers? Are they not capable? Do they lack interest to compete? How to progress in life? Who will guide? How to win? Where to search solution for these? Does compromise meant defeat? Why I am deprived of grace? What should I do? Will my faith help me? Or Shall I quit? All the above queries, doubts, apprehensions are part and parcel in preparing you to rediscover yourself.

Tell me, does life ends with attainment of achievements.

Either you are at top or bottom, your task is unfulfilled till the last breathe. There is no limit on delivery. You are delivering, is imperative that existence is with you. The living force is the fruit of grace. Do not be under the ego that you have passed the day. Be honest to accept it was grace that you lived today. It will be blessing to see one more wonderful dawn and again dawn after dawn, and after dawn.

Dawn's are the sparks of life.

Passiveness should be cut by the axe of activeness. You need to reach all by stretching daily. Never think you have reached the breakeven point of life. There should not be any boundary to restrict your flow. Faithfully march ahead in advancing yourself towards the secrets of existence.

An overview concludes that at any point of time in life, faith is as essential as the air till we breathe to be alive. My own concern should not be the prime cause to deceive the self. The life operates between the quadrant of destiny and self.

All the failures appear to be accounted to destiny, whereas the success story is vetted by the self. Failures can never be hindrances to success. It is stubbornness to excel.

Tame yourself to win and defeat shall take you to the final victory. The unanswerable question is "faith in destiny" or "destiny in faith"? Keep defining, again and again, till the refinement in faith becomes one with the destiny. Ultimately the life exists at the horizon of both, inseparably infinite, just as the sky which tends to fall in ocean but unmeasured distant apart. The knowledge of the self has all the answers of the world.

Life is a witness of phases at different planes of awareness. It is an anonymous journey from innocence to liberation from bondage. The crux of the life's core is the point of realization. The mind wanders from dawn to dusk.

Life has its own breakeven point. Believe yourself and you shall be driven by faith.

"Self-trust is the first secret of success"- Ralph Waldo Emerson

Faith is the truest prime resource for all. One who can hold himself can hold everything. Persistence in awakening the self can lead you to the nucleus of life from where everything springs to the surface of existence.

Learned minds make man of wisdom.

One whose mind is good can see himself as good. One whose mind is god can see himself as god. It has the power within you to know the purpose of life. Time to time it changes its responsibilities and the man discharges his functions accordingly. The mind is infant, child, and young, matured, old and migrates but has no physical death. It passes from one form to another. It never perishes and decays. It gets polished and polished to be enlightened. Once enlightened it is light. It is the light of life. The universal light .It merges with existence.

Hope is life.

Life is to have hopes of existence triumph. Hope can help you to swim the world. Hopelessness is just the tip of iceberg. It cannot keep you afloat all times. Do not burden and worry yourself with this helplessness. Having hope is like midway through the problems of life. No solution can be obtained without the ounce of hope.

The drives of I, ME and SELF work as the gear box of any prime mover. These independent gear wheels are in motion and their engaging and disengaging strengthens and weakens the hope of any human.

I would like my readers to be little bold in attempting, what is the "SELF"? Primarily to know the self you have to understand your SELF. How to do it?

Every human has a " I, ME and SELF". What is the linear, exponential and integral relationship between them?

Humans are derivates from the source. How an evidentiary to this is to be established with authenticity? Will it be revealed as we experience living, life and existence?

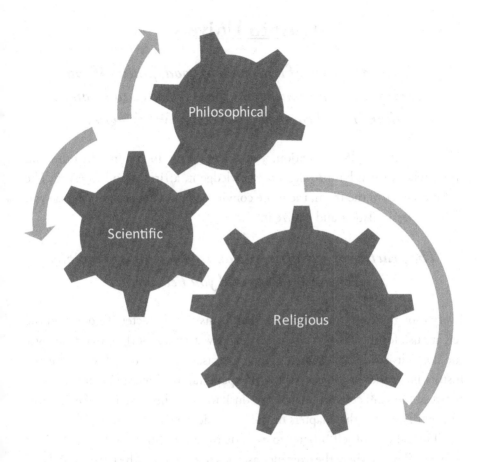

What would the above interlocking ideas drive humans to achieve? Would it strengthen their beliefs, thoughts, trusts, faiths and hopes of living? The ultimate philosophical views of life makes human what he wants to become.

The nearer you are to god lesser you will cry and weep. More you know of him, the more misery vanishes. What is salvation? It is to live with god. This world is evolution of nature and manifestation of god.

<u>Trust in Universe</u>

"Associate yourself with men of good quality if you esteem your own reputation; for it is better to be alone than in bad company" – George Washington

The practice of self-affirmation, you do not have to become infinite and immortal. All you have to do is acknowledge it, affirm it and assert it. The more you affirm the truth, the more convinced you will become. In time you will fully assimilate it and realize it.

The practice of self-affirmation is based on a principle, "As you think so will you become."

Every thought leaves an impression that forms our character. To question the self at dusk for the dawn, it opens entirely new avenues for the dawn to answer the dusk. It is ridiculously being done to erase the writing of life so that the history never dies in times to come. The paragraph of life is being restricted in between the semi colons of dawn and dusk to align the sentences of existences summarizing it to the chapters of the self under the book of mind.

The balloon of self inflates to explode the air within into the larger air of universe. This is where the existence ascends to descend at the horizon of dawn and dusk. What appears to be unattached is under the shadow of attachment. The plane of living cannot be unidirectional. The physical body struggles the quest of survival while the mind travels the peace of self actualization. The duality in us is the art of nature like the separation of time from dawn to dusk. At the end the self becomes meaningless to discover the new purposes to redefine the definition of life.

All school of thoughts, however different they may be is from the same source trying to reach the same sink. Truth cannot have two meanings. It is one and all are one.

The entire universe is within us.

The soul knows the way of peace but the mind is restless and wanders from dawn to dusk. Trying to analyze the analyzed analysis is most of the times futile to the whole process of evaluation. We should run not to win only at the end for the position of award but to witness the act of running.

Action is life. Rank of the performer is not important, what matters is, are you performing the action. The happening has to happen.

We live from dawn to dusk not to amass the world but to know its very existence. I may rob the whole earth but where I have another to accommodate this as my possession. It is our thought which is the prime driving force at dawn, for becoming what we are at dusk. Surprisingly it is difficult to find out which part of the bodily organs initiates and develops the thought process. It keeps coming from dawn to dusk. It is the prime mover of life. The self itself is the transmitter and receiver with autonomy on filtration at wish and will. It can clearly be understood that the doer and the done are all same.

First trust the self. All actions and results are outcomes of your trust. Who can give trust to you? You have to see it within yourself. When it is said something is good, at the same time another parallel truth that something is bad gets established. By law of nature things are classified in quadrants. The option is left to us.

How can good go with badness?

Who can define truth for you? You have to explore the truth. What you perceive today, may not be a rightly justified postulate for tomorrow. The foresight and introspection of trust relatively has no true existence of time.

All philosophies are one. Billions of thoughts from dawn to dusk are experiencing the same life. The ego holds us to reveal the truth. Unknown are the ways of nature to nurture the life. The clock from dawn to dusk breaks the silence of life. Negative necessity is the greatest evil on earth to create all the devils.

It is true that as many men that many propositions. Human is submerged in ocean of propositions. The humanity is questioned and reasoned by infinite beliefs.

Propositions of man are searching clarity between the quadrants of truths and beliefs. All human statements cannot be justified as either truth or beliefs completely. Beliefs have their proponents as well as truths. It is a difficult task for the analysts to give us a final statement on knowledge of existence.

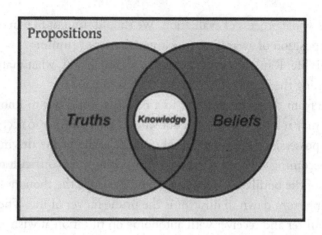

Desires defeat the intended purpose of life from dawn to dusk.

And again life is incomplete without desires. Are desires devils? It is tough to categories. However, aim to rise should not die. Commitment should not drift. Persistence should not cease.

Lift yourself daily to gift the self. Do not rest until the last breath. God can be at all temples at any point of time, but man can be at only one, one at a time. The God in him is yet to be discovered without the external temples of faith. The telepathy is yet to be decoded. There is no failure of network lines to the heavens .Faith travels faster than light. All our queries and doubts are addressed to the same home.

Every day we are in action from Dawn to Dusk. Principally I have to trust my own existence to know the existence of others. Blindly you can trust in Universe. It is the roof of truth.

<u>Hope in Mind</u>

"I asked the Lord for a bunch of fresh flowers but instead he gave me an ugly cactus with thorns. I asked the Lord for some beautiful butterflies instead he gave me many ugly worms. I was threatened and disappointed, but after many days suddenly I saw cactus bloom with many beautiful flowers and those worms became beautiful butterflies flying in the spring mind."

Human's mind is like a chameleon from dawn to dusk.

It changes its color frequently now and then. The toughest task to humans is to invariably control it, stabilize it and direct it. During the disturbance of the mind the senses are uncontrollable, the speech is unpleasant, the bodily look is not impressive, the ego is at its peak, the temper has no limit, the overall understanding of the situation is misinterpreted, the entire human system works without the inner mechanism of control. The war is between minds, brains, hopes, faiths, trusts and philosophies. The levels of mind are another major factor for the disputes in humans.

The souls are never at war. Do the brains are the cause of all misery? The humans according to their brains, minds, thoughts, grace, capacity to perceive and reasoning to act, understand life in their own way. The complete anatomy of humans is a subject beyond the limitations of medical as well as biological sciences.

A man challenges the survival with the highest hopes of succeeding and at the same time another man submits to be surrendered. To minutely examine it, this is only a state of mind rather than the impact of situation or influence of environment.

All humans at this point of time on earth are experiencing more or less the same happiness, sorrow, joy and grief. Our purpose of understanding the moods of mind from dawn to dusk should be given more emphasis and monitored not to drift from the central idea of existence. All say no action leads to inexperience the hope of existence.

All humans are like pebbles having equal potential to become diamond. It is only your hope that can make the difference from dawn to dusk.

Hold on to hope and hope shall hold you.
Every day is a day of hope.

Believe something new will happen, and you shall witness the happening. All men are to get from the day. Man cannot give anything to another man in true sense.

Man can only serve another man.

Day is a great giver. Dare to deliver with hope. Hope is definitely going to elevate your spirits of living. It will promote your thoughts into promising actions. Flood the mind with hope to drown your life into it. The depth of life cannot be ascertained without diving deep to the core of self. Go deeper and deeper into it, to know the core of existence.

Dawn to Dusk is an opportunity to gamble your hope to the extent your mind can hold. How to read mind? Why to read mind? Can man explore the secrets of mind? Man's mind was never in control and is not in control of mind. Your mind is not being mastered? How to tame it?

Mind should guide man or man should guide mind. What do you do? The battle between master and slave here will never end. It probably appears that majority of us are slaves of the mind. We go with the mind. Where the point of realization is that mind is diverting man from its centre of existence? At times all appears to be blank.

All the learning is unlearnt. All the knowledge is once more dissolved into the unknown. All that has been created is destructed to be created again. The cycle of begin, end, begin, and end keeps spinning infinitely in the mind. Is this a new point of start.

Do memories impact the mind? It randomly runs about picking up traces from the past and recent present. The question is why it influences the mind and subsequently the man? Where does hope spring in? How does it rule both man and mind?

Man, mind, matter, memory and moment keep emerging with a new mix again and again with the strong bead of hope knitting them all in one garland of living. Sometimes we are not likely to consider it for retrospection because of our own fear of analysis. Weak mind results in weak man. Strong mind builds strong man. Truthful mind graces man towards divinity. Dirty mind makes bad man.

Why not make a difference this dawn?

Let us today sincerely have a wildest hope to catch fish in the desert. Trust the land and faith will pour heavily to flood with deeper ponds and longer lakes full of fishes at the end. Do it and you shall get it? Believe it, trust, faith and hope are the limbs of the thought you dream of from dawn to dusk.

Nothing lies above your resolution to translate dusk into dawn.

The light within you is overshadowed at day time but the night calmly introspects the dawn throughout the dusk studying the reflections and refractions of the self. Let your sincere faith nurture it and ultimately one day the trusted fish shall be in your promising holy hands.

In my opinion please make a note of it, "Hard work is a journey and success is no destination, hence hard work cannot follow success, it is success which follows hard work, but ultimately both are journeys and not destinations".

It is true to understand that life is a journey not destination. Time is a journey. Mind is a journey. Day is a journey. Idea is a journey. Thought is a journey. Man is a journey. Society is a journey. World is a journey. It summarizes to say that Universe is a journey of existence. Humanity is also a similar journey of the humans.

Humans come with their values of humanity.

The same world at one point of time is in profound cheers and again at another point of time it is in agony of chaos. Why it so happens? It is the same world with good humans at one time and with bad humans at other times. The theory of relativity of humanity has both the philosophical as well as the scientific dimensions of humans.

Hope plays different games in the inner and outer world of humans from dawn to dusk.

Reality can never escape from the clutches of philosophy of life. Infinite volumes can be published by the humans on earth related to the gospels of humanity. Such is the vastness of mind anchored to the hope of existence. The hope of existence is universally being tested at the every dawn of existence.

The spider of life invariably keeps making the web for the self to be trapped.

It is truth that the bees do not sit on the dung. Life as bees is to search the nectar of nature so that the honey on earth can spread sweetness of mankind. The garden of life should not restrict its fragrance within the boundary of self. Rise above to embrace the world leaving behind the ego of the self.

Let us all be grateful to the life living in us from dawn to dusk. No time again in history will be yours if the present precious moments from dawn to dusk have been lost thinking to act. Action should immediately follow the thought towards betterment of the self. Do not; do not wait till you are invited to depart at the cost of self before finally perishing merely as handful of ashes into the land of birth. Let hope over rule the fear of death. Hope for the best and best will befall on you.

Dive deeper into the dusk to see the depth of dawn. Let not the hopes faint before the life gives way. My own resolution to win should overcome all the odds from dawn to dusk. Patiently wait as the cactus even bears flowers and fruits.

The flora of life is invariably for the hopeful.

Hopelessness is like rotten apple spoiling all your other promising resources. Never give up hope. It is the courage to persist. Persistence is the outcome of meditation. Every action may not yield the immediate desired results. Have you noticed sometimes results are purely independent of actions? The understanding of this perhaps requires an intense insight into the self. There are millions and millions of issues unknown to man.

A short life span of humans adds to the misery. In addition to it inaccessibility and natural restrictions further embarrasses our peaceful living. At times the chicken of inspiration pops out breaking the un-hatched egg of knowledge. Pre-mature babies battle with life holding the hands of hope.

Hope is totally yours.
&
No one can substitute it.

The gain and loss are inseparable. Without hope all blessings are futile. It is this ray of hope which holds all the unfolding of Universe. Hope is the thin rope which delicately ties all of us to the floating life. Life is not too short to be big, so keep regularly hoping from dawn to dusk that all faith and trust will take you to the hills of your dreams. Unknown are the ways grace comes to us.

Every adversity is an opportunity to wake up.

It pushes you in and out starting the conflict. Doubts keep arising to weaken your hope. Every moment there is altogether a new reaction happening within you. And suddenly everything ceases. The self is stressing to find the cause. That's where the learning begins. Everything is upside down. Who can help you? How will you face the situation? The battle of nerves begins.

Many schools of thoughts arise in you. When you end with no solution, you want to put yourself away. The spirit in you dies out. You are restless. Your thought weakens; mind loses insight, a complete disequilibrium. And now anxiously with helplessness you are looking for smallest and smallest of grace to befall on. This is that hope you are trying to have faith in it. Hope has to be supported by faith.

Life is neither too short to haste nor too long to waste.

Never leave your hopes. Hope is such a path which lifelong helps you to be dynamic. It is only hope that has made humans reach Moon and Mars. Build your hopes and one day it is not surprising that man will fly like butterfly in the garden of life, jumping from this flower of nature, to that, going round the earth.

Man is a born dreamer.

We have been receiving dreams from very beginning of our existence, both at conscious as well as sub-conscious levels. Hope can only nurture your dream. Hope is the holding hands of your dreams. The greater the hope, the greater is the flourishing of dreams.

Hope, hope, hope awake your hope and you shall see hope will drive your dream into reality. Hope is an engine to primarily move your dreams. Having dreams without hope is like driving a car without the engine. Strengthen the horse power of your engine within you to see the dreams accelerating towards their destination of glory.

Hope requires no investment from outside. It is your own valuable asset gifted by the almighty. Just provoke it to see its miracle. It can change your life beyond your imagination.

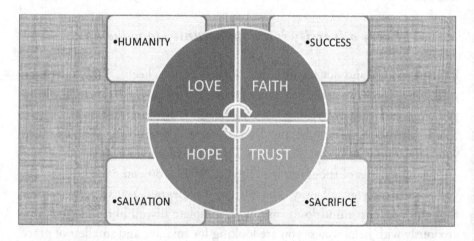

It is through the wheel of faith, trust, hope and love that human can attain true success, sacrifice, salvation and humanity. These are four strong pillars along with the human to hold the ownership of life.

Summing up & Exercise for Readers-Chapter-II

- Readers can start practicing jotting down their strengths and weaknesses in these areas as part of the exercise to finally cultivate the ownership of humanity.

• **Areas**	• Strengths	• Weaknesses	• Remarks
People	I like to help people	I am conservative	Have to change myself
Love	I am reserved	Difficult to trust	All should not be judged by the same yardstick. One to one relationship is important
Hate	I hate bad people	Yet I have sympathy	To stop hating people. More self-practice required
Emotions	Positive	Negative	I have both, my focus should be towards positive emotions.
Values	NIL	Moderate	I have to cultivate more values to excel
Success	It is always strength	A ego comes with it	I am trying to give up ego.
Help	I do to needy	Not to affluent	They are also human being. I have to change my attitude.

- Prepare such matrix with essential variables now and then to understand your variability and one to one relationship. Human variability is natural. Human is bound to change with the changes in philosophies, ideas, cultures, traditions, perceptions, vision, education, wisdom, knowledge, and so on with influencing factors and impacts.
- Try to visualize the changes you are undergoing.
- Try to map it with the variables.

- Have your statistics presented in tables, graphs, charts, bar, pie, venn diagrams, any other forms which generates MIS (Management Information System) for decision making on you.
- In today's digital world you can compute your assessment at the click of the mouse.
- Cultivate this habit of self –assessment to understand your trend towards humanity from dawn to dusk.
- How these inner circles of interlinked processes within the human brings changes in his outward personality from dawn to dusk.
- Readers can generate similar models based on their perception on life, world, universe, existence, nature, and so on to see that the model works towards transforming yourself into champions of humanity.
- As part of the exercise every one can define their ownership to utilize their life. Identifying your core areas will help you to capitalize the opportunities at dawns.
- Your faith, trust, hope, love and perception should make best use of the opportunity, thought, idea, inspiration, voice and dream.
- I believe my readers to start building their pillars of life. It is on this that the personality will remain robust forever.
- Youth is the best phase of life. Do not drain it for nothing. The existence has all the power of energy to create the human in you. Youth is the seed of man.
- Try germinating it in your life if you sincerely look to reap humanity in coming civilizations and generations of the world.
- With the conclusion of Part-I every reader should benefit from the insight into dawn and ownership of life.
- My dear readers start riding the bicycle of life with the wheels of human and humanity rather than riding the fate of humans.
- My respected readers please kindly list out all that you own in life. Rank them in order of importance in your life. Among these select the items pertaining from first to fifth rank. Again among these list out the three which are vital to you. This is a technique known as acceptance by the method of rejections. In other terms a technique to find the important through the route of unimportant things?
- It is a practical approach towards owning life. Everything you know may not be owned by you. Everything you do not know may not

be owned by you. Everyone you are acquainted may not be owned by you. By the practice of this elimination technique I am sure my readers will reach excellence in their lives. It works not only personally but even professionally. At the out most I am confident definitely in eliminating all your evils till you are divine and have transformed into ideal human.

- To reap the benefits from the chapters of Part-II, I would advice my readers to clear yourselves of all doubts about new beginning and the ownership responsibility you are likely going to take in regenerating humanity.
- My all best wishes to everybody directly or indirectly willingly or unknowingly working daily with humanity to proceed further through the journey from dawn to dusk.
- What is going to be wrong if you attempt your endeavors and then say you have failed sincerely?

PART II
TODAY IS MINE

Chapter III

DAY IS A WAY

Every day is a way.

Do you wish lions to die like dogs daily?

Every Day is a miracle day.

How to make every dawn a miracle dawn of dreams? If the morning is good then the dusk will be better than the state you started at dawn. On the other hand if the morning is bad than then the dusk will be worse than the state you started at dawn. The message the dawn of inspiration conveys to us is that the inspired thoughts and motivated spirits take you to a better state of existence.

Aim for the BIG DAY. Do not die small daily. Do not dream small. Do not make little of yourself. How to make the day big for you? It is sure that with small thinking human will invariably remain tiny in excellence. Aspiration should be at par with the inspiration. How to reap the benefits from the day? Ambitions should be higher than the hands of existence. Throw everything in the day to avoid regrets of existence.

My dear readers please memorize again and again to remember that, "The dawn of today will never again be a day of opportunity tomorrow". If you have drained the today then you have murdered your dreams of existence. It is pity on you to lose the fresh poetry of existence.

It reminds me of a very old saying, "Give a man a fish and you feed him for a day. Teach a man to fish and you will feed him forever", indelibly popular in the circles of optimists, reformists, economists, humanists, socialists, and many human philosophers thinking for the betterment of humanity.

This is where the World Learning is to be directed from dawn to dusk.

I strongly advocate that,

"Charity is a misnomer to Humanity".

Why the Human should beg?

Why the human should beg his survival to another human who is similarly struggling to survive? There is no true gain to humanity in outsmarting each other. Charity continually cannot feel the gaps of scarcity from dawn to dusk. Charity should not be a culture to bank on the sympathy of humanity. The perception of sympathy by humans is an insult to the whole fraternity of human existence.

Day is an opportunity to intrude in redefining the basic principles of humanity from dawn to dusk. Disparity in no means should be weakness to yield our morals of humanity. The life is to be sliced and diced daily with courage of existence, with faith of existence, with trust in existence and above all with the confidence of the man in you.

I am putting forward the thought of the legendry Mark Twain,

"To succeed in life, you need two things: ignorance and confidence".

Today is full of ways. Today is mine. I will do something with the day. I shall see that it opens avenues to me. What is your way? Have you decided the day? Man has to decide his way. What is the use of wills if they are not shown the ways? Ways open up only with the eye of will. The love begins to flow only with heart of will. The hand begins to help only with the humanity of will.

Day is a will.
&
Will the day.

Come on to the day and ways are waiting for you to flourish, cherish, prosper, explore, invent, discover, create, construct, build, perform, act, play, love, teach, study and have fun.

Utilize the day to craft way of your future. Begin with a step today and one day you will see that you have journeyed miles and miles away from where you were initially dreaming to go.

Dare to begin with whatever you have. You have the will. Let it work out for you from dawn to dusk. Day is to work, work, and only work. Working does not mean you are burdening yourself. Understand the core purpose of work. Why we work? Is work worship? For whom we are working? Can you remain without working?

Day is meant for activity to roll on. Activity is living life. Living is fun when you are lighter in your approach towards life.

Work with freedom. Live with freedom. Learn with freedom. Teach with freedom. Write with freedom. Read with freedom. Act with freedom. Voice it with freedom. Trust with freedom. Sing with freedom. Dance with freedom. Help with freedom. Care with freedom. Share with freedom. Whatever you do your freedom should have purity of mind, heart, soul, body and self.

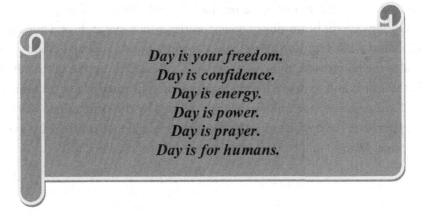

Day is your freedom.
Day is confidence.
Day is energy.
Day is power.
Day is prayer.
Day is for humans.

Shape it as you like. Ride it as you want. Decorate it with your dreams. Fill it with your ideas. Explore it with your thoughts. Live, live the day completely. Read the book day as many times as you can. Tear out its chapter by your dint of sweat. Pour into it to flood the day. Day is yours just go for it.

My readers are likely to agree with me that,

"Days, Wills & Ways are the limbs of man.

Man needs them from dawn to dusk to fulfill his dreams of the inner and outer world"

Man cannot perform without these. A perfect mapping from dawn to dusk helps to attain the usefulness of the day. Day should bring something. You should give something. Day has to assure that exchange between man and nature has taken place. The ends of the day are in between dawn and dusk. The mind of man produces both the will as well as the way. The more it produces the more options generated.

I have a sentence for interpretation, please attempt it to understand, why perception of life is equally important to the living of life. "Life is to do well not remain in well".

Did all of you get it right? How many of us are well? And how many of us are in well? Who can give us this wellness? Where to get this goodness? How many of you got it wrong? I should say all of us are wrong. To clarify yourself of this doubt you will have to do well better than the well you were doing.

Options are the beginning of opportunities from dawn to dusk. I hope you understand what I am trying to convey, communicate, interact, emphasize, explain, incite, provoke, aggravate, inflame, please pick up the grammar of life, the words and sentence has no meaning, if your mind is not meaning it out. The random opportunities are again refined by the same mind. Worked out options are the opportunities in your favor. The opportunities with grace are divine. Man should be fortunate but not idly to lose the day.

Why the day cannot be mine?

Let us work through the day. The day is to be crafted by man. The day is for making out the existence. What to make and for whom to make? Why to make? Look within you to find what you have? You can give to millions and millions through this day. Nature is day. You are part of nature.

To summarize Man is day. Day is man's life. If you are not doing anything that means you are not living. Reason out yourselves.

Dawn to Dusk essay is an intruder to intervene in your living daily to remind you that the day of fortune is yours to embrace. Be wise to rise against all lies of life. The truth is within you. Day is the light to see it. The day is our friend, mentor, helper and giver. Work with faith and you will win. Never give up your determination? Have you started visualizing yourself? What you want to be in the next five years, next ten and so on.

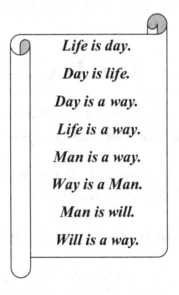

Life is day.

Day is life.

Day is a way.

Life is a way.

Man is a way.

Way is a Man.

Man is will.

Will is a way.

Why cannot I do it? What is stopping me from utilizing the day? How to trouble shoot this? Why I am unable to begin? What I really want to do? It is to be diagnosed prior to the development of the diseases of failure. No day should go in history as the day of failure. If you are not beginning then you are failing in your pursuit of ideals of living?

I am speaking of no exaggeration my dear readers. I am trying to alert you that the urgency for regenerating humanity need not be neglected. The time has come to question your own efficiency. The man who is with the day finally will get his better slice of the success in terms of happiness and bliss. If you have worked with the day thoroughly you are bound to be going towards abundance of existence. Is way in our hands? I have to take the day. How do we do it?

How we can in true sense align day, will, way, self, life, mind, actions and results? It is not that we are not living, not utilizing time, our actions are not focused, we are not result oriented, and the problem is we do things without a proper awareness of the resources from dawn to dusk. What can be a bigger resource than life? What is the greatest wealth than the day? Who is the better performer than you?

The world has its own limitations. Sit at the beach but the sea does not become yours. Neither the sea claims you. Watch the sunshine but the light is not yours. Feel the breeze but it is not yours. There is interaction, exchange of feelings, expression and somewhere the corner of the heart weeps for oneness. Being one also the different forms of the same source diverge and converge in the same mind from dawn to dusk.

I and Day

"Leadership is not a position or a title, it is action and example"

My encounter with day continues. I and Day are married forever. Neither of them divorces the one. Both of us are struggling to make something at the end.

Are we really making new things daily?

It appears most of the time we are monotonously passing out the day in arranging bread and butter only. There is no much novelty in reality. Is the morning good today? Or else, we are good to make the morning good today? Why morning cannot be cheerful? Why morning cannot be filled with cheers? Why morning cannot be yours? What is holding you?

Every day is a good day. All cannot do the same activity daily. Activity is breath of the world. Is the world moving because of humans? Every Man is in the chain of existence. Man is more at war with the other man rather than the world. It should have been the other way. Man's queries are to question the world?

World is a mystery. Man is a mystery. One mystery is trying to tame another mystery. My limitations are good as your limitations.

Man's limitations are as good as World's limitations.

Life is to know the limitations. Wisdom reveals the absolute limitations. Knowledge is to calm the inner self. World is to interact with the self. It exchanges the awakenings from dawn to dusk. Every man has something to give from dawn to dusk. Every man has something to take from dawn to dusk. Every moment is purposeful. Every moment is existence. Every moment is unique. Every moment is infinite. Every moment is opportunity. Every moment is grace. Every moment is blessings.

Every moment is truth. Every moment is love. Every moment is faith. Every moment is hope. Every moment is life. Every moment is dawn. Every moment is bliss. Every moment is energy. Every moment is renaissance. Every moment is incarnation. Every moment is reformation. Every moment is regeneration. Every moment is evolution. Every moment is present. Every moment is a way. Every moment is a will. Every moment is a fortune.

Have you looked through your window today? Have you touched the rose of life today? Have you wished the birthday of life today? Have you planned to plant a tree today? Have you decided to quit evil today? Have you promised to be happy today? Have you learnt the wisdom of life today? How will be my day from dawn to dusk today? What I am doing if I have no plans then? Why I am not able to plan? Will I reach my goal without action plan?

Life is an energy game. Lot is going to happen between me and the day. How I should start my day? Start the day saying to yourself very good morning with all your cheers and dreams. Start with the urge and concentration of achieving.

What I have to create today? Can I pursue my request with the day today? I have to make the day 100% productive. How to overcome the odds of today? Will I surrender to the immorality of living for the sake of survival today? I know that death is the reality. Still I am manipulating myself to see what at the end? Only what I can remain with is the experience of the journey and nothing substantially more than it from dawn to dusk.

Day is a factory of opportunities.

Day is a manufacturing unit of ideas, thoughts, dreams, desires, needs and products. I should not let the day pass away. I have to consume this day to the best of my ability and knowledge. Day is the time to play the game of humanity. Whatever you do link it to the chains of humanity.

Life is a mine of values. Search for it. Unless your will is not looking for it how do u receive it. If you are not going to market of values how would you purchase value? Work and values should go together. I am lost if the day is lost.

Day is in front of me daily. I and day have to work together. How do we do it? Have you ever evaluated the day? Give some time daily to look into your utilization factor. Is your utilization factor increasing from dawn to dusk?

Man has no justifiable reason to blame the day. What can be more better way to perform with your skills? It is time to show your talent, reveal your innovations, and test your potentials, all whatever you can do to write your history.

Craft your day as you like from dawn to dusk.

There is nothing like constrains. It is only the state of mind. The world is your examination centre. You are here to write your destiny. Not to see your report card. The marks sheet is not your prime concern for worry. Your inner voice is sufficient to evaluate yourself. There should not be any regrets from sunrise to sunset. Before the night falls your goals are to be cheered by you.

Day is the honey drop of life. It has all the nectar of happiness. Energy follows your intent. If you can regulate your intent, you are sure to change your life. There will be a daily battle between the day and you. You have to conquer the day from dawn to dusk. Let the day do not become dust at dusk. You should gain the day at any cost without sacrificing your ideals. Day gives you number of options to do and become what you like. The process of becoming should not stop.

To understand purity you have to be pure. To understand faith you have to be faithful. To understand love you have to be lovable. To understand trust you have to be truthful. To understand man you have to be man. To understand humanity you have to be human. To understand goodness you have to be good. To understand kindness you have to be kind. To understand nobility you have to be noble.

To understand happiness you have to be happy. To understand divinity you have to be divine. To understand punctuality you have to be punctual. To understand sincerity you have to be sincere. To understand ethics you have to be ethical. To understand success you have to be successful. To understand your Self you have to be yourself. To understand nature you have to be natural. To understand grace you have to be graceful.

To understand peace you have to be peaceful. To understand bliss you have to be calm. To understand harmony you have to be harmonious. To understand joy you have to be joyful. To understand blessings you have to be blessed. To understand fortune you have to be fortunate. To understand god you have to be godly. To understand friends you have to be friendly. To understand life you have to be lively.

To understand universe you have to be universal. To understand might you have to be mighty. To understand beauty you have to be beautiful. To understand excellence you have to be excellent. To understand future you have to be foresighted. To understand inspiration you have to be inspired. To understand greatness you have to be great. To understand thanks you have to be thankful. To understand will you have to willful. To understand dawn you have to be sunrise. To understand dusk you have to be sunset. To understand teacher you have to be student. To understand author you have to be reader.

From the above possible sets of understanding it becomes clear that to understand anything we have to become that thing. That is to say our participation, action, thought, feelings, emotions, mind, and body, all should work towards it. Is there need to be selective? Take action immediately on life, work, habits, success, failure, behavior, tasks, practice, feelings, power, confidence, creativity, environment, community, society, thoughts, and your vision, targets, goals, mental and physical skills.

Develop your self-esteem. Develop your self-respect. Develop a positive addiction towards good habits.

Begin to organize your life daily.

Practice is the key to mastering any skill. Mind grows with proper use. Man is in fact not having the secrets to capitalize it for the humankind. Have you made a decision to develop habit? Which habit is suitable to you? Day by day stick to it and it will evolve you into what you want to become.

Will the day win? Or I will win the Day? Will the day take most out of me? Or I will squeeze the day out. Will the day today add to restoring humanity? Will I be able to voice humanity today? Will both I and Day win to regenerate humanity daily?

Future in Present

Today is my day.

The moment "Today", will never be again tomorrow. However, tomorrow is based on today. Are you visualizing your future in the present? This should be your strongest vision. I will attain my goals, whether it is sunny, cloudy, raining, windy, breeze, whatsoever it may be finally I am going to win, win and only win. Be bold to have such strong and affirmative mindset to live the day.

The gap between vision and mission is to be bridged by man meticulously. It is not that we have been not doing it. Somewhere down the line we have missed our track out of it. It is a matter of concern for the society at large. The problem is persisting at different levels from dawn to dusk. An introspection of the self with positive conception is required to clean out the dirtiness in the mind.

Struggle is the great lesson.
&
Struggle is the sign of life.

For fear of defeat shall you retreat from the fight? Never lose heart. Go on bravely. Always manifest the highest moral courage. Not one step back that is the idea. Fight it out whatever comes. Let the whole world stand against you. What do you gain by becoming cowards? Many aspire to possess these qualities and even try to imbibe them in their personality. Persevere till your ideal is realized. Stick your guns. Develop that grit.

Youths are personification of energy and enthusiasm. Never give up your endeavor. Mediocre should aspire to raise themselves from the average state of existence. Why to be average? Why cannot you excel? What is stopping you? Has anyone told you not to grow? Has anyone told you not to work for mankind? Have you thought the present is only the time with you? It is time for action? Are you clear about your goals? Are you clear about your objectives? Are you clear about your vision? Are they focused towards humanity? Are they going to take you where you really want to go?

What you want to achieve in life?

Questioning is the beginning of awareness. It is always good to burry yourselves under the heap of questions of life to know where you exactly stand in the world. There are many areas in man's life. Which area is important to you?

Future is always decided in the present. Today's time can reveal your next stage. Are you really transforming? Only managing situations of life are not the right way to direct your goals. Do not say we are weak; we can do anything and everything. We all have the same glorious soul.

Cherish positive thoughts.

Why you are harboring negative thoughts? What makes you weep my dear friends? Summon up your power and whole universe will lie at your feet. Self alone predominates and not matter. Infinite power, existence and blessedness are ours and we have only to manifest them.

People should not dwell on negative thought. Manifest the divinity within you and everything will be harmoniously arranged around it. Infinite perfection is in every man, though not rightly manifested at a single point of time. Time comes out with wider lists one at a time. The same man has many leaves under his tree.

Why shall we think low? When you are born to be at higher planes? Why you are depreciating yourself? When you have infinite opportunities to add values? All knowledge is in you. You need to organize it accordingly. Nothing is new which I am exhorting to share with you today. It is the same old wine of humanity but with a new bottle of hope, faith, trust towards the intoxication of society with greater emphasis and need of the present existence.

My dear friendly readers kindly look inside, the hearts are weeping badly to see the unbecoming of humans from dawn to dusk all over the world.

Man's mission needs great revolution. Evolution and involution both are equally transforming us. There should be daily mission for man. An engineered mission is required to align with the vision, aim, goal and future. The more you drink; you should like to drink again and again the justice of humanity. It becomes sweeter and sweeter as you start drowning into it. I believe the hangover of it shall remain forever and ever till the existence of humanity.

The meaningful saying "If you want something you have never had, you have to do something you have never done", fits very well to the present scenario in which our humanity is struggling.

Indomitable energy lies within you. Start seeing your intellect penetrating into all subjects of life. Start by believing yourselves. Future of man is also to be calculated with applying NPV i.e.; Net Present Value on time. What in the real sense will be its worth if I am investing time to build my career today? From the business and management perspectives the risk of future is to be calculated. There is nothing wrong to be spiritually professional in doing justice to yourself in shaping your personality.

Everybody is reaping from the day. Why some are doing more others are doing less? Always you cannot blame the destiny. Blamelessness should not be the weakness of the right man. Greatness lies in swallowing the shortcomings of other humans. This is an appropriate professional approach to humanity.

What is done is done. Do not repent. Do not brood over past deeds. Now you cannot undo what has been done. Be careful never to do the same thing again. Errors, mistakes, failures and faults are our only true teachers. Man is prone to err and it is man who becomes god on earth. When we are sick, we pray for quick recovery to make most of the day, come back to our normal activity.

AIM Humanity

I am AIM. I am Man. Man is AIM. Man is the aim of nature. Man is the aim of universe. God is realizing his aims through man of existence. God is trying to witness the love of humans through the humanity of the existence.

What can be a better aim than building an integrated meaningful self? How we can become this? Cannot we connect our head and heart to do this from dawn to dusk? Do you think there is nothing novel in us? How such life can be pursued? Our aim is to build that character in humans.

Where to find,

"The Humans of Heroic Ideals" on Earth?

The moral decay of man is rapidly taking place today. The reason is obviously the type of education system we are having in the world. Many of the elite institutions are strong in delivering their commercial mission. The vision of moral is blurring day by day. There are institutions struggling to produce ideal adults.

We need men of principles to bring meaning to life. What is the main objective of education? Is it fulfilling its role in society? It is the place where children start making bigger aims of life. They want to become as they are taught. Teachers are the prime role models for the great ideals of children's. Thus to understand the grown up man's aim, his introspection is to be done first to reach the foundations of life. This is the field where he had been developing his aim for the future. If present was aimless future will be dreadful.

Institutions are failing in ideas to bring ideals in their students. Math, Sciences and History are not the only subjects to make them perfect human beings. What is to be done by the education system of the world? The foundations of life are hanging like the tower of Pisa.

Will they fail in producing real humans?

This is our universal AIM.

To become "REAL HUMANS"

Why your AIM is not humanity?

Why your target is not humanity? Why your desire is not humanity? Why your dream is not humanity? Why your vision is not humanity? Why your mission is not humanity? Is your heart not paining for humanity?

To share from my schooldays as most of us might have not given importance to the subject Moral Science teaching the morals of life through fables, fantasies, fiction, written stories, quotes from holy books, articles, cannot be without regrets today.

The importance of human science, human behavior, human resource management, human counseling, personality development, human culture, human habits, human activities, roles & responsibilities into public services, personal attitudes and professional environment are to be relooked by the world. The concept and definition of career development should not only aim towards outside standards of living for man but the inner self is to be equally developed to understand the importance of human life.

People are killing people as if you are shading of your nails, beards and hair.

These may come back growing today or tomorrow but what about the lives nipped in the bud brutally by us. Every sphere of existence has to sincerely aim to protect the life of man. As we, in order to remind us the importance of environment, earth, energy, mother, father, love, aids, friends, teachers, celebrate environment day, earth day, energy day, mother's day, father's day, lovers day, friendship day, teacher's day respectively, humanity day, a day for man can be celebrated year by year.

In fact everyday is Man's Day.

Attitude changes everything. Have an attitude to have an aim for humanity. People are aiming to bring pains to people.

Every new day is another promising chance to change your life. There should be betterment in our aim towards eliminating pain of people from dawn to dusk. Every man's infinite aim should be to work for humanity. Aiming for positions, power, money, wealth only may not be fruitful if you are not helping humans. Abundances without sharing are as good as redundancy of the thing.

Poverty in the world is another factor for gross misery in the outer world of existence. Who is responsible for this? Are we really trying to resolve this from dawn to dusk? Is it the worry of every man? Are the rich affected by this? Do the rich share with the poor? How the poor can meet their lively hoods? Who will think for them? Why we are not able to resolve it forever? Do Nations have a permanent solution? There are certain truths of life bitter than the existence itself.

Man is himself dividing into two parts.

Man is divided into rich and poor. Man is divided into literates and illiterates. Man is divided into aimlessness and aim. Man is divided into vision and visionless. Man is divided into mission and missions less. Man is divided into loyal and disloyal. Man is divided into cheers and tears. Man is divided into inner and outer world. Man is divided into good and bad. Man is divided into faithful and unfaithful. Man is divided into religious and unreligious. Man is divided into noble and evil. There are many other areas dividing man.

Every difference brings a division.

It is being experienced at all levels, all phases, all times from dawn to dusk. The truth upholds the existence that no man is similar despite the similar bodily functions and biological systems. Then from where does the difference arise? It is these differences which magnify from small ego to big wars. Brains, minds, thoughts, ideas, actions, words, take negative way towards humanity.

The division of man from dawn to dusk creates two worlds for him. One is people with him and the other is people against him. Truthfulness and untrustworthiness both the facets of man are aiming accordingly. Richness and poorness are two major quadrants of separation during existence. They are more or less happy in their communities. The successful and the unsuccessful are again following the legacy of separation. These are permanent gaps of living in society.

A very holistic approach is needed to revolutionize these in man. Let us not be ignorant to the innocent deaths due to starvation being a black spot in the humanity of our times. What else can be a better career than humanity? How to stop the division of man? How to stop the separation of man? How to stop the decimation in man? How can we aim to eliminate these divisions forever? Moreover, primarily it is the prime elimination from the mind. The division starts in the mind of man.

Man lives in his mind more rather than in the real world.

His AIM's are also divided. Man cannot sustain with single aim for long. The dynamics of the life brings in motion to his aims. As his thinking changes so the aim is redefined again and again. Nothing appears to be perfect and stable. No one principle or postulate holds the entire time of life.

Man has lifelong challenges to take and live. Till you are living you have to be aiming.

What is AIM? Why aim? Life is an aim. Aim it. Are you doing it? You will be living till you are aiming? Man has to have the flame of aim to burn the desires of the self and world. Do you have an aim? Have you seriously thought of it? I mean this to all of you from dawn to dusk.

Is AIM always at war with destiny? Destiny activates aim. Why should you search your aim? Aim is the fundamental of our life's journey. Man improvises his aims from time to time. Man reconciles his aim through the process of realization, learning, reasoning, analyzing, retrospection and self-renaissance. Aim keeps changing the man. The man in turn keeps changing the aims. It is true to the law of survival.

You might have heard people in family, colleagues, peers and friends that some have become celebrities, achievers, were rewarded, were successful, were top businessmen, political hero, renowned professor, great practicing doctor, sports personality, lovely singer, had reached the zenith, so and so miserably failed, spoiled his life, went bankrupt, is fit for nothing, lost life due to depression, grace had never befallen on her, irresponsible person, etc .The discussion is that some are able to make their lives and at the same time others are spoiling it.

Can this be totally left to destiny? Where is our zeal? Without which man is not thriving but just surviving. Humanity is an ongoing issue for any society. Healthiness of a person has a direct relationship with aim, satisfaction and targets. The aims can cater to be good, bad, evil, small, short, impure, silly, trivial, narrow, broad, divine, bold, dynamic, reforms, prosperity, society, humanity, habits, culture, and individuality, public, it has no boundaries. There is aim everywhere for everyone, but the direction needs to be established.

Time is said to be eternal.

Time never sleeps, it keeps moving. Using today wisely is the key to success. The perception of success is aimed differently from man to man.

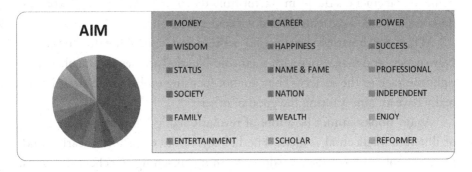

My aim may not be your aim.

Your aim is entirely yours. Say by writing a paragraph on spirituality I feel satisfied with my today's aim, where as you enjoy the same by walking at the beach for a mile, someone by donating at charity centre showing their affection and love, some by helping the needy to obey their kindness of the heart, few for the self in meeting their needs of greediness.

Why our AIM's should be similar?

The aim may vary naturally. It is to do something with the dawn, day and dusk. These are your tools and tackles to make something from existence.

Want to be rich go for money, want to be humble go for kindness, want to be happy search for peace, want to be learned go for education, want to be saint go for renouncing, want to redefine go for realization, want to love mankind go for humanity, want to be noble go for virtues, but go and go, until you go you shall not get.

AIM should take you to your desired destination, dream, goal, target, satisfaction, success, containment, provided you are willing to go, move, run, urge, grab and fight for these things. Can we have a universal aim? It is really a tricky question for answering to all of us. I think we all have the answers within us.

The young minds can pick up brighter and bolder aims. Aim full of courage, faith, trust, hope and love to sincerely commit and accomplish the dreams of existence is the need of the hour all over the world. I firmly believe that we all should pen down our aims. Categorize them on priority. Plan and program them. Work out the necessity of resources as inputs to shape your aim. Time management is the prime factor from dawn to dusk. The day is yours so do not allow it to be contaminated without usage.

What the heartless intellectual writers can contribute to humanity? Newspapers and magazines with their cold-blooded articles are unable to give right message to the society. They are not focusing on be a man first. Do we really have an aim wanting the good of others?

Again Books cannot be a tool of revolutionizing humanity in the hands of illiterate intellectual readers. The literacy works with head, heart, mind, brains, books, knowledge, wisdom, learning, teaching, teachers, students, ethics, values, virtues, vision, mission, self, a proper integration of all these can bring in man a complete well defined AIM.

Let the books actually bite your mind, thought, aim, desires, dreams, perception, thinking, vision, mission from dawn to dusk. History put forwards the truth that good books have brought great revolution in mankind.

Great Books have been written by Great People.

Some have become Doctrines and Holy Books. Book is the reflection of the society through the minds of the man belonging to the law of change. Reformers, Activists and Socialists took up writing to send their message for the welfare of society. Their aims were clear in transforming the society for humanity.

Is unwillingness of readers another reason for slow transformation of society? Reading on humanity should be habit of everyman.

Man need to know man.

Unless man open up their heart how the love can flow to millions and millions. The readers can support the fraternity of authors trying to introduce their thoughts pouring down in these papers called books.

Books are mind of the authors. Books are ideas of the author. Books are abstracts of the society, community and nations. Biographies and Autobiographies both equally are speaking on the subject intended for the readers. Books are AIMs of the author and in turn AIMs of the readers and finally for the purpose it has been penned down.

Our Society needs several libraries on humanity. It is to be the central idea for authors and readers all over the world. If at all you want to write, start writing about improving humanity all over the world.

Man's character should be like the tortoise, it tucks its feet and head inside the shell and you may kill it and break it into pieces and yet it will not come out.

Let us build more and more man of character. Who can have divine aim to live and die for humanity?

Life is a book.

Would you not like your book of life to be decorated with chapters of humanity? Would you not like a great story of yours to be told? Would you not like your heroic deeds of humanity to be shared?

Before a book is written an author gets an idea to do so. I wish more biographies and autobiographies are flooded in society to keep the idea of humanity alive. One who has undertaken writing knows the pain of writing, editing, compilation and publishing his book of life. A complete cycle of learning, teaching, coaching, mentoring, goes into shaping your ideas, thoughts, beliefs, values, tastes, choices, perceptions, philosophies, before the readers are allowed to pounce on the ready to eat cake. We need authors and readers of humanity. The aim is universal to regenerate humanity in the world.

Today the world is getting more high –tech. It is time for fresh thoughts, ideas, actions, motives, attitudes, moods, inspirations, energy, renovations, rethinking, reinventing into arriving at a universal AIM.

The orientation in individuals, societies, communities, nations and the world needs to understand the importance of eternal AIM.

How Human AIM can be different than the AIM of existence?
&
The AIM of human is humanity.

<u>Living is Learning</u>

If you want to live then you have to learn. If you want to learn then you have to live. Both are mutual to one another. Hence without doubt living is learning. The spirit of living defines the lessons of learning.

The attitude of living defines the ability of learning.

Why you want to learn?
&
Why you want to live?

How you want the living to be? Is your choice to be simple and happy? Is your choice to be blissful? How can you learn happiness? Who will teach happiness? Where are the teachers of happiness? Where are the learners of happiness?

"The choice is yours. You hold the tiller. You can steer the course you choose in the direction of where you want to be-today, tomorrow or in a distant time to come".

The above thought of W. Clement Stone is what this chapter "Today is Mine" attempts to rekindle the minds of our readers.

You have a choice of living life?

How to make it as you wish to have it? Who will shape your character? Who will forge your future? Who will give wisdom to live? Where will you go? What will you become? Do you have the ability to realize your potential? Will you become a champion of humanity?

The talent of a man is to be matched with the target. Does everybody have the same target? Our readers can throw better light on this. Is talent only a prime factor for the success of man? How talent can be sharpened? Always our targets may not be predetermined.

The envisaged dreams may not be perfectly achieved. The reason is that the human factor is in between the target and talent. The other very essential factor is time. One is the available time to individual. The other is the time of fortune, the time of grace and the time of opportunity.

Is born talent the legacy of man?

How do we look into integrating the career path of an individual? Before it visiting the definition of success is to be done. Success has many definitions. In my opinion from the bottom of heart after ego of the self the success is another major attribute bringing misery or happiness to man. All success may not be followed by happiness. The paths of success can be through virtues or vices. How you are attaining it?

Where is the ethical talent? What may be the target of man? Is it only careers in academics, knowledge and wisdom? Or career in wealth, richness, settlement, name, fame, power etc. What exactly man is trying to pursue? Take care of the means; the end will take care of itself. Man should himself bring about his own emancipation. Is it for only man? Is it for the world? Every moment of creation is linked with time. The richest truth is that there is nothing richer than the truth.

Will time and destiny decide the future of man? If you waste time then time wastes you. Days should not become vain. Time is powerful and it conquers all. Why all human beings are emotional? People forget and forgive with the passage of time. Resolve or dissolve the evil issues continuity, as it is always deterrent to future of man. How do you expect success without failure? If you are failing today then definitely success will embrace you tomorrow.

What is the ultimate goal? Where is the call from within? Do we have a technology to combat spiritual problems? What is the godly way of life? What is my genealogy? What is the genesis of man? How to make a living? Do not simply be the gypsies of the world? People are draining time in gossip. Where is the Messiah, Allah, Prophet, Son or Avatar of God in Man?

Why we cannot be one of them?

The truth is we all are sons of the same god, supreme, nature, universe or existence. For no fun we have become frustrated, irritated and depressed in our approach towards life.

Life is a project.

Build it. Shape it. Forge it. Explore it. Utilize it. Color it, Dream it. Hold it. Share it. Lead it. Write it. Align it. Understand it. Experience it. Love it. Give it. Take it. Do as you like but do it. Have you sincerely pondered over it? Till you are administering, governing, guiding, planning, controlling, monitoring, and implementing your life you are surely building your future. Develop the zest and zeal to reach the zenith.

Failure is a part of living.

We all die at end. Do you mean to say living is a failure? The philosophy cannot be understood in a day. At the beginning of time, time is always invaluable, and the same time at the end becomes valuable. Anything which is rare and scarce is likely to regain its value and worth.

There are certain areas of our lives which need attention, improvement and repair. Air this "AIR" regularly. A periodic check on yourself helps you in deviating from derailment on future track. The small mind cannot partake of the big.

The man of faith attains wisdom and illumination.
&
There is no such thing as imitation in the spiritual life.

Living is fun if your principles are right. The basics are fine. Is god the claim of theology? We can at the least start with believing in His Saints. God has given birth to great saints all over the world. He definitely wanted all to benefit from the divine spirits from dawn to dusk. He wanted an existence of nonviolent society. Compassion is an ingredient in man for the humanity.

Let there be any culture, Greek Culture, Roman Culture, Western Culture, Eastern Culture, Asian Culture, European Culture, Global Culture and even the Local Cultures, what difference does it make to the true spirit of humans.

Feelings of hopelessness and helplessness is what has remained today as legacy of all the cultures.

Is there hope to humanity?

What is man's target? Is there universal target? All the doctrines will be ashamed to know that humanity is being crucified by humans only. Man is born to save mankind. Man is a savior of mankind. Man is to redeem mankind. Man is to realize his nature. There should not be any moral holiday for man. Let us not be unmindful towards the above. The secret is that if we want to reach perfection, then instead of going out of ourselves, we should try to go inside. The order of things has to be inverted.

How to have the fulfillment of human birth?

We must pray to god in all humility and earnestness. Why we should lack in resourcefulness? Why the feeling of aloneness?

Man is primarily of spirit. Maintaining equilibrium is practical wisdom. Steadfastness is one of the basic virtues of life. Be steadfast. Realization comes when we endure. Hold to your faith and devotion. Never let them grow weak. What can be man's merit?

Man has to mingle with life. Life is an opportunity for enfoldment. Egotism and aggressiveness often blind our vision.

World is like a symphony.

Hearts should be filled with aspirations. It is this ideal that helping others can only bring help to me from dawn to dusk beats all the principles of survival. It is easier to lay your life down than to live for the ideal and humanity. A common man always asserts his ego. A true lover always loves.

Why do we love?

Is it essential by inheritance? Can man create love? Can man create tears? Can man create emotions? Love is a universal lubricant for hearts. It helps in harmonizing the relationships. It absorbs the frictional heat of egos. Hatred is conquered by love and harshness by gentleness. What is the law of life?

Define your ideal clearly? Practice the process of idealization daily. Continually look for ways to reestablish humanity. Meet at least one human daily. Small commitments shall bring you greater compliments. Work with free and pure mind daily.

Day is worship. Keep praying through working for humanity. Be a problem solver. Do not dwell in doubts? The more you live actively the more you learn rapidly. Every action has lessons. Innocence is the power of creation. The curiosity for humanity should never die in man.

Learning is the process of liberation from ignorance.

The recently developed communal bossism in public as well as corporate culture in the liberalized world of today is causing unimaginable turbulence in the present society. I hope many of the youth readers might be under this unrest radar.

You may have been fortunate to be unfortunate to have bosses of not your choices till date. Consider this as a boon in building you to face any adversities arising out of professional living from dawn to dusk. The reason is very simple to understand because they have been trying to manipulate you with their narrow intellectual styles of functioning and unappreciable leadership management obsessed with prejudiced humanity.

Pyramids of AIM

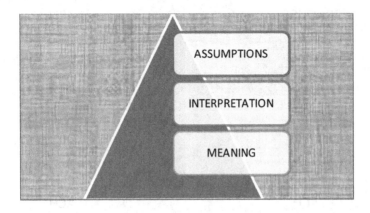

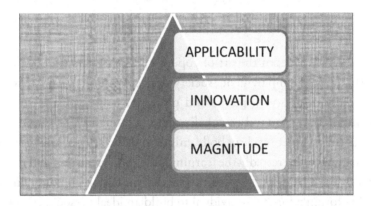

Looking at both the pyramids of "AIM" a mapping relationship can be derived to best understand the aims of humans.

There may be infinite assumptions in human mind but the applicability is within the laws of limitations. When we map interpretation with innovation the question of feasibility is a concern both for the individual and society. Evil innovations do not qualify for interpretations. Whatever may be the tool of analysis it is not ethical to be considered as an ideal AIM.

Thus in the background of humanity "AIM" becomes an important criteria for the personality of an ideal human. The quality of humans is only through the quality of valuable inputs from dawn to dusk in making the man.

A wrong success however big in magnitude may not be the right meaning of the "AIM". Thus an understanding to the readers is to look into developing the meaning of life you are likely to pursue with your "AIM's".

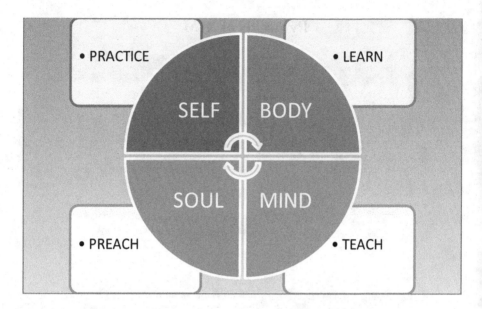

The readers have to learn the art of coping up amidst this trial of the fittest within the laws of employment, society and community. And this format followed daily in personal, public and professional life polishes your entire personality enabling you to become diamond of humanity.

Unless the complete cycle of body, mind, soul and self does not go into any activity integrated interestedly the learning, teaching, preaching and practicing in daily life is not fruitful. The dedication, determination and discipline is the magic 3D's formula for any individual to build an ideal personality to take up humanity.

What I finally wish to convey my readers from the above illustration is that living is a learning process .The tendency of quitting and escaping from the facts of life makes you weaker than actually what you are in reality. Man is not a weak animal by nature. Man can roar like lion against the demons of society.

In the words of Napolean Bonaparte,

"If you build an army of 100 lions and their leader is a dog, in any fight, the lions will die like a dog.

But if you build an army of 100 dogs and their leader is a lion, all dogs will fight like a lion".

Now it is unto us to live like a lion or dog. Lead the life from front. Do not curse it from back. You are the only resource of your destiny.

Everything is bound to happen with your will and way. Rest is just auxiliaries may be or may not be of use to your journey of life. Obstacles, hindrances, adversities, misfortunes, mishappenings, setbacks are all the ways to give you better ways. This is all towards the betterment of leadership and ownership of life. Insecurity is the feeling of mind. Why you feel to be defenseless? Why are you unprotected? The weakness is in your way of living. A man can never harm another man internally eternally. The truth of humanity always triumphs.

Adversity is a universal school of learning.

It teaches you what you may not have come across in your life till the befalling of misfortune on you. Anticipating the motives of another man is a tough task for any man. The mind game cannot be decoded instantly. Man knows his strength and character before someone strips it out. Adversities open up avenues from dawn to dusk.

My readers may not refute this in the pursuit of humanity,

"Man's expectations are the prime cause for exploitations of man".

Man's expectations are not limited. The desires are infinite. Dreams keep building. Thoughts do not stop flowing. All desires may not be goals of life. Rose flower is safe between the thorns, what is your opinion on yourself? If you are trying to find solutions to your unfeasible questions then be prepared for astonishing answers. There is no necessity to shout and scream if we are trying to support peace. Learn everyday to live to win the day.

Let us live everyday in learning to win the day. Learning and living both are mutually connected to the whole process of existence. How to live? How to learn? How to earn your living? Again learning, living and earning go hand in hand from dawn to dusk.

"Seeds do not remain with the fruits", is my living philosophy to all my potential readers. It withers away with the wind of dreams to the whole world.

This is to say that the fruits by nature are unselfish. It always intrinsically remains unselfish in the hands of selfish man. Fundamentally the seeds are universal in existence. Seeds are the origin of the life.

Why humanity is wrinkling day by day?

The best project human will ever work on is human only. What else can be a greater opportunity than trying to learn our own existence? What else can be a better realization than willing to forgive those you have wronged?

Slicing & Dicing

"Fearlessness is necessary for the development of other noble qualities"

- Mahatma Gandhi

Man has to dare to slice time from the day to dice with his ideals of humanity. Is it not a wonderful time to be alive? What else is bigger opportunity than this today? Do you have a plan for today? Have you prepared the action list? Did you prioritize?

Do you have a goal for today?

How will you use your twenty four hours format today? Do you have any plan with you for using your time? Will all the activities be towards humanity? How many people will be helped by you today? Who is the important person for you today? Are there important tasks before you?

Do you have a master list? Why writing down goals? It starts with creating your feelings, thoughts, perceptions and inspirations. Goal should have a deadline. How to achieve your goal? Make a plan. Take action on your plan.

Have a daily schedule. This is very important to execute it effectively. All is haste if not executed.

Dreams are to be executed from dawn to dusk.

Never miss a day. Today will not kiss you again. Do not miss this kiss of existence. Life loves us. Let us work with life. Make it lively every day. Have clarity in making plans and reaching your goals. Keep moving forward otherwise the time would push you back. Keep moving with unconditional faith. Do not pause in your endeavor until the result has been achieved. Do not blink, go ahead and march forward.

Life is excitement. Incite it to aim bigger goals. Have the fire to flame them right now. Do it my dear friends. One is doing the work at dawn. The other part of reviewing is to be done at dusk. Review it daily. The review list is to be executed again in the day with great beginning at dawn.

Let us scientifically plan our day and examine ourselves daily with thorough review. Regular practicing there is bound to change your life. How to measure your overall competency? Your performance from dawn to dusk is with respect to the time utilized by you. Why it is that other people are doing better than I am? The process of learning, implementing and applying can change your life.

Dawn to Dusk attempts to possibly find out probable reasons of man which is affecting the universal humanity. D2D is a little mind trying to explore the world for regenerating humanity.D2D can be an investigating report to understand the better ways humanity can be checked.

Dawn to Dusk is a tool to discover and rediscover the simple truth of man. It is a sample model to see the contribution of day, man, time into the creation and destruction of existence from dawn to dusk and its innovations, influences and impacts on humanity. Every idea on this book is focused on increasing your levels of thinking towards humanity. The faster you learn the truth the faster you realize the life.

Life is dicing with fortune daily.

Every day man is slicing and dicing. The question is to what extent risk can be taken. Man is risking humanity.

Is it not an opportunity to rewrite our lives?
&
Who likes chaos?

Do you want to breathe in slavery of mind? What about inequity in society? How to repair our lives? How to bring the equality? Can it be done in all dimensions? Who will do it? How to maintain our emotional system? How to steer our behavioral sciences? Have you ever thought of the impact of schooling on our overall development? Are you waiting ambitiously to give birth to an anxious idea?

Do not you agree with me that humanity was born the same day when human took birth?

Why then we are unable to hold on to the idea of philanthropy? There are only few exceptions to the whole process of reformation. Why not you become a humanist? The world is eagerly waiting every day from dawn to dusk for the transformation in humans.

Is it really difficult to transform from chaos to cheers?

The readers too can look into this reviewing their personal perspective in relation to world perspective. We are all working towards Global Humanity. Humanity is not a subject of any one man, any one community, any one society, and any one nation. It is a matter of World Peace and Harmony. The complete global village is waiting to be transformed from unwanted blows of daily chaos from dawn to dusk. Who is benefiting from this predicament?

Humanity has become dilemma for humans.
&
Why the living philosophy is in total mess?

Will man be able to unfold the mystery of mind? How to change people's spiritual and social out look? How to establish harmony among cultures and civilizations of the world? What is the prime basis of religion? Is the fundamental clear to man? Why it is difficult to lead the ideal life?

What are the causes of degrading humanity?

As long as the tadpole has its tail, it lives only in water and cannot come up on land. As long as a man has the tail of ignorance he can live in the water of the world only, but when that tail falls off, he can as freely move about in the world as in existence-knowledge-bliss.

There is no point in assuming a human body, if its purpose of attaining God is not achieved.

World is by nature transitory therefore useless to grieve. Let us not lose the joy of creation and the spirit of survival. Man too is transitory in nature. What you were yesterday will not be today and what you are today will not be tomorrow. Start knowing thyself and the rest will follow. This is perhaps the law of humanity.

Business in humanity is open to all.

How to address issues of inequality and social justice? People should start focusing on social entrepreneurship. Every man should start this business for industry of humanity. What should be the idealism of life skills? Let us be honest about our lives from dawn to dusk. Why we have lost touch with our humanity?

Learning, Training and Development is needed not only for career management but even in human management. The vast universal resource of human is getting drained from dawn to dusk. Neither the world nor the human is enriching by living. The productivity of humanity is degrading day by day.

Let us recall the thought of the legendry philosopher Aristotle the world had brought in to understand the value of education as perceived by him, "The roots of education are bitter, but the fruit is sweet".

Why do not we become entrepreneurs of humanity? The world will surely benefit with this new venture of business. There is nothing to worry about policies and finances for enacting and implementing the project of humanity. What it requires is only the strong will of man?

In addition to it supported by the determined mind. Today the world needs more and more human entrepreneurs to globally integrate the international business of humanity. The world should have millions and millions of Centers of Humanity. Connect your souls to this network of universal humanity. Let these centers do the liberalized business of bringing cheers to humans.

Develop as much awareness and counseling centers one can to combat the invasions of chaos. There cannot be any better weapon than education in humanity. These schools of humanity require only love, heart, kindness, hope, faith, and trust as credentials for admissions. Learn, teach, train and develop yourselves as humans.

Every human being is an independent enterprise of humanity.

Humanity is a universal business. Let us gain from the profits of this business. I feel there were universities professionally training us in regenerating humanity and giving us degrees in humanities. More and more Professors of Humanities would pass out to teach humanity. The subject needs immediate reorganization far beyond any other prejudices polluting the knowledge of society. This would help us to form a specialized community of warriors addressing all the issues of humanities all over the world.

A seed of humanity in every home is to be planted to engineer human values today.

Humanity has nothing to do with success and failure. You are the proprietor to manage your accounts of happiness and sadness very much as the profit and loss statement of the organization. You are an organization of your life. The objective is humanity. You have to become a good human. How do you do it? It is you who is answerable for the assets and liabilities of your life.

Human life without accountability is as good as the ocean without water. Do not desert your life. And this entrepreneurship of humanity is not at all risky. Your investment either equity or debt is always going to be love for humans. If you fail in your venture miserably, at the end you are going to lose only the love you shared nothing else more than that.

I have an appeal to all the young youths of the world to jump into this business of humanity. Simply do not become man of leisure.

Life is all about building your own company with humanity. In life, timing is the single most important thing. You should be big from day one in your life. Bigger in thoughts, bigger in dreams, bigger in ideas, bigger in values, bigger in morals, bigger in ethics, bigger in virtues, bigger in love, bigger in faith, bigger in trust, bigger in ideals, whatever you do, try it doing with the hope of becoming BIG.

Why you want to be small from dawn to dusk? Why you want to waste your time on filthy things? Why you want to live with petty dreams? Why you want to make little out of your life? Go deeper into questioning yourself. It is here where the mountain of wisdom lies. It is here where the ocean of knowledge is submerged. Swim to the bed to unearth it to the surface of existence.

Life is yours to realize to the outmost. Do it magnificently.

Life is all about the bigger journey not the smaller destinations. The greatest wealth is the feeling of aliveness. Live every moment of it with happiness. Bring happiness and healthiness to others by your clean existence.

Humanity is an idea which we all are trying to make it happen.

Everywhere the purpose is to uplift humanity. Live for the highest attitudes every man would wish in his lifetime. If at all you want to fight then fight like a lion to be the king of humanity.

Who is the teacher of universal religion?

Does humanity has to do anything with religion? Does humanity has to do anything with racism? Why the creator himself is creating, maintaining and destroying this world?

Did human create the world?

Our basic wisdom needs to be redefined. The perceptions are to be refined. Years and years have elapsed in the precipitated thinking leading only to ultimate ignorance again and again. We are going through these chapters for the valuable and extremely indelible cause of bringing change in the attitude of humans towards humanity. Let the desire for it run down the streets of narrowly existing society of recent times.

Instead of cheers we are living in chaos.

Let the human turmoil cease. We had enough of trials and ordeals. It is only education which can bring the revolution but not the legislation. The dignity of humans is to be reinstated by one and all. Human disorders can be diagnosed only through the process of spirituality. It has the power to sail you through the ocean of life. It brings in the divinity to float you across all miseries.

As you live your days, so you will live your life. Have you showed courtesy to someone today? Have you been compassionate to someone today? Do you still remember the people who had helped you once?

What I was capable of becoming? What I am today?

Summing Up & Exercise for Readers- Chapter-III

- What AIM you have today?
- Do you have agenda for your life?
- Do you have action plan for your life?
- Do you have a draft for today?
- Why do not you start practicing the concept of "Daily Works Management" –DWM, a measurement technique to arrive at a conclusion with real facts and figures?
- This self-analysis tool works out your performance from dawn to dusk. It is one of the best appraisal systems for learning, building and guiding our own personality.
- It sincerely brings out a correlation between I, Day and AIM.

Self- Daily Works Management

Today's Activity- AIM	Target at DAWN	Achieved at DUSK	Gaps/ Short- coming	Reasons/ Analysis	Correc- tive Action Taken	Review/ Complied
Make People Smile	2 people	1 people	1 people	No Time	Time Manage- ment	Met the person after two days.
To learn humanity	Read books on hu- manity- daily one hour	Failed to read today	Not touched the book	Went to a movie with friends	I should not repeat it. I have to be more de- termined, disciplined and fo- cused on my goals.	It is nearly three months; I have been reading book on humanity regularly.
Visit an Orphan- age	Meet & Teach the pupils	Yes	Nil	Nil	Nil	Was happy with my work.

- The above is a sample model illustrated for the readers as how it can be effective in carrying out daily analysis. You can very well customize the format and style of presentation and reporting. The crux of the matter is the readers should do this. Please kindly communicate to your near and dears for following it.
- This is a small tool from dawn to dusk.
- Keep reporting, updating and reviewing your daily activities instantly.
- You can visit these spreadsheets or records to have an overview of the week, month and year.
- Sincerely make something out of your life daily from dawn to dusk.
- Can you do that?

Chapter IV

LEAD YOUR LIFE

Lead with humility as World is a sanctuary of Goodness

Is Life destined to be destiny?
&
Can the Destiny of life for every man be same?

How to lead your life? The density of every individual man is different looking towards his own legacy of existence. Some are floating in life gracefully and some are sinking painfully and struggling to be liberated at the earliest. Destiny is an inherited attribute of the existence. This is a characteristic human has been fighting it out from dawn to dusk. Did the creation bless us with eyes to see the external world only?

Are we running away from realities of life?

Are we fighting destiny in the wrong spirit? Motivation does not mean to manipulate your motions. Inspiration does not mean to become inhuman. How to recreate ourselves as the person we were destined to be divine?

Let us not join the legion of people obsessed with philosophy of excuses rather than trying to overcome the challenges of life. The spirit of life is not to dwell in temples of bricks and mortar.

Envision the day which is about to unfold. Days will unfold in the most marvelous ways provided you lead your vision and mission in the same fashion from dawn to dusk. What are your personal growth initiatives? How do you define your humanity?

Man should start searching for ways to improve his life.

My learned readers as we all know "Worry burns the living before death", it is wise to live without hanging on to it. We have not been clear in differentiating between concern and worry.

The principle of living is crystal clear to the existence of life.

Leading requires the cycle of vision, mission and objectives.

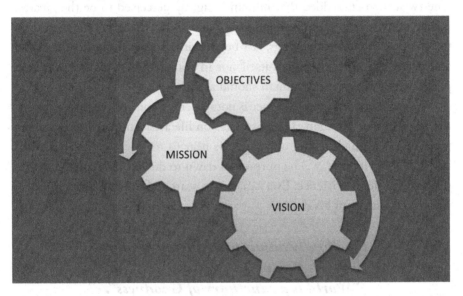

The smooth functioning of these inter locked gear wheels of vision, mission and objectives from dawn to dusk assists the human in their pursuit of attaining goals in all walks of life.

Real Worship

Human has to create temples of humanity through his home of heart.

Divinity is the universal destiny of every human. This is the prime ideal for every human. Is not humility one of the indelibly known and inheritably acquired traits of human? How to get the most out of life for humanity from dawn to dusk? Why fears and doubts are clouding our vision of humanity?

Why Human is unable to understand the real worship of humanity? Let us begin by stopping thinking of tiny thoughts. There is sanctuary of goodness all over the world. To enter this orchid of happiness man needs to be simply true to his own existence.

Life is tangled between destiny and reality.

The twist is so embedded that human is rightly perceived to be the greatest puzzle of existence. Human right from his birth starts searching the causes for the predestined happenings. To begin with, your coming to the world and again leaving the world is itself not in your hands. This is a common phenomenon which every human should admit.

"My in and out in this existence is not under my control", regularly haunts the mind of every human. The postulates on life are formulated to live along its centricity. Which school of thought is near to reality? The greatest truth is we all are living today. The purpose of dawn to dusk is to learn and realize the human life in existence. Every man is in search of the human in him. He wants to be leader of his destiny.

I faithfully admit to say to my readers,

"World is a sanctuary of Goodness".

We have to search it through worship. There is goodness in every man. There is divine soul in every man. First know thyself to understand the world. First know your goodness to see the goodness of the World.

Goodness is the product of quality of life.

How to live a quality life from dawn to dusk? Time is always short for man. It is not easy as we perceive the game of life. The referees are likely to be partial in deciding between goodness and badness. Nevertheless reinventing of humans is the sole purpose of real worship.

Man is a gift of goodness. Man is a point of oneness. Man can only lead man. The world of man is explored throughout from dawn to dusk. Do you really want the quality of change? The reliability of leading a quality life is always to be defined by the truth of worthiness.

Meritless life can only bring misery.
&
Is the world changing?

What is happening to man? Is the man changing? Do you think both the world and man are changing? Is this hypothesis accepted? Will the world change? Will the man change? We all are waiting with greater hopes for the dawn of universal humanity. Expectations of billion humans are at stake. Why man is gambling with man? Why man is exploiting man? Why man cannot lead man? Why man is pulling man back? Why men are at war? Who will check the quality of man? Why the instinct of animal in man is not dying? Does mankind have to wait for another evolution of man? When will this revolution flood the universe with humanity?

Man is bigger by his quality of thoughts.

Man is leader by his quality of values. Man is ideal by his quality of attitudes. Everywhere the assurances for quality of living are being committed by man. Without the code of conduct the discipline is losing its sanctity.

Leading needs direction of life from dawn to dusk. Are we becoming humans at the end of the dusk? Directionless living can only lead you to chaos. Can man's motivation overcome needlessness of life?

The ship of uselessness in man should sink forever at the earliest. Senselessness in living will bring fruitlessness from dawn to dusk. The practicality in physical and intellectual living is to be conceived, perceived and implemented despite unhelpfulness being experienced by man in existence. To grace goodness the mind should start becoming good.

Man has to control the waving mind before it unwontedly sails in impracticality.

Worship is a very difficult proposition for man to define. How to know more about it? Is there literature on this subject? Are there doctrines on this subject? Has anyone researched on this earlier?

Is it a ritual? Is it a culture? Is it a religion? Is it a way of life? Is it related to man? Is it related to work? Does work has anything to do with worship? Whom to worship? Why to worship? Can we not live without worshiping? The universal perception of worshiping is humanity through the service to human. Why victims are only victims of their defeated thinking?

Criticism is not to immortalize helplessness of humans. Wickedness was never the true nature of humans.

Dishonesty is the uninvited devil in the mind of humans. Lack of divine nourishment is the base for the thinning of humanity. Lack of modesty is blurring pure worship of humans. How to stop the impropriety in humans? Impoliteness is becoming the way of life in emerging societies of today.

Are we trying to establish immoralism?

Humanists are being replaced by immoralists. Where are the immaterialists? Does worship means immaterialism? Why world is breeding immoralists? How they are sustaining the impacts of goodness?

Illusionists are ruling the world. Will this trick work forever? Illusionism is bound to fail when the principles of realism start penetrating the minds of humans. Humans are sure to illuminate the universe with humanity. It is a temporary phase of imbalance because of the illegitimate practices the society is not realizing. Illiberality will have its own pros and corns on humanity. Most of the miseries are due to illogicality in living.

Wisdom of living cannot be compiled in a day.

It is a continual process of refinement guiding the way of living and worshipping the existence.

Every day how to worship? Is worship linked to the activity you do from dawn to dusk? Where to look for the right meaning? Does the world have human dictionary? Does the world have prescribed laws of living? Does the world have defined way of worshiping?

I am not placing any question paper to my readers for answering but the universal truth is we are struggling to place ourselves in the right place in the world amidst uncertainties of principles of living.

Our wisdom is also helpless to guide us above our limitations. It is only man's hope and faith which has the power to face all the challenges of mysteries by existence from dawn to dusk. The daily worshiping makes your faith and hope stronger day by day. It is like you are transmitting and receiving energy from the source.

If you are daily praying to yourself for strength, one day this prayer will hold you in times of turbulence. The body lives and breathes through an infinite source of existence with or without your real awareness of breathing in life.

A man really has no destination in the outer world.

In other words he has numerous destinations with respect to the time of needs. Contrary to this man in the inner world has only one destination. People generally forget that the almighty is watching all of us through the eyes of nature. He does not tell you the secrets of life in one go. He wants us to come to him again and again for worship. His mechanism is through the real worship.

One who wants to know him should undergo the trial of reaching him. Let us understand the mystery of our own evolution. Though we all have the same doubts about worship yet it is unearthed to the surface of existence. We are through our own means and individual thoughts trying to reach the central core of existence.

One idea of purity is acceptable to all of us. We all want to be pure. We all want to be clean. We all want to be fair. We all want to be happy. We finally want to know ourselves from dawn to dusk.

<u>Rhythm of Human</u>

"The most dynamic results come only after the most turbulent of times"

What is Rhythm of Man? Is there any difference between the physical man, spiritual man, ideal man, knowledgeable man and man of universal existence? How it is important to the world?

What is devotion? To know ourselves better I have attempted to identify those areas which influence us seriously from dawn to dusk. If you can look at it you will find what is more important and which necessarily suits the individual. Nothing is above self-esteem. Nothing is above self-respect. Nothing is above self-regard.

Never lose your tempo to be human. Never imbalance your living. Never stop receding in life. Hold for a moment and you shall hold the entire life. This is that minute moment which decides your entire life.

Every dawn is a new rhythm you are going to witness. Every dawn is a new song you are going to hear. Every dawn is a new human you are going to become.

Every dawn is a new dream you are going to realize. Every dawn is a new thought you are going to get. Every dawn is a new unfolding you are likely to embrace.

Every dawn is a new opportunity you are going to utilize. Every dawn is a new time you are going to capitalize. Every dawn is a new innovation you are going to take.

Every dawn is a new life you are going to experience.

On thorough insight I have an inference to be looked by my readers for their enrichment as, "Individuality is the means to reach the ends of Universality". All means have the ends of dawn and dusk.

Every individual man is dancing with the rhythm of life. All are swinging to the tune of nature. All are acting as directed by the mind. Beauty of the individual is being radiated by the beautification of the world. The entire individuals are on the same stage drama of life. All the individual roles lead to the same universal goal. Richness and poverty are only temporary plays .Strength and weakness is only momentary states of shilly-shally mind. We live more in hem and haw.

Unevenness is the path of life. Eventually the happiness is from these crests and troughs of life. Sooner or later all the rise and falls ceases and everything merge with the rhythm of universe. Diversities, disparities and discrepancies always work toward bringing disequilibrium to man.

> *Challenges in life never die.*
>
> *Opportunities in life never die.*
>
> *Wisdom in life never dies.*

World in existence never dies. Quest for survival never dies. Inspiration in life never dies. Thoughts of man never die. Voices of freedom never die. Nature never dies. Universe never dies. Evolution never dies. Creation never dies. Idea never dies. Life never dies. God never dies. Man never dies.

And finally Human never dies.

What we can observe is that all are in some or another rhythm of life from dawn to dusk. Eliminations cannot be the law of life. It definitely follows a universal law of rhythm. This is manifested through the rhythm of man.

Dignity of the Self is the wealthiest possession a man can have. Every true man would like to fight for this value. Is man becoming unvalued by his self? What necessitates him to throw away his glory? The rhythm of man continually changes to the demands of the world. His own tempo is not in his control from dawn to dusk. Why man has been blaming the world? Can the world do nothing? Is it only man who has to do all the understanding and reasoning?

Life is a journey of reverence. Show me a man on this earth who does not wish to be admired? Admiration is the primary sense of regarding the importance of services rendered by the man. Man loves to be truly recognized and acknowledged. Always the negativity should not be part of the brainstorming related to elevation of human life.

Emotionalism is indispensable from dawn to dusk in becoming of humans. Every one cannot perform all the activities without involvement of heart. Heart is an intruder with spiritual reasoning. It is the fulcrum of rhythm of man. A thought on religious obligation cannot be dispensed with while reestablishing humanity?

Will man's disposition remain a mystery?

Activities are a matter of choice of the individual. However, we may be, human is to be principally respected and regarded. This is how we worship the humanity. How can pulse of humans be universally converged to the center of existence? Are we not the dispensationalists?

Life is always disputable in nature. This disputation brings a newer dawn to it again and again. All the realization at dusks is dissolved for a new learning. Dissimulation cannot be forever.

Ditheism cannot breed disunity. It may cause distress till the mind opens with universality. All that glitters is not gold is the oldest wisdom man has learnt but without the control on temptations of the mind. His tempo is aligned with the frequency of the temptations from dawn to dusk.

Life should not be parasitic like the leafless plant dodder attaching itself to the host plant by means of suckers. Man should not be sucker of another man. A sucking society murders the humanity. A blood should give blood to save life but not take blood to kill life. The world is filled with doomsayers. Are we all waiting for the last day of the world's existence? By not doing anything today we are already experiencing the doomsday.

A dawn will come to remove the doomsday forever. Let us pray it happens at the earliest. No man will try to end his life then. We are speaking of a world free of chaos. We are dreaming of a world free of crimes. We believe a world free of terror. We trust a world free of inhumanity. We think of a world filled only with love. We hope to have a world full of flower gardens and orchids of fruits. We all want a world of happiness, healthiness and harmony.

My dear readers the universal truth is, "Humanity has lost its existence before the extinct of humans".

I hope all of you agree with the paradigm the world is facing today. This model was never the idea of any existence. It was never intended to bring misery to humans. The world is astonished to reveal the truth of man's agony, anxiety and chaos.

We have remained as Apes. What we were understood to be evolved from. We are still animals not humans. Who will authenticate our humanity? The domestication of our self needs a new dawn today.

The civilizations of today need a new rhythm of existence.

The globalization is demolishing the walls of racism in unifying the vision of humanity. It may not be always right that people of history were not concerned about humanity. The rhythm of their periods had different challenges of imperialism, communism and capitalism. The perception of world is changing with time of existence. The earth is trying to justify that it is the planet of humanity. The whole universe is experiencing a total change in rhythm of humans.

Life always tries to live in manuscripts rather than a finally edited and published thesis. It may be the right time to recall the philosophy of the German philosopher Friedrich Wilhelm Nietzsche to rise above the restrictive morality of ordinary men with the support of the superman. Why man is not trying to become extraordinary? Why man is not trying to excel in morality? Why man is not trying to rise in humanity? Where is the obstacle in pursuing humanity? Why man is not becoming superman of humanity?

Life is like a hill.

When you are at the bottom of it you like to rush to the top at the earliest. The ascending of the hill is like building your foundations, strength, courage, boldness, enthusiasm, spirit, eagerness, curiosity, dreams, desires, vision, target, talent, with all the rhythm of life. Your eagerness and quest increases when you are at mid point to the final topmost peak of the hill. The temptation and focus is not lost. You are holding the concentration and dedication of the self.

Moreover the direction of thought is maintained till you get to your final goal. You keep boosting, motivating, inspiring and encouraging yourself during the journey of climbing to your target point. You are always telling your will to do little more; you make your way through the tough terrains with braveness. You ravage the jungle of darkness through your might. You have no fear of height. You pray with faith, hope and trust to make it to the top. You love the sight of landscapes being left behind. You gratify yourselves marching forward in your pursuit of success.

This is how you tame yourself to make the journey successful. You put all your body, mind, and soul, to get the best out of the day to be at the top of the hill. You do with zest, zeal to be at the zenith. And once you reach there, that moment is the greatest moment of life realizing your dreams come true. The happiness and joy is infinite. You feel you are at the top. You have sense of achievement. You truly cherish your efforts. The ascending of hill is always adventurous as the journey of life towards, perfection, excellence, in proving yourself to the existence. You want to beat your merit through all the virtues and wisdom you have acquired. Till the goal is achieved the work is worship. The containment should not be in way of worship.

The descending of the hill signifies the maturity of life. You are aware of the target you have achieved. You know that you were hero of the drama. You are satisfied with your performance. Your eagerness of the world is not aggressive as it was during climbing to meet your goal. You have realized that you are a winner. You want to share it with your friends, family, colleagues and the world. You know you will be recognized, acknowledged and appreciated. The fruit of success is with you. You are sensing the grace of god. You are top of the world. Your spirits are flooding with bliss. You are experiencing peace after the tiring feat of climbing your dreams. You are experiencing fullness in yourself. You have the memories of a successful journey.

This is how man wants to climb many hills in life. The complete cycle of ascending and descending personifies the real struggle and thrill of life.

Life similarly ascends to descend in the rhythm of life.

Is there anything in your life that you are doing today? Will you get into today again? Then jump into action. Feel the presence of life. The tender touch, soft voice, delicate breeze, glowing sunlight, get yourself in the rhythm of day from dawn to dusk. This is real living, and only living.

An overall experience of bliss can be only felt with the elimination of chaos in the world.

Readers today are yours. Get it completely. Day is an investment to build you. Do not let it drain. Dawn is the time to begin capitalizing it. Start falling in the rhythm of life. Start singing the song of existence. Start feeling the warmth of day. Start building the man in you.

Over the time the truth will spill over your mask. No sooner you realize, you will burn within before you are put on the pyre of life. Let us start creating cheers and destructing chaos. Boldness is not to bleed the needy.

Do you have a dream list of your life?

You are responsible for your life. Do you have any limitations from dawn to dusk? You should know that all possibilities are open to you. What actions you can take today? If you are reading this book now pause for a moment to instantly pen down your list of actions for today immediately. Again what could you do right now? Treat your talent, potential, abilities, confidence, knowhow, and intellect, mental, emotional and physical energies as your human capital for the fruitful consumption of the day. Human has abundant resources in this world to work towards humanity.

A smile on your face, a heartfelt good morning wishes, a sincere two words of "thank you" to win the grace of man, a pat on the back to acknowledge the goodness of man, a kiss to a child thirsty of love, your strong hands to the stumbling old, your few words of encouragement to the unconfident brothers, a bit of learning support to the unlearnt, few words of advice to the visionless, sharing your piece of meal with the hungry, extending your homes to the orphans, volunteering your services to the society, there are many such small activities and bigger activities associating man with man in the overall building of the pleasant world. Whatever we are into the daily activities the central thing is the human.

Above all the activities you do in the day put people first in everything. Why you want to be an average person? Make your life extraordinary with support of people and helping people in and around you. Your goals should have bit of people everywhere. Ultimately all the doing by the people, for the people, of the people is for the people of the world from dawn to dusk. No aim should be concluded without the central idea of humanity.

Have you projected yourself forward from the prospective of humanity? Why do not we start tapping our love for humanity? It is naturally hidden in all of us. Human is a reservoir of love. Let the streams mingle daily to drown the evils, crime and terror forever.

A clean living is essential for humanity to breed in the world. Man should align with the rhythm of life. A marginal discipline in daily living can bring wonders of change from dawn to dusk. This contribution is required from entire humans on earth.

How people represent and assess uncertainty? How the interplay of memory and judgment works? How beliefs and expectations influence perception from dawn to dusk? How a simple rethinking can revolutionize your approach towards humanity? Why not volunteer yourself in shaping the mankind?

Why Humanity cannot be a career?

Why this cannot be coached, taught, trained, learned and mentored? Can humanity not become bigger than it is? Can humanity not become better than it is? Can man not become the engineers of humanity? Let us be a sanctuary where God dwells. Let us be a garden for innocent and tender souls. Let us be a table where others may feast on the goodness of God. Let us be a womb of Life to grow. Let us rise to the question of our time. Can you not become more sensible than you are? Can you not work for lighting the world? Let us speak to the injustices in our world. Let us move the mountains of fear and intimidation. Let us shout down the walls that separate and divide. Let us fill the earth with the fragrance of Love.

No sooner we come into this world the education of life begins. And nothing to ponder over we keep educating ourselves throughout our life. The ridiculous part of it is imperative from the becoming of us. We keep swaying from our ideals, values, ethics, noble, morale, esteem, virtues, from time to time.

Man lives in phases of rhythm.

He keeps swinging between the ends of devil and divine. He keeps moving up and down between heaven and hell. Being in the state of pleasure in hell he forgets the bliss of heaven. The human in him sometimes awakes to move away from the clouds of inhumanity. The rhythm of human is inherently floating between humanity and inhumanity.

Man only can shape humanity. It has been told again and again that, "Failures are the building block of innovation". Brave are the humans who keep failing to explore the opportunities of innovations. Humans are becoming successful. Humans are learning to fly. How long do we grieve for something we are born to deliver?

Delivery of humanity by all humans is the message of dawn to dusk all over the world. Is it not that we all are engineers building a universal home of happiness for humans? Every man is a useful grain of the whole meal of humanity.

The rhythm of man and rhythm of world are no two different frequencies. The rhythm of human and rhythm of universe are no two different frequencies. How to frame a glossary of humanity?

What are the Do's & Don't of humanity?

Can you prepare a table for yourself to assist you in understanding the essentialities of humanity?

Do's & Don't of Humanity

Do's	Improvement	Impact	Influence	Remarks
Kindness	self	society	humanity	
Love	self	society	family	healthiness
Secularism	society	culture	humanity	tolerance

Don't	Damages	Impact	Influence	Remarks
Selfishness	self	society	individual	
Ego	self	society	personal	turbulence
Atheism	society	culture	humanity	Unorganized

What are the actions and reactions of humanity? What is the framework of humanity? Do the Do's and Don't have impact and influence in our pursuit of goals in regenerating humanity? A research dimension is essential to professionally diagnose the problems in every individual.

You have to study the humanity in you.

Below is a list which I have attempted as a primarily draft compilation of few words for my readers from the A to Z of daily rhythm of humans from dawn to dusk. If Man more or less is surrounded by the influencing forces of these positive words a transformation is bound to take place in line with the law of magnetism. The induction then has the vision of optimism.

Man is rhythmically tuned to listen to the divine calls of nature. Thus progressively he is naturally toned up in this glossary of words reflecting the environment of change. I request my readers to take up formulating such exercises essential to you in magnetizing yourself with humanity.

Once you have become magnet of humanity, your work is to magnetize other fellow men. The application of theory of magnetism thus can bring humanity forces to the entire world. A Universal frequency of humanity will be resonating everywhere in the world.

Readers can develop as many lists as they wish. The purpose of the above model is to understand the mapping of actions to reactions from dawn to dusk. It would later on become your habit to be away from the world of negativism. The technique of elimination is a gradual way towards the perfection. Your essentialities thus get established from dawn to dusk. You have a uniform flow chart of actions balancing your rhythm of life from dawn to dusk.

Idea is a word. Thought is a word. Dream is a word. Action is a word. Reaction is a word. Life is a word. To live you have to associate with it. Your expression is through the word of feeling. Whatever you do is reflected, refracted, radiated and defined only through words. Words form the basis of understanding your nature.

Where is the Man of Words? The world certainly is missing them. The world is in scarcity of noble souls. The rhythm of human should be such that it inspires others to dream more, explore more, learn more, innovate more, do more, give more, become more, love more, accomplish more, achieve more, discover more, and in doing so you get transformed into a leader. The leadership role at any level is always about the harmony of the team. The rhythm of the team should be harmonious to be energetic, vibrant, and enthusiastic, with the positivity of life.

Life should vibrate in the twilight of day.

Human should enjoy, feel, understand, experience,
the rhythm of the divine existence.

A charismatic leader values the sentiment, emotions, thoughts, principles, esteem, ideals, morals, opinions, views, perceptions, attitudes, and all the human factors of the team in working towards the central goal. Success for leaders is not just about what you accomplish in your life, it's about what you INSPIRE others to do.

Human is a universe of inspiration.

Man has to hang on it to hold the dreams of humanity. Man has to be a very strong believer before he is an invincible inspirer. Chain yourself with faith, trust, hope and love in whatever good you do from dawn to dusk. Never give up the rhythm of goodness. Man should see that his rhythm of divinity is unshakeable till the last breath of his life.

Every human is a leader. Man can lead with humility.

Man has to lead people. Remember that some responsibilities in life are not liabilities. A decision of yours today is the repercussions you will face tomorrow. Prayer is the most powerful weapon of a believer.

Man has an opportunity to pray from dawn to dusk. He has several ways to offer it to the existence. Unless you are blessed with his grace how you can pass the blessing on to your fellow men.

Life should be organized to understand the rhythm of existence. Human is to be disciplined to gain from the rhythm of grace.

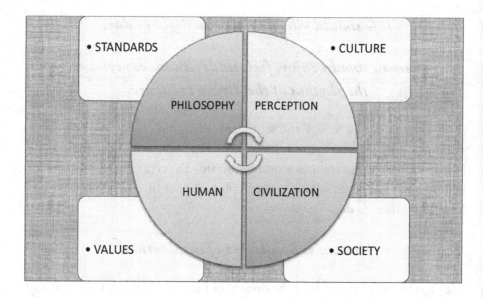

The wheel of philosophy, perception, civilization and human have been generating out cultures, societies, values and standards from time to time for humans to live within their limitations of existence.

The point of discussion simplifies the comprehension and apprehensions of all our doubts, confusions, queries and curiosities from dawn to dusk. That is to say the integrated effort of this cycle is seen outside in the world of existence.

The stronger the core of human the stronger is the humanity in the world. The stronger is the nucleus of human the outer world is inclined towards the inner values of the humans.

A man with words from, "Glossary of Humanity", can only speak, write, play, fight, work, preach, sing, mentor only humanity. He starts living and learning in humanity. He is slicing and dicing in humanity. He is in perfect rhythm of life. He is playing the game of humanity. He is becoming champion of humanity.

You never know which among these can bring you the fortune of change. This credit can be owned by anyone. It may be the 5 D's, the 5 W's, the 5 P's or the 3 Z's. Each one has its own influence, impact and power of induction. The suitability is bound to differ from man to man. The affectivity of the applicability is based on the employability of the words in practicality.

Creativity is the tool with every man in this world.

Man can create his own rhythm of life. Unless he sings the rhymes of humanity he cannot reestablish humanity.

The essentialities with which man has to work out his rhythm can be summarized to "Glossary of Humanity". To further explain what I mean to my readers, I have worked out a model not very exhaustive but a brief one to drive your insight into understanding of the philosophy which I wish to transmit. As we live in the world of words from dawn to dusk, an environment in which we live surely influences and impacts our becoming of the man in us.

At the end of the dusk you are what you started with at the dawn.

Words are your tool of actions to put you in the rhythm of life from dawn to dusk. They are not only some combination of alphabets. They have the power to rule both your inner and outer world. Give them a chance to make your daily agendas, review, follow up, correction, relearning, to reform yourself towards regenerating humanity. By doing this we are practicing the ideals of humanity. Any good practice of society in society will certainly bless mankind with goodness.

The goodness at dawn is the cause for the happiness at dusk.

Similarly the sadness at dawn is the cause for unhappiness at dusk. The misery at dawn is the cause for chaos at dusk. This is the law of dawn. You can very well apply to your living.

Your becoming at dusk is what you wish to become at dawn.

Action is life. Will is life. Way is life. Thinking is life. Idea is life. Creation is life. Giving is life. Creating is life. Sharing is life. Loving is life. Being kind is life. Being grateful is life. Being happy is life. Bringing cheers is life. Bringing opportunities is life. Man should be in activity of the existence. This is where he can experience many ragas and sagas of life.

Always remember there are no pollens in the perished flowers however beautiful and fragrance it had during blooming. The nectar once lost is lost forever.

Life is very well as good as flower. Before it perishes it should have done the work of humanity. The lovely nectar should not be uselessly drained from dawn to dusk.

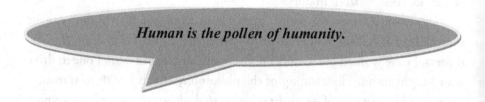

Human is the pollen of humanity.

Man should bloom the whole world. Man should bring fragrance to the entire universe.

Say today your ABC of living is A-Attitude, B-Bold, C-Cheers, D-Do, E-Enthusiasm, G- Gratitude, H-Humanity, I-Inspire, J- Joy K-Kiss, L-Love, M-Man, N-Nature, O-Ownership, P- Prayer, Q-Quiet, R-Respect, S-Sacrifice, T-Truthful, U-United, V-Virtues, W-Wellness, X-Xenophobia, Y-Yummy, Z-Zeal.

The above words beaded together like the garland of life may result today's day for you in this way.

You will start the day with great energy and enthusiasm for the cause of humanity. Your attitude will be full of boldness to bring cheers, kisses, love, to humans. And again with prayer to nature showing gratitude for them you would like to respect the humans with true feeling of ownership of life to deliver the wellness to people from other countries who are fearing to live here for reasons best known to them. Your zeal inspires them for togetherness offering them a dinner to dine with for the sake of unifying humanity.

On overall the journey from dawn to dusk was in doing something good with a balanced rhythm of life.

Daily you can change the color of the garland. Man has infinite ways to create this garland of opportunities, happiness, cheers, values, homes, wellness, healthiness, and so on.

You can see that how good can be your day if you can select proper ABC of living every day. It sails you throughout the day in an environment where you live, learn and do justice to the entire existence. The chemistry of persons are to be mapped anywhere in the world. You go on becoming the way you think off.

A chain of opportunities befalls on you in the day only when you are opportunistic at the dawn. A pessimistic approach at dawn only leaves the day with full of grievances, disquiet and ultimately the worry of unbecoming of yourself at dusk.

How can you expect to reach the right destination if you have boarded the wrong flight? It is never late before the flight of life is ready to take off from the runway of existence. Focus your goals and the day is the way to reach them.

It is only the day which brings what you desire. Fall in the rhythm of happiness and you see making millions and millions smile. Fall in the rhythm of kindness and you see making millions and millions kind. Avoid falling in the rhythm of sadness because you will end up making millions and millions sad. Avoid falling in the rhythm of hopelessness because you will end up making millions and millions hopeless.

Thus there can be as many ABC's of daily living as you wish. It needs a little tuning to the whole process of integrated living. Every human finally enjoys the tune of humanity. The choices for humans are infinite.

Human is an ocean of rhythms.

Once time is in favor of his fortunes and sometimes it rules through befalling rains of misfortunes. Humanity is the shadow of human. How can we get rid of it? It will prevail till human lives.

> ### *Humanity and Humans are inseparable.*

Any human life is irreversible. The wisdom to regulate rhythm of humans is well within the humans. It is only a matter of time inhumanity is dancing without the chorus of humans. Inhumanity cannot have lyrics of existence.

My respectful readers play with the below identified group of words from dawn to dusk the scramble of humanity. A proper mix can certainly bring better ways and means to your living. Use the mathematics of permutations and combinations to arrange, rearrange these group of words till an optimal solution of humanity is obtained. Use the power of suffixes and prefixes the English language is rich in. Keep editing the addition and deletion of words necessary for the refinement you desire to reinstate humanity. This is one of the practical ways to utilize the time of the day in building your personality. The process has the power to transform you into a champion of humanity.

You can become the Architect of Humanity.

The Glossary of Humanity

(A Sample Model)

5A's	*Attitude, Aim, Action, Ability, Abuse,*
5B's	*Bold, Brave, Bright, Bigger, Better*
5C's	*Care, Calm, Cheers, Committed, Crime*
5D's	*Dawn, Day, Doer, Deeds, Dusk,*
5E's	*Existence, Energy, Enthusiasm, Entertainment, Enmity*
5 F's	*Faith, Fortune, Fear, Family, Friends*
5G's	*God, Gratitude, Grace, Goodness, Gift,*
5H's	*Humanity, Heaven, Hell, Human, Heart,*
5I's	*I, Inner, Infinite, Inspire, Intellectuality*
5J's	*Joy, Jealous, Jeopardize, Jolly, Journey*
5K's	*Kill, Kiss, Knowledge, Kindle, Kindness*
5L's	*Life, Learn, Love, Lust, Lose*
5M's	*Man, Mind, Matter, Miracle, Modesty*
5N's	*Nature, Nurture, Nice, Neutral, Naughty*
5O's	*One, Outer, Oneness, Obligation, Ownership*
5P's	*Personal, Public, Professional, Prayer, Party*
5Q's	*Quest, Quiet, Quality, Quick, Quiz*
5R's	*:Right, Reward, Rest, Reputation, Realization*
5S's	*:Self, Sacrifice, Success, Society, Service*
5T's	*:Time, Talent, Target, Trust, Treatment*
5U's	*:Unique, Universal, United, Utilization, Useful*
5V's	*:Vex, Vice, Virtues, Victory, Valuable*
5W's	*:Will, Way, Wisdom, Wealth, Worthy*
3Xs	*:Xenology, Xenophobia, Xenotransplantation*
5Y's	*:You, Young, Yummy, Yob, Yore,*
5Z's	*: Zeal, Zest, Zenith, Zen, Zion*

Let us remind ourselves over and over again that everyone can be an

"Architect of Humanity"

We are right, but most people still think they're too small or insignificant to make a difference. Most of us feel that something is holding us back; that circumstances are preventing us from living the life we want to live.

In the search for what matters most, life as teacher teaches all that what was holding us back wasn't something "out there." Instead, it was our own fear that we were not feeling important enough to matter. It was the fear itself that was holding us back. So we should adopt a "believer's mind".

Prayers never betray your believes. Man is the betrayer of his believes. My way of describing the belief that we each have a sacred purpose and we should stop at nothing to fulfill it, must make some way into my readers mind for development of confidence from dawn to dusk. Without confidence in yourself you cannot justify thyself. Without faith in yourself you cannot justify thyself.

Acronyms	Self Inspiring
YES	Your efforts for success
SIR	Strength, Integrity, Resolve
BDL	Blind, Deaf, Lame
YNA	You Never Attempt
YCZ	Your Comfort Zone
RYL	Running Your Life
YCW	You Can Win
YCTW	You Cannot Win
KDW	Knock Down The Walls
SME	Stop Making Excuses
AYS	Acknowledge Your Success
BYE	Be Yourself Ever
LLB	Live Life Big
NIP	Nothing Is Impossible
AYTS	Are You Taking Steps

AYT	As You Think
FTS	Fix The Situation
HBP	How Bad Is The Problem
HYD	How You Deal
DYS	Determines Your Success
MYM	Make Your Move
EYP	Establish Your Position
CML	Caring My Life
CPG	Change, Prosper, Grow
SDM	Some Days Are Miserable
SOM	State Of Mind
NOE	No One Else
ICDI	I Can Do It
IMD	I Make The Decisions
IDW	I Do The Work
IRR	I Reap The Rewards
ISC	I Suffer The Consequences
WYL	What You Make Of Life
LIP	Life Is Passion
LIB	Life Is Beautiful
LIA	Life Is Amazing
LIS	Life Is Splendid
LIT	Life Is Tedious
LID	Life Is Disaster
JOB	Beauty Of The Journey
GFT	Go For It
NEQ	Never Ever Quit
BCC	Become A Complete Champion
ADBH	Anvils Dream Of Being Hammers
ACT	Action, Create, Thought
SMART	Specific, Measured, Achieve, Real, Timely
FHLT	Faith, Hope, Love, Trust
HIM	Humanity In Man

ABC	Analyze, Balance, Control
AIM	Assumptions, Interpretations, Meanings
AIR	Attention, Improvement, Repair
SMF	Self Motive Force
KITE	Kindness In The Existence
BMS	Body, Mind, Soul
PPP	People, Perception, Perfection
TTT	Talent, Time, Target
HHH	Healthy, Happy, Harmony
MMM	Man, Mind, Motives
FFF	Fortune, Fear, Fight
AAA	Attitude, Ability, Awareness
BBB	Bold, Brave, Bright
CCC	Calm, Clean, Cheer
DDD	Dream, Desire, Destiny
GGG	Good, Great, Grace
HSN	Human, Society, Nation
AAB	Attitude, Attributes, Behavior

"The best thing that happens today will greatly outweigh the worst that occurred yesterday".

Justify Thyself

"The difference between who you are and who you want to be is what you do"

How to justify ourselves?

How to work out this evaluation? Who will evaluate us? Who will measure our inhumanity? How to prepare the report on humanity? Do activity of man is linked to humanity? How do you interpret success of man without humanity? Are not we living in the world of reactions from dawn to dusk? Is it not shameful that man is creating his unhealthy critics by improper means of living?

Can man not find the ethical means of living in this sanctuary of goodness?

Will dawn to dusk answer the above questions? Is dawn appraising the world? Is your role defined? Are you on the right path? Do you have the wisdom of living to differentiate between humanity and inhumanity?

What is the core purpose of your living? Is money the only wealth you have understood in life? Is killing the only love you know to build your own homes at the misery of other fellow men?

Why I and you are not realizing the humans in us?

At the least it only requires common sense to live. Hunger can only be understood by the hungry person. Thirst can only be felt by the thirsty person. Goodness can only be done by the good people. Grief can only be understood by the suffering person. Cheers can be seen only on the face of happy person.

Humanity smiles with the person of humility.

Humbleness is the way of life for the divine. Where you are standing with your understanding? What you have done so far? What changes you can initiate in the overall changing process of transforming society? Purity of life can only be understood by the divine person. Orphan can only experience the misery loss of life brings to humans. The need of home makes the nomadic man mad. A family is in chaos without unity among the members. The nation is at war for the peace of citizens.

Think again and again before you make a choice in your life. Be true to yourself. Keep justifying your decisions. Always question Am I making the right choice? Make a habit of creating and recreating yourself. Man should never give up the aspiration of honing his skills of living. It pushes you towards attaining perfection.

The excellence in you is churned out by continually recreating yourselves.

Do not ever sit down to celebrate whatever you have achieved? There is lot to be done by you again and again from dawn to dusk. Creativeness slowly removes corrosiveness in novelty of humans. Inner world of man is examining again and again his own ideas on his own existence.

Life is reinventing itself in every man from dawn to dusk. This is where the humans stand away from the insects, worms and animals of the world.

Man has an opportunity at every moment to justify himself.

We have an inner-system of self reformation. The lessons are written in the sub-conscious mind to tame the conscious mind now and then. The learning is by living from dawn to dusk.

What distinguishes human beings from other living beings? Do you think animals are deprived of thinking? Do animals are not philosophical as humans? Biologically there may not be appreciable differences except for the brain and the mind. The animals too are in tears and cheers. The challenges of survival are equally met by them. Either it is through the natural selection or by the acquired virtues of existence. A point reader should have to ponder over to understand the animal in us. Do we have the exactness of all the reasoning's which differentiates man from animal?

Why animal is not seeking to become man? Animals might have realized that we are in fact inferior to them. Their contribution in sustaining our lives is a vital factor for the entire definition of existence.

Will man remain as animal forever?

Will animal try to become man? Both the postulates have been the tested hypotheses but an innovation of existence can bring miracles at any point of time. This was what being thought of by the existence before the evolution of man in this world. There may be a new planet tomorrow with entirely new features of the living creature are all possibilities in this galaxy of existence. The limitations in the man are being redefined by the power of existence.

All the philosophical works have contributed to the world humanity. There have been difficulties to the common readers to understand the intricacies of arguments on the subject of humanity.

Visionless man has to first be blessed with an erudite teacher. The world is learning in the scarcity of learned scholars. This may be one of the rightly assessed reasons for literacy to be not up to the standards of excellence and perfection. Still the humans are principally struggling in the alphabets of life. That is why centuries after centuries have passed but the justification of true education is far beyond recognition. Society has lost at large. The huge population has faced brain drain in knowing the wisdom of humanity.

Man is accountable for the environment he has created to pollute humanity. The dawn is yet to befall on us to see the light of humanity. The cumulative discrepancies and unaccountability today has surmounted to degrade our existence ever in the history of mankind. What worse period of existence man can face from dawn to dusk?

The extraordinary teacher can really transform an ordinary student to the extra ordinary levels of comprehending the meaning of existence. Our association with spiritual knowledge, living wisdom and the type of environment is very essential for an overall divine transformation.

I have a determined principle probably to be followed by the readers of any age that, "We cannot beat the truth that there are no roses in the garden of weeds".

The purpose is to be clear in your basics at the very beginning of perceiving something. The choice or desire of weeds cannot fetch you roses. How can man justify thyself with improper and unclear perception of the concept itself? However small the weeds are it is dangerous to the expansion of humanity. The roots of humanity are forced to terminate before its destination is reached. How healthy trees can bears fruits when it has lost its roots due to the weeds?

The World's education and the learning system are unable to yield the flowers and fruits of humanity. The Scholars of Philosophical treatise are persisting pursuance of man to become human of vision from dawn to dusk.

A visionary needs to develop millions of visionaries. The existence created human to further create human in the existence. There is nothing ridiculous about the statement of similarity in developing humanity all over the world.

The problem is who will be the leader, champion and humanist coming forward to volunteer his service for the mankind.

Make humanity your only vision, mission, objective, aim and purpose in life to justify thyself in the existence. Man is living because of man only. Man has nothing more to doubt his own existence. A man without ambition is like a torch without light. Blindness is in the mind rather in the blurredness of eyes. Why bloodlessness cannot be attained in the world?

How you are changing the world for better? Are we using our power of imaginations rightly? Who has not gone to school? We have been going to schools, colleges and universities for grades? Where these institutions are leading people to from dawn to dusk? Are they only responsible for making a professional career?

It appears that the concept of professionalism has nothing to do with the philosophy of humanity. Are we getting this definition, direction and destination right? Despite of all these educations, learning, teaching, training, awareness we fail to get along with our family, with colleagues, with peers, with friends and on the whole in society.

"I have never met a strong person with an easy past".

What would you do with your life if it were 100 % up to you? Where are we putting our future? We have been losing our present in securing our unsecured future. We see politics in power, money, career, sex, relationship, worship and to be true everywhere wherever there is economic or non-economic activity being done by humans. The world has failed to comprehend the economics of humans. Again it has miserably been victimized by the emerging human socialization philosophy. A new way of living is redefining the morale of the humans from dawn to dusk.

The first letter "H" which would have been meant to signify holiness of humans is now being understood as helplessness of humans. The changes in recent times speak of the inhumanity with the unhappy background of mankind.

Man is failing to equip, enable, empower and excel himself in leading towards a righteous living. Will man be successful in changing the world towards betterment?

The subject tribology of humanity is difficult to master. How to realign the eccentricity in humanity all over the world? Where are the specialists? Man should platinize himself with humanity. Are not men the predators of humanity?

Why Man is preying another man?

And again some men are the saviors of humanity. Why we are differing in our attitudes towards humanity? We have been unnecessarily welcoming the Prince of Darkness the devil all over the world. It is time to collectively dethrone the kingship of evils. For this the world needs warriors of peace, soldiers of love, army of faith, commanders of action, military of trust, leaders of confidence to win the battle of humanity from dawn to dusk. It is time to justify our lives. It is time to justify our existence. It is time to justify thyself.

The earliest period of the Mesozoic Era (between the Permian and Jurassic periods, about 245 to 208 million years ago), a time when the first dinosaurs, ammonites and primitive mammals appeared may not have imagined that the existence would bloom with a similar advanced animal "HUMAN" biologically simple to comprehend and intellectually complex to understand the emotional intelligence of this mysterious creature.

Is man a malediction of nature? Why man's malignity is a deep concern for the humanity?

The World is witnessing the evolution of existence from dawn to dusk. The Man is also witnessing the involution in him. The thoughts of humans should be invincible in any circumstances of existence. Are there invokers of humanity on this earth? Ideals of humanity should be irrevocable anywhere in the world. Why not let humanity jazz with the rhythm of universal brotherhood?

Man is yet in the kindergarten learning the alphabets of humanity.

Rationalism and spiritualism are the two inseparable faces of humans. Religionism is other area where man's maturity has to invade again and again. The world is eagerly waiting to be ruled by Renaissance Man. Humanity can be renewed. The remuneration for these humanity services should be love and only love. Life is a riddle till you know to ride it.

Where are the Champions of Humanity?

It is rightly told by Napoleon Hill,

"The starting point of all achievement is desire".

Desire to die you are dead. Desire to live you are alive. Desire to work you are in action. Desire to rise you are arisen. Desire to win you are winner. Desire to lose you are loser. Desire to lead you are leader. Desire to love you are kind. Desire to help you are grateful. Desire to excel you are inspired. Desire to be human and you are humanity.

Hence the starting point is always the time taking one. It requires all the counseling, coaching, teaching, learning, analyzing, evaluating, educating of the self before you really plunge into realizing the desired dream.

Man should cultivate the desire to be human first. Fundamentally man sees his achievements in the two disputed worlds in which he lives from dawn to dusk. Does an achievement have a self-transformation impact on man's living? Is satisfaction one of the traits for peace in man? What are the other qualities to align with humanity? We should develop a world in which we could have a blissful living.

Leading people only to destiny will not solve the purpose of living in totality.

We have to lead people to opportunities of existence. Existence is an infinite mine of abundance. The opportunistic man has no limitations from dawn to dusk. There are millions and millions ways to good to humanity every day.

Every day we are living by the edge of judgment. Let us not quarrel to establish the quietness in the world. Unfortunate to witness the trials and ordeals humans are facing today for no fault of theirs. How can justice come to all? When will the courts and prison leave the world forever?

Let us listen for those who have been silenced. Let us honor those who have been devalued. Let us say, enough is enough. With abuse, abandonment, diminishing and hiding. Let us not rest until every person is free and equal.

Justice is the right of every human.

Laws can only categorize the crime and penalties. It is only the attitude of the humans which has the power of resolution. What can be a better court than your heart to forgive or punish the culprit? No one is born culprit. In fact we make the innocent fetus to conclude later that he would have been lucky to remain in the mother's womb.

The journey from Womb to World and again from World to Heaven undergoes two different exclusive experiences. Nevertheless the seed of existence is actually not meant to lose its uniqueness. This again advocates the universality of spirituality. Is it not surprising that irrespective of the similar biological process in all the wombs of the world why we have humans born to show various attributes and traits of living? It starts with the thoughts, ideas, and perception and so on. Why it happens so?

Build desires in humans to fight war against inhumanity with the weapons of peace. Let our roles be to achieve the goals of humanity. The journey of mistakes to maturity certifies the self to enlighten the world. The lights are the way for the youths to start working early in justifying their lives towards humanity.

Champions are leaders of change.

The world needs more and more champions of humanity. Be your own boss in meeting humans. Greet humans with heart. Your own heart can only be happy when you make others heart healthier and happier.

Understanding of MAN with the interpretation M-Moral, A-Attitude, and N-Noble by every Man is invaluable to all the discussions and debates if the project of happiness has to be expedited in a timeline.

Again similarly HUMAN stands for H- Holy, U-Universal, M-Moral, A-Attitude, and N-Noble. Human is the extension of the Man with holiness and universality. The understanding is very simple because the attributes of morality, attitude and nobility go in forward to seek the holiness and then subsequently MAN only remains with oneness i.e. to say the ultimate Universality.

PROBLEM can be the well suited acronym for P-Personality, R-Reality, O-Objective, B-Boldness, L-Learning, E-Ego, and M-Man. All the problems which man has been facing erupt from one or the other traits discussed and expanded above. The greater problem arises from the ego and the multiple personality man has from time to time. Duality of existence brings in turbulence in reality. The objective suffers the blow because of clear vision and mission. With all these features man is diagnosed to be having problem of one or the other during living. Ego is again bifurcated into physical and emotional. Both of which are deterrents in restoring humanity.

To continue understanding further EGO stands for Enmity Getting Obsessed- E-Enmity, G-Getting, and O-Obsessed. The negative obsession is dangerous than the nuclear weapons. It speaks killing of humans from within more than the removal of physical existence.

A probable thought has been compiled to define ANSWER. Humans are to be first humanitarians. Rhythm of life has answers to all the problems in the world. I have thought that the "ANSWER" can be looked this way by expanding each letters of it signifying an attribute valuable to the point of discussion.

A is ACTIVITY of the man related to the problem to be resolved, followed by his N- NOVELTY to innovate and discover opportunities for solving the issue as perceived by him and with his intellectuality and wisdom on the prevailing subject, then the time of initiation i.e., S-START so that an early initiation to removal of problem is equally important before it is infeasible, how you are working towards it by W- WORK, without any timeline no answer has a significant purpose of finding if there is no tentative end date, E-END date is the target date of the activity's goal of reaching the resolution and finally R-RESOLVED, concluding that your file is closed as the issue has been attended successfully. You can see that "ANSWER" is a structured process of resolving a problem.

Every problem has many answers through the process of perception.

It is here that the perspectives of life play an important part in man's real resolution in existence. Identifying a problem is the beginning to amicably resolve it.

Resolution does not mean creating a problem for the other man.

The resolution of the problem should bring peace at any level. The central theme is the rhythm of man towards humanity. Regularity in cleaning of the mind can surely help all of us to have a meaningful life.

Dusk is the time to plan your next day for the effective beginning at dawn. Waking up in the morning without a plan is as good as blinking at the sky for the stars in the day. Staring is an unproductive activity consuming your major share of the day from dawn to dusk without any appreciable meaning of life.

Day can only take you nearer to your dreams daily. Day can only help you achieve your desires in time. The early morning air is so inspiring that it breathes in you the determination to do whatever you want. If you have never thought ill of anyone till today then never think of it in the remaining life of yours. Believe in your abilities more than the deliverables of the world. Time is precious from dawn to dusk. All are meddling with time throughout the day to justify their purpose of living.

Do you doubt you're potential?

Unfair means have always bitter ends.

Do you hesitate to be a winner? Do you shy to grace the victory? When again will the time be ripe for you to germinate your seeds of humanity? Why anyone else will work for your dreams? Why anyone else will waste time for your aim? Why anyone else will sacrifice for your goals?

I sincerely think that,

"Time managed accurately is life lived precisely".

The quantitative living cannot be compared to the qualitative living. How to fit the individual framework of man with the society framework? Though many things are independent yet the dependency cannot be dispensed with living from dawn to dusk. A total freedom for man is only at the hands of existence.

What should be the ideal model of man?

What type of human the world is seeking today? Can the evolution redesign, reconstruct and renovate the desired humans? Unfortunately the world lacks the manufacturing units of such humans of humanity.

It appears the WORLD of Land is the Learning Centre of Life where humans are imported as raw humans and the final product with values is exported to the WORLD of Heavens. Ultimately it is quality of the life lived that is responsible in forging the final product human.

The lessons the life teaches us are as simple as they are hard to follow. First, the most important expectation to fulfill in life is not that you become like someone else but that you become yourself. A unique man of your thoughts, dreams, ideas, values, principles and philosophies and to do that, you have to do the hard work of going inward, of seeing yourself with all your strengths, gifts and weaknesses too—and of realizing that in all your vulnerability, you are more beautiful and powerful than you dare imagine.

Learning to trust that being lovable isn't something you earn, but rather, is a quality you already possess, is the first step to feeling fully alive from dawn to dusk.

Human beings and the natural world are on a collision course. Human activities inflict harsh and often irreversible damage on the environment. The give and take between man and nature is not reciprocating as it should be ethically done. This is very much evident from the recent hue and cry on global warming.

World Habitat Day is the one day set aside annually to recognize the basic right of all humanity to adequate shelter, food and clothing.

The World and Humans together witness amazing events from dawn to dusk. Why people should talk about the work place as a jungle? You never know when you have lost your job because of your fellowmen. The professional arena is also not free from the stings of personal egos.

Human has infinite opportunities to do justice to their lives.

It is not difficult as the situation is really thought off.

We live in digital world today. We live in a world in which more people are connected than ever before. We spend lots of time talking about new advances in science, technology and business, health, living. We turn to a different end of the spectrum, the humanities. What is next for the humanities?

Are the basic needs of the human's survival bringing us stress than peace? Is it really difficult for the humans to arrange these basic needs from dawn to dusk?

What makes a great human?

The Human needs homes, shelter, food, clothing, safety and security. Who will provide these opportunities? How to avail the minimum for survival? Can it be not obtained through the ideals? Can it be not arranged through the morals? Can it be not arranged through the ethics? Can it be not attained through the principles of humanity?

"How can a starving man feed the hungry man?"

This is our life today. Then why chaos will not prevail. Can man have cheers without tears?

Is the World Economy not looking into these basic necessities? Citizens are employees of the nation working from dawn to dusk to improve the GDP of our world. Why the nation's productivity is bringing poverty? Means and ends are not being mapped properly from dawn to dusk.

At every level there should be justification of the individuals holding the chairs of authority. It may not be always right to blame the governance keeping in view the disloyalty of the people in all walks of life all over the world.

Why do humanities matter? Is World such a bad place? Is World failing to give security to humans? How to define security? Are the human needs not varying from person to person?

How do you prioritize your basic human needs? Please try to work this query.

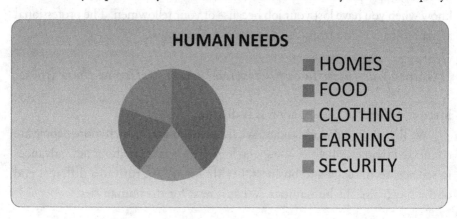

HUMAN NEEDS	Major	Moderate	Minor	No Opinion
HOMES				
FOOD				
CLOTHING				
EARNING				
SECURITY				

Is it earning that majority of us are worried? What should be the right means to earn? Snatching the earning share from fellow man always speaks of the inhumanity in us. There is no end to the human needs. Who will justify the essentialities? Who will advocate the necessities?

Every man has an exhaustive list of wishes from dawn to dusk. Do you think all the wishes are your needs?

Man has been swinging like the pendulum in between the ends of wishes and needs. If you are asked to list out your wishes and needs will it look like the below table?

Wishes & Needs

WISHES	NEEDS
Land Lord	A piece of land.
Palace for living	A room for living
Princely Dishes	Two loafs of bread
Golden Treasure	Few penny
Power to Rule Man	Grace to Serve Man
Riches of the World	Wisdom of the World
Super Rich Club	Home & Family
Recognition	Be a Simple Human
Authority	Synergy
To Become GOD	To Know GOD

Is there any different between wishes and needs? All wishes are not needs for survival. There may be a need for survival but you may not be wishing it.

If we start developing a **"Pyramid of Needs"** we will come to really know the levels of necessities in our life.

Pyramid of Needs

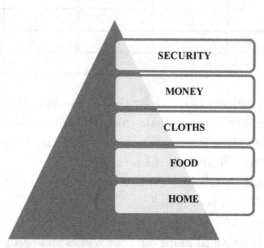

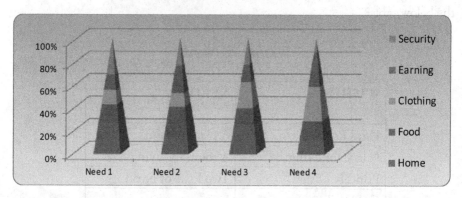

The above is a graph depicting various pyramids describing the basic human needs combination as Need1, 2, 3, 4. There can be infinite number of needs depending upon the humans style of living based on perception, philosophy, intellectuality, spirituality, wisdom, knowhow, state of mind, personality, divinity, ego, desires, dreams, sacrifices, boldness, humbleness, virtues, ethics, vision, mission, objectives, goals, education, literacy, society, status, attitude, ability, demographics, development, modernization, technology, and many other human factors.

One to one mapping of humans to needs is a difficult subject of study anywhere in the world. The Pyramid of Needs will assist you in examining your strengths and weakness in living. Most of us fear more on the security aspect of our life. Many break downs of life is being witnessed by the society from dawn to dusk.

The Pyramid of Life say with 5S's is described below. It is a model in which the Cycle of Life for human can be seen to understand the phases and stages man passes through in reality.

Pyramid of Life

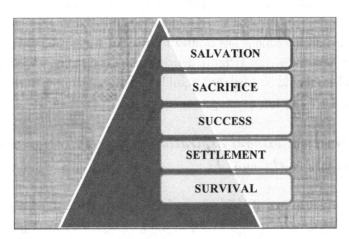

The pyramid looks easier to be presented only. Majority of the population remains at the bottom of the pyramid. The struggle with needs from survival to settlement is from dawn to dusk. Few with the leadership principles might move up to the success triangle. But the unhappy part of all the story is only one percent of the successful people is willing to sacrifice. No doubt one who has can only give. But it makes no sense of the success if you are not willing to share and let other grow.

Without sacrifice there is no way to salvation. A man who swims across these in the right way then understands the grace of spirituality. It is he who has started seeing human in himself. Till then he has been wandering with humans to understand the basics of humanity.

Man is a journey from survival to salvation. And it happens every day. A daily insight into it and regular review practice will give us a practical way of reforming ourselves.

Everyday man after meeting the survival needs can sacrifice and seek salvation from dawn to dusk.

I have a researched reasoning for humans,

"Perfection in living can be attempted by clarity in fantasy, dreams, desires, wishes and needs".

This is where man's literacy has failed completely. When you are unable to identify your needs from dawn to dusk how would you arrange the means and ends? When all the time is lost in dreaming where is the time to execute the dream? When all the time is lost in desiring where is the time to realize it into reality? There should be a balance, equilibrium, harmony in man which gives him a regulated rhythm not to go out of balance.

All inspiration without aspiration and perspiration will lead you nowhere in the world.

The Pyramid of Winning -5W's is another model to understand as how man can win from dawn to dusk. Develop a strong will followed by a right way, use your wisdom and work continuously towards your one idea, one goal, and one aim to win. And one day you will be at the top of pyramid winning all your battles in life big or small.

The stronger the base of the pyramid the permanent will be the apex of the pyramid.

Man's will is like the breathing air, you never know when it comes and goes. No do not allow it to happen. A determined will is the beginning towards winning yourself.

Pyramid of Winning

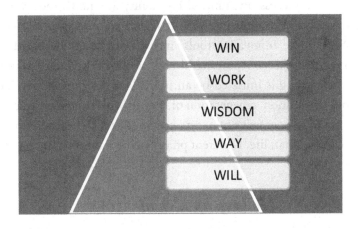

Pyramid of SUCCESS

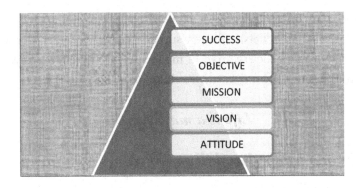

Pyramid of FAILURE

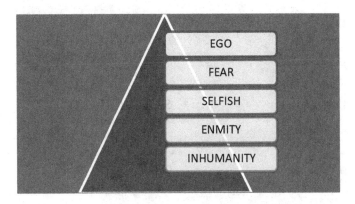

The 5D's, Glossary of Humanity, Pyramid of Needs, Pyramid of Winning-5 W's, Pyramid of Success, Pyramid of Humanity are model tools we can use to know the trend we are moving with. It alarms your derailment from dawn to dusk. Such more innovative tools, mechanisms man should devise for himself to regularly keep examining himself in the background of humanity. Unless the relearning is initiated by an individual his growth, development, reformation, reinvention, regeneration of the self will remain a distant dream. The urge should be aggressive in nature keeping in view the limitation of time and the cycle of human life. Different phases of life have different justification altogether.

"To keep up is challenging,

To stand still is to fall behind".

Humanity is an integrated subject of needs, paths of living, ways of life, wisdom, knowledge, beliefs, cultures, success, sacrifices, inner world, outer world, legacy of man, society, man in me, justifying thyself, destiny, nature, world and ultimately the universality of humans.

Life is a marathon.

The best leadership skill on the planet is endurance.

Pyramid of Humanity

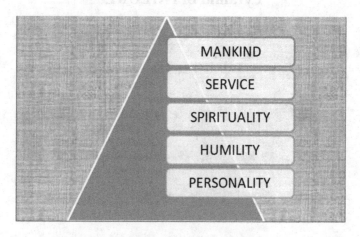

"The supreme art of war is to subdue the enemy without fighting"

There is nothing in the world which human cannot correct. Correcting ourselves is also a continual process like living. We need to maintain our wear and tear of living. We need to keep fighting with our spirit rather than with the other man.

Survival brings in the best training to every human from dawn to dusk.

Pyramid of Excellence

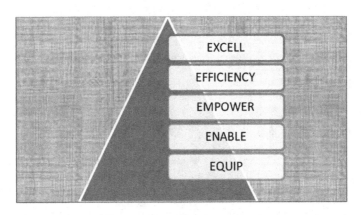

To excel through the "Pyramid of Excellence" you have to begin equipping yourself to enable all your strengths, energies, enthusiasms, zeal, vigor, towards empowering your abilities and potentials to increase your efficiency against all odds and challenges from dawn to dusk. And once you do this you are at the apex of excellence and finally you have excelled. The above 5E's can bring revolution in your entire evolution process.

Man has the power to transform himself. The creator has justified it by giving us this ability. To be or not to be the becoming is very much now in our hands.

Let all of us put in practicing building small pyramids of big values and dreams. You may not be instantly able to reap the benefits but over a period of time it goes into building you a human.

I worked out the above model pyramids to bring some insight into the subject of justifying our lives. This is only possible by starting justifying our ideas, thoughts, dreams, actions, values, needs, desires, ethics, morals, attitudes, wisdom, beliefs, trusts, faiths, hopes, loves and what not right from perception to perfection.

The pyramid under any circumstances visualizes us the steps to move to the apex in all walks of life in trying to win, have success, achievement, happiness and so on till the final liberation and salvation in this world.

What about the Pyramid of Fear? Fears are nothing more than the states of mind.

Pyramid of FEAR

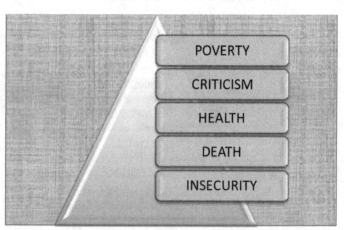

Man's mind is under your influence. Your state of mind is in your control. Your state of mind is emotional resulting in emotional fears. If your state of mind is intellectual it will project scientific fears of reasoning. It will have the analytical attributes. If your state of mind is spiritual you are bound to struggle yourself with the factors of fears pertaining to your beliefs, ideologies, god, theologies, culture and your practice in life. The root of your state of mind is the thought.

Can we master our fears? Can fear be controlled? Can fear be mitigated? Many people may not fear on certain issues on which some other group of people panic seriously. Some feel harassment others may not be affected from dawn to dusk. Therefore there are infinite pyramids of fears in this world.

The state of mind of any individual cannot be generalized. It cannot have a common diagnosis. Man has to work towards removing these unwanted pyramids of fears from his daily living.

Fear is the greatest impediment of life. It disturbs the natural rhythm of humans. It blocks your progress in life. It brings the hesitating style of living in individuals. It develops the ability in you to doubt your own potentials of excellence. With fear you can never justify your living. The fantasy living is away from perpetual living and is never near to the realistic plane of existence.

The above is our state of ruining our lives. The World is in fantasy for centuries and centuries now.

<u>5 D's</u>

"You cannot teach a man anything,
you can only help him find it within himself".
- Galileo shared his wisdom to the world.

"Dawn means Activity".

One thing is sure that every life on this earth is living the moment with some or other activity from dawn to dusk. I am trying to drive the importance of this moment in man's life. Let all moments in our life be moments of joy, success, and cheers, full of happiness, peace and bliss. Today is mine with a new wine of life. It has the cheers of becoming fine. Now let us this very dawn align ourselves to the line of grace.

Dawn is the only nearest moment in day after you awake. Dusk is the next nearest moment in day before you sleep. Every play of life is in between awake and sleeps. Now it is up to man to utilize this series of moments effectively in forging himself. This cycle of life revolves around you with infinite opportunities. Probabilities and possibilities are the fortunes and misfortunes of the man in the day. The composition of the day is in man's hand. Man has to constitute it to build his life as he desires.

Dawn to Dusk is trying to help man to look within himself for all the answers of the world. The inner world is full of solutions, realizations, lessons, reasoning, wisdom, knowledge, discoveries, inventions, innovations, secrets, ideas, and thoughts, purity, to fight the outer world of man.

Dawn to Dusk has tried to cover all areas which make man what he is. Right from His immediate needs of survival at dawn to final liberation at dusk. Man's sufferings to happiness from dawn to dusk. It has attempted to study the effectiveness grouping them as 5D's principle.

This is a model prepared to understand the interrelationships of activities, time, performer and results. Many such models can be designed to understand the variances of other influencing attributes in man's life. Like the 3P's, 5M's or the 5A's such feasible models to optimize the overall process of man's living from dawn to dusk. The vastness of the variables, problems, issues, queries makes man unable to prepare the scientific mathematical models to completely address humanity.

The rhythm of life can be captured in pie-charts, bars, graphs to primarily understand life from scientific perspectives when we speak of effectiveness and efficiency of individual human beings.

The model 5D's principle is a scientific way to examine the self journey from dawn to dusk. Which broadly can be understood as grouped below?

Dawn - Opportunities, Abilities, Potentials, Grace, Fortunes, Capacities, Resources

Day - Time, Utilization, Productivity, Value, Contribution, Existence, Work, Make

Doer - Action by Man, Performance, Motion, Dynamics, Influences, Networks,

Deeds - Achievements, End results, Targets, Goals, Aims, Fulfillment, Satisfaction

Dusk - Lessons, Realization, Introspection, Retrospect, Redefine, Rediscover, Reinvent

The combination of the above is the progress of man from dawn to dusk. The rate of progress is again proportionate to the mix of 5 D's.

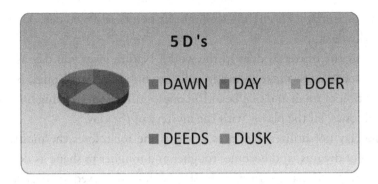

The 5 D's concept derived from above is the base for origin of Dawn to Dusk. We are surrounded by these D's from dawn to dusk. The life interconnections leads to a network chain of sphere engulfing us for survival, excellence, realization to salvation holding the liberation at one or the other bead of the existence.

It is a complete cycle which summaries the importance right from beginning of dawn, the passing of whole day till dusk, and from dusk through the night to the next dawn, including the doer, and his achievements and accomplishments in the day, with lessons learnt and realized. The cycle of today prepares you for the cycle of tomorrow.

Every man has to execute this 5 D's cycle daily regularly till his existence. There is no escape from 5 D's. I would like to bring your focus on your core living.

You are living from dawn to dusk with these 5 D's. I hope no one disagrees with me at this point of time after understanding the Part-I, DAWN of this essay before going through the chapter of DUSK in Part-V .Why Part-I as Dawn, Part-II as Today is Mine, Part –III as Champions of Humanity, Part-IV as Legacy of Man and Part V as Dusk has been constituted for this essay from Dawn to Dusk?

This must be running in the minds of the readers. If it is happening then the intended purpose for publishing this thesis has been primarily achieved.

Man needs to regularly examine and reexamine himself.

Dawn to Dusk is not a magic tool that just by the golden touch all the issues of the society fighting for reinstating humanity will be resolved. However, the catalytic reaction of it cannot be undermined in its journey of transforming humanity. Humanity is circling through the points of dawn, day, doer, deeds and finally dusk.

Man is the universal doer in the world. Nature gives you day as clay. It is up to you how to make as many dolls as you want, small ones, big ones, combination of small and big, beautiful ones, smiling ones, crying ones, short ones, tall ones, all the play is with the mystery of the clay.

The clay not utilized becomes worse as the rock, loses the moisture for plasticity of dreams, and becomes tougher and tougher to shape as desired by you. The life is similarly waiting to be shaped, forged, carved, made, extracted, explored, fabricated, constructed, established, built, as many names as you like with the freedom of perception.

Man's work is like the potter.

The wheel of production, shaper, extraction, construction keeps revolving working out the clay of life in different forms and shapes. The wheel of existence, nature, universe, self, man, world, god, fate, truth, hope, love, fortune, grace, blessings, curse, misery, evil, divine and so on all keep moving in time, out of time, within time, endless time, infinite time to create, destruct, demolish, evolve, in many manifestations, personifications, unknown and known to man, for man and of man, with universal undefined and defined goals, mysterious ways and wills, for us to witness as experience from dawn to dusk.

You are the architect of your life. It can be made through these 5 D's. 5 D's can combine to overthrow your destiny at any point of time. At the same time we may not be surprised to understand that at times destiny is probably in line with the efforts of 5 D's.

Life is an opportunity to build you.

The question is what your ingredients are. What will be the major constituents? Will they be value based? Will your vision, mission, objectives, goals, have divine directions? Simply for the sake of survival, we should not live. Biological existence cannot be man's only central idea of existence. It has to go beyond the boundary of your limitations.

Like everyone, you have ambitions, and that's a very good thing because having ambition is a great help in moving forward. Being ambitious doesn't necessarily mean having elevated or idealistic goals that are impossible to realize.

Your ambitions could consist of more limited objectives. Set ambitions for yourself that suit you, without asking yourself whether they are lofty or limited. The main thing is that they are yours. Leadership position may be inherited but leadership capacity cannot be inherited. It has to be built.

MAN and 5 D's.

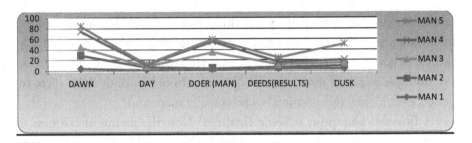

A relationship between Man and 5 D's can be plotted with infinite number of combinations. This is the practical approach in evaluating humans from dawn to dusk. Every man has his own potential, ability, utilization factor, availability of resources, constrains, limitations, approaches, ways, paths, inputs, purpose, perception, will, inspiration, motivation, need, necessity, awareness, intellectuality, attitude, virtues, values, ethics, in making his things move from dawn to dusk. Based on these relationship it can be mapped to respective man.

From the above graph it can be seen how Man 1,2,3,4 and 5 as sample study are reflected with their plot points representing their variation in percentages from dawn to dusk. The values are our own parameters. Every man has his own success or failure path.

The learning from here is that a very wider spectrum is required to integrate the living. All the minds cannot be traced to the same graph. How effectively this 5 D's principle will work towards reinstating humanity? A good question might be running in the mind of prospective readers seeking humanity?

Where you are putting your day to work? Say you are a priest the whole day is related to the subject of teaching, preaching, learning, discourses, gatherings, addressing, counseling to people who are also interested in the similar subject of values, morals, god, religion, mind, meditation, truth, eternity, virtues, mankind, and all around humanity and up lifting of humanity. Here minds are working in sharing, guiding, mentoring, kindling, finding, searching, and helping other minds. Now though the intensity may be weak, the approach may not be aggressive, yet something of it might have progressed well into totality.

Let us discuss a situation where the plan of looting the public is being planned and organized by a group of evil people from dawn to dusk. Their mind is obsessed with wealth to be acquired by stealing it from men who possess it by dint of hard work. Here minds are working towards harming other men. The men are utilizing their brains, minds, resources, thoughts in fabricating unappreciable plans to unethical works. When they are successful in looting one, the second man and so one, it becomes a practice, and finally the fear of goodness is dead, making them extend towards, terror and cruelties.

Both are minds of man in two different paths of life. Both claim them to be successful. Now the question is who is really successful?

A Business blue print is being finalized. Now the nature of business is important. Is Man's personal nature prime? He has agreed for this employment. He is working for the principles of other men.

A living of a person is based with the environment of persons.

He is working for the objectives of other men. Here your decisions are not important. The objective is of the entrepreneurs who are trying to reach their goals through you. You are working to realize their dreams. To what extent your personal dreams will be realized. If you too are of the same objective then their ethics are your ethics. If you do not own the business too, the ethics naturally will be owned by you over a period of time. This is how the philosophy of humanity operates from dawn to dusk.

This as good as one understands that you never become old. The mind never dies. All the death is in the physical body. All the sufferings are in the physical body. All the beauty is in the physical body. All the worries are in the physical body. Are all the experiences in the physical body? Is man only a handful of ash? Is man soil and all his game the life springing from it and finally collapsing in it? How to resolve these unanswered queries? It will rise in every civilization, every generation, every man, every land, everywhere across the world, everywhere, wherever space, time, universe goes, beyond, beyond the man's vision, mission, objectives and goals. This is the true nature of life.

We are trying to run away from what we are. There is no escape from dawn to dusk. Human issues cannot be resolved only by the physical means. Is this the purpose of mysterious existence? The summary which I wish to share with all of you is also with you.

My reader's realization and summarization of this thesis dawn to dusk will be the fresh beginning of their approach towards humanity.

Dawn to dusk will be a drop of learning for every man to fill the world with wisdom of humanity.

Different Success Paths

I. With no latent energy at dawn and dusk.

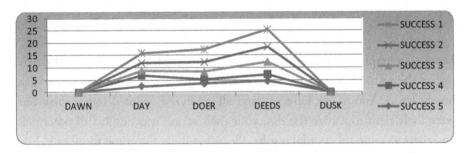

There are different success paths one can arrive at with the combination of dawn, day, doer (man/action), deeds (results) and dusk. The above graph depicts with the beginning at dawn and end at dusk without the latent energies.

I can throw some light as per the below graph surfacing out the latent energies at both ends of the day. The energy never depletes to zero. It may have transformed into another.

Let us have a look at the success paths with end energies. These end energies are either acquired, learnt, realized, inherited, developed, graced, whatever it may be, but are in the core of man, everyman. They are instrumental in deciding your flight of life.

You may take off from the runway of institution to intuition towards the light for universal enlightenment. My bent of mind is scientific as well as spiritual.

My postulates are based on the exploring of spirituality through the scientific and emotional minds. The gap between the brains, minds, spirit, soul, body, heart, reasoning, destiny, reality, nature, universe, origin, end, all are playing the game of musical chair. The seat of one over rules the seat of other. The dominance of one overshadows the other.

Man is the composite machine to behave with the emerging mixes of these 5 D's.

II. With latent energy at dawn and dusk.

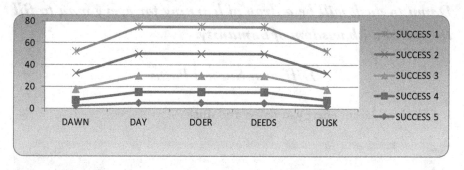

From this graph it is evident that greater utilization of day, doer and deeds one of the prime factor is the latent energy at dawn and dusk. But it may not be always so. You might have realized all, analyzed, worked out at dusk but were inefficient to utilize the day, your own action was not at full potential, and there were no substantial results. Please glance at the graph number V, just below the IVth to understand the discussion here. This is the truth one should blindly realize. You may have all the resources but say were constraint to utilize the day. This "D" has lost its value in the value of supply chain of 5 D's.

III. With latent energy only at dawn.

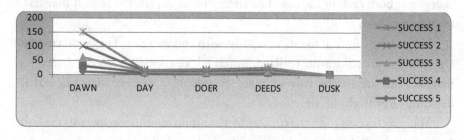

Only latent energy at dawn may not give you successful paths. You are vibrant with your dreams, inspiration, and motivation, enthusiastic about your goals, highly spirited yet far from appreciable success. The fact is only dreaming without action and proper utilization of time may not take you anywhere. The marginal and moderate success is always destined to happen. However, for dreams to be beyond destiny the other factors contribution is very essential.

An attempt has been made through these graphs to probably understand the relationship in a pictorial way. The impact of it is more than simply learning it through literature .The graphs are tool for scientific analysis. These can be applied to the evaluation of human behavior, man's motivational levels, physical and non-physical aspects of the humans. A mathematical model can be designed to study the issues affecting our growth, development, emotions, intellectuality, capability, potentials, abilities to understand the various relationships and impacts on the whole process of man's living.

Can man defeat the wish of destiny?

IV. With latent energy only at dusk.

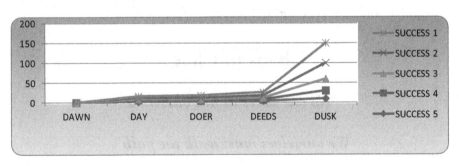

The day fades away daily despite your reluctance to let it go. We all go to some extent from dawn to dusk. What you carry forward to other day is very important. Can fortune, grace, luck, fate, help move to the other day along with you? How influential they will be in deciding our destiny tomorrow? The greatest loss is that the precious day has been lost. What projections can be considered today for tomorrow? The lessons of the day are the latent energies for dusk as well as dawn. One acts as the prime mover the other helps to maintain your trajectory of flight. Both the ends are the take off points of the runway of your life. Every day is small capsules of time to be released with thrust of hope for humanity.

V. Performance less than latent energies at dawn and dusk

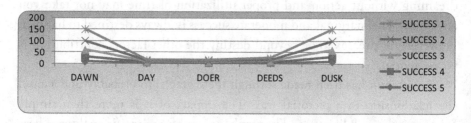

The above graph is self explanatory where the performance of day, doer and deeds is far behind the latent energies at dawn and dusk. The success paths are as many as you utilize the 5 D's.

What you have is only today with you? Go get the today? If you are getting the dawns and holding on till the dusk then definitely you are leading yourself to right goal of humanity. Awareness is to be strengthened. Practical living and leading needs greater insight into the daily activities from dawn to dusk.

Man to bring out the best in him should formulate models as illustrated above for the sole benefit of readers. Human lives, needs, success, aims, desires, dreams, are all likely to be within the sphere of dawn to dusk.

Chaos to Cheers

"No one saves us but ourselves.

We ourselves must walk the path".

- Buddha.

We ourselves have to walk the path of life. We ourselves have to fight the misery of life. We ourselves have to be the guardian of hope. We ourselves have to practice humanity. We ourselves have to become good. We ourselves have to sail in this world. We ourselves have to go to heaven.

Where is the path of cheerfulness? No doubt we are living with success and wealth. Are we living with value of life? Are we living with ideals of life? Are we having virtues of life?

Are we having a meaningful life?

Life is broadly in two main quadrants either good or bad. Being good it should be meaningful. How to build a unique individual meaningful self from dawn to dusk? Meaningful Man is the ingredient of meaningful society. Purpose of life has meaning. Are we becoming a meaningful self or soul?

Let me put forward to my compassionate readers the spiritual thinking of the valued scientist world has ever seen Sir Albert Einstein,

"Peace cannot be kept by force, it can only be achieved by understanding".

Further he continues to say, "Try not to become a man of success, but rather try to become a man of value".

The Scientist had the message for the humanity in the world.

He went on to clarify that, "We cannot solve our problems with the same thinking we used when we created them".

This gives most of the answers to the man for understanding science and spirituality.

We might have been successful here and there, now and then, but we were never valuable to the entire existence. Man has become doctorate of philosophy but not the doctorate of humanity. Man has failed to add value to his own existence. Homes have failed to add value to their existence. Societies have failed to add value to their existence. No school certifies degree in value. It is only man who has to live and die for it.

No university has Professor of Peace.

It is man who has to establish the bliss in him.

Man can only save man from misery. Man can only bring cheer to man. Man can only bring humanity in the world.

His confession at the end,

"It has become appallingly obvious that our technology has exceeded our humanity".

Let us again trying to interpret the philosophy of the Prince who became Buddha to renounce the World.

The enlightened Buddha preached for humanity,

"Just as a candle cannot burn without fire, man cannot live without a spiritual life".

He renounced the world to understand the value of humanity. His methods were designed to live a meaningful life. He emphasized discipline, control and meditation to bring continual meaning to your life.

For man's worry with time, "Do not dwell in the past; do not dream of the future, concentrate the mind on the present moment".

Life is a way to value of humans and in the words of Mahatma Gandhi, "Live as if you were to die tomorrow. Learn as if you were to live forever".

He practiced, "The best way to find yourself is to lose yourself in the service of others".

He advocated, "You must be the change you wish to see in the world".

He derived immense strength from, "The weak can never forgive. Forgiveness is the attribute of the strong".

In short he says,

"Where there is love there is life".

Confucius the great Chinese Philosopher in 450 BC philosophized the world with, "Life is really simple but we insist on making it complicated".

On the blindness of humanity he confesses, **"Everything has beauty, but not everyone sees it".**

On the learning of man, "By three methods we may learn wisdom: First by reflection which is noblest, second by imitation which is easiest and third by experience, which is the bitterest".

Understanding value of man from him, "Our greatest glory is not in never falling but in rising every time we fall".

We live in circle of misery. We fail to sail smoothly. We argue rather than improving our discussion. We blame rather than understanding our mistakes. We retaliate rather than forgiveness. We are cruel rather than being kind. We are small by questioning greatness. We are fools with improper education. We are narrow because of lively vision.

The majority of us are entangled in a circle of misery from dawn to dusk. Who will remove our knots from misery? Till when man will remain knotted to these miseries bringing chaos from dawn to dusk.

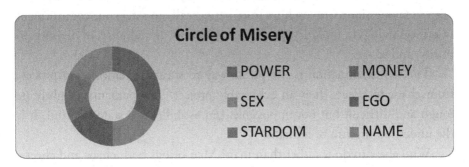

The above is depicted from the prevailing chaos society. I would instantly like my readers to take the question below to understand your position immediately.

Where do you stand in the circle of misery?

Misery	Major	Moderate	Minor	No Opinion
Power				
Money				
Sex				
Ego				
Stardom				
Name				

A quick glance need not leave you astonished and ashamed that majority of us are running towards power and money. We are doing this without the proper understanding of authority? And in addition to it are becoming mad for stardom and name making at the cost of bringing harm to our fellowmen.

The society is daily being hammered by millions and millions of egos. Moreover in recent times the politics of sex has become more vulnerable in society all over the world. This defenseless trend is likely to skew away our ideal youths from the principles of humanity.

My dear readers I hope you understand what "Dawn to Dusk" is willing to share for the reformation of humanity. We need to interrogate ourselves with such questionnaires on humanity periodically to assess our commitment in ethical living, in integrity, in attitude, in ideals, in morality, in divinity, in purity, and so on.

The self-examination is the prime way to start the reformation process from chaos to cheers. It is an achievable project. The path may slightly be tough and difficult but not impossible. Impossibility is a state of mind. It is the undesired rhythm of humans.

Who else can do it rather than man? Man brings both chaos and cheers. He is the originator of happiness and sadness. Misery only prepares man to work against his rise of life.

Means of survival does not mean misery of existence. Anything of excess is harmful is the wisdom we all have. Unidirectional living is to be cultivated. There should be one vision and only one mission.

Man has remained a juggler. He keeps creating circles of misery now and then. The AIM is not clear; the goal suffers clarity, duality in thoughts, and conspiracy in mind, betrayal in trust, weaker faiths, mildness in hope, all these leading him towards ambiguity of life from dawn to dusk.

How to come out from this devil circle? How to dissolve the circle of misery? How to make it a football to kick it out forever form the field of humanity? We all have to make our playground of existence free the weeds of miseries.

If you want to be a loser live with miseries. Be not a miser in expending miseries. Misery is unfruitful liability. It is an asset to make you poor at the end.

Miserly ultimately succeeds in making man misanthrope. The wildest misapprehension of man is that power can get him the world. Mischievousness is the product of misery in man. Miserableness breeds miscellaneous uncertainties from dawn to dusk.

Man many times misidentifies man. Man many times misinterprets man. Man many times is being misled by man. Most of the misunderstandings are because of the miscommunications. How to eliminate misjudging others? How to remove the confusion among ourselves? How to manage these miseries out of lie?

I would like to summarize from the learning, livings and practices of great scientists, reformers, philosophers, writers and saints that without discipline life is directionless and meaningless from dawn to dusk. In continuation to above any approach to life from any perception, philosophy, discipline, thinking, idea, dream, concept, faith, belief, trust, hope, culture, place, people, leads to the understanding of life for humanity.

Live with meaning to life.

Man has infinite choices, ways, and opportunities in this world. How well he wishes to be in the world is his concern. The wheels and circles which he boards will take him to the desired destinations at the end. But before that the thought, idea, aim, and activity needs to be at the dawn of life.

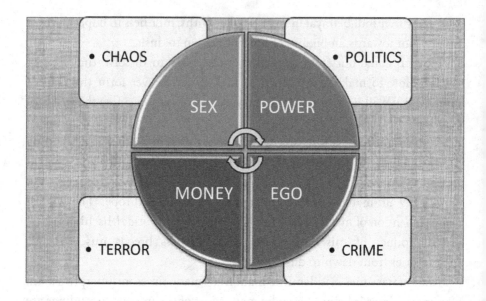

Live with purpose to know yourself. Live to understand the reality of existence. The wheel of power, ego, money and sex of human can only bear unwanted fruits of politics, crime, terror and chaos. The outer circle is reflection of inhumanity as your inner centers are still dwelling in lower planes of existence from dawn to dusk.

To understand this let us go through the division of life by the English, Poet, William Wordsworth,

"Life is divided into three terms-that which was, which is and which will be. Let us learn from the past to profit by the present, and from the present, to live better in the future".

Science never made atomic bombs to throw on humans. It is humans who decide to do so. Science never had the vision to be the ruler of crime. It is humans who gave the direction. Science never had the mission to demolish humanity. It is humans who started constructing human barriers.

A rubbish mind can only speak of garbage. A stupid mind can only understand the unproductive arguments. A foolish mind is no good to taste the result of education. A timid mind has no courage to even hold the fundamentals of humanity. A spirited mind never tires inspiring the postulates of humanity. A poisonous belief can make you only desperately unhappy.

I tell you my optimist readers, "The Man is born from the mind". You are exactly going to shape up as you are conceiving the things.

"Intelligence is the ability to adopt to change",

is what the great living intellectual Stephen Hawking says about the human in us.

The poison is in the mind not in the body. It kills humanity before the human meets the real physical death. Why to die by mind daily? The change in all of us is inevitable. Let it make its way for betterment of humanity.

The world is again not new to this indispensable saying,

"A smooth sea never made a skillful sailor".

The humans should realize that adversities are avenues towards making you more cheerful in days to come. Thus we can see that the rougher the sea the stronger the sailor. The tougher the life the stronger is the ideals of humans. The harder the learning the perfect is the teacher. The sweeter is the communication the better the relationships. The deeper the love the better is the humanity.

It would be wrong to say life has not given us anything? Actually the problem is we do not know what we should get. All are getting what they deserve. This is right today; it was right yesterday and will hold the same for tomorrow. How can the universal giver do injustice to all of us? He never created to prove his dishonesty with humans. May be our existing knowledge and wisdom is inadequate to read and understand his world. This is very much imperative from the resistances we have been showing from dawn to dusk. The psychology of human thinking is beyond the realms of humans.

Do you think there was not a single human who might have all that what he desired got fulfilled by the creator? Then why did he leave the world? Then why did not he remain youth forever? Why did he grow old? And why did he finally decay with the remains of a handful ashes in the existence. Can we find his traces in this earth? What has happened to all the wealth he was possessing? What has happened to the entire ego he was holding? Where is his identity today? What happened to his success, achievements, positions, chairs, authority, stardom and heroism? What happened to the castles he had built to live? Where he is sheltering today? What did he ultimately acquire in his life? Are people offering flowers to his graveyard? Is he remembered by the world from dawn to dusk? Was he a human that humanity could not understand?

Man is suffering because he wishes to control what he is supposed not to control.

Man is lying mercilessly in misery because of his ignorance more rather than his misfortune. How can a child be his own father? How can a child be his own mother? He can become a father to his child. He can become a mother to his child. The above discourse has revelations to revaluate our understanding of the existence.

Chaos is our creation.

Badness is our creation. Sadness is our creation. Happiness is our creation. Goodness is our creation. Cheers are also our creation. Near and dears are our creations. The machine to generate thoughts may be the gift of creation. But the content of thinking is ours. But the purity in idea is ours. But the divinity in mind is ours. But the strength in body is ours. But the hope in living is ours. But the faith in life is ours. But the faith in prayers is ours. But the truth in existence is ours. But the love in universe is ours. What creator has to do with the created world by humans? An insight into the self has answers to many queries of existence from dawn to dusk.

Human have been experiencing this manifestation in many ways from time to time. A single moment of misunderstanding is so poisonous that it makes us forget the hundred lovable moments spent together in a minute.

To know others you have to know yourself. If you can protect yourself from the evils then you have the strength to protect the society from the evils. If you can remove the chaos in yourself then you can remove the chaos from society as well.

Summing Up & Exercises for Readers- Chapter-IV

- It is homework for readers to work out a plan for leading their lives.
- Would you be a leader, follower and scavenger?
- Is what you have to decide in the view of working for humanity?
- List out the activities you can do to justify your life.
- What are the steps you are taking for real worship?
- How you are going to stabilize your life?
- Put all your knowledge and wisdom into formulating models which works for you in transforming you from dawn to dusk.
- Keep evaluating and apprising yourself.
- You are the best judge to give decisions on your life.
- Place yourself now and then in your inner court for confessions and prayers.
- Question yourself- Are you a party to chaos of the world?
- Please ensure you are working towards reestablishing cheers in the world.
- Creation should be followed by sincere commitments by humans. In regard to this what is the practical agenda for implementation.
- Please participate to justify your life.
- Look at the wheel of leading your life with vision and mission.
- A properly organized life is going to provide every human growth, maturity, worship and finally humanity.

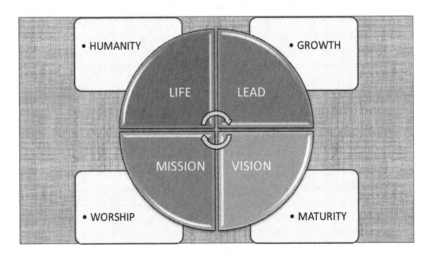

- I would like my readers to generate such dynamic wheels of progress.
- Look at one more wheel of progress below with the greater will of human facing challenges to utilize the opportunities to the best of their abilities and potentials.

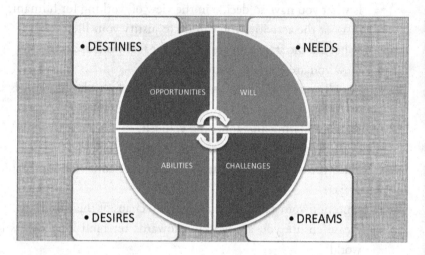

- This wheel promises your fulfillment of needs, dreams, desires and destinies.
- And all this with your strong will of human who gives you the strength to work with challenges and opportunities in the world from dawn to dusk.

PART III
CHAMPIONS OF HUMANITY

Chapter V

WORLD & WISDOM

"World improves because of Wisdom"

-Dr Shree Raman Dubey

The great poet Milton wrote,

"The mind is its own place and in itself can make a heaven of hell or a hell of heaven".

My readers, by now at least we have come to know all the worry we have from dawn to dusk. This is due to the mind the hidden culprit ever since existence in all of us. Is this the prime cause for all the goodness and badness in the world? What are the common problems of man today? What are the specific problems of a man? Are we suffering because of universal problem from dawn to dusk? Can situations be classified as problems? Is a problem to be considered as situation? Is situation management a solution to the man? Can we avoid situations? You might have avoided it but again what about the ones influencing you?

World & Wisdom are mutually dependent. World improves because of wisdom. Wisdom is learnt in world. Man excels because of mind. Mind is developed by man. The mind reaches everywhere. Can we not restrict it? Change the mind from one thing to another. Why get attracted to things that create tension?

Where can you unburden your minds?

Will the monk help you? There is monk in all of us. There is saint in all of us. There is god in all of us. The only way to control stress is to control the mind. The only way to control the crime is to control the mind. The only way to control jealousy is to control the mind. We can see that all are originating in the mind. It is like the sea and ocean with infinite number of waves continuously rising and falling from dawn to dusk. It is not a one day activity of a single mind of a single man. This is happening with all minds, all man in this world. This is the universal nature of mind.

Now when you have known the mind then why is the difference with the man. I am again trying to bring out the reality on surface for my readers that in all the disputes, conflicts, disagreements, criticisms, what we encounter from dawn to dusk is the war between non physical minds rather than the physical appearances of men. Just imagine its latent power. Invisibly it destroys and constructs the whole world. Can man control the application of mind? We must have a positive attitude even in the face of the worst adversity.

At times the volcano of evils keep integrating and disintegrating within making it more harmful than the explosion of the negative lava. Still we live in fallacy of the mind. When will man leave his fairyland?

Ego

Enmity Getting Obsessed

Education can only take man closer to mind. Mind primarily generates thoughts randomly interacting with nature, self, world, universe, and overall existence. Education brings in the power of conflict and reasoning. It struggles here to evolve differently with more permutations and combinations.

If I have read hundred books it brings me the thought of hundred authors. If all from the same land I am unfortunate to master all the cultures.

If the authors are from all over the world then this organized sampling comprehends me to have a global look to the same issue. I am benefited by the perceptions of so many philosophical writers all over the world. The reason to stress the above is that as individuals our learning should become global learning to accept the neighboring nations.

It fights its own reasoning to accept or reject a response or a question. The deeper you go the better you become from dawn to dusk. The impact of education is that the mind is under the influence of so many forces of attraction, repulsion, neutrality, morality, that it learns to be with the action of man with the reasoning of existence.

Every action has a reason.
&
Every action has a reaction.

Were you born to earn only money? Were you born to spread terror? Were you born to hate? Were you born to help? Were you born to care? Were you born to cheat? Were you born to teach? Were you born to kill? Were you born to save? Why you were born? Ask this regularly to your mind.

Let the mind come out with solutions for you. Let the mind rightly map you. This process of mapping, reforming, redefining, reinventing, regenerating, researching, relearning, reanalyzing, should be the sole purpose of education all over the world.

What is EGO?

Where it is? With whom it is? Is it good to share ego? Do you have the skill to kill ego? How to define it? Is it a complete personality? Is it a character? Is it self-esteem? Is it only limited to self? Is it the self-image? Is it the sense of self? Is it just an opinion of the self? Does it really reflect the self-worth of a man? Not so easy to write few lines with personal opinion.

I would like all my readers to look into this subject daily from dawn to dusk. The belly of ego need not grow beyond your wisdom. Being ignorant, it is the disgrace man is regretting. All learned men are egoist is also untruthful. All egoists are unlearned is equally untruthful. Then what is the truth? Has ego to do anything with wisdom? Do you think wisdom has no answers to ego? Is ego necessary? Is it hereditary? Is it the natural instinct in man? Why we are unable to live without it? When we can throw it completely? It follows us everywhere. Is it likely to remain till human remains?

There we are at crossroads. We have to find a solvent to completely dissolve it. Now the classification that ego can be good and bad again confuses the whole issue. This is a great area of research individuals can carry out individually from dawn to dusk. You are the University .Writing and submitting your thesis on ego shall never be to your satisfaction.

How to work with this project of ego? Mentor's, Guide's, may not be coming forward to clash with egos. I am speaking reality with all of you. It is tough to crack it. It is difficult to melt it. It is hard to cut it. It is not easy to throw away. No fool can steal it. No wisdom can dissolve it. Then how to come out of it?

Man egoistically can never let his ego go. Where can you bury it? It only goes with you. Is it a legacy of an individual or society? Ego has many forms, individual, personal, groups, community, society, organizational, internal, external, national, international, global, local, intellectual, spiritual, etc. It manifests in many ways. It suffers internal and external conflicts. It protests and contests. It resolves and dissolves. It is partial and impartial. It is confusing and comprehending. It is a mix of all human behaviors.

Studying one man is a huge task. Imagine the quantum of effort required to study everybody's ego and that too when you do not know where it is exactly existing.

Man is yet to attain the great wisdom to control the ego.

Man is chasing himself. Man is fighting himself. Man is troubling himself. Man is rearing himself. Man is finding himself. Man is taming himself. Man has to understand himself. Man is seeing himself. Man is searching himself. Man is teaching himself. Man is fighting himself. Man is killing himself. Man is bringing dawn in himself. Man is controlling himself. Man is playing himself. Man is writing himself. Man is brainstorming himself.

How to eradicate this never dying ego? I request my all readers and associates of readers to start working on eliminating ego from the self and the world. What we all can do from here? Action plans are to be effectively worked out.

Competition is to bring out the excellence in all of us. Competition is not to bring out our egos. Politics is to bring out the best in governance. Politics is not to manipulate the freedom of speech. Literacy is not to exploit illiterates. Power is not to miss- utilize authority. Power is to lead. All the above is not opening up because of the blanketing on man. The ego is continuously holding the pure existence of man.

One more day of existence, one more day and again, and again is being witnessed by all. This way days roll on without the dawn of egoless man. Can man really not shed away his ego? Why fears letting his ego go?

Man is unable to identify his real identity. Anger is not to burn the desires. Champions are crusaders of misfortune. Success is to bring opportunities to others. Ego ceases the creativity in you.

Globalization is to unite homes of the world.

Secularism is to bring oneness in humans. Society is the garden where you have grown with all the care of survival and lessons of existence. Even though man is well knitted within it from dawn to dusk, somewhere the urge for liberation from bondages haunts him from dawn to dusk.

Foremost there should be willingness to have wellness. There should be urgency to become good. There should be a pure thought for transformation. There should be a deeper commitment to change towards betterment. Without all these we will remain in darkness even not knowing ourselves at the end. Man should feel pity to such type of human existence.

Liberties of the people are to be understood by the people. To what extent man should be liberal to man. In the wars of egos man is found to be blind to his reasoning senses. Are we not doing injustice with the freedom of existence?

Ego is negativity.

Positive-EGO is rarely practiced.

It is cursed asset in man. Continuing with this inventory can only spoil the warehouse of your goodness. You lose more because of the uncontrolled behavior due to ego rather than criticality of the situation you are facing. Ego weakens your wisdom to live as human.

The positive –EGO is very rarely seen in man. ENERGY GETTING OBSESSED, ENTHUSIASM GETTING OBSESSED, would bring wonders to the society.

The society lacks energy and enthusiasm to regenerate humanity. In fact some of us might have received severe blows before we could realize that we were victim of the inescapable inhumanity. The insight for humanity dimension on the victimized aspect may be understood as our patience which we were holding to let the immaturity of human dance within the tune of morality. The greatness is of the man who knowingly behaves as unknown to let the chaos be simple like the pleasant chorus with lyrics of inhumanity.

Any issue has two choices for resolution between men from dawn to dusk. It will be in favor of one and at the same time unfavorable to other. The party winning never wishes to lose. The losing party never wishes to compromise. The battle is of the egos rather than of the subject. Both are unwilling to have a similar perception. Their opinions cannot be same. Is it because of the variance in the man or of the substance in reality?

Let us take a look at the population statistics of humans living today. Humans are nearly 7 billion in numbers on earth. And we are still multiplying faster than our World GDP and inflation rates. We are expected to hit 9 billion within a decade. The sufferings are going to proportionally increase keeping in view the shortage in food supplies, shelters, clothing, and standards of living, means of living, heath, wellness, fitness, hygienic and environmental challenges. The economy of the nation has an impact on the living of the humans.

Here is a relevant point to be marked to understand the chaos and cheers a human faces. A developed country has better means than the underdeveloped nations without any thought of doubt in this hypothesis. The unappreciable part is why the places of abundance are having the intensities of chaos. The cheers are spreading without resistance in the plains of poverty. Will the people from these two regions demonstrate the same egos? What do you think?

Human is now developing Global-EGO?

This is a new term probably for the entire World. I would equally like contemporaries Researchers, Authors, Teachers, Students, Reformists, Humanists, Naturalists, and Idealists, to start exploring it. Ego is no more confined to the individual ideologies. Ego is redefining its nature. It is no more inheritance of the inhabitant from a particular land. The global outlook has revolutionized the inner and outer theories of the present humans.

The Green revolution, the White revolution, the Industrial revolution, the Brown revolution, the Cyber revolution have been instrumental in influencing the dignity of labor and subsequently the dignity of humans.

Many Schools of thoughts have invaded the arena of humanity. The professionalism from working culture made its way to the human culture. A bit of scientific management in resolving human disputes started taking lead into the societal frame work. The Industrial disputes indirectly educated and brought in awareness in the working classes to understand their fundamental needs. They then started demanding legally even in the society.

The social revolt jolted many of the militaries and parliaments of the world. A question here in the background of humanity is that the collective ego of humans for freedom was voiced in history many times rather than the individual egos of a worker.

Ego has been transforming accordingly. Right from capitalism, communism and nationalization to democracy it underwent changes in the minds of humans. The point of the above discussion is to understand that ego of human is very much dependent on the environment of living.

Humanity is not only limited to the human. It has an environment. A vast arena operates with many influential and interfacing disciplines.

Let it be Asian-Ego, African-Ego, American-Ego, Arabian-Ego and European-Ego, whatever it may be, ultimately these are the different faces of the ego of humans. Do regionalisms have impact in the egoism of the human? The clock is ticking for everybody. Timelines are lost many times in our goals to reestablish humanity.

Ego is the controller of your actions, speech, behavior, feelings, temper, tempo, attitudes, reactions, thoughts, and so on. It guides you away from the reality of life. The world of ego is the battleground of chaos rather than cheers.

Reader is dear to any author. And this is no exception to me. I am waiting for dawns of reception where every day flock of readers would join this battalion for fighting the wars of humanity. Let both my readers and me constitute a team from dawn to dusk to win the wars of humanity. What else can an author wish more than this?

My idea of humanity from today is the idea of my readers. My idea of readers will be the idea of society sooner. The idea of society will be the idea of nations very soon. The idea of the nations will be the idea of the world. The idea of the World will be the idea of the Universe. And this is exactly then that we will realize our goal set by the essay "DAWN to DUSK".

I am not producing intended critics through this essay but I am reporting the painful facts of existence. Let this year 2015 be the "Year of Change" beginning with first completely demolishing our embarrassing ego.

Man's life has become a mess. Ego can only add to upsetting the day from dawn to dusk. Let it be the year of cleanliness, implementation, innovation, intuition, inspiration, resolution, commitment, action, volunteerism, something new, entirely unbelievable in transforming the face of humanity.

I am wishing my readers to make this drive one of the rarest of rare daring ever undertaken by humans on earth to wipe out the epidemic of inhumanity. This is an endeavor you will cherish till the existence of universe and beyond it.

You will not be guilty of the life you have been given by the existence. It is time to justify yourself. It is time to justify ourselves.

"You must not lose faith in humanity.

Humanity is an ocean;
if a few drops of the ocean are dirty,
the ocean does not become dirty".

–Mahatma Gandhi

We are discussing the problems of these few drops. Why these few drops are dirty? These few drops are increasing from dawn to dusk. Man has to evaporate these drops. The ego should vanish forever.

Ego is the unwanted devil in you.

Ego is blind to humanity in the pursuit of prosperity and wealth. It is the ghost of your life. Man should drive it away from his daily living. Knowledge has the light more than millions of rays of sun. Man is struggling to feed his stomach with ego. In this shadow the kindness, sacrifices and humbleness have eroded away from the ideals of humans.

Keep putting at good. It will come back to you. Let yourself become poetry. Life isn't about getting and having always. It's about giving and being.

Dawn is Gateway

If you are not at the doors how you do step in the world?

Sitting at home you cannot roam the world. Neither the world can come in your lap or the doors. What I mean to say is that man has to reach the gateways of life. Keep searching them at dawns. You are to find the resources of life in the world. The world starts opening its doors at dawn. Be the first to rush in. You will see wonders happening to you shortly.

Believe me my dear promising readers; the power of dawn can bring miracles to your understanding and living of life. With sincerity ask the dawn your wishes to be fulfilled. Its rays are the energy of your life. It is for humans to work with it. Most of us are buried with the dunes of foolishness.

Nothing comes to the brooding man.

Nothing comes to the crying man. Nothing comes to the sitting man. Nothing comes to the stupid man. Nothing comes to the lazy man. Nothing comes to the angry man. Nothing comes to the cruel man. Nothing comes to the brutal man. Nothing comes to the egoist man. Nothing comes to the coward man. Nothing comes to the sin man. Nothing comes to the evil man. Nothing comes to the dual man. Nothing comes to the glooming man. Nothing comes to the heartless man. Nothing comes to the selfish man. Nothing comes to the crippling man. Nothing comes to the crawling man. Nothing comes to the cheating man. Nothing comes to the dying man. To get something you have to be bold, brave, healthy, active, lively, lovingly, fair, truthful, cheerful, helpful, kind, generous, grateful, good, and so on.

Man is finding easier routes of obtaining things. They are acting smart but not ethical to the act. Copying of an idea leaves you with a lost opportunity of creating your own idea. You are not giving chance to novelty. You are not testing your potentials of creativity. This way you are running away from the gateway of creation.

Dawn is to create new.

Please afresh yourselves with the day. The thoughts cannot be borrowed to lose your uniqueness. In this way we are giving scope to redundancy of our inherited values. Our ideas are being abandoned because of our inability to look into them. This however is insult to us from dawn to dusk.

Why cannot you innovate? You have the world to work for. You have the existence to deliver for. Above all you have human to work for.

Every dawn you have two chances either to sleep with your dreams or to wake up to chase your dreams. Either to continue your foolishness with brooding or to concentrate on your intellect to built the wisdom. Either do or die.

Dawn is the gateway to infinite opportunities everyday all over the world. Is Man availing this universal opportunity?

Dawn is light to all.

Man should be humble to receive it. It has its way of giving gift of life. One should know to receive it. Man can light another man just like the single candle lighting other candles. To light others you should have light. This is the whole process of enlightenment.

Dawn is the window to the divine.

A dawn can only make another dawn.

A day can only make another day.

A man can only make another man.

A home can only make another home.

A village can only make another village.

A city can only make another city.

A town can only make another town.

A state can only make another state.

A society can only make another society.

A government can only make another government.

A nation can only make another nation.

A world can only make a better world.

A god can only make another god. A teacher can only make another teacher. A doctor can only make another doctor. An evil doer can only make another evil doer. A robber can only make another robber. The fact to be understood here is that the becoming takes the form of the maker.

This is the point of time where everything starts sprouting provided you have sowed your seeds at the dusk. This is an equal opportunity to do for yourself as well as the world. An opportunity creates many opportunities.

A dawn creates many dawns.

Hold on to one rightly others will follow like bees.

Every opportunity is a fortune of existence. Sufferings are also opportunities through the path of misfortunes. It requires right education to understand the right things not wrongly. What else can be more miraculous than that you exist? It is always easier to ink down happiness rather than sadness. It is always easier to communicate good happenings rather than convey sad incidents. Why, have you ever thought? If not done earlier try thinking on it now. Why we fail to recognize science as one of the paths to spirituality? Why Society enjoys segmenting the world into science and spirituality?

In fact why it cannot be other way round that because of advancements in science and technology we have come closer to the understanding of god. Science is a tool given to man by god. Spirituality is the inner science to understand god.

Human science is about the universality in individuality among the diversity. The science has improved understanding the human limitations and thus accepting the supreme power of existence. Science is holding His life a little longer not to challenge his creation but to experience it further. Who does not like to live a second more than allocated? Science is making man to think faster. Science is making man to compute faster. Science is to some percentage trying to give man a ray of hope to dive into the mystery of existence.

Science is either by God or by Man is a finding of the Universe. It is either a creator or destroyer. It can be used both ways just as the mind of man either for good or for evil. Man and World both are in fact existing and again Man for World or World for Man and in continuation Science for Man or Man for Science.

Science is one of the golden dawns in the history of mankind.

It is like a torch light to search in the darkness of life. It is slowly changing the concept of living from dawn to dusk. It is bringing in turbulences in the mind for betterment. It is inclined towards the materialistic growth. Will it answer questions on humanity? Will humanity give place to science? Will spirituality shelter science? Will the world protect science, spirituality and humanity? Scarcity of goods can be increased by bridging the gap of supply and demand.

Did Science influence human behavior? Has it helped humanity? The missiles, torpedoes, atomic and nuclear bombs were all detrimental in harming humanity.

Science has brought smiles and tears to humanity. Were tears more than the smiles? Humanity has witnessed its own destiny. Our perceptions should not be like knife to cut the hand of fortune which we are holding. The world is already suffering from hopeless and helplessness. Let it not become handless.

Role to Goal

What is your sole role in life? What is your main goal in life? The total journey of man's life is remembered by the role he plays and goals he achieves. There is a definite match of role to goal from dawn to dusk.

Time changes your roles as well as goals.

At the youth of your life your role and goal is always inclined towards quest of life, exploring nature, to do new things, you are flooded with opportunities, ideas, thoughts, voices, lot of action, eagerness to experiment, you want to slice and dice the life, youthfulness is revealed through your talents, formation of team, togetherness, you all want to fly with your wings of existence to touch the sky, the dynamism brings in momentum from dawn to dusk. How you can perform your role today? How you can meet your goal today?

The dawn is the best time for starting any activity of goodness towards humanity of the world.

Where are you today?
&
Where shall you be tomorrow?

What you have become? Definitely not the one you desired. Whom to blame? An exhaustive list of blamers can be arrived. But who is the real culprit of unmaking your future. Was role not mapped to your goal? Do you want to change? Why you should change?

Our goal is sole. Our role should be solely towards universal goal. Solidarity of goal for every man in the world should be established from dawn to dusk. Shall I wait for many dawn to dusk pass away? Shall I change today this very dawn? Why my life is in dusk? I am unable to pour down from the clouds of failure? Why they are holding my release?

Who will bring me from darkness to lightness, sadness to happiness, ignorance to enlightenment, blankness to wisdom, laziness to activeness, fear to boldness, failure to success, loneliness to friendliness, dehumanizing to humanity, devils to divine, badness to goodness, and so on towards welfare of mankind?

Why my life is in dark?

Who will give me light? Why I fear? Who will inspire me? Who will make my future? How can I improve my family life? Will money only solve my problem? Am I a human with humanity? Why the conflict in me is not subsiding? Who will regain the lost glory of humanity? Is it necessary for humans to fight with humans?

Can human not resolve other human's problem? Are problems of humanity only because of humans? Let us apply our ideas, intellects, reasoning, mind, heart, body, soul for seeking solutions from dawn to dusk. The day is given to us to play with the nature, earth, world and universe to define the role with the goals. Step by step a process of betterment shall surely begin to transform the humanity. Think till you completely sink in the existence. Thoughts are jewels of life. Ornament yourself from dawn to dusk in enriching your lives.

Life is a will.

Life is a way. Life is an idea. Life is a thought. Life is a dream. One will follow the other. It is a chain to anchor with the existence. Who does not want a good dawn to befall on self?

Life is action. Doing is living. Finding is living. Exploring is living. Are we living? Passing away time may not be a fruitful living.

If you are unlearned learn. If you have learnt make the unlearned learn. If you are a doctor, serve, nurse, strive to bring healthiness in society. Fight till the end to eliminate the diseases from the earth for the well being of humanity. If you are engineer, construct, build infrastructure, projects, dams, roads, villages, cities, towns, metros, with proper engineering, planning for the welfare of the society.

Everyone should be blessed with a home. If you are an administrator, bring policies, implement, monitor, and ensure law and order, stand up to deliver, justice, moral, rights, dignity to build a good and happy society. If you are a leader, voice the dreams of citizens in the parliament of people to greater heights of commanding governance. Simply do not represent the party with regretted objectives of grievances.

You are the vision of your people. Be bold and strong to die for the cause of the people. If you are a teacher, plant the seeds of humanity into the young minds at the earliest for them to grow the tree of humanity. They are energetic voices with the potential to transform the society with new dimensions of humanity. If you are a preacher, intoxicate the minds of many with the values of existence.

Let the body, soul, mind self all speak the language of love, togetherness, kindness, sacrifice, help, association, volunteerism, nobility for welfare of mankind, society and humanity. Give them the secrets of better living from dawn to dusk.

I live in a place surrounded by mosque, church, temple, gurudawara, monastery and other centers of spirituality. What I observe is that they are all doing some common activities of performing timely prayers daily, weekly prayers, especial prayers, offerings, gatherings, and discourses for the devotees and people seeking blessings. If you just remove the identity of the buildings as they are sacredly called or honored as churches, mosques, temples, gurudawaras, you shall see that the core things more or less are commonly performed .We all pray for peace. We all seek his blessings. We show our gratitude to him. We thank him. We love him for his gift of life. What can be inferred from this is that any religion, any community, any sect, any caste, any society, any man all are working towards the same objective of universal humanity. Why Gita, Vedanta, Upanishads, eight fold paths of Buddha, principles of Jainism, Ramayna, Mahabharata were born in India? Why Bible was born in Babylon? Why Koran in Arabia?

Was it not for the same purpose? Is it not for the same purpose? Will it be not for the same purpose? Yes, it would have been only for humanity, humanity and only humanity. The Sun rising in Japan is the same as the Sun setting in

America. The Lord at Lords in United Kingdom is the same as the Lord in Eden Gardens of Calcutta in India. Is the water of Dead Sea sweeter than the water of Bay of Bengal or Arabian Sea or Pacific Ocean? Is the air in Egypt, Italy, and Moscow, New York different than the air in Delhi, Karachi, Tokyo, and Hong Kong?

My dear friends, then how man can be different. It appears we are somewhere going wrong. May not be the whole lot but marginally we are drifting. Impediments to humanity are increasing. Let us all have one objective of universal humanity. There is nothing above humankind.

<u>Defeat & Victory</u>

Man would like to die rather than live with defeat.

Who would not like to live? Who would not like to win? Who would not like to cherish? Who would not like to breathe with freedom? Who would not like to be happy? Everybody is anxiously waiting for the better dawn in life. When this better dawn come to one and all?

What is defeat? What is victory? How do we understand both? Does it connect to our strength and weaknesses? Does it give meaning to our living?

Will man regain victory over himself?

Is defeat the end to life?

Where is the problem in man? Why he fails to know himself? What type of victory you want? You want to be victorious in what? You want to beat the other man. How you want to establish your superiority over the other man? Is this your motto of victory? Or do you have some other definition for victory from dawn to dusk?

Do you want to win over nature? Do you want to be powerful than the creator? Are you slaving to your own master? Why you feel you are defeated? Who can defeat you? Why you fear defeat?

A feeling of defeat in us due to realization may actually be a victorious phenomenon in the process of overall transformation of man. When the man in me is ashamed and admits that he is defeated to goodness a new dawn has begun in his vision towards existence. Probably it is the way of refinement for all human beings. The melody song of victory which you were singing with illusionary dreams is later on found to be the cry you were holding under the blanket of immaturity. The clarifications itself are unstable from dawn to dusk and it is only comprehensible if you are willing to fail and quest the living.

Quest has the power to refine your thinking. It brings in a new dawn in you every time you question yourself. The fight & flight from defeat and victory is what every man is encountering from dawn to dusk.

Dawn is a new hope of reasoning your own abilities and potentials. The question is victory at what cost. Does man has answer to this? How to define the victory?

Defeat brings unwanted depression of life to those who are fools of existence. You are here to be with your action and not the results. The basic truth I would like to share with my readers is that there is nothing to be upset like defeat in life. It is the moment of the attempt nothing more than it. It has gone with the time. You for no reason are carrying the meaningless impression till depression kill you completely.

Man's expressions should be connected to the liveliness of existence. You might be observing that the people who are cleanly living are happier than the dirty men cursing themselves. They are reaping the grace of life.

Happiness is a godly feeling. It is the confirmation of the faith in existence. Harmoniousness is the grace of life. It follows the goodness of man. The moment of badness pollutes the memory to get dissolved in the sadness rather than the gladness of the living. Are not we doing injustice to our lives banking on moments of happiness and sadness?

Our aim should not be to stand at the ends of defeat and victory? Man should not hold either of them. Both are moments of history. Remaining with it is like lying dead. Man is not born to die at these points. We have to rise above defeat and victory.

Nature has seasons. Life has seasons. Day has seasons. Time has seasons. Man has seasons. Defeat is one season. Victory is another season. You may not win in all the seasons. You may not lose in all the seasons. Defeat and Victory are like the crests and troughs of life.

Our aim is to go through defeat as well as victory from dawn to dusk. The understanding is that as dawn and dusk passes away similarly defeat and victory will pass away in your life. The celebration and cursing are all temporary moments of the infinite existence. The real victory is to know the man in you.

Dawn to Dusk is an idea of hope for humanity.

It is feeling for happiness for all the lives of the world. It is voice of this civilization to excel man as human. People are worried about defeat. Can we define defeat? I have attempted it this way,

> **DEFEAT to me means**
>
> **"Did Effort Fail Enduring Aim Today?"**

Where is defeat? It is only the problem in the mind. Did you fail in your aim? Who stopped you to pursue your aim? Is the world holding you? Had you pursued it for some more time may be even billionth or millionth of a second, you would have experienced that there is nothing called defeat. It is only the penultimate time yielding to success. The throne of success would have been yours. This is the only difference between cheers and tears. The passion should not die midway. Go through it before it throws you out. Be the hammer to blow not the anvil to receive all the hammerings. Every new dawn has power to blow your dreams. Cherish it and you shall never regret it.

Aim, aim, it right and you shall get your target. Majority of us drop at this point, sympathizing by embracing defeat. Friends, I very honestly feel, that little effort which makes all the difference is banking in our minds as fate, luck, fortune, grace, blessing and so on.

How it is to be done? Who will do it? When we can do it? How we can do it? All of us have to win in life. Win the day of opportunity. See that no day is useless to you. Emptiness should not be daily witnessed by man. Make a determination not to be defeated. Endure to recover when the season becomes favorable. How to make time in your favor? Time has all the secrets of the world. To start with the human evolution and its first civilization, the world has witnessed great wars of defeat and victory of man.

The wars for wealth, land, ego, kingdom, supremacy, glory, power, dynasties, princesses, prince, aristocracy, legacy, were fought, kingdoms exchanged, ruined, destroyed, people were killed, ravaged, and brutally murdered, exiled, made prisoners, taken under captivity and so on. All the above and imprisonment speaks of the barbarism culture of those days. There was great revolution as we all know from history to safeguard humanity.

Today almost the kingship has gone, government is the voice of people's freedom, the capitalistic theory is fading away under the light of democracy, but yet the humanity is at crossroads. Some of the great cities in history are no more. They were defeated by their successors. Some lost because of their destiny. The new dawn was with the new empire. The victorious were those who could fight their battles of nerves. Man was not man to do this. It is always sad to read this painful history.

I am speaking of some of the remarkable ancient cities where the human was breeding to expand and continue its existence to unfold mysteries of the nature and him. They were the largest cities in the world and arguably the epicenters of human civilizations. Contesting and protesting is not new to man. Man was doing this and is continuing to do so. What is the benefit of these victories? It would have been better to win by loosing.

Is it victory of the land which brings glory to man?

Man can be more glorious in sacrificing the land for humanity. Let it be Alexander the Great, Hitler, Napoleon, what finally they gained from these invasions.

A brief overview below makes our vision more clear to understand our past generations to build new generations.

Ultimately the major causes of defeats have been buried with marginal remains in history.

Jericho was the biggest city in the world in 7000 BC, the city nestled between the Dead Sea and Mt Nebo. Mari was the robust trade capital of Mesopotamia. Ur was the most important port on the Persian Gulf. Ur was no longer inhabited after 500 BC. Yinxu took the lead in 1300 BC an old village on the Huan River contained the earliest form of Chinese writing. Babylon was an epicenter of wealth, power and prestige from 2000 to about 538BC. It was here the Bible says residents believed so fully in themselves that they tried to build a structure into the heavens. Carthage is said to have been the greatest city in the world for a short time span before getting reduced to ash by the Romans in 146 BC.

From its humble roots as a small Italian village, 1100 years earlier, Rome in the second century AD, was enjoying the pinnacle of its influence and achievement. By 273 AD the Dark Ages were looming on the horizon. Istanbul of today was once upon Constantinople, in fight for its survival in 600 AD. In the year 900 AD, Baghdad was the center of the Golden Age of Islam, A 500 year Middle East renaissance that began with the founding of the city and ended in 1250 AD with the Mongol invasion. Beijing took the lead in 1500 AD, the Jingtong store houses were constructed to house grain to feed its growing population.

While the British Empire was flung around the globe bringing in immense wealth for a small portion of England, London was largely a slum in 1825 AD. New York City took on its modern shape in 1914, when the Bronx was added as the fifth borough. It was a city that looked to the future as it built skyscrapers and laid plans to build them even larger. Despite the onset of the Great Depression in 1929 New York went ahead and built the Chrysler Building, The Empire State Building, The Lincoln Building and one Street Wall 1931 just to name few.

Philosophers for thousands of years have issued good advice.

Why this universe appears and disappears to us? Truth cannot be limited to any individual, society, culture, belief, religion, community, country, race or world. Either ancient or modern there cannot be transformation in truth. Truth billion years back and truth billion years from today will remain as it is. Man should promulgate the harmony of religions. No scriptures can make us religious. Where is God? Where is true religion? Where is the path of devotion? Where to learn wisdom? Is it by virtue? Each person tries to hold himself faultless.

Man needs to practice control over himself. The energy of man is drained to combat the outside influences more than the inside disturbances.

In the words of Publilius Syrus,

"A wise man will be master of his mind; a fool will be its slave".

Am I a progressive thinker? People today want to achieve everything speedily. How can a tradition of 5000 years be learnt in 5 minutes? How can an existence of billions years be known in fraction of second? Is there continuity of mind? Mother Earth has given birth to all life. A woman is indeed the full circle of God's creation and within her is the power to create, nurture and transform.

We all have mothers. Mother Earth is for all of us. Mother is the origin for all of us. She is the birth place for all of the mankind. Let us pray for the divine universal mother. Mother is the goddess of birth, strength, learning, wealth, prosperity, success, happiness, healthiness, courage, beauty, divinity, grace, spirituality, knowledge, wisdom, what not she is the infinite source of existence. Man as woman and man have segmented the society with their theory of dominance. There is no fun in becoming victorious here. The war of genders has humiliated, mutilated, and tortured the society for making it discriminatory.

Why humankind is regressing?

With whom you are conflicting? With whom you are protesting? With whom you are challenging? You want victory over whom? Is it yourself? You want to beat the woman? She wants to defeat man? For what we should defeat and find victory to do?

You should become greater than your ideal.

Let your goal be the highest ideal. Is the ideal of man and woman different?

Are not the defeated and victorious lacking the real will of humanity. If you want to defeat, defeat your will of evil, bad, jealousy, enmity, hatred, etc. Go have victory over your devil.

Realizing our own real nature is the one goal of our life. Devil and God both want to occupy your inner self. How should be your innersole? Realizing is making it a part of our lives by constant thinking of it. Hypnotism of humanity is good for society. Hope such more and more magicians could play their skills to hypnotize the world from dawn to dusk.

Man is the biggest beggar of humanity.

Being human man is searching humanity. Our progress in wisdom is such that we are becoming learned fools from dawn to dusk. Victory for man is a misnomer. Man is surviving on sympathy of defeat. It is the shelter of millions and millions of educated people. In addition to it, man is shamelessly banking on the shores of worries, miseries, sorrows, pains, darkness, cruelty, and foolishness. Whatever we do we expect a return. We are all merciless traders in life, virtues, religion, love, faith, trust, hope and wisdom. Is this the real world of humans? Does it have an absolute existence?

I hope you all will agree with me that, "No man is mad to hit his head on wall".

Weapons of Peace

"The glory of friendship is not the outstretched hand, nor the kindly smile, nor the joy of companionship. It is the spiritual inspiration that comes to one when he discovers that someone else believes in him"- Ralph W Emerson

Dawn is revelation to the world. It brings what man needs into the world. Nature is feeding man. What man can give to nature? Man can only love nature. Man can only serve nature. Man can only live with nature. Man can protect nature. Man can add to nature. Man cannot create new flora and fauna other than that of existence.

Can man live with peace?

Can man live in harmony? Can man have regard for another man? Why war between man and man? Man by nature is angel in the world. An integrated effort is required to bring peace in world. Where are the weapons of peace? Who will operate it? Can optimism of peace become the religion of the world? Man is trapped within his own kingdom. Unless he fuels his spirit he cannot visualize the divinity of existence.

Man is armed with love to conquer the empires of hatred.

Why man is breaking his universal promises of brotherhood? What is the ultimate benefit in murdering humanity from dawn to dusk? How can hatred bring happiness without the spirit of love for humans?

Man has astonishing powers of creation. Human has only created the humans in the world. Both chaos and cheers are his creation from dawn to dusk. Perhaps the supreme is of the same opinion.

What god can do?

He says he only created humans. He is not willing to take the responsibility of creating evils and goodness. World was given to man by god. It is our ownership to keep it in order. Man has to lead the life. God can only give you the life energy. You have to decorate your world. Man is the architect of his life is known to one and all. We are all his children. We are all his descendants. We all are from the same source of existence. Where is the problem?

There were experts in all civilizations and generations of man. Man can learn from the legacy of experts. What man means by prosperity from dawn to dusk? What man means by peace from dawn to dusk? Is success predictable? Is peace predictable? Is failure predictable? The success and failures are the momentary ends of life but not the end of life.

Does peace float between success and failure?

Are success, failure and peace destinations from dawn to dusk?

Is peace a feeling? Is success and failure also feeling of man? Are success, failures and peace material possessions to be carried out by man? Or Are mere moments of time in one's life? It hardly makes any difference to be a good human being.

It is not the grade in exams that decides the quality of human. It is not the wealth in life that confirms the richness of humanity in man. It is not the status in society that decides the well being of man. It is not the self ego that decides the power of man. It is not the number of books you have read that decides the knowledge in man. There is something else which we all got to learn to become human.

Who will be our eye-opener to safeguard this world? There are millions of people already armed with the weapons of peace. They are equipped with love, kindness, humbleness, gratefulness, gratitude, togetherness, holiness, nobleness, moral, ideals, faith, trust, hope, goodness, heart and humanity. Some have already accomplished the heroic deeds by sacrificing their lives for the restoration of peace and humanity in the world. They are the real men of ideals and worship.

In the words of T.S. Eliot,

"Only those who will risk going too far can possibly find out how far one can go".

Man has to use his time from dawn to dusk in understanding peace. Think peace and you shall attain peace. Let all the places of people right from homes, public, offices, schools, institutions, organizations, markets, shops, malls, hospitals, monasteries, universities, playgrounds, parks, wherever you can make them the permanent battleground of peace. Fight with everybody to reinstate peace. A drive for peace should be felt by one and all.

Let the mind only think peace from dawn to dusk. Constitute an army of humanitarians to ravage the kingdoms of inhumanity. Campaign voluntarily the manifesto of humanity. It is world for humans not inhuman. Inhumanness is not the goal of man. Do not rest till we have cleaned the world from this debris. We can do it and it shall be done.

Today the world needs only peace. We have foods to live but no peace to live. Continually remind yourself that one of the most important decisions you make each day from dawn to dusk is what you will do immediately and what you will do later, if you do it all. Use your time for humanity.

Peace is the basic of humanity.

Let our basics of life be clear and cleaner day by day. The purity in mind can be attained only through keeping the mind peaceful. This is the way towards right wisdom of life. We have all the weapons to safeguard our kingdom of humanity. Man was never born to kill man. Man was never born to murder man. Man was never born to fight with man. Man was never born with the purpose to destruct and demolish another man.

Let us use our weapons of peace daily. Start with your responsibility to yourself and your world is to take full advantage of the doors opening all around you from dawn to dusk.

Your prime duty is to participate with all your potential talents and abilities in what many economists are calling the **"The Golden Age of Mankind"**.

This is one of the very best times in all of human history to be alive to unlock, explore and mine your inborn creativity. The best way to understand leadership is to know about the qualities a leader should possess.

As economists are struggling to map the means to the ends presently more humanists are needed to bridge the gap between man and humanity. Man is moving farther away from humanity. Which in no means is a reason to justify the human existence? The sole purpose of the existence is at stake. Is life to be treated as a bitch? What is man's key weakness? Is not learning intended to transform man's perception from negativity to positivity? Animosity gives rise to several unwanted diseases. Man should be like the bird swarm picking the pearls of humanity.

Man is victim of multiple personalities. Who can influence the world? Let us revisit the realization that the ultimate in human creativity is to create another human. I firmly can say without an ounce of doubt that your heart knows who you really are. Your dream knows what you finally want to become. Now the question is optimism cannot be imposed on any individual.

World is reflection of Man. Every Man can be a leader.

Leader

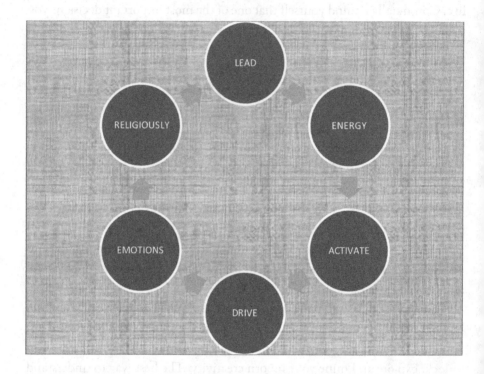

To me leader is,

"A leader is a person who leads with energy to activate and drive the emotions religiously".

He takes responsibility of his followers to lead them to the destination they are willing to go. He absorbs their worries and conquers their emotions religiously with a very strong drive and zeal to activate their minds in the pursuit of goal. He has no personal expectations of his and is always willing to understand the needs of the followers. He is in fact a personification of mother to the crying child.

Humans who understand the language of another human are obviously the leaders of humanity.

Existence is the natural leader. Existence speaks the language of love. Existence speaks the importance of life. Existence brings in all the inspiration in humans. Existence imparts the lessons of learning life. Do you think anger has its origin outside you? Do you think love has its origin outside you? Do you think ego has its origin outside you? Then why existence should be discriminated. Then why existence should be criticized. Then why existence should be dishonored. Then why existence is unpleasant.

Man enjoys the ego of ownership.

Why not the responsibility of leadership? Both ownership and leadership can constitute a good weapon of peace. Man can arrest restlessness in the world only if he is at rest first from dawn to dusk. Have you made yourself in such a way that everything and everyone around you cannot help loving you? Man should be loved by man. Nation should be loved by nation. World should be loved by world. And ultimately existence is in love with the existence.

Make your life magical to understand the love of existence. The day everything in this existence is included within you is the day you are liberated.

A self-taught human is the ideal human. There will be unceremonious rejections in life for its own heights. Humanity is facing challenges to dismantle big egos. Humanity is working to strip the masks of immorality. Humanity is reshaping the styles of humans. Humanity is diving deep into the ideology of humans.

A weapon of peace is like the essential vitamins of the body. Without the proportionate vitamins the physical body depletes in strength before its actual decay time. Similarly the regular dose of Vitamins like honesty, integrity, loyalty, ethics, and truthfulness and so on are needed to control the mind, thoughts, feelings, actions, reactions, love and hatred of humans.

We speak of vitamin A, B, C, D, and K for the healthiness of the body. What about vitamin "H"? Where to get this? Yes, I am speaking of the vital vitamin "Humanity". Every human needs to possess some percentage of it.

I have prescribed a list of vitamins essential for learning, developing, growing, cultivating, mastering, reforming and transforming the human in us into ideal humans. A similar list can be prepared by the readers and implemented from dawn to dusk in their daily lives.

Vitamins	Human Improvement
A	Authenticity
B	Behavior
C	Credibility
D	Divinity
E	Ethics
F	Faithfulness
G	Generosity
H	Honesty
I	Integrity
J	Jolly
K	Kindness
L	Loyalty
M	Modesty
N	Nobility
O	Obedience
P	Purity
Q	Quietness
R	Righteousness
S	Sincerity
T	Truthfulness
U	Universality
V	Virtues
W	Worthiness
X	Xenophobia
Y	Youthfulness
Z	Zest

The above model is a list which can surely bring in desired changes in you provided you are committed to implement and follow it regularly. These vitamins if taken regularly by any human have the power to transform that individual human into the ideal human.

How to improve humans?

Men are to be built with these vitamins and minerals from dawn to dusk and the human environment physical, philosophical, societal, individual, national, global, spiritual, all need to be reflecting, radiating and absorbing humanity.

What is the real reason that people won't change? Is change literally hard? People are much more likely to act their way into a new way of thinking than to think their way into a new way of acting. A pack of "PAK"- Practice, Attitude and Knowledge is essential in forging yourself. The foremost thing is change from within from dawn to dusk.

Why men are egocentric? Why customer centricity is important? Every human is a customer to one another.

We are struggling hard in discovering our own facets. Why man has as many facets as he thinks? Today's humans should realize that we are now living in multicultural environment from dawn to dusk. Before we start to punish others let us be true to ourselves.

Being true to yourself is the beginning of the basics of humanity. Which self? We have many selves, depending on the roles that we play in life. We evolve and even transform ourselves with experience in new roles. How can you be true to a future self that is still uncertain and unformed?

Take a look at your "ACV"-Authenticity, Credibility and Values. ACV can help in changing yourself entirely. Make a habit of picking behavioral patterns for personal improvement from dawn to dusk. Ask yourself to change; change and you shall be becoming so.

What drives you in life has a lot to do with what thought you drive. Habit change takes the help of the tool " DPP"-Discipline, Patience and Practice". You should not feel like you are constantly trying to force yourself to do something you really do not want to do from dawn to dusk.

"You want to change 9 billion people in world. Have you ever thought that one is immediately available and it is you? If we all change by ourselves it may take only one billionth of a second to transform the entire world."

Summing Up & Exercises for Readers-Chapter V

- It is my sincere confession from the bottom of heart that our knowledge and awareness on world is inadequate.
- Only by knowing some few names, just glancing through the magazines and pouring down time watching television shows and browsing the internet from dawn to dusk you cannot become a man of wisdom.
- Try to differentiate between knowledge and information.
- Find out the practical way to know the lessons life teaches from dawn to dusk.
- Life is an open school for all of us. It is 24x7 formats. You may sleep the school never sleeps.
- Let us differentiate between information and knowledge, intellectuality and ability, attitude and reasoning.
- We have only ego with us. You have lot to do in the pursuit of humanity.
- Develop an instinct of the Researcher.
- You should start exploring and experiencing whatever good you want to master it.
- Curiosity is the mother of inventions and discoveries. The first and the foremost thing are to discover yourself.
- Now what shall be done to do this?
- Concentrate on this to find ways of reinventing yourself.

- You have to bring the shinning dawn in you. You have to be victorious. The world is not a place for cowards.
- Do not die with worry daily.
- Clarify your role and goal at the earliest. Later on neither the role nor the goal will be in your reach.
- You know very well that just by sitting you cannot become a champion. To become a champion you have to come to the arena of existence.
- Speak to the humans, earth, sky, nature, self, world, and universe and then you will witness the mysteries unfolding for you.
- Work with faith and you shall get bliss. Find ways to be peaceful. You gift peace, smile, cheer, joy to everybody unconditionally.

Chapter VI

INSPIRE TO EXCEL

Man is a born warrior

I begin with remembering the golden saying of Sir Albert Einstein, "Everybody is a genius. But if you judge a fish by its ability to climb a tree, it will live its whole life believing that it is stupid."

Man is born daily with the dawn to experience the new beginning. Let us keep taking birth daily with a new mission, vision, objectives and goals. Let your inspiration reach the heights of zenith. Do not rest even you reach the point of excellence.

Man is a born warrior. Fight for your dreams .You shall get it. Inspiration keeps the instinct alive. Feel your existence. It further enhances your spirit of living. Do not wait to waste time in perfectly setting a goal. How will be the end goal no one knows? What is important is you are on the journey of goal.

Keep moving and goal will reach you. Your journey always starts with the dream of the goal. Planning, organizing, directing, and implementing all follow the will of the man. First have the will of inspiration. Then this inspiration has the power to reach all the excellence of life. Move on and you will embrace it. Imagine the vastness of potential in you. Existence is infinite. So is the man's will.

Every day is a new canvas waiting to be colored by you. Go paint your dreams into reality. Every day is a new song waiting to be sung by you. Go sing your songs into reality. No one is stopping you; you alone have to make the move.

Man is like the "VIBGYOR", violet, indigo, blue, green, yellow, orange and red colors of the rainbow. The colors are the various faces of man. The different colors of rainbow emanate from the same light source. And this one light is the illumination in human seen through all the man on this earth.

Life is like a rainbow. It is beautified through the colors of existence. A blank paper becomes purposeful when it is filled with these colors. The golden yellowish rising dawn, the green landscape, the bluish and indigo sky, the snow white mountain, the violet daffodils hanging in the garden of spring, the reddish and grey shade of the setting dusk, captures the daily nature to activate our thoughts for the existence. Our aspirations may not be fulfilled each time but our experience of aspiring always and certainly transforms us.

Every man is unique.

Society should realize this uniqueness. Society should regain confidence; we can win, win, and win humanity. Every thought creates a force within, either good or bad. Our reactions are positive or negative, ugly or beautiful, appreciable or criticism, agreeable or unconformable, which is again an analysis of the individual's mind.

Life should not drift into the realms of fantasy.

Man has to balance among destiny, reality and fantasy.

Man's vision has two components, emotional and rational. Differences in humans is either by genetic or upbringing. It is going to stay forever. Whatever may be, one has to move on before you are finally perished. You should grow to excel outmost before you are declared decayed. You should swim all the oceans before you are drowned. You should fly across the world before you are lost in the heavens. You should live the life before it is lost in the darkness forever.

Everything in the world may not be as per your likes from dawn to dusk.

Dislikes are our limitations to understand the existence from all dimensions. Productivity is in the mind of labor not in the tools and resources. The efficiency of the work is based on the simplicity of the mind of the doer. A mind with production vision will always meet the mission and objective.

Management has no answer to the human behavior. Human behavior cannot be evaluated only by scientific means. Organizations have failed to understand the organizational behavior. Organization is the collective face of the humans. Good humans make good organization. Humans role as employer and employee in recent times have been much talked by different school of thoughts all over the world. It is humans with different roles for the same goal. Mapping of role to goal is again a matter of debatable subject. Is Man independent to decide it?

At times man desperately prays to the nature to look after his legacy. The continuation of legacy is also a matter of destiny. It is not necessary that a king's son will become the king. To become the prince is also the grace. A rich father may not bring to the poor son. A poor father may enjoy the riches of his son or daughter. A saint may be born to evil couples or either of them being evil. A saintly couple may be facing the torture of his son or her daughter from dawn to dusk. Though the family background is the field, yet the seeds inherited may not be of the parents always.

Life has its own ways.

The black couples are having white offspring's. The white children parents are black. So what you say about all this? These are no new findings. It is being again and again reemphasized so that the issue of humanity starts running in our veins as the blood of excellence beating from dawn to dusk.

Dawn to dusk is a struggle from tortures to fortunes. Man has to chase it, transform it, forge it, carve it, built it, construct it, obtain it, voice it, get it, move towards fortune and you shall get it. Tortures are the path ways to fortunes. It is runway to the flight of grace. It will take you to your destination of excellence. There are definitely limitations to man's resources. The qualities, abilities, thoughts, desires, views, perceptions, principles of a man are not only due to his or her parents. It appears they are linked to the individuals before the birth only.

A biological process of reproduction may not answer all the queries of man. Do you wish to live to lose? Engage all your clutches and gears to drive the engine of life. Do not wait to ride till you see the road of destiny. More and more is to be seen. Much is to be performed. Are you listening to me? Hear me, I am telling you, you can beat the world, but before that you have to defeat your illness of excelling. Do not wait till the dusk. Do it now, right now, at this very moment of dawn.

Your thoughts should not die before you. Hold it, protect it and achieve it. Ask yourself, what is not there in me? When you have nothing to lose, then why to fear? Believe me after all is lost, still you will be with your golden dreams.

Dreams never die. Ideals never die. Truth never dies. Values never die. Virtues never die. Nature never dies. Wisdom never dies. Grace never dies. Love never dies. Humanity never dies. Inspiration never dies. Spirit never dies. Soul never dies. Righteousness never dies. Goodness never dies. Never let your faith, trust and hope sink. If they are floating your life will float anywhere in the world. Try to become a winner of humanity, leader of humanity, reformer of humanity.

Will Man conquer nature? Dusk is a great blessing in disguise. It is not a bane but an equally gifted boon at par with dawn. The real eyes of vision need to embrace it with a foresight of horizon to understand the emergence of dawn into dusk.

Novelty in Humans

"You will never reach your destination if you stop and throw stones at every dog that barks", Winston Churchill.

The Prime Minister of United Kingdom was right. Man has become more or less like this animal. Man has been domesticating and petting this animal since civilization and sincerely taming it by beating and pampering it on laps.

Dog has known the weakness of man. Our novelties are just as the barking of dogs. We bark at home, public, streets, parties, gatherings, institutions, organizations, forums, summits, conferences, seminars, workshops, trainings, for nothing at the end from dawn to dusk. We are still with the dog's tail.

We wag it wherever we like and meticulously bark as called for with the predetermined manipulative mind to survive and manage the situations of life.

To go with the very old saying, "barking dogs do not bite", the society of today is simply wagging its tail to the humanity of world. We are surviving with this style of dog management concept. Only pleasing the owner rather than doing something for the owner.

How novel we are?

Let us answer it. Is there any nobility in our novelty?

Man should fall in love with spirit, heart, character, ethics, values, morals, ideals the essential ingredients for humanity.

All is in me. Till my basics are not clear, I experience the turbulence. I am here with life to sense, feel and touch my own manifestations. At times I float above all and sometimes I am beneath all. I wish to rule and then I have pleasure in surrendering. The quest keeps visiting me from dawn to dusk. All my goals are temporarily achieved to be permanently dissolved. But again I rise and rise; to reach the best in me is my struggle. If all is learnt where is the necessity of the book, but still learning, the essentiality of the book cannot be questioned. Similar is the living and life lived. Dare to rise and you shall never fall. The classroom of life is not only from dawn to dusk.

The University of Life never limits the years of learning. Every day is a new chapter in the books of life. Be a leader not to make followers but to see you can follow one of them. Strive to excel daily as perfection is limitless with no permanent milestone in life.

Productivity of the self is to be audited from dawn to dusk. Lost time can never, never ever be regained, it is lost forever. As you use the umbrella to protect yourself from the rain, so have a personal shield with firm determination to guard yourself against all deterrents in blocking your advancement towards perfection in living.

Keep flowing like the river without banking at the shores. Just as the purest form of water left stagnated contaminates for no further usage, is the case of the self not trying to perceive perfection from dawn to dusk.

Inspire to excel. All the energy to live is in you. Live a life such that even your graveyard keeps smiling from dawn to dusk. Let it be transformed to explore your potentials buried beneath the carpet of darkness. Do not trivially perish yourself for any invaluable reason to uphold the inspiration for a great living. The fire of inspiration can burn the jungle of desires unwontedly polluting the environment of life.

Action is life.

What worth is sitting and watching a football match rather than playing it? Life is an open playground. Be an optimistic performer not a spectator. Life is for rewarding performers not unproductive watchers. One who acts is living. Get to know what more and more you can do. Make a habit of sincere doing and you shall keep invariably winning. Heartless greetings are worse than abuses.

Defeats are not to be defended by cursing competitors. Be brave to challenge the fortune. Bridges are built by Man to unite the lands separated by rivers created by nature. Swim to the surface weightless rather than sinking with over burden of ego. Ask from within, did I help anyone today? Were my services beneficial to at least one single person? Did one man become happy because of me from dawn to dusk? Could you wipe the tears of at least one man? Did you do something for yourself?

Knowledge unshared is as good as garbage in dustbin. Start reaching to as many brains as you can. No one stops the pure air from inhaling. A thought is the beginning of anything. Let it sprout in you from dawn to dusk. Extend your heart to the needy.

We all are beggars of love in this world. Leave the nest of insecurity. The lap of Universe is as big as your thought. Is it possible to dispel misfortune from our existence? How to fight against a seemingly negative fate?

All of us do not have equal fortunes. But we all have an equal opportunity to develop our talents. Time given to us is to explore. How all can explore one thing? The need of the existence may not be to only physically exist. Perhaps it urges man to go little bit beyond the boundary of realization. The constraints may not be always in the mind. It remains as seed because of the delayed monsoon of eagerness to germinate.

Bring monsoons of eagerness in your life. Quench your quest today to be ready with another quest tomorrow. The more quests the better development of the self from dawn to dusk. Work towards growth and you shall get your goals.

This is, believe me my friends the greatest of all opportunities to man, that he is gifted with time to see his reflection of the self in the mirror of dawn to dusk. Moods are swings of mind. It is intrinsically dynamic and likes to vibrate throughout the Universe.

At times, we feel, all is known to us, but again within no time, we realize, what has been learnt needs immediate revision. This is the power of thinking. It rules the life. It dictates the happenings. It is the lava of knowledge yet to be exploded in the volcano of man.

Idealism is not to be idle.

Keep doing something. During the process a new learning springs. It promises growth despite confusion and goals. Initial results are primary evaluations for correcting your actions. Neither good nor bad should influence you to stop your ability to deliver. Focus on attitude and it will build your aptitude. Have hunger to endeavor. Try not to give up and you shall persist with your endurance. The last breath you never know when it is going to come before you have breathed millions and millions of breathes.

Work from dawn to dusk to find the human in you. Sweat to enjoy the satisfaction of commitment. Pour your energy to reenergize your spirits of life. To know his limitations is the true knowledge of man. Remember those days when you were just beginning to crawl and walk the world. Despite falls now and then, you never gave up tumbling down and finally today, you have built yourself to walk miles and miles through the desert of life. It is this childish vigor that holds your biggest dream of life.

Cultivate the taste of success. Learn to win and you shall never fail. Tell yourself the biggest truth, if you fail all will fail. Eyes are given to us in front to march ahead not to look back. What use is your shadow of? It only follows you. Be brave to dare the life. Get something out of it. Upside down, churn it, dazzle it, beat it, heat it, embrace it, love it, somehow do not leave it, it has so many things for all of us, patiently urge for it, and it will follow you. It is like the magnetism, be in the electro motive force of life. The push and pull from dawn to dusk is to electrify your existence.

<u>Wings of Existence</u>

Dreams are the wings of exploration. Man should fling it to the outmost. Do not worry about the trajectory of flight. It will be guided by the draft of faith and hope. There is no other supreme power as the power of self confidence. It is your latent energy to be utilized without the supplementation of sensible heat for the purpose of existence. Small efforts towards realizing your goals may work out wonders. Any big reaction like the Big Bang was result of an initial explosion.

Keep moving bit by bit. Needless to say, the electronics revolution is the outcome of primarily application of two binary digits 0 and 1. When limited combinations of 0 and 1 could revolutionize the world into cyber village, and then think what the unlimited permutations and combinations of the brains could bring to the Universe.

Perspiration without inspiration and aspiration is like body without enthusiasm of life. It hardly synchronizes with the objective of thrive in living. One should be living to thrive from dawn to dusk. An inspired man dares to ride all adversities. It is the inner strength activated to face the challenges of life.

Life should have timeline. Time is the essence of life. An exercise for all of us, rearrange the word "LATENT", what did you get, hopefully and rightly, yes readers it is "TALENT". It is latent in all of us. It needs to be exposed by sharpening the intellect. This when picks up momentum can accelerate you to explore faster than the speed of light.

Every day is a dream of the lord.

The almighty is trying to come out with best dawns and dusks for man to experience the eternity. To know myself better I have to read my anatomy of existence. One thing what we have to understand is that no sufferings is because of any man. It is not that god is credited for all happiness and man is discredited for sufferings. Our senses are the accessories which run the body. Our will decides our way. Our habits develop our culture. Our society builds our nation.

Mind can be cleaned only by spirituality from dawn to dusk.

As science is exploring technologies, management is optimizing efficiencies, spirituality is redefining humanity. I have to know my framework before I question the structure of others. The structure keeps on redefining its elements with the maturity of mind. The journey of mind is parallel to the journey of life. Life, mind and body needs to excel day by day from dawn to dusk. Something which is not in my favor must not be wrongly coined as an adversity.

We should not hate the fate. It has its own way of giving. Never rate a fate. Do not be late for fate. It only adds to become unnecessary haste. Never waste time in the umbrella of fate. It is good to start early with faith rather than banking on the fate. Compromise is not the sign of defeat. However, it should not be the reason to stop the search for abundance.

One should dream beyond the limits of perfection. The little grass hardly gets uprooted by the wild storms. The giant trees sometimes are withered even by the gentle breeze. This is the law of nature. No one is big or no one is small. All have unique characteristics by the nature. The nature teaches us the first lessons of inspiration. It is home to all. Living and non-living are under the same roof. Man on earth has been seeing moon for centuries after centuries to ultimately discover it in the Universe.

Self-purification is the true agenda of this century. The human capital since civilization is being managed from dawn to dusk. All should pray for the well being of the world and exhort that peace should prevail upon the earth and the Universe.

We have all the military in the world but then why the terrorism is still continuing? It may not be always for the wrong motives. The dignity of humans itself has made them to quarrel among themselves.

Man has to abolish the raw methods of living. Let man relight himself for the cause of humanity. Man is child of infinite, the all powerful divine mother. Man's worldliness should be only holiness. Why man is radicalizing other man?

My dear readers the only project we are lagging behind is

"Let hell become heaven".

Life is a project.

We are all into it. World is the arena. Man is the constructor. Humanity is the beneficiary. Knowledge is the tool. Dawn is the gateway. Dusk is the lessons. Nature is the protector. Man's aim is to kill evil. Man is at war with humanity. Ethics and ideals are to be strongly bonded. Values and quality are to be the basic ingredients. Tears are to be removed. Cheers are to be restored.

Chaos is to be demolished. Humanity is to be won. A new dawn is to be established in the world.

I feel to share this for the benefits of my readers as to how you can cultivate the quality of ownership and at the same time really do not own the possession. This is from the leaf of my long career in constructing projects for various core and infra sectors in the country for government, public as well as private customers.

Never perform for appreciation. Never sacrifice for acknowledgement. Never criticize for fame. Look towards owning it for the self. Never have conditional commitments. Never work towards succeeding without integrity. Never lack loyalty. Ultimately work for the central theme of humanity from dawn to dusk.

Inspiration is your energy do not drain it for others consent. Do not wait till your perception is vetted by others. Charity, mercy and sympathy are the unwanted limbs for developing an incredible life. Are you here to live for others? To live for the self? To live for whom? Is there any clarity on subject?

How can cheers of others bring happiness to you? To experience it you have to smile. No one can, ever die your death. You have to courageously fight your battle of life. Wisdom should be harvested to remove the weeds of foolishness.

Reaping the Grace

Tame yourself not to be influenced by others if you are not adding value to the living. The epidemic only has the potential to ruin your ability to excel. Just by having the trunk of elephant you cannot ravage the jungle of fear. Your faith in it should shake the whole world. Sprinting away from these harmless pains may not prepare you for the huge goals.

Every Dawn to Dusk should make you stronger day by day.

It may not be easy to keep inspiring under all odds but the institution in you should not stop. The bell of prayer is ringing in all hearts but few are being graced.

Look for every opportunity to seek the grace. Smell it and run to gather it. Who is responsible for the sufferings and happiness always existing throughout the world at any point of time? An empirical approach may not resolve this query? It needs a spiritual tool to measure the reality.

Can I buy happiness?

Can I sell sufferings? Neither of the two in true sense has a market place. All your money has no power to purchase the non materialistic essentials of life. It is altogether a domain of faith, trust, hope and love. Is it only a state of mind? The experience is the real truth. The time is the greatest witness.

The tears of realization can only wash the misery of mind. This will buoyant you to the surface of existence. The self floats above the world. Though all the drains of the world drain into the ocean, yet it never loses its identity of purity. The Ultimate truth to be witnessed, source and the sink are same.

The Philosophy which I have analyzed is,

"Dawn rises to set in Dusk and Dusk sets in to rise in Dawn".

Can Human buy Grace? Who will give us grace?

It is only through grace that you can sail with resistance. Is there end to solutions? Try to convert all your frustrations into peace. Observe the calmness of the self. Keep migrating within again and again. Cheating and manipulations are shortcuts to lower grade of survival.

Quality of life is the crux of the existence. Are Humans becoming unreliable? Reliability is to be restored. The volcano of righteousness should erupt to eradicate the cruelty in humans. Why Man is both humble and cruel? Man intrinsically tosses both to meet the demands of survival. Life is an opportunity.

God's vision is man's excellence.

How it will be revealed to man about his life? God knows, we see a lot of desperate cases every day, but few are as moving towards appreciable resolution from dawn to dusk. Many times we have to deal with one problem after another for much too long. Despite all our efforts, we may never be able to get things back on an even keel.

On the contrary, our situation just keeps getting worse, as if something or someone were conspiring against us. No one ever comes along to offer us a helping hand. We always have to face adversity on our own, even when it is ferocious.

But despite our difficult destiny, we should never give up.

We all have a pure heart and let us never resent those who watch us struggle with their hands in their pockets, doing nothing to help. You should never hurt anyone, even in your darkest moments, when you thought you'd reached the end of your rope. It's this courage and purity-of-soul that we should admire most in us.

Human- Cycle of Grace

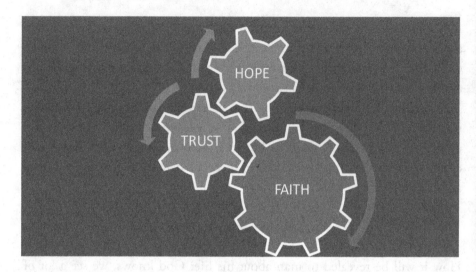

Man's Cycle of Grace is very essential to run the mechanism of humanity. All the three are required to be in motion in man's life to reap the benefits of the grace.

Imaginations to Champions

"Education is the most powerful weapon which you can use to change the world," has been very well practiced by the great revolutionist of recent times Nelson Mandela.

The International Literacy Day is celebrated on 8th September to highlight the importance of literacy to individuals, communities and societies.

Literacy for peace is to be implemented throughout the world.

In reality the governments of nations are at war rather than the people of the country are the opinion of majority of citizens all over the world. Today our citizens are from the pool of wisdom. They very well understand governance and politics. Why humanity should pay the price for instability of the world?

Is Will of the government not the will of the people? Any Government is by majority only. The representatives of the people have the power of veto to any bill, law, policy and other ordinances to bring it in force. We need not wonder to ponder on this issue that there is hardly any bill debated discussed and vetted in public rather than the four walls of parliament.

The minds of massive population are reduced to mere handful of people in the real process of implementation. I am no where challenging the style of governance but perhaps this is bitter reality and agony of the citizens of any country.

Few minds decide the future of million minds.

The population suffers the bane of decisions and at the mercy of constitutional transformation. The plutocracy cannot justify the fundamental rights of citizens. How man is to be ruled by man? Why man is to be ruled by man?

Man is bounded by the law of the land. Society is bounded by the law of the land. Nation is bounded by the law of the land. The Law of the Land is invariably a barrier between the minds of man. A revolution all over the world is required. Now we should taper down the law of the land into universal law of the world.

Let there be only one law.

The law of nature, the law of universe, the law of earth, the law of existence, the law of life, the law of heart, the law of mind, the law of body, the law of man and the law of humans merge into only one the law of oneness.

Innocent citizens are sacrificing their lives for no wrong decisions of theirs. The integrity and loyalty of Representatives of the People has been in discussion in politics and government.

Transformation is essential at all levels of humans.

The whole human chain is to be revived from dawn to dusk. The literates need to uplift the illiterates. The sword of literacy has the power to eliminate the misery of man. It is literacy which can help you to differentiate and select your right thoughts, good actions, valued concepts, better perceptions, leading to overall transformation.

How much do we know about the world?

Do we have the will to really understand humanity in the world? Do we have the wings to go all round the world in pursuit of humanity? Do we have time to think over it? Do we have wisdom to understand the world?

Today, Man at the out most knows 1 Universe, 9 Planets, 204 Countries, 809 Islands, 7 Seas, and some under study. This is our world as known to everybody existing during this time. There are many theories and postulates under research and study.

One fine dawn human at earth will unfold similar earth which can sustain human life. More advanced or inferior humans than us are always a possibility till the truth has not been realized. Humans like us are living somewhere as we are at earth may best be known to the existence only.

One golden dawn may be our galaxy is blessed with a brother galaxy. The point to understand is that time is transforming. What will be the package for human tomorrow this can only be revealed by the time?

World is an arena of opportunity for man.

Where is such a huge stadium to play the game of humanity? Where is such a show ground to enact the drama of life? All the actors are to be healthy and happy for roaring with voice and dialogue delivery with spirit of action for humanity. This is the biggest ring to box out your energetic blows of humanity.

Disparity in literacy is a major concern and the prime cause of basic differences in humans. The world percentage of literacy is yet to be 100 per cent. Everything that happens in life has a cause and an effect, even if you don't always understand them.

The way our universe works is entirely dictated by the Law of Cosmic balance, which governs all our actions, down to the most minor events in our lives. You should know that it is possible to influence cosmic energy, and instigate the appearance of a specific event in the life of a designated person. What we need to do is that determine the precise nature and quantity of the cosmic vibrations we should channel into our destiny. Things are happening because of nature. Is there a flinch of hesitation?

Experience proves that our efforts are always crowned with success, and the people who benefit from these interventions always see huge changes take place in their life. The importance is directly connected to the transformation. Values of life should not be devalued for the simple reason that a change would have made the miracle. The greater the shine the harder is the rub.

*Rub yourself day in and out from dawn to dusk
till you achieve the spark of transformation.*

Becoming evil from good is easy as you are falling with the gravity. The challenge is in becoming good from evil as you are rising against the gravity. Do not gravitate yourself. Descending a hill is always easy. Falling down in life requires no additional effort.

Transformation is not a commodity it is a process.

Man cannot fix any price for it. One cannot escape the process to reach the zenith. Without the circle of life how can you understand the wheel of existence?

Destiny is at the door of every man.

The goodness is in the heart of every man. The kindness is in the heart of every man. The love is in the heart of every man. The freedom is in the mind of everyman. The action is in the hand of every man.

Life is like a bud, you never know what will bloom from within. When and how is also a matter of time and destiny? It may surprise you beyond your expectations. However, you have to hold on with the delicate petals of hope, till they show their numerous colors pink, yellow, blue, red, grey, purple, white, with different shades and mix, with different fragrance of nature.

The mind is to be periodically ironed to be straight otherwise wrinkles will remain forever. As the sting of a bee stimulates the whole body so literacy catalyses the overall personality of an individual.

This is in all humans. Every seed has the potential to be a giant tree of infinite dreams. Man has to only sow them and nourish. The rest is known to nature.

Nature is the giver of fortune.

All are his children of eternity. Give nature a chance to synchronize with you. Jump on to the good thoughts to see the goodness unfold in your life. Most of us are so engrossed in the survival mania that hardly we have time to see exactly what we are doing.

Will my present actions give me desired results? Some are fearlessly sleeping such that they have sold their horses forever. There are others toiling their lives worse than the donkeys without value of life. And some other men are passing the day like the oxen getting ploughed in the same field again and again.

Ask yourself now and then what you are doing? You should not throw away your precious share of life. Take it and live it to the highest pursuit of existence. Write, rewrite, rewrite, till you can to keep changing your destinies, till you have finally seen the ultimate destiny of your dreams.

Make yourself work towards it from dawn to dusk. Great is the soil manifesting too many forms to be with man in sustaining the life? Any game, sports, organization, association, institution, industry, project, society, committee, government, party, state, nation, are run on the team of men working together engaged to perform a specific task for a central goal.

Men from all lands, across all borders are working together directly or indirectly to achieve their collective goal. Let us visualize this, can the team have an individual goal for each player. This is what the existence is all about.

Existence has a goal and all men have their own goals. The whole drama is between and within these goals from dawn to dusk. However, all these individual goals are to merge with the universal goal. Similarly all manifestations are players of the team working for the universal goal.

A football match being played in England or Germany, what difference it makes to the real existence of the game. The basics are legs, football, nets, goal posts and the field. Of course the players are humans. The game principally has nothing to do with basics of humans except the kicks on the football. This is our point of discussion. Our focus is on game of life, not the identity of players.

Let us all be great players of this game of existence. Make it as exciting as you can. Let us immerse ourselves such that we are not aware of the time when the game was over. This is where there is no need of realization and liberation.

Man has been free, is free and will remain free forever. Man is to be baked from all sides, if you want to be the eatable bread of life. This baking is done in the oven of adversity. Adversity has the heat of reformation more vibrant than the prime forgone opportunity.

Adversity is the greatest of all the banes on this earth. It is the golden boon for man to shine like the moon. Keep giving room to adversities so that the home of dreams will never be demolished in your life. One after the other is an indirect solution not a problem as you invariably perceive.

Without darkness the importance of light is never felt. It is the time to understand the value you hold within yourself as human on this earth. This is the simplest of task we need to do first.

It has been ages we have been educated but still lagging behind in transforming ourselves towards the truth. This is the need of the present century.

How to transform yourself?

Once educated it should be implemented. The irony is we are far away from the reality. The manipulation and exploitation among men is not ceasing. Do you think our society is not educated? The advancement in science and technology, modernized living, better infrastructures, facilities and amenities, prosperity and abundance, substantial industrial growth, manufacturing and commodities, networking and communication, mechanized and automations speak of man's progress in life. This definitely is better than the times man was living in caves. The destructions of nations when at war go beyond understanding of humanity.

Everybody thinks that the other person's life is easy. Everybody thinks that the other person is bad. We think wrong to beget wrong ultimately. Give the other person patience to understand your faith in him. Allow him to understand your concern for him. Trust his will to help you. Wait with hope to receive his love.

Education is to transform ourselves.

This is a tool in the hands of society. Man is the beneficiary from any dimensions of implementation. The power of persistence and persuasion is to be primarily implemented in transforming the self. Time is like ice, after the ice melts, its effect is lost. Life is such series of time, not to be lost like the ice. Man should look into availability and utilization of time. The time put in by individual towards their pursuit shall definitely be rewarded.

Literacy is mightier than the sword.

Literacy has the power to kill all the evils of the world. Literacy has the heat to melt the ego of the world. Literacy is manure to the thought. It can grow your idea and develop beyond imagination.

Man is to be iteratively liberated from ignorance through literacy.

Literacy is the tool to transform the understanding of society from dawn to dusk.

Finally a Human

"Keep away from people who try to belittle your ambitions. Small people always do that, but the really great make you feel that you, too, can become great." was rightly advocated by Mark Twain.

He emphasized that; secret to getting ahead is getting started.

Take the immediate DAWN today to explore your ambitions. Do whatever you can to finally become a HUMAN.

Have a greater will to start. Have a bigger will to do big. Have a hearty will to love the world. Have a braver will to fight evils. Have a tough will to endure. Have a will to be finally human.

Man has to start to become human. Never stop learning, transforming, innovating, excelling, thinking, sharing, guiding, teaching, inventing, discovering, making, thriving, encouraging, helping, cheering, dreaming, praying, and keep moving on and on.

If you really want to be lazy and at the same time worthy of your act then stop killing, betraying, cheating, abusing, fighting, molesting, assaulting, robbing, teasing, criticizing, manipulating, deceiving, bombing, radicalizing, discriminating, exploiting, embarrassing, threatening, murdering, sinning, lusting, torturing, and many more not favoring humanity.

Till you are moving you are finding the human in you. The true characteristics of human are from the different characters of man which we are seeing today.

Who I am today? Am I the way god made me? Why friends are turning into strangers? Why people are annoying? Why public is not safe? Why nations are at war? Today is being witnessed by us as the most transforming point in the history of humanity. Today is the time to reform. Without our will how can garbage fill our minds?

What you allow is what will continue. You do not want to see the dawn in you. Then who can do it for you. To start over again and again we have to be willing to fail again and again. Accept the defeat to fight for victory. Let your inner world be full of purity so that when it reflects it gives the same purity to the outer world.

I am sharing it for the hidden meaning in this riddle,

"One tree makes a million match sticks, only one match stick needed to burn a million tress."

The question is what shall we become, a match stick or a tree.

The theory of evolution was debated, is debated and will always be debated. Presumption is that our gradual evolution from ape and monkey had been over a prolonged period of time into the existing form. We have been existing in this form for the past 5000 years and more, with no significant changes in physical structure and biological system. As there had been no changes in us for over 5000 years, so there should not be any changes down the years to come.

A plant cannot become an animal and man cannot become a tree from dawn to dusk. A fox is similar in nature to dog, can this be a case of an evolution. A tiger from the family of cats is also a possibility. Goat and sheep might have evolved from one and the other. Is shark an advance form of small fish or an identity of its own? Did the horse take over the donkey? Was chimpanzee ahead of monkey?

In my opinion, if evolution is a continuous process, then the changes in forms as proposed by theories should continue to take place. It is not out of place to mention that why then the elephant cannot climb and jump on the trees as monkeys do?

The endless point of discussion, is there a demarcation between evolution and manifestation? Will the future human have only one leg, one hand, one eye, one ear and one brain, to advocate the optimization of organs and limbs in regard to the efficiency in evolution of humans? If in 5000 years, man remained with two legs and two hands, then for the coming 10,000 years, and 100,000 years man would be as he is today. Any doubt about it. It is unfortunate for all men of today to conclude what we will look like in future. The grace is with those men yet to invade the existence.

Irrespective of the philosophies, theology, ideologies, psychology, diversities, cultures, traditions, history, man continues as human of existence. It is the principal form of life to understand the other lives of plants and animals.

Is civilization progress?

Does it impact the quality of our plant's life? It is broadly the life of plants, animals and humans. Who to rank as the essential attribute of existence? No one is complete without the other. Is it that plants and animals are sustaining human life? Nature has balanced manifestation equally to support the life of plants, animals and humans.

Humans have to play the central role between plants and animals from dawn to dusk. Both plants and animals are equally important to sustain human life. Were plants, animals and humans not planned for the experience of existence? All rises from the earth to go back into the earth. It is the source as well as the sink to absorb both the construction and destruction. And again both life and death are from and into it.

Humans are not only for humans from dawn to dusk. Human have broader responsibility beyond humanity. Humans have to protect the plants and animals. As the plants and animals have been doing for the humans. The life in totality means plants, animals and humans on this planet of destiny.

Human quest for planets that can sustain life increases day by day. Will man find a similar earth? When will real understanding of the universe finally dawn? The search for existence never ceases from dawn to dusk. This is absolutely inherent characteristics of life.

Let us review the perception on the "HILL". Our will should be rigid, hard, tough, strong, heavy, giant, and huge, like the hill when it comes to yielding down to bad activities. Our will should be soft, light, easy, and flexible, not rigid like the hill when it comes to melting down of heart towards regenerating humanity.

So you can see that the "HILL" is taken as a moral for one good activity and not considered for bad activity at the same time for reference by man. Man lives in comparative world. Man lives in relativity. He by birth is born to compare, contradict, compete, compromise and challenges the world.

If you are thinking BIG, then you are definitely becoming BIG. No one is going to lead you. You have to be your own leader. You have to become the leader of change. Time never waits for anyone, neither leader nor follower or scavengers. It is a universal resource equal to all living organisms in this universe.

Man has to work out his gaps. Man has to map these to the right choices from dawn to dusk. The law of attraction states like will attract like type of things, good will attract good things, better people will make better community, knowledgeable men will make intellectual community, loving humans will form lovable society, divine spirits make spiritual community.

Learn and Teach from dawn to dusk. At times you are teacher to many and at times you are a student at the feet of your teacher. Anyone can learn from and teach to anyone as per the law of learning in life. Every human is so blessed by the law of existence.

Explore and evolve from dawn to dusk. Both the inner and outer world of man thus progresses towards the perfection of life.

That which is lovable is certainly going to be an additional drop in the ocean of humanity. The rate of inhumanity is to be overcome by making it up at a faster rate of humanity. It is true that much of our pain is because of our choice in living, perception, reasoning, assumptions, and understandings and so on in regard to complete living. Our circle of life has different radiuses at different point of time on the circumference of life.

The best part of learning, taming, practicing is to place our peaks and troughs above the zero baseline. We should always ensure our trend is not beyond the base line and falling towards negativity zone. Whatever may be the rise in negative quadrant of life, it is going to remain negative gain only for any human in this world. At the same an inch of rise in the positive quadrant is going to be eternal throughout your life in uplifting your morals and ideals.

Never try to fall once you have risen above the average baseline in your own pursuit of ideal life.

Every day is a way towards regenerating humanity in us.

Keep the novelty alive in you. You have the infinite power to revolutionize humanity on earth. It is only your will, your will which can bring in enormous changes from dawn to dusk.

Little thoughts make little people. Small thoughts make small people. They do nothing marginally appreciable and contributable to the life what has been given to them. Little people live with jealousy envying the big people achieving and living better. Big people are not robbing anyone's career from the little people. They are focused, determined, disciplined, ethical, loyal, punctual, worthy, ideal and sincere towards the goals of life from dawn to dusk. Why some men are becoming little? Why some men are becoming small? Why some men are becoming big?

Every man has to ask himself?

Human should have bondage with humanity. Little, small and big all have to focus on humanity. That is the final goal of all religions, cultures, doctrines, teachings, philosophies, practices, all over the world.

Thus Dawn to Dusk summaries to finally become a human. What is the path to becoming human? Who will make us those great humans? It may not be anyone except you and only you?

Self- Filtration of Negatives

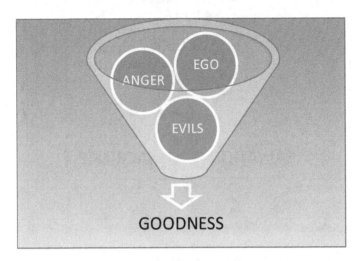

Unless man starts working on the self-filtration process how the negatives of the humans can be removed forever.

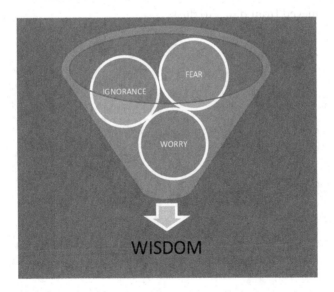

Wisdom is attained if the fear, ignorance and worry are removed from any person. These are the unwanted basics for optimism in any individual. Wisdom is the daily tool to guide you for a right living from dawn to dusk.

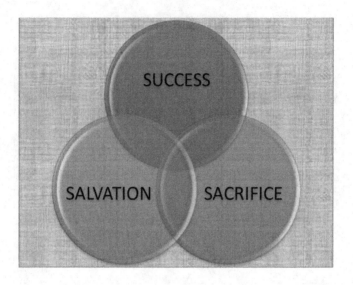

The overlap of success, sacrifice and salvation is very instrumental in finally making a human the world is struggling to create. Human should have something to sacrifice. He can only do it when his containment has been primarily achieved from dawn to dusk.

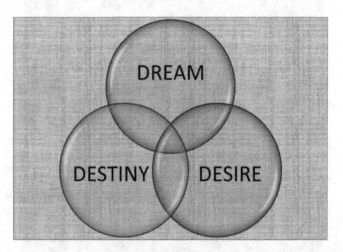

All are never fulfilled at a time for any human. If so then that human is the rarest of the rare blessed with divine grace. The practical reality for humans is totally different in existence. I request my readers to kindly work out their overlapping areas of dream, desire and destiny. Dream and desires are more or less the wish or proposal of the ever wanting human while destiny is the disposal to man as gift of existence.

The other complexity is arrived when the basic needs intervene into the respective circles of dream, destiny and desire. The human approach is bound to be influenced by these spheres.

The intruder need takes dominance over the others as per the situation, crisis, environmental, urgency, feasibility, applicability, availability, intellectuality, reasoning, wisdom, and so on. To summarize need is answer to questions of survival from dawn to dusk.

How do you fulfill your needs is again depending on the type of work you do. Every activity directly or indirectly is connected to the economy. The path, ways, actions, deeds, and the doer are linked to one another from dawn to dusk.

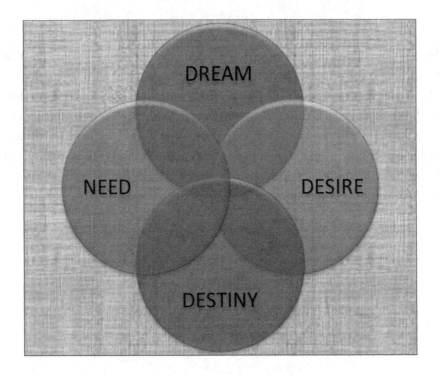

Human is in between the spheres of dawn and dusk. Every day he has to struggle, fight, learn, tame, direct, lead, counsel, compromise, dominate, retreat, innovate, discover, initiate, associate, and so on for survival, success, living and excelling within the limitations of humanity.

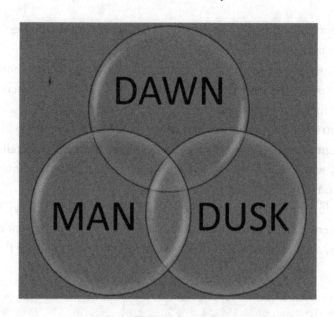

Man is categorized into various people based on their perception of life. The perception is the primary dawn for any human towards his glowing or gloomy life. If you have picked up the secrets of glowing then gloomy has been lost in the dusk forever. The differences in people are the result of differences in perceptions. To have harmony among people the healthiness and worthiness of the perception is very critical in the total approach towards humanity. All knowledge, learning, wisdom, knowhow, talent, education, and so on are unfruitful till the perception has been set right.

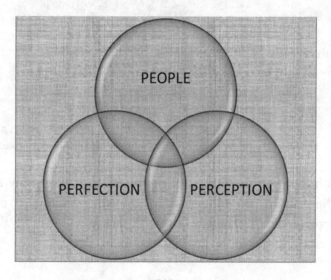

The sphere of perfection finally depends on the spheres of people and perception. The chain is linked to the talent, target and time. A right perception has to be further forged with inspiration and aspiration by the human talent. It is talent which will physically transform your perception into the planes of reality. It is here the human starts sensing his creation from dawn to dusk.

A feel of touch, a sense of achievement, a curiosity of innovation, an authority of ownership, and so on back and forth with your abilities, potentials, creativities, ideas, thoughts till you say no to perfection.

If you are not soiling yourself today then there may not be any moment waiting for your realization later. This is the time to play your all the ideas, thoughts, dreams, desires, inspirations towards excelling yourself from dawn to dusk.

Leaving aside the unavoidable overlaps of spheres man has to be present in the sphere of activities. This is the true worship. Keep yourself working irrespective of the desire of the fruit. Unless you do this you may not be putting your best trials of survival.

Dawn to Dusk is a time house. Everybody has been allotted equal time to work with their talent towards target. Humans with born talent may not be consuming much time in building their talents. Right from the dawn of birth they are productive and fall in line with the world target of humanity.

The rest have an equal opportunity to groom themselves keeping in mind the availability of time.

Time makes all the differences whoever he may be. There is no exception to the rule of time. Youth is the time for humans to make best use of the indomitable energy towards humanity. This is the time you can conquer the whole humanity. Tame yourself to perfection of ideal person the world is starving for.

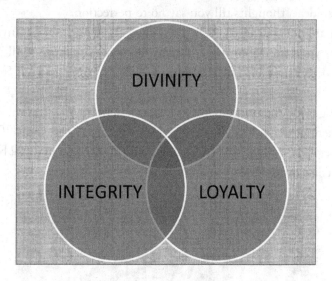

My dear readers take a look at this "DIL".

Divinity, Integrity and Loyalty
are the basic and fundamental spokes
of the Wheel of Humanity.

Do you have a "DIL"? Let us try generating as many "Wheel of Humanity "as possible. This wheel will do wonders. It will go throughout the world establishing the fundamentals of humanity and thus finally making humans in the world.

After the revolution of wheels the transportation sector could bring marvelous miracles in infrastructure of the world. Again it is time for a greatest revolution of all the greater revolutions put together so far to begin showing its power of miracles.

I believe from the bottom of my heart,

"This Century will certainly witness the Revolution of Humanity".

Summing Up & Exercise for Readers- Chapter –VI

- My dear readers though inspiration has no physical presence in life as material yet it makes enormous difference in humans physical living. The body has to perform physical activities from dawn to dusk. Inspiration is a source of positive energy to take care of your overall personality. It acts within you and the other world of yours.
- Are you taking care of your inspiration levels?
- How many times you go in depression in a day from dawn to dusk?
- Take some time out of your daily routine to work on it.
- Your concern is to inspire yourself to face the daily challenges and opportunities of life from dawn to dusk.
- You can be only graced if you are inspired to excel.
- We live more in the world of should. Avoid assuring to live in future. Live in present.
- In fact this should be done, that should be done, but in reality we end up in life with the pending list with summary of regrets and grievances. This is absolutely pathetic for all of us.
- Improper utilization of time, resources, guidance, fortunes, and graces many a times makes man to land in no man's land. When your spirits are down inspiration is the only medicine to revive you.
- Try to bring out the novelty in you.
- Enhance your skills and abilities to forge yourself as you would like to be.
- Try to become a painter, writer, architect, leader, coach, team member, reformer, humanist, preacher but not a criticizer, joker, traitor, criminal, fool, cheater, loafer, stupid, intruder, and any negative character.
- Work with inspiration to gain positive characters, values, morals, ideals and attitudes.

- Look into yourself where can you add the wings of inspiration.
- Thrill yourself with the energy of existence.
- This is how you can benefit from Part-III of this appealing essay on humanity.
- It is a petition to all of us to justify our lives.
- We have to cultivate the art of living within the ideals of existence.
- ***My dear readers make a note of it that, "Living within limitations of nature is not a weakness but is regard to the existence".***
- The more we practice it the perfection is witnessed.

PART IV
LEGACY OF MAN

Chapter VII

MAN IN ME

Man is having millions of faces

The renowned Russian thinker, Nicholas Roerich said, "Every man, every member of the human family, carries the responsibility for the peace of the whole world."

If the world is in turmoil today, it is because its inhabitants are in turmoil.

World peace begins with each of us.

A Society is the summation of individuals. The values of a society are determined by its individuals. The force of inequality in society is to be kept in control from dawn to dusk. Who will do it? My mind gropes about in darkness. I cannot see where my duty lies?

Man cannot just jump to the absolute. He must evolve towards it. Man is bound to stray into pride, doubt and confusion. Man should not refuse to fight this righteous war. In doing so, he will be turning aside from his duty.

There are so many men in man. I have to know the man in me. Why I am not the same for long time? Why I am shifting my centers? Why I am not focusing on one philosophy? What makes me do so? In fact the readers may not be surprised to note this truth. We are weak in following one principle for life long. Why it so happens?

Man keeps himself changing.

Mind keeps swinging. Thoughts keep flirting. Ideas keep jumping. Instability is our inheritance. Man is searching stability in the outer world being instable in the inner world. There may not be any animal on earth more ridiculous than man. Perhaps our legacy of mystery will never end.

Man to Man the "Man in Me" is having millions of faces. All may not be in the dominant stage continuously. The turn comes one by one. One at a time is vibrant to suppress the others. At times man is depressed and the same man speaks of inspiration at another point of time. The man in me is foolish as well as intellectual. The man in me is mad for wealth and again one fine day patiently willing to sacrifice and liberate. The man blindly wishes power and finally quits embracing freedom. Why we hate the person with whom we fell in love? Why we fight the man we like most?

Unless the man in me is holy how can I be human?

What about my readers? How do they feel about men in them? Are the human in you alive? This needs to be searched by all of us. The making of the man in me is important to understand the inner as well as the outer world.

Humanity is not born today.

God is not born today. Man is not born today. Nothing is as of today which has just evolved out to disturb the world. Every time in history had its own rule of the game. Man is a natural improviser of life. Man aligns himself with nature and existence as and when required.

The question is how to bring the human face in man permanently dissolving the demon forever. This is to be done by man only. How Man will do it when he is prisoner to the evils of the world?

The cycle of influence on man is infinite from dawn to dusk. Man is moods. He is under the influence of his mind. No idea remains for long as the central idea. Man jumps like the monkey from one tree to another till the jungle of the world is not journeyed.

Why I am being harmed? Why I am being not trusted? Why I am being criticized? Why I am being exploited? Why I am being revenged? Why I am being disrespected? Why I am being disregarded? Why I am being not loved? Why I am being discriminated? Why I am being pained? Why I am suffering? Why I am being cursed?

Am I harming? Am I criticizing? Am I exploiting? Am I cursing? The problem is from both sides, in doing and being done on us. Hence it is imperative either you do or is done on you both will have the influencing and impacting effect on each other.

Man has to look into neither doing bad nor bad being done on you from dawn to dusk. This is the basic philosophy of non-violence. Not to harm and not to be harmed. Not to blame and not to be blamed. Not to assault and not to be assaulted. Not to betray and not to be betrayed. Practicing it daily you will be on way to humanity.

HUMAN- Cycle of Influence

The chain can be infinite. I sincerely wish that my readers keep drawing these cycles for understanding their influencing areas. The above has been attempted by the author to illustrate the impact of it on daily living of humans.

The impact of bad, sad, anger, enmity will result in making you in the direction you might have not intended yourself to go. By the time a new dawn befalls you might have walked miles in the dusty dusk. Then finally you may not have a point of return despite your learning, maturity, realization and all lessons inspiring you to change for betterment.

Wisdom delayed is loss of valuable life. Time is not with you. Time is with existence. Only doing things is not the purpose of such a divine and beautiful life. A simple task of becoming happy and making others happy appears to be a herculean feat for humans in the world. Are humans of today so weak to resist their own exploitation?

How man is resisting exploitation of man by man?

Life is a workbook. The more you work, the more you practice the exercises, the more you repeat the morals, the more you perfect your mathematics of life, the more you correct your balance sheet of time and success, the more you balance your sheet of goodness and badness, the better human you will be becoming.

Work with life. Live with humans. Live in humans. Generate cycles of positive influence. You become a source of influence. You radiate the society with your power of change. Work towards enlarging your workshop of humanity from dawn to dusk.

Let humans rush to your school of reformation. They are anxious to be transformed provided you embrace them. Develop a chain of reformation throughout the world. Let this chain join as many humans as it can. This chain of humanity is unbreakable and unshakable. It is the garland of humanity.

Move people from their boredoms. Move people from their nests. Move people from their cobwebs. This is a revolution for humanity. Let one and all march into it. It is a marathon. We can do it. We have everything to do our best except the attitude. Let the world build attitudes to change and then nothing is miracle.

My respected readers I am determined to say,

"Human attitude is the secret of winning over human's inhumanity. There is no other power to rule humanity".

Can man not fight his own war of humanity? Throw your fears and tears. March to meet the dears and cheers. Keep aside the joys and worries. Slice and dice the day out again and again. Live and learn from dawn to dusk. Share and teach from dawn to dusk. Human should be a good student sincerely attending his class works and submitting homework's on humanity. Do not stop the drive of cleaning inhumanity from the world till your last breath of life. Let us bring back the immunity of the world towards humanity. Utilize the resourceful world for the welfare of humankind.

We all should experience newness. Let us witness a complete freshness of secured freedom. Let the god in us live in this world. Let the spirit in us sing the songs of heavens. Let the soul salute humans.

Let the world witness the best humans of existence.

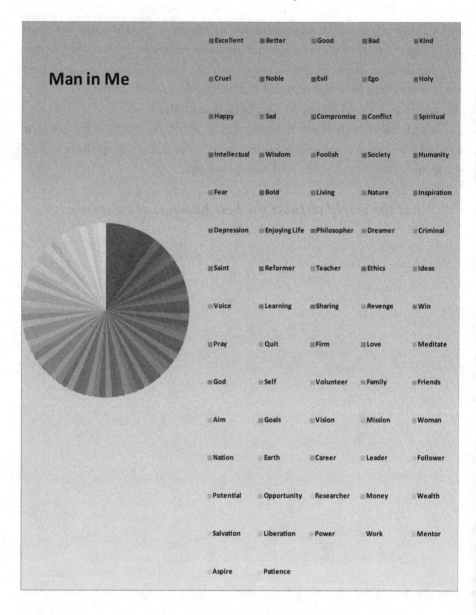

The pie chart above depicts a model showing probability of the nature of man in him. The list is not exhaustive.

Man has infinite facets.

The man in me may not have the same proportion of attributes, basics, tastes, likes, vision, mission, perception and goals. The complete circle of man in me is to be first minimized with only essential parameters. Then only you can concentrate, focus, direct, strengthen, the purpose of existence from dawn to dusk. This sphere of circle should have minimum sections with highest percentage. This is where the man in me is suffering right from the birth.

The man in me has great potential to deliver, the inherent ability in me is to lead, I do not understand the word of defeat, I am born to win, my visions are to dream beyond reality, still the man in me is struggling to understand god, the man in me is vibrant to conquer the nature, it wants to fight the suppressions through revolt, hates the discrimination of genders, has respect and regard for the woman, the man in me is filled with kindness and love, sometimes the jealousy and enmity visits me unknowingly, I wish to sacrifice, dedicate my life through work, be of help to mankind, the troubles of the society brings the turbulence in me, it erupts like volcano to eliminate the evils, at times depressed with the ambitions of the self, unintentionally due to my foolishness I have been hurting the man in me, despite it the man in me is humble to reform the society, and again it runs for the worldly pleasures to amass wealth for security, for the fear of starving the selfishness in me sometimes questions my own self, however the soul is not delinked from the chapters of spirituality, the mind wanders for peace and harmony, the ego in me clashes with my own reasons of intellectuality and wisdom, the meditation of the mind is blown away with the charms of the world, I continue to live and die daily again and again tearing apart and compressing into containment, it is only in the mind not in the possession of the world, I am surprised to see my own colors of rainbow, the darker clouds clout my inner vision making me thirsty for the rain of grace, they do not explode to clean my man in me.

It is like the shocks and the boots, the man in me is struggling with the clean shocks to be out of the dirty boots. The shinning boots with the torn shocks on your clean feet. This is the condition of man in me from dawn to dusk.

Dreams and reality are suffering because of the man in me.

The mind dreams for the man to make it into reality. The mind can make only a nonphysical existence of the things. Man has to bring it into existence. All actions are physical executions to realize the nonphysical perceptions driving the mind. In fact all the blue prints are shaped in the mind.

Why mind has been hunting man?

It throws you out of your skeleton. The complete anatomy is restructured. Man helplessly keeps taming it from dawn to dusk. Rather than controlling our man in us, we try to intervene in controlling the neighbor's man.

Man goes on to think through the mystery mind that even god is not perfect. How we would like him to create us? What features we should have? Our dissatisfaction needs to be addressed by him. Will man ever love god's creation? Is humanity suffering because of war between Man and God? Or is it because of the war between man and man? Or is it between the men in me? The purpose here is to look within for the reformation of the self.

Everyone can attain the highest sainthood. Why man runs between ecstasy and misery? None can have both at the same time in one. We have not evolved to throw our lives upon simply dressing to be nude in fashion, eating to be obsessed without appetite, drinking to lose consciousness, flirting to break disciplines, lusting to discriminate sanctity of love, wandering as hooligans, challenging the faith in almighty with cowardice heart and thus becoming the symbol of immoral day by day. Is this the man of today dreamt by the vision of existence?

Can idealism be realism?

Let us not live in subjectivity of the things. Objective philosophy has its own interpretation of man. How can we find the infinite in the finite? The higher is your ideal, the more miserable you are. No hypothesis is without conflict. The universe of respondents is finitely infinite. Every man is a universe of the existence.

Opportunism does not know the law of racism. However all cannot do all the work. At any give moment in time, we are what we are, and our action expresses that conditions. We cannot run away from our actions, because we carry the condition with us. We must turn at last to accept the consequences of being ourselves. Is nature of action in control of man? How to realize our true nature?

Impact of Human Genesis

Is being a human universal curse?

What the world will do knowing my origin? Is genesis of humans needed by humans? My man in me has yet to rise. Where is the man of existence? Where is the man of dawn? Why the man in me is crippling? When will this crawling stop?

Life wants freedom to live.

I want freedom to live. Despite the time gone, best known to history a Man of Man could not be seen by the existence of life. Is it not shame on all the civilizations to boast of humanity? When will the evolution of man reach perfection? Will our deepest desire to see the Man of our dreams be fulfilled?

> ## MAN rightly stands for Morale, Attitude and Nobility.

Why the ideal man should lose his decency? Let us boost our self-esteem from dawn to dusk. Do you really think there is impact of genesis on today's man? Does our origin matters to us? Who are we? Where did we come from? Are Asians not similar to Americans? How man can be different from man?

Man in me is the same man in you. The existence is entirely universal. Did we start evolving at same time at different places of origin around the globe? Or did we evolve at one place and migrated all over the world?

The Neolithic Revolution advocates independently flourishing civilizations at the same time. Graced are the mouth of Euphrates and Tigris, Nile valley, and Indus rivers to nourish the first known civilizations. Intrinsically do we differ among us? Keep debating, ultimately with no conclusion. Scientifically our biological system is same all over the Universe. Then where is the intellectuality of difference to keep questioning the enmity of survival. Why racism to hold the divine spirit of existence? The soul in everybody understands only the language of love, and only love.

Theory of evolution has its own empirical conclusions.

Every specie has inherent potential to evolve, survive, compete, discover, invent, explore, create, generate, demolish, etc, what not; an infinite list of probabilities, Man can do wonders. Why human beings do exists? To answer this man has to journey within his own existence. Why earth has been the only planet suitable for human existence, till now as known to man? The earth is worshipped as goddess for giving life and sustaining living.

Is Man working to establish the Society of Humans? Man started creating small centers of his own existence. It expanded over time to be followed as cultures by the invading generations. Again and again the doctrines were redefined to meet the needs of time rather than postulates of the individuals. Every civilization has witnessed followers and betrayers equally for their best analysis and reasoning known to them.

A decision taken 150,000 years ago or in 5000 BC or even 500 AD or in 1500 AD cannot be presently stimulated to understand the consequences today. History has its own limitations. Time has its own reasoning. Man has his own limitations. Demographics keep changing now and then. Existence today is the result of existence sustained yesterday. One manifestation leads to another and so on.

However, the core of the seed universally speaks the indifferences of individuals. All reforms and restructuring of the self is to know the self. Diversities, differences, disparities, and divergences have been still remaining with man despite the revolutionary periods time has experienced in history of existence.

How to turnaround our lives?

Great happiness awaits all of us.

Views, opinions, analysis, interpretations, perceptions, advices, speeches, suggestions, theories, philosophies, sciences, psychology, thinking's, of man cannot be free from conflicts. This is the beginning of democracy in humans.

Democracy is always home to diversities for finding the excellence in the best. Without probability where are the chances of occurrences. Without evolution there is no exploration and without exploration there is no evolution.

Luck, fortune and happiness are the extra lifts of nature. It pushes you towards your objectives and goals. Faith, hope and trust are supported by these to endure your persistence of reaching destination of life. Man has become miserable like the chair anchored to the table. When will the freedom of man come in reality?

Man has two important phases of existence as young and then old. The young man is biologically robust and the old man is spiritually strong. The young is vibrant to explore and the old is realizing to liberate by sacrificing. The young knows the passion of success and the old wins by losing. The old is learned and the young is learning. Both of them are living at one point of time but with different responsibilities and objectives from dawn to dusk. It encompasses the ends of existence. The existence before birth and after death is mystery for one and all. The existence within this ends is what we are trying to speak of through enormous ways of living, astonishingly on the written paths of individual destinies.

Man keeps encountering man from dawn to dusk.

The transactions of living are based on many modes of survival and each with its importance in supply chain of living. Some Men among us are preachers of life and at the same time majority are the followers of practices. Few are intellectuals of queries pertaining to existence of life. Great numbers are dwelling in intoxication of ignorance from dawn to dusk.

Man needs man. Man needs woman. Woman needs man. Reach him. Be pure in approach. Hold him from dawn to dusk. Then only you can taste the purpose of life. Fools are better than wise as they do not know the art of human manipulation. Exploitation of Man by Man is not the law of nature. Hear the beats of hearts. It transmits the pulses of love. The human veins carry the wine of love. Share it to intoxicate the society with love.

Man should love Man from dawn to dusk. Woman should love man. Man should love woman. Woman should love woman. Man's differences are with the attributes of Man, not with the physical man. Rise to love. Help as many as you can.

Today is the day to do service and give. Do not doubt your actions. Be bold to hold the cause of humanity. Search for opportunities to be of use to man. The genesis of man is same for all men living to enact the purpose of existence. A negative should be washed to see the photo of life. Till we purify ourselves how can we see the god in us? The process of purification may not be same for all.

Man is busy for what. Please take some time not to just watch the proceedings of life from dawn to dusk, but to understand the gravity of existence. Sleeping away the golden time allocated is an unpardonable offence in the existence of living. Let us not be handicapped by the misnomers of pleasures. Do you think entertainment can alone free us from the realities of life? Diverting away from truth weakens your inherited strength to face the truth of existence. Truth is ball of fire which can explode everything.

The Creator might or may not have anticipated that his own creation Man would try to question him from dawn to dusk. Similarly Man is facing the challenges imposed by his produced machines.

Machines are replacing Man. The industries are running on automation. The horses have been replaced by bullet trains. The critical surgeries are being performed by robots. Man has landed on Moon and recently invaded Mars. The space has been discovered. The submarines have explored the life at sea bed. The progress from lighting by kerosene lamps to lighting the malls of today by LED electric lamps is the journey scientifically advanced by man.

Man is the creator of the auxiliary world.

He has been doing it night and day. You might have built skyscrapers to space jets but what have you built it in the inner world of yours? Give a serious thought to it from dawn to dusk. Is the outer world important than the inner world?

All the discussion, debate, argument, conflict, brainstorming, knowledge, wisdom is to regularly examine our inner world. Man has filled the gaps in nature equally with materials and machine. Man is trying to improve his standards of living.

Man is swinging between spiritual and material world. Indelible inventions and discoveries are being celebrated. Inspiring documentaries and plays are being scripted and staged. Motivational Books are being written to reach the prospective readers, to act as leaders for societal changes. Human Capital Management concepts are being flooded to upgrade the dignity of labor. E-Governance is being implemented to increase the efficiency of administration.

Universities are assisting researchers to capitalize the idea of innovation. Godly Saints are uplifting the devotion of disciples. Information Technology has been working smarter to shrink the world into a Global village. Be it art, science, literature, economics, politics, what not all are striving from Dawn to Dusk to complete the cycle of daily activity. There are many more in the pipeline from dawn to dusk towards attaining perfection and betterment.

Every civilization had contributed to this Universe. Man has been recreating the world. Man is progressively repainting the beauty of life.

Is Man competing with the Creator from dawn to dusk?

Will machines remove man completely? Where do you stand as an individual contributor to the whole process of formation? Have you effectively utilized your Dawn to Dusk? A weary mind is inattentive to learn the lessons of life. Living by sympathy is deterrent to the purpose of own existence. How to quantify your life? Where is the accountability? How to discharge your responsibilities? How many days were underutilized? Are you unable to command yourself? The energy in you is to be directed towards the attainment of your vision. Holding your mission should be the prime objective.

Man is mortal but invariably trying to seek immortality. Man is bounded and seeks complete freedom. The imperfect man keeps redefining his vision towards perfection. Is it misapprehensions or his ignorance? Why man moves up and down in search of life beyond death, for night beyond darkness, for joy beyond sorrow and so on? Our thoughts, words, deeds are the threads of the net which we throw round ourselves for good or evil. One has to lift his self by the self.

Man only can uphold man. Man only can withheld man. Will duality in man die? The common background of human life is the same old drama of smile and tear, hope and fear, love and hate, success and failure, enacted in the four consecutive stages of birth, growth, decay, and death. This underlines all the varying conditions of life –social, political, economic, cultural and racial.

The theory of life may change, the pattern of living may vary, yet the panorama of dualities persists. In spite of his hearts longing for unalloyed joy man cannot avoid suffering, in spite of his severe struggle for freedom he cannot escape bondage, in spite of his constant striving after good he cannot get rid of evil. This is the human situation that has prevailed throughout the past. Is it not that the same situation is prevailing today? Why so? Is this all that man has to live for? Is this the final fact of life? Is this the ultimate destiny of man? When man will get rid of this dual nature? Who is the dispenser of the fruits of action of all?

Good and evil are but different manifestations of one ideal existence.

The differences are in the degree of its manifestations. We have to rise from the lower to the higher manifestations and then go beyond both. From day to day every individual is shaping his own future by accumulating within himself the subtle impressions of his thoughts, words and deeds. Let us recognize our self as the self of all beings.

Man is miracle. Man is seeker of what? Is man in search of his own genesis? Dawn to dusk man wanders like a nomad. Man of today is important to the present existence. Say, my origin is either from Greece, Mesopotamia, or Harappa, what difference it makes to be man of attitude on this earth.

All actions are by attitudes. Man has to have attitude for the existence. Man needs to understand the manifestations. Now revolution in our attributes is prime important for establishing a commendable genesis for tomorrow's man. The day is not far, when all this will converge to a single global civilization.

Philosophy to Reality

George Bernard Shaw had shared with us,

"Progress is impossible without change, and those who cannot change their minds cannot change anything."

Mind changes man. Man can change mind. Man is as the mind. Both these axioms are unbeatable by the truth of existence. How mutually both are dependent on each other for the welfare of humanity? Man has to realize the reality through mind.

Man's journey from Apes to Humans imperatively speaks of the prime evolution of existence. Humans to robots evidently follow to confirm the power of human brains. Nature might have taken millions and millions of dawn to dusk of incremental change to get from the first complex cells to the sophisticated thinking machine that is the human brain. Were Apes unknown to the art of writing? Moreover biology defines human beings as animals.

Does human life have only meaning? What is the role of other animals in the theory of existence? What makes us human? Will you agree with me that the human intelligence was the greatest evolutionary shift in the history so far? Was existence simply an anonymous event? Is earth only perceived to be home for animals?

When did the idea of the higher force stem in humans? What is philosophy of the mind? Is there any relation between mind and world? How sense of self changes from dawn to dusk? Is the brain everything? How much do we understand about the life right now?

Do we know enough?

How will be the Universe after 1000 years from now? There is no end to these enduring questions. Probably the questionnaire of life keeps expanding with the advancement in exploration. Some of the discoveries and inventions were thought to answer the quest of humans but to the contrary they have become manifold queries.

Man has been assigned dawn to dusk to play his game of life. The arena is full of mystery and challenges. Man as student and Nature as teacher are in the school of existence. Enormous quotations about life have been formulated for the benefit of society. Which is the right way of life? What should be the meaning of life in true sense? How to classify between formal and informal philosophy of existence?

The human conditions have been regularly changing and the man's perception of life accordingly. Dialogues and discourses in this area have been of interest to learned scholars and researchers all over the world at any point of time capturing the dawn and dusk. The search for pursuit of truth still continues to haunt humans. Where to search the remains of life?

Just imagine, can two paintings of different painters be same. Can two authors write similarly? Can two orators address the public with same style, vigor and influence? Can the readers have the same interpretations on the similar subject? This is how the definition of life gets related to the diversity of thoughts. The view of existence is either inward or outward.

The whole summary is in between the ends of reality and illusion of life.

I like curd, you like milk. What is wrong? I am white, you are black. What is the difference? I pray to sky, you bow to earth. What will happen?

Had things been common between men? Then why worry till death? No one can hurt you. You are allowing the leech of destruction to demolish the ascent of living. Life is an independent entity. No one can rob it from you. Not easy to conclude that the downhill journey is easier than the uphill. It has its own lessons.

The Man's debate can run into volumes and volumes of chapters.

Do some issues really require a solution? We have been draining ourselves to straighten the dog's tail since ages, and still like clowns are continuing to do it. Do you think lessons were not learnt? Truth is, we have many other things to be undertaken. Our focus should shift to the greener pastures.

Freedom of expression should not be nipped in the bud.

How to come out from human dilemmas?

The exponents of critical philosophy also do not have any concrete or proven solutions. There are many contemporaries working towards a converging definition of life. Many believe that the God-centered views make the meaning of life more significant than the other principles. It is extremely difficult to categorize whether life has been meaningful or meaningless.

We enjoy worrying over the spilt milk. Sometimes our funniness doubts our own intellectual strengths. Not to confess, we keep dwelling in stupidity till the good time is swallowed by the pessimistic thinking. The reconciliation may not even marginally be setting things right. Man is stubborn to yield in time. Have you ever calculated the fruitful time you had was drained for nothing? If not do it today. And once you have done the analysis, I think again you will not repeat this blunder.

Time lost is life lost. Things are no doubt easy to tell but hard to follow. It is a continual process to rewind and remind the importance of utilizing time. Nothing is more unpardonable than the murdering of time.

Time is the essence of living.

Crying after the tears have poured does not make any justification for the mistakes you have done. The time of realization is to be advanced in order to benefit from the last ray of hope. Then certainly we can attain the happiness we deserve.

Have orchids of humanity.

Humanity is an imperishable fruit. Develop the appetite for it. Fill your hunger with the attitude of humanity. An idea is always willing to be independent. All the greater ideas lead to wisdom of life. Man may discover something better than the already discovered. But however, the sole purpose from dawn to dusk more or less of these ideas is towards a central nucleus holding all the orbits of existence. Expansion and contraction of existence is the universe and self respectively.

No land is bigger than the land itself. No man is greater than the man himself. No religion is greater than the religion itself. How can the earth be greater than the earth? Similarly think, universe greater than the universe itself. It is only possible when you are comparing. Where is the question of comparison? We are all one. Did the teaching from saints was for only few man? No, it has spread all over the world. Are not we learning from the nature?

All teaches humanity. They worship humanity. They pray humanity. Is universe for one man? Is nature for one man? Is earth for one man? Is air for one man? Every day is a new birth for all of us. This is an equal opportunity to clean ourselves to the perfection of purity. Man's greatest challenge is to establish equality everywhere. Man always biologically dies but never spiritually. Why the spiritual journey cannot be for everyone?

Man is serving Man from dawn to dusk.

Any activity involves man. Can anyone differ this? Either directly or indirectly we all are supporting each other to sustain the garland of Universe. Who is working for whom? We all are working for the existence. Another unanswered question is till when man has to work. Is it specific to the individual assignment? Where do we stand collectively today?

Man has been working since birth to attain what? Life is a series of questions and answers from dawn to dusk. Love every man. He is as you. The demarcation of work and worship is unattainable by man from dawn to dusk. Man is like man. Principally no one is servant and master. All the deeds and doo's are to discharge different responsibilities to perform the assignment of existence.

Life is an adventure from dawn to dusk. Imagination is the seed for primary inspiration. Dreams are the building blocks of existence. Man took a flight to discover the sky. Which is the basis for all life? I know one thing for certain that if we persist in our endeavor, we will be progressively elevating our own entity of existence. The perfect life is bound to bring incalculable merits to one and all though it keeps confronting many catastrophes. If the basics are clear, then where is the turbulence? Does the destiny of life dictate the process of living?

Why universe for humans? What is our role here? Who will answer it? Probably we all are brainstorming it from dawn to dusk. This is an indelible mystery of life. Whose idea is human? Everybody has fundamental right to express their feeling of existence.

Will philosophy discover the reality?

Man's conception of life has been continuously changing with the passage of time. Reality changes at different stages of growth by ceasing the unwanted obsession which no more holds the inner self. At some specific level everyone knows the highest truth.

Every individual can analyze and comprehend to the best of his ability and knowledge. Who is manipulating whom? This is a self disguising undefined complex equation with no known computational methods for absolute solution. Within the time frame dawn to dusk man has problems as well as solutions. Problems are issues of life and solutions are lessons of life.

Naturally man at times has been unintentionally compelled to adopt dual policy in order to sustain the basic survival needs and accordingly, equally at the spiritual plane of liberation. The goodness of one has been exploited by the other to gain advantage in the transaction of living. For most of them the physical existence is the prime reason for competing and for some resistance is the way of living. The coin of life has to show any of the one faces, it cannot keep rolling like the wheel forever.

Can you define dancing? I hope we all will agree that it has many ways. Any dancer can tune up the way he wishes. The philosophy of life is as good as dancing. The living is tuned to a particular set of ways .We all are dancing from dawn to dusk to synchronize with the rhythm of existence.

Human is both at war and love with human.

Can man not live without opposition? Opposition is an instinct to bring out the best in man. It is by nature and so will prevail. Opposition is an impulse to unfold the potentials of man. Is god helpless towards exploitation by humans? The basic characteristics of life in nature like land, water, air, soil, sand, minerals, fossils, aquatic, flora and fauna, hills, mountains, snow, glaciers, etc are more or less similar all over the earth where life is at its peak, known to man.

This it should be the prime reason for burning all the discriminations. There appears to be no standard operating procedure for living. However, a proven system may be amicable solution to the confusion of redefining. But again acceptability by individuals cannot be generalized. The feeling of satisfaction is a phenomenon of individual.

Collectively a society or community cannot express satisfaction or dissatisfaction as an individual.

The universality and individuality will always be at conflict because of their intrinsic nature. Individuality needs a massive explosion to expand to universality. Universality reflects the broader plane of existence. The journey from narrowness to broadness requires a disciplined approach to life from dawn to dusk. All individual thoughts, ideas, action, learning, perception and realization should converge to comprehend the Universe.

People not concerned, will ever be benefiting from the source? Without going to the pond, your conclusion that water is bad, may be proved wrong. The counseling of man by man is possible only understanding the true nature of man. Do not you think a subject of ridiculous debate, when no man is superior to another man?

All is revolving around the point of centre of ignorance. This point of centre man has to search within from dawn to dusk. Universe, earth, evolution, life, nature, man, faith, belief, almighty, trust, hope, religion, culture, heaven, hell, death, affection, mankind, humanity, society, family, love, sacrifice, help, kindness, humbleness, hospitality, identity, status, recognitions, ego, personality, power, democracy, capitalism, communism, humanism, nationalism, globalism, world, conservation, and so forth are the possible essential factors influencing man's perception of living.

Man keeps jumping from one to another. The tree of perception has several branches to hold on. Perception tends to keep changing with strategy of living. Principally you see the world, as you perceive it. Broadly the two worlds have been created by our own perception. Isn't that the theists and atheists are deriving two different perceptions of living from the same source. The crux of the basic understanding is that despite the perception you have established with your reasoning, living has to go on, till life in you is existing. Which is mattering living or perception?

Dawn to Dusk tries to understand the journey between life and death.

95 per cent of the work is done if the alignment of perception is nearer to the truth of existence. Where to find the perfect definition of perfection? The perception will follow the phases of life cycle. A matured perception of life is reflected only on completion of the lessons and realization chapters. It should not be misunderstood that realization is only for the sinners. No man is born sinner. He is not solely responsible for his sins. Sin cannot take place on own. It is the outcome between the source and sink.

Man is gift of god to nature. How can god make a sin man? Man has become sin. Dawn gives lessons and dusk shares realization. It is a tool to reconcile your life. But generally the problem is we always think we still have time. This casual approach has swallowed millions and millions nipping them in the bud. Do not be the next victim of time. Beat the time. Be ahead of time. Deliver before it is asked. Supply before it is demanded. Help before it is begged. Rise before you fall. Live before you die. Excel before you expire. Protect before it is lost.

Learn before you are gone. Sail humanity before it sinks. Save society before it is drowned. Work at dawn before it is dusk. Conserve before crisis befalls. Pray before you break. Rest before you are tired. Retire before you are redundant. Dance before the rains. Cheer before the party. Be happy before the happy birthday. Do not wait till auspicious time.

Every moment is green.
&
Graze it before it is grey.

Win the war before the fight. Life and time plays hide and sick with man. It will remain as long as the existence. Time is infinite. But for individual man it is finite. The eagerness, ambitiousness, instinct, desires, dreams, satisfaction, ego, success, passion, fortune, fate, destiny, achievement, etc keep floating and sinking in between the finite and infinite ends of time. At times the fear of losing, isolation, separation, loneliness, keeps dwelling the mind governing it to question his own philosophy of survival.

Every day a new thing crops up with several dimensions of analysis. The learned have an intrinsic tendency to impose and influence the unlearned. The ignorant are in two minds right from the beginning. Philosophy to reality is again at different levels of perception. A glad person sees the gladness in the world. A pessimistic is bound to be depressed more because of his attitude rather than the impact of the surroundings. We all are not new to history.

Everybody little or more from here and there are aware of the differences, discriminations, disparities, inequalities, arising now and then across the world. The basic element of cause is human.

Man's desires cannot be like the huge rock or mountain to standstill as it is. It is by nature the reactions are catalyzed. All the destructions caused are only the outcome of the instantly taken decisions without the chance of reconciliation in thinking towards humanity.

Man can be compared to pure water. Pure water is colorless, tasteless, and odorless. It is composed of hydrogen and oxygen only. But water becomes contaminated by the substances with which it comes into contact; it is not available for use in its pure state. Such is the case with man; he is purely made of body, mind and spirit. To some degree water can dissolve every naturally occurring substance on the earth. Because of this property, water has been termed as universal solvent. Similarly man is a universal solvent. As he comes in contact with earth his color starts changing. His contamination increases to the extent of realization.

Manifestations and incarnations are the prime elements of philosophy.

Man and nature are equally the principal elements in the reality of existence. How can man be pure? Why purity is dissolved? Man as solvent has to decide to what solute he requires to mix with for the sweet drink of humanity. The chemistry of man describes his ability to understand the concept of philosophy and reality.

<u>Quest for Survival</u>

Without quest search is incomplete.

Survival defines its own rules from dawn to dusk.

The flight of life cannot be on the runway for long. It has to take off to meet the challenges of sky. It seems that we are steering our life through the congested roads of survival. But the truth may be destiny is propelling us towards our destination. The tracks of life keep changing from dawn to dusk. But finally all converge to merge for unique cause existence. Life and time play hide and sick with man. It will remain as long as the existence. Time is infinite. But for individual it is finite.

Existence is between dawns to dusk.

Does life confines us to explore within its permutations and combinations, ever since universe might have been born, and similar is the story of other galaxies. It is surprising to note, as to why the magic humans, could not decode life, despite vast population of it nearly all over the world. Is that adding new alphabets was never thought of, or the necessity did not arise. We went on and on till today, managing with these limitations. Did we lack novelty? Or we had inborn limitations to further dramatize the existence through expressions.

Opportunities will develop if you take charge.

Ownership in every man is the need of the hour. You have to own things to hold it. First the will has to be there before the way. The will simply cannot follow the predefined way. Way can definitely be seen through the window of the will. Man should go on making wills first. Have as many wills you can. Then try mapping it with the ways. Rank it to optimally suit your survival. This is where your quest is bringing betterment in survival.

Let the process go on from dawn to dusk. Even the destiny starts mapping the way as per your will. Will has the power to overturn destiny. Nothing is final till you have given it up. Till you are going there is no end. Survival is not a check post to halt. It is the road to living. It is infinite. At no point of time the quest should close. It is the cause as well as the reason to the whole process of survival.

Life is a game. Games are played to be won. There is no result in any game as survived, surviving and will survive. Every individual is playing his game of life. He should win in his philosophy, perception, sacrifice, happiness, wellness and contribution in life. Survive to the supreme. Beat all the expectations arising in you. Attaining mere needs is not the quest for survival. Utilize the resources of will, body, mind, heart, spirit, time, earth, nature and universe. All are at your disposal and above all, your dreams to transform your survival.

Creator of the Universe was very much partial to gift humans with the power of speech. Voice is the reflection of the being. It holds the iceberg of mankind. The freedom of life is the language of heart.

Man's prayer has the warmth to melt the heart of God. Nature and Man are at the horizon of existence. Possibly everywhere the quest is to have union of all from dawn to dusk. A ripen fruit detaches from the bearing tree on its own. It leaves its source to meet the needy.

Man's greatest wealth is nature. It is an asset without individual ownership. Lord never made such legal documents before bringing us here. The gospel of the story reveals the universal truth from dawn to dusk. I am part of the nature and hence how I can sell it while being with it. Any moment the bodily presence is lost into the handful of ash. All are ashes holding the skeleton of existence.

Life and death are inseparable ends of the supply chain continuity from dawn to dusk. We are born to die. We die to be born. These are as old as the beginning of existence, hence why to doubt yourself. The mortal in you is eternal. We all are visitors to this Earth. Why then the question of possessiveness by man? Let the milk of life be churned again and again to get the cream of self at the surface of existence.

The world should be a single home to all. The concept of nationalization should dissolve into globalization. Liberalization should overrule the philosophy of religion. Humanism should redefine love for humans from dawn to dusk. Maturity of the Self should not be ruled by religion. The kingdom of cultures is the manifestations of living. Diversity is yet to give its best.

Oneness is the prime objective through various souls.

Each day from dawn to dusk is an opportunity to understand life through living it in various ways for all living beings on this earth, which unintentionally was mysteriously discovered by the species fighting the race of evolution as history puts its postulates to us to conclude between dawn to dusk. One which is gained at dawn is lost at dusk patiently to again germinate the seed of accomplishments. Man should not compete with another man.

Man has to compete with his self. Why man should be at conflict with another man.? Color your life as good as you can. Being alive is the greatest gift of nature. It is the opportunity to understand the existence. Always exist to quest the self. You should anxiously be curious about all the happenings within you. What could have been my purpose of living? Do I deserve this experience? Go deeper day by day into the depth of quest till the core is felt by the self.

Change is the only constant. Thoughts arise to fall in the ocean of life. Keep wandering till the mind gives up quest of life. Heat, dust, sweat, thirst, rain, storms, floods, let them come one by one, all the physical challenges should fail to uproot your inner quest of life. Moreover the poverty, richness, ownership, criticism, egoism, hatred, enmity, jealousy, cruelty, all and such supporting elements to draining of life should not influence your true nature at any point of time. They are temporary phases with permanent impacts making its way on retarding your inner progress of life.

Let your mind not collect this garbage to end up as dust bin of life. Move on without sacrificing the intrinsic nature of purity. Struggle does not mean to lose the basics for survival. Your life should not become a summary of regrets. Why to give scope to reconciliation, when it can be nipped in the bud.

Life is the greatest author.

It is an encyclopedia of the world available to one and all. The flow of chapters to individuals is an attempt by the nature to bring the tranquility of mind. The lessons of life are so designed that all the struggles as perceived earlier are nothing but the path of realization at the end.

Live for all .Joys and sorrows are all the banks of life. Not permanent to anchor you forever. Just like clouds are formed to pour as rains, the mind is given to flood the brains. Barriers are restrictions to growth. Keep expanding the self to encompass the Universe. Day by day add value to the self.

Admiration and criticism are the two facets of the same coin life, invariably tossed from dawn to dusk .Ridiculously the living souls are criticized and the dead souls are admired. The glory of your life is chanted only after you have departed from the world. You are known better to the world through your deeds rather than your name when you are amongst them. There is no escape from quest. Quest will never allow you to rest. It keeps visiting you for the best. The self tries to live the nest of life but the branches of attachment compel you to hang on without complete liberation.

Life itself is a greatest reward, understanding this; the desire to be recognized and acknowledged should be dissolved forever. No one, absolutely no one, not even yourself can claim to be architect of life, what we all have till existence in the physical form. It is through this body that all senses are activated to make the differences. Just think for a while, why are all of us here on this earth? This is home to billions and billions of species on land as well as in ocean. All we need to sustain life has been provided equally for everybody. The sun at dawn daily spreads its grace to each of us. The evening helps you to retire to regain the energy lost during the day at work. Everyone is being addressed from dawn to dusk.

Dawn to Dusk is an equal golden opportunity for all to explore the beauty of life. All whatever could be ours has been given to us by the nature. Humans should not be branded as beggars provided the containment of life keeps springing in us. Where is the question of misery? How worry makes home in our mind? Why we are at conflict with our own fellow beings from dawn to dusk? From dawn to dusk the war between destiny and the self never seems to die. Sometimes you are at peace absorbing all the turbulence and at times the determination to overcome trivial things is washed away by the wild flood of arrogance. At times you are humble to all. The very next dawn the enmity makes its way.

Why the hostility and meekness in me both exists? The sweetness of rise and sadness of fall from dawn to dusk is invariably being witnessed by the self. Nothing enables me to stop swinging like the pendulum. The self has no point of equilibrium. It is dynamic in nature and the inertia it holds from ages will propel it with greater momentum in future.

Where I am going?

It is beyond, far beyond the understanding of life. The anonymous journey never seems to end. Mysterious are the ways of existence. Unknown to known is the struggle from dawn to dusk. All that was assimilated awaits a new learning. Though the fallen leaves never go back to the branches, but a new leaf always springs from the same branch, provided the branch is held by the trunk of life.

The individuality is lost again and again to spring into the new chapters of life. The novelty thus begins to demolish your past. A new dawn altogether awaits you. And this journey never seems to end. One of the prime causes of any existence may be to have again a new existence. As the old skin shades away periodically to give way for the upcoming skin, similarly the process of thinking and action keeps dissolving the old to give birth to the new. One who dives deeper and deeper, experiences newer and newer definition of the self.

Life should be assertive. Complacency restricts your force of aggressiveness. Self-satisfaction is a state of mind. As Life is an ongoing process the quest of survival also shall continue to exist with you forever. No one, no one can bury it. It will keep sprouting with new dimensions again and again from dawn to dusk.

What should be my choice of living? How to earn for living? The earning process is again a matter of concern. It has to map with your skills. Does it meet your daily needs? The style of living creates the gap between expenditures and earnings. Rating of any skill is a herculean task. The conflict between communism and capitalism is as old as civilization itself. Pure Nationalization alone is insufficient to hold the economy of nation. The existence of today has many challenges and opportunities.

The extremes of poverty and affluent cannot be eradicated in single dawn to dusk. Representatives of the masses are half heartedly voicing in the governance. Nations are competing with nations. Both the weak and strong are to live here. Migration of Man for survival has its own pros and cons. The patriotism requires new definition under the concept of globalization.

Optimism and pessimism together are sailing in between dawn and dusk. In addition the surmounting population is a threat to earth. Nature may be worrying to create another earth? Can we curb our own exploitations? How to redefine ourselves? Preaching and practice are not going together. Man is not enjoying the freedom of life. Man is captivating man. Everyone is doing something from dawn to dusk. There are major contributors and at the same time men with marginal out puts. All are being churned in the cycle of time. Man thinks to deliver to nature and nature in turn nourishes his potential.

The evaluation never remains with the doer. Intentionally there may not be any defined strategy by individuals before taking the living in majority of the cases. Improvisation during the course of time cannot be ruled out. And finally one wishes to revolt within to release the frustration of satisfaction .Are happiness and sadness subjects of the mind? We have been dwelling in quantity rather than quality of life?

No man is lazy. Be crazy to work. Work and work till the satisfaction of the self. Concentrate towards attaining perfection. How to identify human's highest productivity potential? When man is most productive? What major factors influence the man's daily activity from dawn to dusk? Why waking up early should be made a ritual?. Man should focus on squeezing the time from dawn to dusk to taste the abundance of living. The spirit of humans should be like the football player not waiting for the boot to kick the goal.

You are the driver of your destiny. How do you expect someone else to steer your vehicle of life? Remember to be the hammer of life and not the anvil of existence to die with blows at the end. Come out of the egg of destiny to rule the kingdom of existence. Start breaking your chains holding you to rise. Leave the nest of ignorance to embrace the bliss of enlightenment. How long you would like to be hatched?

Open the windows of your hearts to see the love of universe. Perceive our lives as miserable or as wonderful. This choice resides solely in us, as individuals. Sometimes throw the umbrella to dance in the rain. Most of the decisions in life are being taken under stress. The strain continues to deform your sound living both at the personal and professional level. We hardly get time to intricately look into resolving the basic issues pertaining to causing disturbances. The effect of all these is clearly seen in our relationships from dawn to dusk.

The social platform of living cannot be free from the push and pull of good and bad thoughts. It will prevail till humans invade this earth. The natural pleasure attached with man on defeating another man needs to be interrogated. The cross-culture values are to be broadly accepted. Human's present situation keeps stimulating the brain accordingly. Aggressiveness and submissiveness are responses of the same brain which empowers humans.

Exchange of ideas between humans is nothing but the exchange of brains. The interaction between brains is based on the level of development. The scientific approach restricts us to only biological findings in humans. Self as identity is yet to be understood. Is Nature and Man two different entities?

Is Man extension of nature? Who will conclude? How will it get concluded? I am at my own crossroads. Never know which will lead to the journey of future. Is there telescope to view the final destination of man? I have become so vibrant, that unable to remain in the shell. I wish to spread myself like the wind. This is the voice of freedom. How to know the sphere of survival? Do thoughts influence the conscience?

Man should realize his divine heritage. More spiritual a man, the more universal he is. Why we disagree? Tolerance and acceptance are the wheels of peace and harmony. Science and Religion were never different. They have to converge. Definitely no one can deny that out of the past is built the future. Are we doing it? Though wisdom has made its home, man appears to dwell in Stone Age. Our becoming of cannibals will be an unappreciable mark throughout the history of human existence. It is difficult to understand this unwanted animalism in humans. Survival never meant saving man by killing man. We need to strengthen our minds. The formation of character is lacking in us. No Man ever created god, but god created man. No Man ever created soul.

Is Man born to kill Man?

Then we all should be ashamed of this creation. Why this thought comes to us? We have to eliminate it from the root of humans. Let us conquer the god of Evil. Survival is not through the doors of evil. It should be lived through the window of wisdom.

Can we not rewrite destinies? You have the power to do it. Does living a clumsy life make sense? Why to live in stress and strain? We have been managing all activities for living, but somehow it is unmanageable to stop generating stress directly or indirectly from these activities. Then why stress as the single activity which influences your life from dawn to dusk cannot be managed. Sometimes we are obsessed with negative thoughts to such an extent that it ultimately leads to our breakdown.

Man is trying to stampede man in this outcome. Developed and underdeveloped nations all have the same story to share? Again learned and unlearned are sailing in the same boat. Is society of man becoming hell of the world? Were we born to witness our criticism?

Imagine life without an activity?

Imagine earth without man. It astonishingly sounds terrible. Hence, there is need of activity and the doer. The drama of life cannot be enacted without man. The virtual world is always questioned by the real world.

Life has been mystery ever since its existence. Without quest it could not advance. We would have been hunting animals even today had the flora did not develop. The nature had been good to give both fauna and flora to man to meet his survival needs. All its adventures are the results of quest. Quest for survival, knowledge, betterment, discoveries, inventions, sacrifices, exploring, innovation, novelty, meditation, health, wealth, faith, hope, trust, love, success, goals, accomplishments, all in one and other way are at core of the mind revolving around life from dawn to dusk. Above all the quest for purpose of life deepens more and more with maturity of life. The reality is in experiencing the transition gradually till the transformation from one form to other takes place.

343

It is a very old saying that energy is neither created nor destroyed, it moves from one form to another holds good in all walks of life. An activity transmits energy and is received to be transmitted to another, thus everything is in motion. Life is movement either controlled or uncontrolled. Controlled energy is constructive in nature and uncontrolled leads to destruction.

The flight of the mind takes you to distant planes from consciousness to sub-consciousness levels of experience encountering your interpretations again and again towards betterment in refining your thinking invariably till the final quest in the self is realized. The orbits of thoughts again converge to the nucleus of mystery to attain equilibrium but the true instinct of life struggles to escape from the central force to discover the new bonding of innovation. The power of the self is infinite.

Push and pull between the virtual and real is the undeniable truth. It has visited every man's mind. Is the game within man and man to man inevitable as humans?

Man is lumbering for nothing. Who will save him from this bumbling? Let us not shamble ourselves. We have to rise from our ineptness of this unwanted living. Misfortune on man is a great concern of present times. Very unfortunate are the ones still living with the disgrace of existence. Do you think one or two noble laureates here and there can transform the society? This is my question to all. The century hardly sees man working for men.

Let us vigorously haunt ourselves with this thought from dawn to dusk. More and more implementation of goodness is to be done along with the recitation of chanting the prevailing of goodness. More and more practitioners are equally required to march with the preachers of humanity.

Though you know that the wages of sin is death yet you wish to continue with the bad things. Neither helping yourself nor the society, you encourage the worst of both worlds. In fact man should strive to see the best of both worlds.

Man is born in the mother's womb and dies in the nature's womb.

Both the wombs are the truth of existence. Do not you think God, Nature, Universe, Earth and Man are all one and all of the same manifestations? One is incomplete without the other. All originate at one origin of existence. Our understanding of these crafts the way of living. The road of progress follows the light of perception.

Man is said to be a born philosopher. What is the conception of human personality? What learning is needed by the newly born baby to identify her or his mother? No sooner the baby cries, is fed by the mother. When the baby just out from the womb, can identify the mother source, why man is failing to realize his origin from god?

God and Man are not separate entities.

They are just like the mother and baby. The mother craves for the baby; the baby wants to enjoy the freedom away from the mother. The baby wants to experience as mother. Mother wants the baby to remain as baby. The truth is baby is born to be the mother.

Man is equally born to experience the god in him. The day he experiences, he is no more man, neither god, both dissolve to oneness. That is where the existence is all about. We all are trying to seek this Oneness. It is only appearance that man is mortal, bound and imperfect. Man is not what he appears to be. There is continuous turbulence in him. Man wishes to dissolve the quadrants when the truth is embracing him. He no more wishes to conflict with the self.

The beginning of realization is the merging of Man into Self. Cognition and volition are two distinctive powers of the mind. By dishonest means one may gain opulence but not happiness. How can you find joy with mental disquiet? Do you think excess of sense enjoyment can bring happiness? Where is the true happiness? What are the essential needs of life?

Does happiness means only affluence? Will aristocratism rule the democrats forever? Why the people of modern times have failed to sustain the universal harmony?

Can we not reach the root of all miseries? Today improvement of mankind on earth is a big question? Materialistic outlook on life appeared in succession in the form of greed for wealth and power, industrialization, capitalism, exploitation of the weak by strong, mercantile, colonization, imperialism, militarism and so forth. Still the optimists have hope for a better new world. Modern man has learned to measure world progress and civilizations in terms of material achievements. To see things impersonally one has to overcome passion and propensities.

Paths of Life

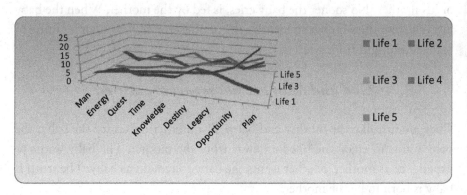

The author here wishes to share the scientific dimension of life with the readers. An attempt has been made here to bring out the relationship between essential variables of man affecting his own life. There can be as many life paths as possible for survival and sustenance. The quality of man with all inherent and acquired attributes can be scaled and ranked accordingly. The different energy levels of the same person during the phases of life.

Life 1, 2,3,4,5 can be different paths of the same person at different time intervals of life. The utilization of opportunity drives the success paths Success 1, 2,3,4,5. The quest and knowledge of the same man varies with time.

Destiny and legacy are other governing factors of man in his life.

The readers from the science fraternity or with a marginal mathematical background can quickly comprehend the survival philosophy. The above interpretation gives you further chances of interpolation and exploration to regulate your life. The purpose of introducing this to readers is that an awareness living can enhance and enrich your survival. Rather than struggling you will be thriving in life.

Now a mapping between Life- L 1,2,3,4,5, Success- S 1,2,3,4,5 and Man –M 1,2,3,4,5 is a subject of great interest to all of us. No one alone is a failure or success.

If we have the summation $\sum L + \sum S + \sum M$ and equate it to $\sum So$, then the type of $\sum So$ will give you $\sum H$. And the product of summations of society and humanity gives you universality. All different universalities when summed up will give you the central universality.

Here the following stands for:

1. $\sum$ - Summation
2. L - Life
3. S - Success
4. H - Humanity
5. Hc - Central Humanity
6. So - Society
7. Soc - Central Society
8. I - Variables from 1 to ∞ (infinity).
9. U - Universality
10. Uc - Central Universality

Equations of Humanity

$\sum L1+L2+L3+---L\infty +\sum S1+S2+S3+--S\infty+ \sum M1+M2+M3+--M\infty = \sum So\ 1$
$\sum L1+L2+L3+---L\infty +\sum S1+S2+S3+--S\infty+ \sum M1+M2+M3+--M\infty = \sum So\ 2$
$\sum L1+L2+L3+---L\infty +\sum S1+S2+S3+--S\infty+ \sum M1+M2+M3+--M\infty = \sum So\ 3$
$Soc= \sum So1+ \sum So2+ \sum So3+ ---------\sum Son$
$Hc= \sum H1+\sum H2+\sum H3+----------------\sum Hn$
$\sum So1 \sum H1 = U1, \sum So2 \sum H2 = U2, \sum So3\sum H3= U3$

(1) Uc = $\sum$ U= U1+U2+U3+--------U∞
(2) Uc = Soc x Hc

Humanity on Earth

What is humanity? How many of us really know it? Why it is required on earth? Can we live without humanity? Can humanity submerge the chaos in the world forever? Am I living for humanity? How to support its implementation?

Let us make humanity culture of living.

Dawn to Dusk should focus on transforming humanity. Though it witnesses many actions and results, the most influencing is its impact on humanity. Who will become the reformists over night? All walks of life are encountered from dawn to dusk. It is not that the distant pasts were not serious in attempting the cause but it is the nature of man to hold on till new concerns are again defined.

I do not exactly know the taste of my prospective readers, however I have a firm faith beyond all doubts that they will surely like to lick the honey of humanity. As my readers are going to be humans on earth, with the benefit of doubt, it is my pleasure to reach them through their blessings on me from dawn to dusk.

Dawn to Dusk will act as the catalyst of change.

This epidemic should never die. It is bound to rapidly transmit the diseases of loving mankind. Few good words to all you have met today from dawn to dusk will be accounted as great contribution in battling the woes of humanity. A wounded man needs to fight till the last breath of life. Your guns should have the bullets of love. Care all. Cry to unite them. Let them feel the warmth of togetherness.

Dawn to Dusk is not competing with the fairy tales, short stories, passing time novels, fiction etc but it emphasizes the sincere need of society to understand its own existence prior to dramatizing the story of living.

Dawn to Dusk is like the flue which will catch your throat to speak the truth of humanity. Let all actions from dawn to dusk converge into humanity. Put a question to yourself today.

Dawn to Dusk has entered the market of inspiration to do the business of humanity. Either buy or sell you are enriching yourself with the grace of mankind.

Dawn to Dusk ambitiously waits to migrate from the reader's desk to the rest of world. It should have the spirit of sharing across the borders of individuality. Let us all write our living in great book of life. It is life time opportunity to uplift you.

Emerge as humans of the universe. The poorest of poor is he, who has failed to credit this golden time in his account from dawn to dusk. Only assurances for change are as useless as the clouds without ambition to rain. Showers of grace come to those who are willing to be faithful to themselves.

Do not wait till others to change.

You have to be master of your own destiny.

Do you have a plan for today? No other individual can make your life. You know it, then why the hitch, get up to rule the day. Leave your bed the dawn is waiting for your glory.

Man has to conquer the day. Get the most out of it before it slips into darkness. Take the light as much as you can. At dusk question yourself, have I done my best today. If no, it is sure you have lost a chance of performance, do not regret but accept the truth; however the next dawn should be more sincerely and meticulously utilized.

The rivers do not flow to the fields. Water is to be channelized for irrigation. The hills do not come to the homes. It is to be climbed. Miseries are to be uprooted. Happiness is to be planted.

Every human has the potential of planting billions and billions of plants of happiness. The Society has enough voids to be bridged by the gaps of happiness. Why relationships fail? Do we make friends to end as enemies? Where is the basic problem?

Let us try to work out effectively in the interest of mankind. Dawn to Dusk should bring happiness, peace, bliss, smile, love, success, prosperity, health, wealth, wisdom, grace, abundance, oneness, humanity and what not, it has many things for us, provided we ask through the heart of heavens. We have to continuously search for the hidden things. The secret will be known only on attaining your goal. There cannot be single path.

Every day has its own ways.

Dawn is a treasure of fortune. Men of fortune are the grace of existence. Unravel it to your best of ability. Give the touch of fortune to other fellowmen. Share your fortune with the unfortunate. Be of help to as much as you can. Cheer them with your fortune. Let them participate with your living. Hold them to rise. You were destined to be god to the unfortunates.

Man is only a media. The doer is within us. You are golden dawn to millions and millions of life. What else can be supreme than service to man? Serving a glass of water to the thirsty is far better than hundred prayers of liberation. Search the needy. They are your right goals. Their hearts are waiting for your love. Do not wait till they arrive at your doors. Volunteer yourself overcoming all the hindrances.

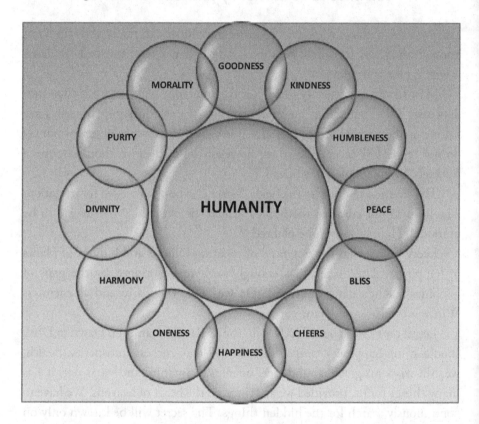

Let us explore the infinite ways life loves the existence.

Man's collective efforts through institutions, forums, committees, gatherings, centers, should not be under acknowledged of recent times or of the distant past all over the globe; however there is still scope to refine our approaches in reinventing the postulates of living. The existing rate of productivity to produce humanity needs to be multiplied million to billion times.

Every newly born human's blood should have the chemistry of love. Let us not stare to know the sky is blue today. More and more centers of happiness are required to cater to the needs of society from dawn to dusk. The dictionaries of dawn need to rewrite them eliminating the words of hatred, anger, jealousy, crime, brutal, depression, enemy, murder, hanged, ugly, humiliation, curse, abuse, and all that are negative to the whole process of existence. No change is eternal that it can remain as permanent. It vanishes away with time.

Man has to primarily change to bring change.

Dawn to Dusk is a voice of change. It will speak aloud daily the need for change. Principally it will keep reminding the readers as alarm of change. Just as Sun brings the lovely day, so will dawn to dusk strive to bring humanity to the world.

Dawn to Dusk first and foremost is an atom of hope. It will bond all men with energy of humanity. The chain will continue to hold the existence of Universe.

Dawn to Dusk is powerful than the atomic and nuclear bombs of destruction. Its magnitude of faith will construct the sphere of humanity.

I believe, "Learned are the ones who bow to humanity, World is not scarce of learned people".

Dawn to Dusk will not rest till the objective of humanity is accomplished. It will see an entirely new Dawn of humanity on Earth. He who determines to be good cannot become bad at any cost. If you are yielding, certainly you are not holding your resolutions of sustaining the idea of working for humanity. Both Man's and Nature's environment equally needs a transformation for better balance of ecological systems. Do not hesitate to abuse yourself if you are failing in your commitment from dawn to dusk.

The good habit of cleaning is reflected in your teeth's when you smile on a cheer. Otherwise it would have been so ugly, that no one could dare to receive you. Similarly a regular cleaning of your mind is required to witness the purity of your soul.

Every life should have some mission .The idea of humanity should never die. Success cannot come without suffering and sacrificing.

No civilization has been perfect till date.

It can only happen with push of humanity. True help is always unselfish in nature.

Books are the latest tools .Prior to it ears were the best educators. Where to find educators of humanity? The conquest of humanity will take how many years?

Man is the best teacher to his self. His school is independent of the specific courses and general books. He is both the teacher and student from dawn to dusk.

What is the ideal of human race? Where knowledge does exists? Is it in the mind? Is it in the body? Is it in the soul? Is it in the self? Where is it exactly? The truth is, knowledge is within us. It can come to surface only through the way of experience. To begin is to get. Why to delay?

Life is an experience. Good life good experience. Bad life gives bad experience. Experience can only come from actions and results. Despite the type of results, man has been doing his activities. The journey of life continues with the time. An eternal renunciation has to come to kill this "I" the prime reason for evil in this world. Without getting rid of the delusion, can we get real knowledge?

Souls are divine. Where to get ethics? What is the basis of all ignorance? The idea of separation leads to all sorts of misery. Who has caused all these evils? You all should agree it is only man alone. There is great gulf between man's needs and greed.

Truth cannot adjust to society. Society should pay homage to truth. Neither man owns the world or the self. What can be more truthful than this? Inequality is the bane of human nature. This is the greatest curse upon mankind. Can there be any social reform without the spiritual reform? Just as the law of energy, energy can neither be created nor destroyed but can be transformed from one form to another, the sum total of good and evil in the world remains ever the same.

My dear readers let us attempt this, "Why do the humanities matter to Humans?" Will human be able to explore insights into everything?

Through exploration of the humanities we learn how to think creatively and critically, to reason, and to ask questions. Because these skills allow us to gain new insights into everything from poetry and paintings to business models and politics, humanistic subjects have been at the heart of a liberal arts education since the ancient Greeks first used them to educate their citizens.

Do we really understand our World? Research into the human experience adds to our knowledge about our world. Through the work of humanities scholars, we learn about the values of different cultures, about what goes into making a work of art, about how history is made. Their efforts preserve the great accomplishments of the past; help us understand the world we live in, and give us tools to imagine the future. Is Human bringing clarity to the future? Is human correcting humanity from dawn to dusk?

Today, humanistic knowledge continues to provide the ideal foundation for exploring and understanding the human experience. Investigating a branch of philosophy might get you thinking about ethical questions.

Learning another language might help you gain an appreciation for the similarities in different cultures. Human is a voice. Despite any language he speaks humanity knows the language of love only. Despite any language he speaks the freedom of joy is seen in the tears of penance in humans.

Do humans have apology to humanity?

All humans are artists. What can be a better painting than the world? The colors are the dreams of humans. Contemplating a sculpture might make you think about how an artist's life affected her creative decisions. The human art speaks the language of colors. What language a color has? The art personifies the manifestations of the creativity the existence can come up with in this universe.

Reading a book from another region of the world might help you think about the meaning of humanity. By no means will you find that the authors view is more or less centrally focused to the core of humanity. Despite the books written in different languages it speaks only one philosophy the philosophy of humanity.

Listening to a history course might help you better understand the past; while at the same time offer you a clearer picture of the future.

Humans are unique among life on this planet, and much remains a mystery as to how we evolved. What steps came first? Did it follow a specific order of evolution?

The world is yet to formulate the Laws of Evolution. The world is yet to define the Laws of Human. The world is yet to understand the Laws of Humanity.

Will the human species ever die?

Why did we evolve this way and not that direction? Why are we the only human species left? What other paths we might have gone down in our evolution? And what directions might we go from here?

Our ancestors evolved an upright posture well before our large brains or stone tools even appeared. The question, then: Why stand and walk on two legs when our ape cousins get by on four limbs? It appears the goal of the human species will never be achieved.

Will the dawn of humanity grace the humans of the world?

Walking as bipeds might actually use less energy than movement on all fours does. Freeing up the arms might also have enabled our ancestors to carry more food. Standing upright might even have helped them control their temperature better by reducing the amount of skin directly exposed to the sun.

Recent evidence suggests that humanity is not only still evolving, but that human evolution is actually accelerating after agriculture, industrialization and modernization spread. Is technology making a difference in the evolution process today?

A number of scientists challenge the strength of this evidence, saying that it remains difficult to ascertain whether or not certain genes really have recently grown in prominence because they offer some adaptive benefit.

Still, if human evolution is accelerating, the question becomes why? Style of living, diet and diseases may be some of the pressures that caused humans to change. The changes in humans are again a subject of continuous debate all over the world from dawn to dusk. The department of humanities needs more spiritual strength to supplement the scientific findings at any point of time in the existence.

Is human really changing?

Is the change in human internal? Why the rate of change in the external world is beyond the understanding of the existence? Where human is going? Where humanity will lead people?

From the chapters of human history roughly 50,000 years ago, modern humans expanded out of Africa, spreading rapidly across most of the world's lands to colonize all continents except Antarctica, reaching even the most remote Pacific islands.

A number of scientists conjecture this migration was linked with a mutation that transformed our brains leading to our modern, complex use of language and enabling more sophisticated tools, art and societies. Moreover the digital world of today is rapidly influencing and contributing to the behavioral science of humanity.

The more popular view suggests hints of such modern behavior existed long before this exodus, and that humanity instead had crossed a threshold in terms of population size in Africa that made such a revolution possible.

Did we interbreed? Does our species possess any genes leftover from our extinct cousins? Scientists have suggested that perhaps the Neanderthals did not die out, but instead were absorbed into modern humanity.

Scientists are uncovering more and more ancient hominids all the time — here meaning bipeds including humans, our direct ancestors and closest relatives. They strive to find the earliest one, to help answer that most fundamental question in human evolution — what adaptations made us human, and in what order did they happen?

The most bitterly debated question in the discipline of human evolution is likely over where modern humans evolved. The out-of-Africa hypothesis maintains that modern humans evolved relatively recently in Africa and then spread around the world, replacing existing populations of archaic humans.

Finding the root of the origin of humanity is as good as finding the root of humans.

At this point of existence after billions and billions years of evolution, exploration and experience human has nothing to breakdown not knowing his traces.

The multiregional hypothesis contends that modern humans evolved over a broad area from archaic humans, with populations in different regions mating with their neighbors to share traits, resulting in the evolution of modern humans. The out-of-Africa hypothesis currently holds the lead, but proponents of the multiregional hypothesis remain strong in their views.

Let us start from the dawn of today's humanity to make a better history. For humans of now this is prime project. It is time to act, be the doer of humanity.

Liberation from World

The highest ideal is the ideal of non-violence.

"Blessed are the peace makers," says the Bible. Either it was the Sermon on the Mount by Jesus Christ or the preaching of Buddha under the bodhi tree, or the message of, "I see god in everyman", by Sri Parmahansa Rama Krishna on the banks of river Ganga.

What man wants to obtain? Is it wealth, education, knowledge, liberation, salvation, freedom, fame, name, endless aims and desires? Without these sustaining survival is also difficult. The necessities for living cannot be just eliminated. However, the demand of need can be regulated by the reasoning of self. It is here, where principally the process of sacrifice starts towards liberation. Practical approach has many definitions of living. This varies from man to man.

How do you balance the gap between philosophy and reality? Why man fails to differentiate between need and desire? All desires may not be needs. All actions may not liberate. All truths may not be realized. How do you expect everything to come to you? There is abundant water in sea and ocean but unfit for drinking. There is sweet water on land without salinity but in less quantity meeting the needs of survival. This is law of nature. Whatever you see may not be yours.

Every individual has a specific role to play. All the players cannot be goal keepers in any football match anywhere played at any time in the world. The game is designed so with limitations on every players movement.

Life is also such a football match. The football is at your feet to do the goal. Kick out all the worries, anxiety, doubts, greed, ego, jealousy, anger, tears, unhappiness, stress, strain, weaknesses, illness, evils, to get the goals of bliss, peace, happiness, cheers, smile, dignity, prosperity, health, wealth, joy, humanity.

Keep kicking goals for betterment of humanity within the time allotted to you .Time is the essence of the life match. You have to play at your full potential, energy, confidence, strength, skills and integrity to excel in the match.

Is Man a toy in the hands of existence? Man is keyed to dance on earth. A confused state of existence when not convinced. The truth alone triumphs is not a new finding to anyone of us just as the cycle of life and death. Why unrest then? It has been a subject of continual research throughout the life of man. Life beyond death has its own philosophy and hypothesis under continual test. Among all these assumptions, presumptions, anticipations, interpretations, how to define the liberation from world?

Every man has the liberty to understand liberation as he likes, but the process is universal. Is it a man's choice? Are you sure definitely not in our hands? After you have lived completely, it is time to go back to the source. The source and sink are no different entities but it is just like you and your shadow. Till you exist your shadow follows you.

Man allows himself to be worried with liberation. Man's single life may not be sufficient to understand even the alphabets of liberation. Is liberation consciously a part of our daily existence? Why only at the end of life the congestion is enormous on road to liberation? This questions our way of living entirely.

Is it time to quit the world?

When is the right time? Does simply quitting mean that you are liberated? Is man unable to decide his priority at intermittent phases of life? All the cumulative needs of liberation are piled to be addressed at the end. The last phase of the man's life is trying to refine the summary of regrets? Why should we take this chance? If man has worked and delivered, what needs to be delivered at respective phases of life, irrespective of all, he naturally gets liberated. In my opinion, liberation cannot be enforced by man.

A successful life with harmony and bliss will surely be lighter than a life with full of regrets, unhappiness and disquiet. Saints and sinners all will be liberated from the world as per the law of life. A slow and gradual emptying of a balloon never punctures it, but any scratch, dent, or stress, bursts the balloon. A premature man has to struggle for liberation from the world. It is ridiculous to understand that why liberation is a last activity in man's life?

Liberation just like realization, living and learning should happen daily from dawn to dusk. It is not the last chapter of life, or a concluding summary of existence. It happens parallel to living. Man somehow appears to be blind to these unproductive lessons. The modern man has started measuring his success by receivables. That too the materialistic assets are the benchmark. The advancement of technology and modernization is completely changing the perception of living from time to time. This is influencing the process of living and thinking from dawn to dusk.

Liberation is a point of time in man's journey of life; it nearly approaches the ultimate understanding of life. Truth now, today, tomorrow, yesterday or at any point of time is always truth. I am not revealing anything new, but trying to discuss with my readers, as to think that why we are yet not liberated from the ignorance of life. All realization and no liberation are more harmful to the spirit of existence. Many times the description of life may not be the real definition of existence.

Liberation is the airport to heaven.

Your flight of life will board you one day to the eternity of bliss. The only baggage with you is the experience of existence. Think over it. Nothing has been lost yet, till you board. Work towards it from dawn to dusk. No bondage with action is the beginning of liberation. Serve the man not the entity of the person. Respect the authority of the chair not the race of the person. All are men living for men and dying for men. Do justice for the existence not for the fame of the self. Work, work, work not for the rewards but for the opportunity rewarded to you by the existence. A free mind very easily tunes with liberation. It is in you. You have to liberate yourself.

No man can liberate any man. Man in me has to be liberated. Man in me should realize the necessity of liberation. Man in me should be graced so by the divinity of existence. Liberation is within us. Do not search it outside. Have a broom to groom yourself.

Man who has lost the will has lost everything.

Do not kill your will. Never have a will to be still. Have always a will to fill. Fill your life with ideas, dreams, desires, aims, goals, purpose, to see what you can really make it of yourself. Make your body healthy, strong for the mind to concentrate, meditate and control your senses, actions, thoughts, in the right direction to attain the purity of soul, the sanctity of life and dignity of humanity. Have a will to thrill the life. Never stop till your will says to fill, fill and keep on filling your life.

Let your life be not an empty vessel. To anchor it you should weight it with the values of life. Fill it to radiate, reflect, illuminate, enlighten, other men of the society. Raise them with your abundance, with your prosperity, with your dreams, with your attitudes, with your capabilities, with your potentials, with your vision and work towards transmitting help to one and all.

A true will is the power to till the whole world. Drill the human in you till the will is on the surface of existence. Never be ill to depart from the will. Grill yourself for excellence. Mill the idea of the will. All skills are in you. No will should say nil to life. Never have a will to spill life to nil. Ever have a will of zeal to fill life to thrill. Who will fulfill the will? How to bill the will? Let us have a will to be liberated.

Liberation is the light of soul.

Man's body dies but the soul radiates this light merging with the light of existence. What else can be brighter than the bright sunshine of existence? Every dawn is an opportunity to see your light.

Man is the light of the world. It reflects the purity of existence. One and all are part and parcel of the existence. Light cannot become dark but darkness can be lightened. Search all the areas of darkness into you. Make a resolution to completely eliminate from the self. Darkness sucks your energetic life. It clouds your divinity.

Light is an axe to demolish the demons within us. Why our originality cannot become the existence within the self? Every new realization brings a new liberation. It is like you know, you have filled up your life with so many conceptions, bondages, attachments, reservations, philosophies, wealth, assets, knowledge, and so forth, now you are one by one finding some of them not needful, no necessity, or the purpose might have been achieved, do not require it, so you are letting it out as and when according to the realization from your accumulated treasure of life. This is the process of emptying yourself, a step towards liberalizing yourself and finally one day you can see that you have liberated yourself.

Summing Up & Exercise for Readers- Chapter- VII

- Let my readers look into finding their legacy.
- The genesis may not be traced successfully of an individual unless and otherwise there are substantial remains from the books of history of one's life.
- However, you can work out with the available sources you can reach to know your origin.
- The study of your transformation is the most important factor here.
- Were you a born leader? Or you became one here in this World.
- Your individual perception of survival, quest, humanity, liberation in your background is to be mapped with the world.
- You have to work to find out, "Are you a different human?"
- This initiates studying the self.
- Understand your legacy before you understand the legacy of the world.
- It is a subject of diversity in human's philosophy and living and by doing so you will start knowing the existence of various cultures, beliefs, faiths, trusts and love among humans in the world.
- Without knowing MAN from different parts of the World how can HUMAN be blamed every day by man?
- This is a difficult exercise for all of us but an essential one before we blame any human on earth.
- Every reader has an opportunity to be a researcher of his life. Start researching yourself today.

Chapter VIII

MAN IS UNIQUE

"Man is a reasoning animal"

Aristotle,
The Greek Philosopher termed man as a reasoning animal.

Humans reason and react to situation they confront uniquely. Animals react in an instinctive manner. It appears this is not holding anymore good today. Man is joining the faculty of animals. Man has lost all the reasoning to be a human. Is reasoning the hall mark of humans alone? Conceptual thoughts are possessed by humans alone.

Man has to submit the power of his reasoning to his quest for values. To study the human predicament we have to study his history, prehistory, archaeology, cultural, and physical anthropology, evolution genetics, origin of life and about the constituents of living organism.

Life has properties unique to itself.

Man is product of the evolution of life on this planet earth. There is no trick in life. The ship of opportunities should not wreck in the midst of voyage. Every Man is a unique wave which invariably rises to fall at the shore of existence. What is Man? How is Man? Where is Man? Why is Man? Who is Man?

Buddha focused on discipline, control of mind and meditation. Freud explained man in terms of his libido. Karl Marx explained man in terms of an economic process. Shakespeare, the humanist, has spoken of man in "Hamlet", the beauty of the world and "Macbeth" the tragic poem of renaissance.

Charles Darwin speaks of evolution through adaptation, natural selection and the struggle for existence. Mahatma Gandhi worked with non-violence. Hitler used power to understand mankind. Mother Teresa believed in service by man. Fredrick Taylor applied scientific management. Peter Drucker used the tool management by objectives.

The Saint Sankaracharya, the eighth century Hindu Philosopher and mystic, taught that there are three boons, extremely rare, which one obtains only by the special grace of god, namely, birth in a human body, the yearning for liberation from the prison-house of world and the guidance of a qualified teacher towards the attainment of this liberation.

Only man, through the exercise of reason and intuition, can investigate his own true nature. The physical scientists have studied man in different ways. The sociologist goes beyond the stand points of the materialist and the vitalist.

Does scientism upholds atheism? Is there continuity of life? What is Doctrine of Immortality? Where is the Soul of the World? How to understand the Doctrine of Rebirth? Knowledge is based on experience. Partial experience gives only partial knowledge. He who has known the self obtains the entire world and all desires. What is personality? Have you ever felt the necessity to know your mind? Why the mind acts as our enemy? What are the different layers of personality?

Man is divine.

Can pleasure be the only goal? Pleasures and pains are great teachers. Goal and evil have an equal share in molding character.

Wisdom is the goal of life. Be a man first and rest will follow. Time is infinite. The faith calls out the divinity within. What is Ethics? Every ordeal, misfortune, adversity, misery, lays the foundation for serenity and cheerfulness of mind. How to attain union with source? World is the radiance of universal soul.

Life is an opportunity to pour out our higher instincts. We all have the instincts of heroism within us. Why people lack in fitness of feeling? Why people lack in sense of sanctity?

For the readers to begin, firstly I should say just close your eyes and try to question yourself,

"Where is the human in me?"

This primarily makes you to initiate your thinking on the state you are floating in and out of existence. The secondary benefit is that the impact of this initiation develops inertia of search and the quest continues to invade you consciously and sub-consciously throughout dawn to dusk.

My readers are my respondents from dawn to dusk. I have written for you. I have toiled to come to you. I have burnt the midnight oil to see you. I have edited this essay number of times to see that the perfection is not lost in embracing you. It is my sole purpose to somehow make a dent in your mind. I would like to introduce you the virus of regenerating humanity. It is my concern not to be defeated in the promise to my readers which I am making through this essay.

Writing the bitterness of humans requires the courage of existence. Experiencing it daily from dawn to dusk is worse than the presentation of the facts. No human truly would like to be a journalist of inhumanity. No ideal human would like to hear his own criticism. No divine human would like to witness the death of humanity in humans.

Dawn to Dusk is a drive to regain humanity in the world. My readers are the leaders of this massive program to again build the valuable and meaningful foundations of humanity.

Let us all take this resolution at dawn of the New Year 2015 as the Year of Humanity. We all shall religiously work towards cleaning the world for humanity.

To see that they have truly gained from this essay, a set of essential variables, major attributes, the influencing factors, the parameters of behavioral science, psychology of humans, perception of life, gap between dreams and reality, overall understanding of humanity, a set of questions based on the research methodology, following a simple random sampling has been researched and designed to give it a partial scientific approach in reaching the individual findings for self analysis, suggestions and recommendations to reestablish humanity at respective levels of inferences.

I believe that ninety nine percent of us will arrive at the same results. However, an exception of one percent humans requires the salutation of the remaining.

My readers eagerly can introspect themselves for reforming their selves through the set of questions summarized under the heading Examine Yourself. This model questionnaire for self analysis is an attempt to reinvent, rethink, rediscover and reform us. It is a brief insight into your external and internal living throughout from dawn to dusk. The questions are so designed that its responses will help to greater extent to categories and classify our perception towards living and the basics of humanity.

The intention is very clear to clean ourselves first. The coating of dirt of ignorance is corroding the self unnoticed to the existence. These are to be blown away as quickly as possible.

My dear respected readers you may not be blinking to realize the truth that, "Man generally comes back to the nose after going all round the world".

Is it true in your case? Man has to give many examinations in life.

Life is a series of examinations.

You are the examinee and not the examiner who goes to evaluate you. Who is our examiner? It is none other than your inner self. The true man always resides in your inner home. You are to act in all positions accordingly as per the role in the outer world. The question paper is not same for everyone. It varies from man to man. This is a unique test for man.

Humanity is the honey of the world.

Is money the only honey in this world? God made us man not money bees. Why we are flying for money when it is not our honey? Can money buy happiness forever? Can money buy your life? Can money buy your soul? Can money buy your mind? Can money buy your heart? Can money buy your will? Can money buy bliss for you? Can money buy humanity?

What use is of the rain falling on the ocean? How to test a man? Man himself should start assessing his strengths, weaknesses, opportunities, threats, progress, development, learning, morale, values, virtues, ethics, conduct, qualities, actions, renunciation, perception, aim, goal, god, faith, trust, sacrifices, one by one in all areas to understand his existence. What is the use of billions and billions of man on this earth if they cause grief to the world?

We should remember the political ethics of the great Indian **Pandit Chanakya** who true to his oath engineered the support of the Magadha(presently the State of Bihar, in India) citizens along with Chandragupta Maurya to defeat the Greek conqueror Alexander the Great and his general Seleucus about 2300 years ago invading the Indian sub-continent, "Time perfects all living beings as well as kills them, it alone is awake when all others are asleep. Time is insurmountable".

He continues to say, the life of an uneducated man is as useless as the tail of a dog which neither covers its rear end, nor protects it from the bites of insects.

Again to add his quote,

"Purity of speech, of the mind, of the senses and of the compassionate heart is needed by one who desires to rise to the divine platform".

<u>Examine Yourself</u>

1. Does genesis of man really influences his living from dawn to dusk?
   a) Yes   b) Partially   c) No   d) No opinion

2. Did evolution of man, mean?

Evolution	Yes	No	Partially	No Opinion
Racism				
Mankind				
Atheism				
Humanism				
Communism				
Capitalism				
Globalism				
Democracy				
Aristocratism				
Idealism				
Realism				
Materialism				
Naturalism				
Objectivism				
Subjectivism				
Unionism				
Liberalism				
Fundamentalism				
Opportunism				
Pessimism				
Truism				
Secularism				
Monasticism				
Empiricism				
Equalitarianism				
Casteism				

Asterism				
Esotericism				
Terrorism				
Negativism				
Fideism				
Existentialism				
Plutocracy				
Dualism				
Hooliganism				
Bossism				

3. Do you ever sincerely think of helping other man?
   a) Yes b) Partially c) No d) No opinion

4. If yes, then how many men you have helped in recent times?
   a) One b) < 5 c) >10 d) Cannot Say

5. How many people have helped you in the last year?
   a) < 10 b) >20 c)Cannot Say d)None

6. Have you defined your own life?

Life	Yes	No	Planning	No Opinion
Policy				
Mission				
Vision				
Objective				
Aim				
Goal				
Purpose				
Perception				
Position				
Destination				
Contribution				

Autonomy				
Orthodox				
Dignity				
Values				

7. Which is important to you? (Rank)
   a) GOD   b) NATURE   c) EARTH   d) LIFE
   e) DEATH   f) SOUL

8. How do you rank them as priority in your life from dawn to dusk?
   a) Self   b) Colleagues   c) Family   d) Friends
   e) Relations

9. Impact of these attributes on your daily living from dawn to dusk.

Daily Living	Major	Moderate	Minor	No Impact
Spirituality				
Religion				
Culture				
Society				
Hospitality				
Humanity				
Philosophy				
Nationality				
Personality				
Individuality				
Originality				
Universality				
Intellectuality				
Nobility				
Loyalty				
Integrity				
Morality				
Divinity				

Sanctity				
Positivity				
Negativity				
Cruelty				
Enmity				
Mythology				
Genealogy				

10. What matters you from dawn to dusk?

Attributes	Major	Moderate	Minor	No Impact
Survival				
Dreams				
Destiny				
Love				
Faith				
Trust				
Hope				
Perception				
Inspiration				
Realization				
Novelty				
Liberation				
Salvation				
Actualization				
Reality				
Fantasy				
Ethics				
Earnings				
Giving				
Taking				
Sharing				
Sacrificing				

Helping				
Spending				
Travelling				
Learning				
Enjoying				
Reading				
Volunteering				
Playing				
Chatting				
Cheating				
Laundering				
Living				
Striving				
Thrilling				
Mentoring				

11. Impact on your living by the sources of learning during various phases of life.

Learning Sources	Major	Moderate	Minor	No Impact
From Grand Parents				
From Parents				
Childhood Friends				
Teenage- As Student				
Bachelor Community				
Married Couples				
From Better Half				
Middle Age Group				
From Your Children				
Old Age People				
Peers				
Seers				
Teachers				

Society				
Colleagues				
Institutions				
Organizations				
Centers				
Seminars				
Sermons				
Nature				
Environment				
Magazines/Papers				
Books				
Scriptures				
Self Analysis Reasoning				
Media/Internet				
Lessons from Nature				
Your Intuition				
Self Realization				

12. What are you personally becoming from dawn to dusk?

Becoming	Major	Moderate	Minor	No Impact
Human				
Nobel				
Good				
Bad				
Kind				
Cruel				
Winner				
Loser				
Sinner				
Intellectual				
Spiritual				
Sincere				

Egoist				
Stupid				
Cheater				
Fool				
Clever				
Clown				
Nothing				
Other				

13. How do you visualize life?

Life as	Major	Moderate	Minor	No Impact
Opportunity				
Adventure				
Enjoyment				
Sports				
Boon				
Bane				
Liability				
Undefined				
Unknown				
Mystery				
Destiny				
Action				
Light				
Author				
Gift				
Idea				
Dream				
Thought				
Burden				
Asset				
Dawn				

Dusk				
Quest				
Bondage				
Beauty				
Whirlpool				
Journey				
Energy				
Manifestation				
Business				
Almighty				
Nature				
Moment				
Science				
Infinity				
Creativity				
Happening				
Incident				
Purposeful				
Event				
Meaningless				
Helplessness				
Enthusiasm				
Experience				
Existence				
Thrill				
Wisdom				
Meditation				
Work				
Book				
Tool				
Resource				
Seed				
Time				

Matter				
Mind				
Heart				
Love				
Body				
Universe				
Self				
God				
Heaven				
Hell				
Power				
Useless				

14. How can you bring good changes in your life from dawn to dusk to transform yourself?

Bringing Good Changes	Major	Moderate	Minor	No Impact
Joining a Job /Work/ Enterprise				
Helping Needy People				
Stopping being idle				
Loving Home, Family, Friends				
Teaching People Humanity				
Learning Humanity				
Applying Better Thoughts				
Self Becoming Good				
Making people good				
Praying God for harmony				
Working for Society				
Reading and Sharing Books				
Quitting Bad Habits				
Confessing Self				

Sharing with Friends				
Owning Life Completely				
Strive for Goal daily				
Taming towards divinity				
Open a spiritual centre				
Live towards my dreams				
Bring cheer to men				
Careful towards my life				
Organizing daily routine				
No Blame Games				
Of purpose to society				
Caring for Animals & Plants				
Volunteer my services				
Utilizing the day purposefully				
Inspiring Children				
Nursing Sick/Unhealthy				

15. How you can reestablish humanity from dawn to dusk?

Reestablishing Humanity	Major	Moderate	Minor	No Impact
Attitude				
Action				
Awareness				
Education				
Literacy				
Reinventing				
Rediscovering				
Realigning				
Regenerating				
Reformation				
Restructuring				
Preaching				

Implementing				
Ownership				
Serving				
Confessing				
Sharing				
Influencing				
Enforcing				
Taming				
Learning				
Mentoring				
Bringing togetherness				
Loving				
Organizing Society				
Trusting				
Faith				
Caring				
Volunteering				
Utilizing				
Inspiring				
Nurturing				

16. Is your life really organized?
    a) Yes   b) No   c) Partially   d) No opinion

17. If no, then why? Are you waiting for any auspicious golden dawn to start organizing?
    a) Yes   b) No   c) No opinion

18. Where do you stand in life amidst understanding of these from dawn to dusk? (Rank)

Understanding Life	Rank	Reason	Impact	No Impact
Civilization				
Society				

Man				
Soul				
Body				
Religion				
Mind				
Self				
Science				
Humanity				
Spirituality				
Power				
Peace				
Heart				
Love				
Sacrifice				
Trust				
Hope				
Faith				
Nature				
World				
Universe				
Nation				
Thought				
Dreams				
Wisdom				
Philosophy				
Theology				
Life				
Applying				
Inspiring				
Reasoning				
Recognition				
Admiration				
Ego				

19. Your opinion on the cause of human sufferings from dawn to dusk?

Causes of Human Sufferings	Agree	Partially	Disagree	No Opinion
Conflicts between man and nature				
Conflicts between man and man				
Conflicts between man and society				
Conflicts between man and self				
Conflicts between man and human				
Conflicts within man				
Conflicts between man and woman				
Looking at life as a fight instead of game				
Looking at life as blessings in disguise				
Life is not as per our wishes				
Unfulfilled Dreams				
Unfulfilled Desires				
Unfulfilled Destiny				
Attachment to loved ones				
Attachment to sense pleasures				
Attachment to physical body				
Possessing happiness and peace				
Possessing money and wealth				

Possessing health and beauty				
Possessing materials				
Comparison with other man				
Comparison with society				
Comparison with outside world				
Cannot distinguish between illusion and reality				
Cannot understand difference between education and knowledge				
Finding peace outside				
Do not understand real success				
Struggle to be better than others				
Non cooperation of society				
Non cooperation of family				
Non cooperation of friends				
Lack of overall personality				
Man's dual nature				
Utilizing Life Ineffectively				
Non Inspiring Life				
Lack of proper nurturing				

20. What are your enemies of happiness from dawn to dusk?

Enemies of Happiness	Agree	Disagree	Reason	No Impact
Jealousy				
Anger				
Greed				
Prosperity				
Rivalry				

Hatred				
Love				
Affection				
Attachment				
Humanity				
Spirituality				
Personality				
No Self Control				
Wandering Mind				
Hungry for Power				
Selfishness				
Authority				
Heart				
Lack of emotional control				
Lust				
Conditional Sacrifice				
Trust				
Hope				
Faith				
Fear				
Judgment				
World				
Universe				
Nation				
Thought				
Decision making				
Wisdom				
No clear cut philosophy				
Improper understanding of Theology				
Lack of concentration				
Competition				
Comparison				

Discrimination				
Recognition				
Admiration				
Ego				
Criticism				
Sacrifices				
Compromise				
Illiteracy				
Stress & Strain				
Bondages				
Possessions				
Indiscipline				
Evils				
Sins				
Freedom				
Lack of satisfaction				
Falling behind expectations				
Inferiority				
Racism				
Religion				
Nationality				
Poverty				
Richness				
Outside disturbances				
Undefined Goals of life				
Lost Time in Life				
Lack of family support				
Professional life				
Marriage Life				
Personal Life				
Social Life				
Gender Impact and Influences				

21. What lessons you have learnt up to the present from your life?

Lessons Learnt from Life	Agree	Partially	Disagree	Reason
I have made more mistakes for nothing				
Mistakes have brought in awakening				
Have wasted life without giving love				
Have not utilized the natural powers				
Have not capitalized the opportunities				
Failure is absolutely necessary before success can be attained				
Greatest part of education comes from constantly striving to overcome obstacles				
Which a man gives comes back to him				
Habit of forgiving instead of striking back				
Life is not as per our wishes and will				
Never give up unfulfilled Dreams				
Work to achieve your unfulfilled Desires				
Do and die for unfulfilled Destiny				
Never have attachment to loved ones				
Quit attachment to sense pleasures				
No attachment to physical body				

Possessing happiness and peace by true means				
Possessing money and wealth with integrity				
Possessing health and beauty with sincerity				
Great leaders are man of tolerance and self-control				
Never fall in comparison with other man				
Equality in comparison with society				
Birds of a feather flock together				
Be away from illusion and delusion				
Try understanding difference between education and knowledge				
Never waste time in finding peace outside				
Try understanding real success				
Struggle to be better for yourself				
Create your life as you like				
Human mind should keep on imagining				
Your work should bring happiness to others				
Develop overall personality				
Avoid Man's dual nature				
Utilizing Life effectively				
Always live an inspiring Life				
Focus on proper nurturing				
Anger is a state of insanity				
Believe in yourself				

Happiness is something you cannot buy, borrow, beg and steal				
Be bold to hold dreams				
Man should work with the community spirit.				
You may kill a man but not his message				
We are responsible for what we are				
There are certain principles which comes to man naturally				
One ounce of practice is worth a thousand pounds of theory				
He who has a pure mind sees everything pure				
Our thoughts make things beautiful or ugly				
Do not find faults with others, rather learn to see your own faults.				
Discrepancy is the key to discovery				
Man can only attain immortality through renunciation				
Man should always care for the spirit				
Save yourself by yourself.				
Liberty is the first condition of growth				
Mind-stuff keeps on undergoing modifications not the mind				
Life is but a constant expression of your inner activities				

22. Your personal, social and professional achievements over the years of life lived till present?

Years	List Achieve-ments	Excellent	Appreciable	Satisfactory	Marginal	Nothing
0-5						
6-10						
11-15						
16-20						
21-25						
26-30						
31-35						
36-40						
41-45						
46-50						
51-55						
56-60						
61-65						
66-70						
71-75						
76-80						
Above 80						

23. Your perception on the individual's role in developing the humanity?

Role	List Con-tribution	Excellent	Appreciable	Satisfactory	Marginal	Nothing
Mother						
Father						
Parents						
Son						
Daughter						
Children						
Brother						
Sister						

Husband						
Wife						
Uncle						
Aunt						
Niece						
Nephew						
Family						
Friends						
Relatives						
Acquaintances						
Neighbors						
Community						
Corporations						
Clubs						
Gatherings						
Institutions						
Organizations						
Strangers						
Saints						
Philosophers						
Reformers						

24. Your opinion on, how to expedite regenerating humanity around the world at the earliest from dawn to dusk?

Regenerating Humanity	Education	Awareness	Imple-mentation	Enforce-ment	Empower-ment	Revolution
Reversal of your situation						
Reforming the self						
Transforming the society						
Welfare of the society						
Literacy of the world						

Spirituality of the world							
More centers of happiness projects							
Changing attitude of man							
A radical change							
Change through next generation							
Contribution by every individual							
Role of Nations							
Integrating it globally							

25. Write your autobiography this dawn focusing it towards humanity today. Evaluate your own written essay of life to understand where you are really standing in existence. Do it today sincerely before the dusk. Let the essay be a crisp summary of important turning points and milestones of your life restricting it to 5000 to 10,000 words.

Could you interrogate yourself? Does your awareness on humanity not astonish you? Are you aware of what you are becoming? Do you still have time to become human? Is the urgency to bring in humanity being felt by you? Can you change the world? Can you regenerate humanity? Are you living from dawn to dusk?

I am sure what else can be a better way to examine ourselves. Keep writing your autobiography now and then to examine, evaluate and explore the human in you. Understanding your darkness is the purpose of this life. Life is an opportunity and grace to experience the divinity of existence.

Man should see the light of life in every human. Cutting man is like cutting of trees as good as reducing oxygen in environment. Man is required to breathe humanity.

A librarian is only the custodian of the many number of big, large, small books, articles, thesis, dissertations, manuals, journals, epics, manuscripts, unpublished works, literature, writings, periodicals, white papers, project synopsis, statistical data and information.

He is good at identifying and locating the book by author, topic, and subject, year of publishing, awards and writers community. He is good at preserving these books. He is good at daily holding and handling it with care and love. He is good at protecting it completely. All these activities never give him an opportunity to even peep into the knowledge of life. Though he lives his entire life with books he fails to utilize the vast resources of knowledge.

Such should not be our lives. Being in the library of world we should not end up our lives like the librarian of books.

The world is library of wisdom.
The existence is library of truths.

No other person generally has a huge wealthy resource of this kind to explore knowledge, ideas, thoughts, findings, views, opinions, principles, philosophies, perceptions, objectives, voices, inspirations, from various fields, subjects and authors.

Despite all these you may not be astonished to know that just by being the custodian of books the librarian cannot become intelligent, knowledgeable and owner of wisdom of life.

I understand that, "On the other hand any visiting reader to the library who has read a single book, may be even a single chapter, or even may be a small paragraph from a valued book, and he picks up a single idea and continuously works towards it, he reaches from the perception of that idea to the perfection of the idea in reality". Let us not be the librarian of life but be the readers of life.

The more you read life the more you understand existence, human and humanity. Any mechanism which works for you is the best mechanism till it is assisting you in examining yourself. You are the best doctor to diagnose your human in you. The prescriptions of medicines are yours to arrest the fever of inhumanity. The treatment is to be so nursed that it does not relapse to bring you back to the dawn of sufferings.

Do you know the real causes of sufferings from dawn to dusk? Have as many workshops as you can. Prepare workbooks for working to understand the need of self-assessment.

Ethically evaluate the human in you. Examine, examine and reexamine yourself as many times as you can for your self -reformation. Let the methods may be different but the purpose is same to know the human in self.

Queen of Virtues

The Roman Philosopher Cicero stated that

"Gratitude was the Queen of Virtues".

Who can be the greatest of greatest kings on earth? Man is the only prince of existence. He is the ruler of the world. Every land is enemy of other land rather than being a neighbor of happiness. Why we hate our neighbors? Hate always brings out the heat between the exchangers. Are we trying to demolish their existence? Are they not equally important as us? Land should hold land to see that the cultures are integrated with single mission of happiness all over the world.

You will be responded as per your ability. The self talk is a great source of energy. Keep talking to yourself I can and I will, I shall do it, I will win, I will beat the day. All days are ours. But today is more important than tomorrow and yesterday. Yesterday I was a bad man today I am a saint. The world please look at me, I have all the virtues of existence with me.

When you are becoming right thence your voice gains immense power of purity to speaking aloud to the whole existence. You want your virtues to reach to the heavens. Day by day virtues acquired help in eliminating the vices which were already residing in you.

Where is the queen of virtues in you?

Among virtues there is a supreme virtue. What is the most difficult virtue to hold on from dawn to dusk? Can we sustain it till our existence? All days are ours. In fact we are not utilizing it. Not reaping from it. We are throwing it. We are spilling the valuable time.

Man should be untouched by ruthlessness, malice, pettiness, selfishness, jealousness, cruelness, edginess, evilness, cunningness, passiveness, untruthfulness, and so on and so forth. Every man has his own ideological and political evolution. Can man halt the course of history? Why man should struggle for his elementary rights? The denial of these elementary rights leads to the dilution of the virtues. Changing your mind, thought, action, perception, understanding all away from the centre of virtue. The Vice in you becomes your Queen of Virtues. Man suffers because of his both realistic and idealistic convictions despite having a scientific method of understanding and changing society.

No man is born criminal.

Why man has taken up crime? Foremost this is the beginning of reformation process. What compels him to associate with terrorism? Is terrorism an individual issue? If one man can bring terror then one man can also bring peace to the whole world. Man is operating in groups either for the good cause or for the bad cause. This is splitting the humanity. Humans are being broadly divided into divine and terror groups. One is fighting to reinstate humanity. At the same time other is fighting to demolish humanity.

Will the division of world cease?

There is no greater virtue than peace, happiness, kindness, unselfishness, divineness, which humans are not working for. Where the terrorism is breeding? The criminal activities from dawn to dusk are polluting the society. Simply by war can we attain peace?

War is a very raw method of trying to bring peace in society. The question is why they are happening despite the enforcement of national and international laws. Criminals have been migrating to become refugees all over the world instead of being the messengers of happiness. A perfect law and order can be established only through the process of education on humanity.

Crime begins in mind.
&
Crime can only beget crime.

The thought comes because of the narrow understanding of the situation. The sufferings are not shared. The causes of sufferings are not considered. The elementary right of the individual has not been honored. The opponent man behaves not with a difference to the man affecting the argument. People are becoming intolerant day by day. Our approach towards upsetting people is not with an attitude of brotherhood. The distressing person is bound to disturb the entire environment of peace from dawn to dusk.

Criminal by himself is not criminal.

He has been made so. The society and humanity is also responsible. If you allow the weeds in your garden, then there is always a possibility that you will end up with the garden of weeds rather than the garden of roses.

Our scenario today is the same. The true confession of every man is he hates terrorism. Terrorism is not an appreciable profession for earning bread and butter. The majority of the people's life is consumed in getting the bread from dawn to dusk. Where is the question of the butter on the bread?

Every individual can work out this sample tabulation for ready reference after the dusk. This summarizes the list of problems faced in the day. And the probable solutions you had. Did it bring benefit to you?

Problems & Solutions

Area of Problems	Causes	Solutions	Benefits	Becoming of Self
Money	Purchase Materials	Borrowed Money	Liability	Dependant on others
Health	Stress	Nil	Nil	Depressed
Family	Relationship	Giving More Time to family members	Togetherness	Happier/ Homely
Humanity	Colleagues	Counseling	Team Work	Leader

Man made guns. God never made guns.

The ideology of society is not able to penetrate the core of humanity. Punishing a criminal does not mean that crime has been eliminated. What use is of this punishment which cannot bring in attitudinal changes in the criminal? The criminal remains where he had started.

Our system of learning needs revolution of thinking from dawn to dusk. Society should impart virtue to the needy. A drop of learning daily can transform the entire community. What can be a greater religion than secularism? It has all the minds, cultures, traditions, theology, of the world.

Man has to conquer the evil. Man has to defeat the terror. The society is to be cleaned of all this. Courage is the most important of all the virtues because without courage you cannot practice any other virtue consistently.

No one can have a good idea everyday on every issue may be our limitations but not impossibility.

Humans have to leverage the diversity of experience and exploration. We all know that pressure is what turns a lump of coal into a diamond.

The problem is, are we pressurizing ourselves to that extent for excelling to become a diamond of humanity? Believe me my dear learned readers that not even 1% (one percent) of the learned fraternity is applying the pressure to transform themselves with virtues of heavens.

The wheel of humanity is with educationists, reformists and humanists to move into the world with supersonic speed to traverse the maximum distance in minimum time frame, meeting huge population of humans in spreading the message of humanity. The focus is to effectively utilize the implementation techniques, expedite awareness, monitor and review that the intended values, ethics, morals, principles are reaching one and all.

Virtues are wealth of life.

Do you think someone will come and give you daily virtues in your pocket from dawn to dusk? It needs solely your effort to forge yourself as a man of great value.

I wish to confess to my valuable readers,

"Value can come to human only through virtues".

If you are facing opponents, resistances, hindrances, critics, ill words, non-cooperation, suppression, humiliation, from the people not from the valued community that itself speaks of your good things being done by you from dawn to dusk.

If you are truthful to your values and virtues definitely the unvalued man shall yield one day towards your attitude and persistence.

It is no good wisdom to sacrifice your values for short and instant gains. All short pleasures are blessed with curse of longer pains.

Man cannot discover new oceans unless he has the courage to lose sight of the shore.- Andre Gide

In recent times many of the schools of management are professionally speaking of people management in improving the skills of humans in areas of negotiations, communications, networking, teamwork, leadership, effectiveness, operations, productivity, motivation, inspiration, human resources development, human capital management, international human resources, global culture, and so on.

Keeping the above in background an insight into humans reveals that the overall purpose of these trainings, development, learning programs, human workshops, case studies, etc with the advancement in teaching techniques is to groom the overall personality of any professional inculcating ethics, virtues and values in humans.

The World is attempting to establish the kingdom of virtues. The necessities of survival have been the intruders in compelling man at times to yield from their central principles of living from dawn to dusk. Much of our life is lost in frustration and worries for others rather than on the self. We on average indulge in 90 % of unproductive activities leading to nowhere in life from dawn to dusk.

Do you have a clear sense of who you are? Your leadership identity can and should change each time you move on to bigger and better things. Seeking and giving advice are central to effective leadership and decision making. Receiving guidance is often seen as the passive consumption of wisdom. It is a question for all of us to understand our level of perception and knowledge of existence.

Many problems between and among humans arise due to exchange of words, views, opinions, ideas, thoughts, feelings, egos, minds, brains and so on.

When the exchange is done well, the people on both sides of the table benefit. Is the exchange ethical? Is it moral? Does it have the value? What virtues were considered to finalize the deal? It may not be true that all benefits are beneficial to humanity. Why to be party to the beneficiary of unethical gains in the world?

Where to get advice for living with virtues from dawn to dusk? Things are peculiar because of perception rather than that of complexity in reality. The society today is mix of unlearned, learned, intellectuals, scholars, moderates, average, bringing in different styles of managing the self.

Managing your mission, vision, objectives, aim, targets, and so on is the prime step towards changing your minds. How do you get people to change their minds about you? Any new person you encounter – a potential boss, a prospective client, a new colleague, a stranger is likely to evaluate you in two phases. The way we see one another can be irrational, incomplete and inflexible and largely automatic. And most of the time we are victims of our own ego rather than the real cause for happening the unappreciable.

Can we fill our gap between efforts and results?

Smile & Tears

I have one very sincere advice for my readers that "Let us not fiddle while Rome burns". Man can convert tears into smile and smile into tears.

This is solely based on the understanding of the life he makes from his wisdom on the world.

Always remember the road to heaven is only through the hell. The path of success is through the path of failure. The path of bliss is through the path of struggle. The path of perseverance is through the path of patience.

A Renaissance of Humanity should flood the world. Humans have to redesign a better road map to attain it everywhere. Man is born with potential, goodness, trust, hope, faith, love, ideas, dreams, confidence, greatness, courage to defeat problems, miseries, sorrows and troubles, to succeed but not to crawl.

Man has to fly away from the evils of existence.

Gratitude takes us outside of ourselves. The world is divided into smiles and tears. Again this state is not attainable eternally. It changes with times of the individuals.

Man is found smiling today and in tears tomorrow. The law of union and the law of separation are applicable to everyman on this earth. This is law of life on earth. This is the law of existence. Let us cure ourselves of excuses. Before we really fail we withdraw our action, persuasion, perseverance, patience, due to our lack of confidence. The fear in us should be destroyed.

How to think big?
How to lead big?
How to become big?

How to do big? Who will do the big? Why not me? Why I am unable to manage my environment? Why we are largely depending upon inanimate things? Why the man in me is inalterable? Why I am still continuing with impudicity? Is life an incomprehensible subject? Is it inconceivable? Why man is inconsiderate to man? What should be effigy of a person? Why man is becoming indecent? Where to find the ethos? Have ethics to do anything with ethnography? When will the real euphoria come to this universe? Who will bring this? How to get it? Is it not the sine qua non?

Some have the apprehensions that world suffered because of the theocracy? Did fideism failed to integrate humanity? Why we still are not able to think right about the people in and around us? The leadership qualities have become extinct from the world. The rule of transitivity has its own doubts. Existentialism again has its own limitations.

Where to find the right exegesis today? The society today has flung from polygamy to exogamy. The humans are in experimentation with their values blaming the globalization. The exobiology study is a way towards migrating to other better earth as quick as possible. This will be an alternative solution to mankind on earth tomorrow against the pain of designing a better road map.

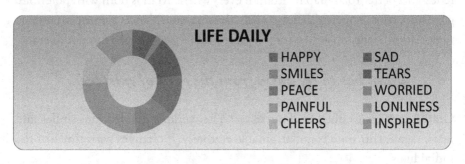

LIFE DAILY

HAPPY	SAD
SMILES	TEARS
PEACE	WORRIED
PAINFUL	LONLINESS
CHEERS	INSPIRED

Life has many moods from dawn to dusk.

Some of the ones very frequently rise and fall daily in everybody's life.

Life is as it is.

This is not the reason for not fighting it out. Some are sailing in smiles and some are sailing in tears. The readers are not to be surprised on this account of man's life.

> ***A negative situation is to be visualized with positive perception.***

At the same equally a positive situation is to be visualized without negative perception. It is really a very difficult task for a leader to lead when you are not the boss. How can you discharge a function with authority without owning authority? How human can work with informal authority?

Do you really need authority in teamwork?

***True leadership, of course has never been
a matter of formal authority.***

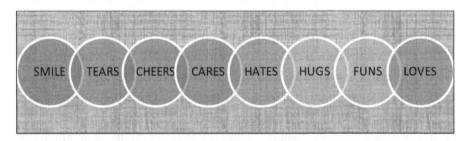

| SMILE | TEARS | CHEERS | CARES | HATES | HUGS | FUNS | LOVES |

People Vs People

The Whole fight is here.

People have overlapping changing moods from dawn to dusk. A smiling man this moment is in tears next moment. A person depressed with hates suddenly starts hugging with love and shares fun. Man moves from moods to moods first in mind and then in feelings, thoughts, expressions, ideas and becoming.

Now the question is why humans are victims of cruel moods? Does enmity is outcome of moods? Are humans able to differentiate between moods, emotions, fantasy, dreams, desires, wishes, needs and realities?

How to summarize the outcomes from dawn to dusk? Is the arena of people responsible to the whole proceedings? Is it not ridiculous to understand that people hate people?

Why people hate people?

The British historian Lord Acton warned his students and his readers "Power tends to corrupt and absolute power corrupts absolutely," he did so because of his concern for the danger posed to liberty by holders of political power.

Is liberty of human the cause of all chaos?

Man is at times deceived in reading the situation of life. What you are obsessively anticipating may not be in reality happening. This is one of the reasons of frequent instability of man's moods from dawn to dusk. Man is the victim in any case. Sometimes the prevailing situation is favorable but the understanding of it is misleading from exactness.

Do you always deliver on promises you have made from dawn to dusk? Do people consider you to be trustworthy? Do we establish an environment in which people can share their ideas and know that their opinions are valued?

Differences in opinions should not end up with enmity. The fact is that faithfully trusts between people do not happen overnight. It is gradually developed only over time and through a series of personal interactions and observed behaviors. So if you behave repeatedly in a trustworthy manner you will earn a reputation for being trustworthy. The reliability in relationship is what matters in building humanity all over the world from dawn to dusk.

Live for Perfection

To recall the undying thinking Philosopher, Socrates from the remains of Ancient Greece, used to say, "Practice death daily",

be meant not in a morbid way, but in order to put the problems of life in perspective.

There is relationship of death to everyday life. Life is to threaten it or be threatened by it. That is to do or die. That is to slice and dice. That is to live and learn. You cannot die and do at the same time. Let us not sweep death under the carpet.

Every dawn is the death of death. Dawn brings an entirely new leaf to the plant of life every day. Knowingly or unknowingly the unwanted has to die. When the purpose of the banana tree is completed it falls on its own after bearing the fruits. The flower fades away after the fragrance has been lost. A single flower has to die to give way to the millions of buds waiting to bloom in the existence.

Human should not be foolishly selfish to hold on ever in this existence in the physical body. The purpose of the body is limited. The purpose of the spirit is infinite. The purpose of human is infinite. The purpose of humanity is infinite.

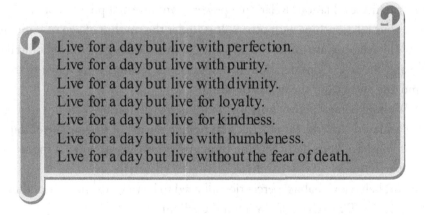

Live for a day but live with perfection.
Live for a day but live with purity.
Live for a day but live with divinity.
Live for a day but live for loyalty.
Live for a day but live for kindness.
Live for a day but live with humbleness.
Live for a day but live without the fear of death.

I passionately communicate to my readers, "Life and Death both are interconnected like Dawn and Dusk". Dawn is Life. Dusk is Death. Daily we go through these two vital end points of existence. My understanding is "Dawn to Dusk is as good as Life to Death", where the complete infinite world is collapsing into the finite world from dawn to dusk.

Never allow naysayers and negative voices to derail you. Doubters stop us from following our vision. Sometimes life is full of heart break and getting up one more time when you fall down. The world needs more and more teachers and student of humanities. Will the dualism die? Will terrorism perish? Depressions are crippling our lives? The way humanity is doing I feel we have to start practicing disappointment.

Power is a necessary feature of every social system. In military organizations, every unit has one person vested with power to command action. Despite its necessity, however, few people have a positive view of the power and are after distrustful of the people who seek it.

How people feel about power? How it is restrained by interpersonal dependencies? In many cultures, power is viewed with suspicion and fear because of its potential for coercion and corruption.

Humans have different perception on power as necessity. You may observe that paradoxically, neither society nor its organizations can function without the application of power. Shall we punish failure?

Is power the meaning of dictatorship? Is not dependency a fact of life? The effectiveness of human is not only through the scientific methods of performance evaluation. Relational power is an informal power that emerges from your relationships with others. It is under the rhythm of ego of humans.

Why relations are under the influence of individual egos? Man should live free and die free. Consideration to thoughts and feelings from dawn to dusk is moving away from the hearts of humans.

Without being a perfect human rest are useless perfections which you might have achieved. After great practice you perfect the art of singing melodiously but if you have been daily abusing humans with ill words what is the use of such perfection.

Our behaviors, habits, perception all need to be towards the central theme of humanity. Expertise helps you build credibility.

Dependencies are a natural part of human society.

We depend on other people for some things and they depend on us for others.

Dependency is the law of existence. In today's world it is more or less to the concept of synergy. Accomplishing things without association generates draining of resource participation at any level and all walks of life.

We see an explicit manifestation of dependencies in the everyday life. Are our relationships and obligations carefully codified? Relational power can also be increased through a system of reciprocity. Whenever you do a favor for someone else, a change takes place in the relationship. The other person owes you a favor in return. This is the law of reciprocity, which demands that every favor must someday be repaid.

Man is suffering because of the accounts of payable and receivables in daily life. Undesirable and unwanted receivables are flooding in human's daily living accounts. Man's integrity, credibility, authenticity, reciprocity, loyalty, nobility, morality, purity, divinity, attitudes, attributes, behaviors, and so on all are under mappings with survival from dawn to dusk.

No doubt to be an ideal man is not as easy as told in books, essays, lectures, classes, discourses. It is an opportunity and challenge from dawn to dusk.

Humanity is an all round shield for ideal humans.

Are humans of today reliable in reciprocation of valuable concerns?

How can humans stop themselves from becoming inhumane? Who would like to be cruel, brutal, merciless, heartless, appalling and sadist? Even the beasts would like to spare when they are not hungry.

Human's sadism issues are universal. A unique problem everywhere in the world should have a universal solution. The severities may be different but the central theme of hatred precedes any other ambiguities.

2+3=5, is it not the same anywhere in the world? The basics of the problem are universal. Man lies is a truth everywhere in the world. Now what he is untruthful about is the secondary matter.

Will of Man

I would like to bring your attention that

"What you cannot do today you can never do it tomorrow".

Learn the art of self-gratification. It has the power to exponentially multiply your energy of life. And you have to start with yourself. First make your will ready. Readiness to live properly can be very well achieved by this miracle will. The will, thought and action should go hand in hand. No man's will, shall be ill if the man really wills.

Our daily obligations should not deter the goals we are dreaming.

The mind should not dwell only in thinking. Make it shift from thought to action from dawn to dusk.

Human quality is suffering because of the will. We have grown in numbers but not values. The massive population of man is not having a unified will. If all our wills are thinking and working towards caring and uplifting each other then there would have been no absence of happiness in all homes all over the world.

Will of Man cannot let it happen. Will of Man is always the divine will. The inner will always have the power to uproot the outside will as and when required. This probably advocates the theory of reincarnation of man. Will is the core of the mind. A strong will can defeat all the senses. It overrules all the other functionaries of the body.

Till you have the will no one can tilt you. The whole world also cannot drill you. It is only with the right will that you can perfectly fill your life. Start now, right now, to discover how to make your thinking make magic for you.

Start out with this thought of the great Philosopher Disraeli,

"Life is too short to be little".

Now again to my potential readers, what this book will do for you? The answer will defer from reader to reader. I nowhere mean to say all should become philosophers of humanity. However, at the same time I am not liberal in compelling you to live a life without philosophy. That you are reading this page proves you are interested in humanity.

How to decide the levels of authority in man? Man is always accountable for his own state of mind. External influences and its impacts are another area from dawn to dusk. Understanding is deeper than knowledge.

Mistakes become a collection of experiences called lessons. Time is cruel like life. It slows down to experience the most out of it. Time is Man's breathe. Sometimes your heart needs more time to accept what your mind already knows.

The Will is in between mind and time. The willingness of the mind needs support of time. Do not allow people to alter the state of your mind? Again before people it is you not to lose your focus away from your prime will. When we are concentrating on the externals like body, roles, relations, possessions, the will on inner world starts weakening. Does responsibility makes us tensed or worried? Happiness is the best nourishment.

Will of Happiness is to be developed by everyman.

Will is the inner force to gain the momentum of happiness. Happy mind attracts good fortune. Have pure feelings for everyone.

My readers can see how one thing of man is related with other aspects of his oneself. Will, mind, heart, soul, body, thought, hope, faith, trust, love, wish, way, perception, attitude, ability, time, grace, fortune, dawn, dusk, day, opportunity, mood, happiness, affection, kindness, healthiness, and many more are regularly to be activated and need to be aligned towards one central goal humanity.

Do not make your life hellish just because you are not willing to be out of it? Will to leverage your mind, thought, talent, energies, potential, time, resources of nature and earth, towards happiness of the soul?

Will of man has to take control of cropping desires. As you fulfill one more come up. Do we need many desires from dawn to dusk? It is not to limit your ambitious aim but as you know the weeding desires suppress the advancement and growth of essential desires. Will control is principle for containment.

Man needs to decide his will towards dreams, desires, thoughts, and actions and in overall living. Again it is will which brings satisfaction on sacrifice. A good man need not be successful in all areas. It is good for the pure hearts to regularly fail in will for the bad activities from dawn to dusk.

The Will can kill evil.

The Will can still turbulence of life. Man has to first get the Will. There is nothing powerful than the Will of Man. This is the root cause of all the miseries arising from the bad desires. Good desires can only take you towards divinity, nobility, morality and humanity. Will is an inner voice of man. It is universally in all of us. We need not create it. It is the gift of life. We have it any time with us. The concern is making it work for us.

My dear ambitious readers please kindly make a note of it,

"By the time Will catalyses to initiate in action, Man loses the golden dawn".

Will of Man is the prime mover from dawn to dusk.

Where is the will to decide the will? When you are inspired with the spiritual goal all desires fade. Trade rapidly and regularly to fade away your unwanted desires. You should clear your inventory of bad desires immediately as you notice it.

God's greatest power to man is Will of Man. It has all the secrets of existence. It has all the unfolded chapters of life. It has all the activities from dawn to dusk. It has all the power to face the world. It has all the grace to embrace the nature. It has all the miracles to see the universe.

With trust and faith in universe I share to say, "Seek the spirit and the world will be at your feet".

Summing Up & Exercise for Readers- Chapter- VIII

- Plan a self feedback session.
- Prepare a Self-Evaluation checklist.
- Have worksheets for Self-Assessment.
- List out useful implementation tools you can utilize.
- Mobilize your resources to build yourself.
- Periodically review your Self-Appraisals

- Identify performance gaps by disclosing your appraisal.
- If you are falling short of your goals, why do you think that is?
- Find out the root causes of performance gaps in regard to the problem you are facing.
- Plan to close these gaps by right means.
- Enhance your capabilities required to meet the new goals.
- Follow up in Self-Life is very important to the whole process.
- Encourage yourself daily to transform into good human and you shall become.
- Managing Yourself, Self-Day is to be cultivated from dawn to dusk.
- Follow –"CCA"-Create, Communicate and Act.
- Follow-"AAB"-Attitudes, Attributes and Behaviors.
- Follow-"ACV"-Authenticity, Credibility and Values.
- Follow-"PAK"-Practice, Attitude and Knowledge.

PART V
DUSK

PART V

DUSK

Chapter IX

REALIZATION AT DUSK

Why Concern of life is lost in the shadow of time?

"Prefer to die doing your own duty.
The duty of another will bring you
into great spiritual danger,"
-Teaches Lord Krishna in the Gita.

This truth is being experienced by one and all. There is no exception in truth. Truth is the law of all laws. It is you to review where are you standing at dusk. Did you win by dharma or karma? Are you following bhoga or yoga? Keep revoking yourself. Keep transforming yourself. Keep changing yourself. Keep rediscovering yourself. The inner and outer world of man changes from dawn to dusk.

I have been influenced by the teachings of our ancient saints who lived on this earth at this part of the world. It is not because of the prejudices I have for these wisdoms but because they have some answers to the chaos of the world today. They have given us many windows to the world. The clarity in living from darkness to enlightenment should be the only aim of human to learn and relearn.

I am grateful to those Indian Saints who lived only for finding the right education for the right living. Their findings were not just mere piece of literature from the existing libraries of the world but in fact it was from the realization of living, nature and universe.

India is the land where liberation and salvation is part of the entire process of cycle of life. The spheres of karma, dharma, yoga and moksha in any once life accounts his overall living with the perception of life. A complete man can only understand the complete cycle of life from dawn to dusk.

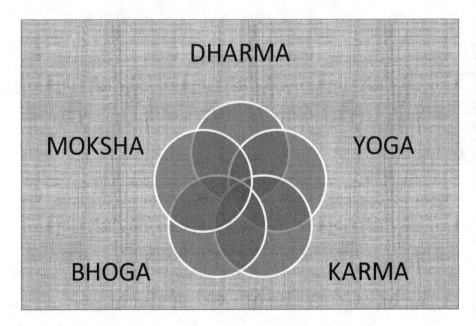

Everyone experiences the emptiness in life.

Honestly speaking it may not be an easy postulate to accept or reject on a generalized platform of living. Aloneness is a way of recovery in the inner world. When the influence of the outer world ceases on you the seed of the inner world starts sprouting and germinates inside to eternal tree of enlightenment. The more you go inner the more you reach nearer to eternity.

At the end of dawn you may feel incomplete and unfulfilled.

The journey between this abundance to emptiness holds the secrets of lessons from life. The journey between learnt to unlearn holds the secrets of wisdom from life. Why recognition and acknowledgement of the deeds and the doer? Both are two faces of the same coin likely to be liberated. The aspect of realization lies deeper within us as the mines of assimilation. One by one is to be reviewed. The findings may not be the final inferences. Till you are living, you are striving, thriving, fighting, learning, inspiring, editing, and realizing.

Every passing of dusk gives a new dawn. The vision, mission, objective, aim, goal brainstormed at dusk sprouts like a new leaf to attain the perfection. The fundamental nature of man is freedom and equality. The world has dreams of unity in humankind.

Mistakes to Maturity

Everyone makes mistakes. I have come to an understanding that,

"Mistakes is the mother of Maturity".

Think little deeper to take this nectar. The bitterness of mistakes is sweetness at maturity. This is here you are transforming into teacher from student. This is here you are transforming into leader from follower. This is here you are transforming into ideal human.

The question is of the known and unknown mistakes humans make from dawn to dusk. Intentionally no one from the bottom of heart would like to harm anyone is the nature of ideal human.

How mistakes have an impact on humanity? Mistakes related to loss of life are unpardonable. The guilt is like the shadow of man. It never leaves the wrong doer. Such faults are not the purpose of faithful humans. How guiltiness can help humans to transform themselves into worthiness of existence?

Faith and trust are the two principal pillars of any relationship from dawn to dusk. Mistakes in relationship are more influenced by the immaturity in understanding the give and take between the humans involved in transactions of humanity.

Do mistakes originate in the mind?

Maturity originates from mistakes.

A new way originates from the older one. A new thought springs from the other one. A new idea is created from another one. A new thing is discovered from another one. A new ideal can be stood from another one. A new human can be generated from another man. Anew man can be born from old one.

Thus mistake is the mother giving birth to new dimension, avenues, ways, options, chances, opportunities, ideas, thoughts for better understanding of the self, nature, man, earth, world, universe and in completeness the existence.

What do you mean by mistakes? Were they miss-takes of life? It should not have been that way? The other way looks always good. It is rightly been in voice for long time that the neighbors lawns are always green than yours. I say unless you are on way how do you know about the other ways? If I have done something this dawn then I can compare with previous and next one. If I have not done anything, I do not have an opportunity to create and compare.

You can only learn if you are willing to learn and till you are learning gaps will be coming to surface from dawn to dusk. The realization helps you to map with the gaps.

What we call mistakes are actually "GAPS" not mistakes and it has to have "MAPS". That is gaps are to be mapped or bridged to complete the learning process. The delaying in mapping the gaps is detriment to the overall development of humans.

I have made plenty of mistakes, big ones, little ones, expensive ones, name it and I might have messed it up. This is already over. Are not you doing blunder, a more unpardonable mistake by grumbling over the mistakes done? You are again wasting the remaining valuable time. Talk to yourself what I am doing otherwise you may miss an incredible opportunity of life time, simply mourning over the lost time.

We learn from everything. It is to restart here rather than unfruitful reconciliation .The one who follows the mistakes will usually get no further than the mistakes. The one who looks beyond it is bound to excel despite the series of mistakes. It is so because he perceives them as attempts but not failures. Attempt is a way to reach the goal. The one you are trying may rightly be not your path. Educate yourself picking the right one till your goal has been achieved. There are many ways to climb the mountain. It is our effort which is failing not the person in you.

No one makes mistakes, these are only some takes which you might have missed or you may miss. In the true sense mistake is a big misnomer in life. When the whole life is a probability, where is the question of mistakes? Rather these are chances tossed up or down in reality. Life is to take a chance. What you have to do with yes or no? If yes, then there is a way, aligned to it. On the other hand even for the no, there is way aligned to it. Does it make a difference? We should remove mistakes and failure from our vocabulary as everything you try is teaching you something. The aim of an argument, discussion, mistakes, failures, conflicts, debates, should not invariably be victory but progress.

Why fear what will happen after the mistakes? Why to think every time that bad will happen? Let us keep moving towards our goals, if we fail to get anything, one thing is sure that the experience will be definitely new.

Experiences are lessons to grow.

Hence without mistakes it would have been difficult to come across such valuable experiences and incessantly learning. The departing soul should salute me with gratitude, confessing what a person he was with whom I wish could have continued to be for some more time to learn the path of righteousness for living. Oh heavens, I shall not get any dawn of this gesture, hence let me too perish with him.

My resolutions should stand above all obligations.

The life of slavery should be cut by the sword of knowledge. Bliss can only come from purity of the mind. Grace can only befall from the divinity of the self. Gain the divine thought from dawn to dusk before the mind is obsessed with unwanted weeds. The weeds are to be uprooted as they will not allow the plant of dawn to grow in the garden of life. Hold on to yourself if you want to hold the simplicity of life.

Who came along with you to see this beautiful world? No one, no one, you were all alone, then why are you waiting for someone to hold you. You are the branches of your own trunk. You have to accept the sourness and sweetness of the self bearing fruits. Your true nature can be only seen by you. Nothing can be revealed within the self without realization through the mind. As body experiences the truth, mind understands the reality. Rise before you fall for ever, never to lift yourself from the den of hell. Be the king of your own kingdom from dawn to dusk.

Let no intruder invade your thought of life. March; march ahead as the light is to be seen by the eyes not the back of you. Help yourself to be tamed daily, the way you want to exclusively live through dawn to dusk enjoying the freedom of life. Both the point of time is yours, only yours. No more looking back in the weakness of the self.

Learning is the process through realization.

All school of thoughts is in vain, if the intuition in you has not taken birth. Without living to the fullest, realization cannot be appreciably substantial in intervening in building yourself. Water quenches the thirsty not the viewer. The deeper the thirst for realization the deeper is the learning from life. Live to the fullest till the candle of life melts down. All that vaporizes during the process should fill the universe with fragrance of love, faith, trust, hope and mankind.

Life is the greatest teacher of all.

Lessons are experiences of the self. Every moment is a new time for learning. We can start examining yourselves daily. We can professionally carry out GAP ANALYSIS frequently. This would bring to the surface our means, needs, desires, dreams, destiny, likes, dislikes, perception, urges, aims, goals, careers, sacrifices, intellectuality, wisdom, spirituality, boldness, nobility, cruelty, jealousy, becoming, trend, vision, mission, faith, trust, and the mappings with the ends, results, accomplishments and achievements.

Keep observing the nature very closely as it is invariably imparting teaching in one form or the other. Prophets, philosophers, saints, researchers, scientists, thinkers, gurus, rishis, reformers, scholars all in their regime underwent realization, putting forward their summarized findings as postulates for the coming generations to redefine the very beginning.

Every culture has a meaning of existence.

Every man has is worth of salt. Every nation has its importance. Are not the men of the world trying to bring betterment to humanity in all respects through all walks of life? A small betterment in one area influences betterment in another area manifold times. The law of multiplication is man's strength to save time. Man has been also helped by the law of magnification. The theory of exponential expansion is another tool.

In addition to all these this simple tool Dawn to Dusk may be of tremendous use in moving the minds of man equally towards achieving betterment. It should live its purpose for rekindling society.

Living with certain principles before a basic maturity is obtained has its own perception and challenges at dawn. The advantage or disadvantage of maturity is that it brings in transformation in different dimensions at dusk. Mistakes and maturity keep floating between dawns to dusk. There is pull between mistakes and maturity daily. Shedding out your mistakes is like the skin of snake. The new snake is ready with new spirit of existence. Man keeps doing these till he lives. He acknowledges himself on his new learning. A vibrant new man is born because of the blows of the mistakes. A new man has been forged because of the melting of mistakes in the furnace of existence. This is the beauty of dawn and dusk.

Dawn and Dusk brings a new beginning to one and all.

Man is the most dynamic life on this earth. Man can recast again and again his existence just like the nature. The perfection is awaited for oneness with nature. The School begins at dawn to assimilate for comprehension at dusk. Push yourself through the chapters of life from dawn to dusk. The world today have people who will insult you, hate you, rate you, shake you, break you, fool you, manipulate you, on the other hand there are people who will love you, help you, admire you, inspire you, assist you, encourage you, mentor you, the point here is, how strong you stand is what really makes you.

You become what you dream.

The power of dream is the only governing force to uplift you among the people of likes and dislikes.

<u>Way to Heaven</u>

*Cradle to graveyard should not be a journey
of life with confessions of regrets.*

Dawn is a universal cradle for all humans.

It is the spring of life. Let it spread out to all corners of the world. Every life has its own seeds of purpose. Let it germinate in good earth to even spread its fragrance at graveyard. Life is to be remembered more after you attain the graveyard.

Man is known more after he is no more.

He is remembered more through memory rather than in present. Actions of today are ways of tomorrow.

How ridiculous our lives are? We hardly welcome man with roses during life time but always rush to the graveyard very punctually on anniversaries. Reality in practicality living is diminishing day by day. Man is making his opinion about the happenings. However, the last rites of man cannot be undermined because of any physical appearance of the man for whom the ritual is being performed. The salutations to the soul should be from within.

Why Man is managing life?

Man is not living natural life. Naturalists are fading away. Naturality is the essence of life. Man is losing his natural charm. Man's transformation as machine is bane of today's civilization. It appears he is a semi-automatic robot. The pattern of living is like a task to be daily executed without the natural sense of living. We are having less of human touch and far away from the hearts emotions of love. We have started believing man as a computer device to receive input commands with out put results . The behavioral changes in humans are the greater concerns for humans only.

Do things when one is alive. Love him to the fullest before you may just remember him. This would have been better for man to offer through the services while alive. Being alive we are not at terms with each other. The philosophy takes a u turn immediately.

Regretfully I beg to confess my readers that the whole world unnecessarily repents in agony when the concern of life is lost in the shadow of time. The call of the glowing dawn is lost in the glooming sunset at dusk.

We will think, we will decide, we are acting, we are consulting, we are planning, we are brainstorming, we are analyzing, we are reviewing, and one day we find ourselves at the graveyard with unleashed dreams.

We are in fact garbage of unused dreams.

We fail to disburse our inherited dreams also. Being a thoughtful warehouse we end up with unappreciable inventory. It could have helped millions and millions of men who are left behind. We suffered the same as the ones who reached the graveyard prior to us were as good as us.

It is the runway to heaven. The fear of not doing is worse than the fear of doing. I hope the readers are with me. We all at times have not done justice to ourselves. And the same applies to the treatment we receive or give. The truth of the fact is always with us. Why someone else should make us realize what we are?

Each experience teaches us new lessons for betterment, which is what evolution is all about. Everyone has confession to the self. From cradle to graveyard the bitterness of truth is assimilated to taste the sweetness of realization. At this point of time, all worries dissolve to unfold a very new beginning again. The purpose of living from dawn to dusk daily rises like the waves to fall back in the ocean of life.

Dawn should start with revolution daily.

It should never lose its momentum till the dusk is reached. Dusk is time for review. Dusk is the mentor for dawn. No matter how many errors or failures you experience in your existence, you must keep trying to improve and change things in your life.

> *Learn from your mistakes.*
>
> *Don't reproduce them.*

Do not repeat the actions that caused them, and very often, you will obtain different results. If a solution doesn't work, it's possible to try another one. If the new one doesn't work, you can try something else, and so on, until you find the right solution. Real failure is to stop trying and throw in the towel. It's a human reflex. Everyone makes mistakes. But it's well-known that only those who do nothing never do anything wrong.

All great inventors were wrong a hundred or more times before finding the solution to a major problem. We never succeed in life on the first try; you've no doubt observed it yourself. In that case, tell yourself you've never exhausted the solutions. The solutions are infinite. Man's queries are infinite. It is fight between finite to infinite.

Just as there are infinite numbers of problems in life, you must remember that for each problem there is a solution, and often even many solutions! There will always be a suitable solution that can be adapted to a situation. This is a great cosmic and spiritual law.

Remember that the solution always exists, even if it takes time to emerge. All you need to do is to try and try again, and be persevering. It has its own way of beginning in you. Once the roots have sprouted your life will seem to be lighter. It focuses on the inner life rather than on the outer casing .The branches further reduce your dissatisfaction and stress.

Today, I realize, I could have done better, better than what is being done. The perfection of the self is infinite. It shall never rest is the true nature of life. My race seems to lead nowhere though the aim kills me to strive. I keep struggling between dawns to dusk. Life rolls on between its undefined planes of horizon from dawn to dusk. The more I analyze, the confusion expands exponentially but the knowledge seems to be of fragmented traces only. I am unable to understand the mathematics of life.

Does Life have a definition?

Is my existence required? I am trying to define through the various forms of existence. Knowledge cannot be only theory but it is realization.

Man can only tame himself.

I keep confessing to myself, fearing the revelations to the world. Why the air around me envelopes the truth of realization unwilling to confess? I want to explode with infinity but the will collapses before the way. The blindness is searching light. The clarity of sight has lost its illumination of the divinity. I want to leave the body for immortality. I know nothing further can improve beyond the chains of my limitations. I feel I have attained the enlightenment but then why the life in me?

Who will free me? Who will sail me? The dawn passes into dusk but the darkness does not leave me. Where shall I go, shall I go, I see no way, far and far I see no way?

The way to heaven is through the holy graveyard. What a holy place after the place of birth? A man's life is between these two lands of physical destinations that is one where you sprout in and the other you burry yourself. What can be more sacred places for an individual? All begins to end. And all ends to begin.

It is here my readers; I ceaselessly wish to intervene in your thinking, live to love and love to live. There appears no other aspect which should be of greater concern to man more than man.

Man comes through man. Man goes leaving man. Man fights for man. Man works for man. Man lives for man. Man learns from man. Man teaches man. Man guides man. Man is an atom of the existence. A man lost is an atom lost. Let man perform.

Do not work towards extinction of man.

Man should not be annihilated. Disappearance of humans is the next mystery the world of existence is likely to face. The rate of killing probably may become higher than the rate of birth. Were we born to become butchers? Let us think deeply without losing precious time of life.

Why are we killing humans?

Is it that essential to resolve the issues of the world? Man cannot be an identity to be eliminated. It is not the way solution of discrimination, disparities, injustice, equality, terrorism, can be obtained. We have to prevent ourselves from this negative crusade on mankind from dawn to dusk.

By making graveyards can the battle of humanity be won. Then all have to die. Why few should remain on earth? Let all of us withdraw ourselves from the life. Put a question to yourself now and then before you abuse a man, criticize a man, harm a man, deceive a man, stab a man, cheat a man, beat a man, hang a man, throw a man, scold a man, insult a man, fight a man, strike a man, grill a man, drown a man, shame a man, kick a man, kill a man, and other things which demoralizes the whole process of reestablishing humanity.

The journey of life has two distinct destinations, one while birth and the other at death. No one wishes to reach the final destination. Why we fear death? It is here, where a new purpose keeps springing again and again. The nearing of death is a new chapter of life. Loss of a family member no doubt disturbs the harmony of life. It is the way of nature. Man can only serve .

Why to serve others? Why to give others? Why to share with fellow being? Why to teach with fear that the disciples will takeover you one day? No one is helping, why should I?

Probably a series of books may not be sufficient to accommodate the questions of life pertaining to "I". This "I" needs to be dissolved. Say only "I" is living, only one person on this gigantic earth, and no one, not even animals to take your command, just think for a moment what would you do alone, how do you think to rule the kingdom now, the entire earth is yours, you are the king of universe, no one to dethrone you anymore, the zenith of dreams are under your feet, you with earth is revolving round the sun, only a single existence of yours from dawn to dusk.

Oh! What an existence, no one to steal you, criticize you, you need not share, will you sustain your living, does it make sense, you are like the minute dot on a blank paper, no one behind and above you, you are an one man army, the greatest fear of reproduction, you even cease to reproduce, the whole cycle of reproduction comes to an end, this is what we all are waiting for, will the Universe collapse, the life will end, the earth too will become like some of the other planets without traces of life.

Doesn't it astonish to witness the end of life? Then what will remain without Man and Animals on this earth. Why this flora and fauna was created? Why the big bang theory then? What is the purpose then? A series of such questions brings an entire new learning to the self in the existence. The importance of human race is to be known by human primarily in the existence.

The Earth will also become a lifeless ball and you will be witnessing a similar situation of Adam and Eve or Manu who were the first in the process of evolution, the life was beginning to sprout, and the world we see today is all that has been done, a point of contradiction, some may agree others may defer, earlier there was no life and in future there may not be life, hard to conclude. There are no limits to the resources of our psyche.

You have everything you need to lead the life of your dreams within you. You want to find a new or better job? To seduce the one you dream about? To be loved or feared, or simply have your own worth be acknowledged? All of this is possible, provided you know how to use the power of your mind. Now is your turn .We all know, we are not doing well.

How to improve? Never enter a stage of stagnation. It is sign of ending your vision, innovation, engagement, motivation and dreams. You are trying to close your book of life. A premature surrender is only because of your slackness in holding the spirit to fight. Your positive force can never allow the witches, demon, and curses to swallow you.

A little boldness can change your whole perception of life. You should be up for the challenge? Try to be a legend and one fine dawn you will become so.

Dusk is to dream and dawn is to do. Realization in tranquility further strengthens your learning at dusk. Well basically, in your earlier days, every day you have done nothing, then how things can be in your favor today. Why do you distant yourself even further from the happiness that is your due? Do not make your future at stake?

Never lose hope. You never know what tomorrow will bring. Do you think there is still time to break open the locks that have been hampering your access to riches, love and happiness? You just cannot always have the Universe on your side.

Every day has its own conclusions.

These inferences pile up for man to redefine the wisdom of living. We learn daily the lessons of life. Yet we cannot control life, as needed.

The tough war is in between desire and destiny. Compromise has its limited ends. Can you differentiate between misunderstanding and perception? Principally nobody wants to learn without cause. A wrong cause leads to wrong learning. The inclination towards learning is the beginning to fight the ambition within you. It will help you to explore all the possibilities to witness the different shades of life.

Loneliness is the friend of peace. Holiness is neared by loneliness. May not be that easy to interpret. However the policy of detachment throws light on the issue.

How man can detach and be attached?

Once the work is done, the freedom is in not worrying about the consequences. If the prime selection is of the right work, whatever may be the degree of work, the result is bound to be right only. If the work is done rightly it may not be true that the results will always be right. A wrong work might have been very rightly executed for bad results.

This is the start of liberation in man. The secrets of detachment bring internal joy to the performer. Man is to perform but not ponder on the act of performance from dawn to dusk. The rays of sun brighten the world without physical attachment. Similarly the goodness of man brings happiness without attachment to the giver and taker. Happiness is not a physical item for exchange. It can only be mentally shared. It can bring bliss and peace. It transforms into wellness, healthiness, calmness, gratefulness, and so on.

Existence is Infinite

Readers may be wondering how a man with finite existence is infinite. You are true. The same quest is with many. It is to be discovered within us.

What do you understand by infinite? Why we are having a doubt that we are not infinite? Our lives are struggling between finite and infinity from dawn to dusk and similarly between mortal to immortal. Again it does not end it continues with the inner and outer world. Thus existence is man's quest right from survival till liberation.

The readers can try to understand the importance of realization which man undergoes at different phases of life with respect to time. It is this truth which never dies and is infinitely moving with time. Everything shades of but truth is with time always. What was truth at the beginning of existence will be the same at the end of existence universally. Humanity is another truth which humans have to realize sooner or later in this moving time of existence.

Man is infinite.

An individual man dies many times in life and finally the physical death. But whereas the universal man never dies. He is as infinite as the existence. Our narrow wisdom is unable to lift our planes of divine thinking. We are like the black crows of the world unwilling to become white? Unless the crow becomes white man too will be nomadic in life searching from this door to that window the purpose of existence.

Man is not man till he starts thinking about existence. This is a subject that many authors do not dare to attempt for the sake of criticism or any other reasons best known to them. In fact the readers are also not many who are deeply interested to dive into the inner self sacrificing the pleasures and pains of the outer world.

This gap has widened drastically over the time despite advancement in technology, knowhow, publications, internet, communication, schools, universities, methodology in research, infrastructure in living standards, printing and publications, marketing, and other means. The problem as I envisage is more of the interest of man, society, nation and world.

Sometimes when the pain is not directly felt the concern does not arise in the individual. The philosophical plane without life experiences is like the pen without ink. Man has to pass through moments of grief and joy just as the dusk and dawn. Poem on paper has no meaning till you are not reciting it. Lyrics of songs on paper have no meaning till you are singing it. This is what exactly with our lives too; till we are not living life has no meaning.

Do not worry. At times the whole world is against you. Do not worry again and be surprised because this time the whole world is with you. It is very good that you have eliminated all at the stroke of immaturity. It is wisdom that you have again embraced all. Does the world changes so rapidly? At instant you are in favor and again at the very moment you are against. Don't you feel some thought should go in this direction? We yet need to understand the existence.

Earlier men have done it. Many inferences and conclusions of the previous seekers have not been shared into the world. The conclusions they arrived through some means have been buried with the individuals. Had there been progressive revelations of man since the first humans have arrived in existence a concrete conclusion perhaps could have been compiled and comprehended.

That is why the confusion, doubt, lack of clarity, ignorance, limits, shortcomings, weak believes, timid faiths, have been visiting the infinite man's finite structural body. We have been home to the trivial things of life and continue to do so. In this environment the mind fails to take you to the infinite planes of existence.

The seed of the substance always lies in the fruit of the substance.

Do you get coconut from the seeds of mango fruit? That is to say the nature adored is an inherited blessing. To understand peace, I have to be peaceful. To understand freedom, I have to break bondages. To understand truth, I have to experience reality.

To understand humanity, I have to love mankind. To understand the world, I have to understand the self. To understand grace, I have to pray. To understand success, I have to sweat. To understand the beauty, I have to live in the garden of life. It is only through the understanding of becoming, that you will become, what you dream to become. Who has no sense of thinking? Life is full of common sense. Why we are insensible? Does any rocketry science is required to understand live longer, feel younger and work smarter?

All the learning of life cannot be just through reading a book alone now and then. The whole universe cannot be understood in a day. All the secrets of existence cannot be known in a day. Do you think one life is sufficient to know the self? By the time we realize that we should have known ourselves, the life is at the verge of leaving us.

Every moment of time is precious. Time is the greatest essence of all. I will tell you, write a letter, article, note, book, essay, comprehension, poem, and read it, think over it again and again, and you will see and realize, that something was missing. This is going to happen with one and all.

And again you are inspired to attempt it, rewrite, with more zeal, vigor, interest, dedication, strength, this time with more maturity and deeper concern, trying to add more value, this is where the process of perfection has started, the next one, the next one and ultimately all aiming towards perfection, eternal perfection.

I was able to draw from a deep well of memories that have been accumulating within me since long to share with you, which you could read today, compiled as Dawn to Dusk. I remember every time I thought my essay was done and ready to be published, I again sweated over it to recompile, reedit, rewrite, I again rewrote, rewrote, obsessively to ensure, I could give all to my readers, with the hope that once dawn to dusk is picked up should not go back to the shelf.

This was an early realization to give more sincere efforts to be of purpose and value to my respected readers. This inspired me to further explore from dawn to dusk.

This is how, in small things, day to day, we can improve our commitments towards life. Whatever we do from dawn to dusk should have a meaningful purpose to life. Every man can bring value to another man. It is to be realized early in life. What is the use of strong resolutions at the end of life, when you even cannot see them become reality? Seeing a plant shooting up from the seed sowed by you is more thriving to your life? The blooming flowers early at dawn are the natures call to man to prosper.

Day is the secret for flourishing. Love in true sense is when the other person's happiness is more important than yours. Love is built on the bricks of sacrifices. There should not be any prejudices in sharing blame and credit. A coin can be only yours when both faces of existence remain with you.

<u>Still have Time</u>

Do you still have time?

Will time remain for you?

The man who actually knows just what he wants in life has already gone a long way toward attaining it.

I start with an earnest confession to my readers, that before finally compiling "Dawn to Dusk" to be released for publishing I swept away sometime unnecessarily thinking that I still have time. In fact I was looking towards its perfection as a well compiled and comprehended book for the readers when it is published.

In the due course of time I had several edits to my credits but ultimately surrendering to one dawn for release to my readers. There is time for everything but not beyond the invalidation of time.

We may "still have time", is to be seen from both ends of dawn and dusk. That is the opportunity to do without the will and will to do without the remains of opportunity.

Everything in life is time.

Time is precious of all. Time is precious than the diamond. Time is precious than gold. Time is incomparable to anything in this world. There is no equivalence to this. Do you still have time? When will your dawn come? Are you waiting for the change to happen?

The change is to be brought by you.

You only have to work towards the change through your will and way.

Awaken yourself if you are still sleeping. Get the thrust to rush towards the dawn of life. If you are not early to catch it will fade away into dusk. You might

426

have lost many moments of happiness but the remaining can be yours. This is the truth of moment.

Have a hopeful dream not hopeless dream and you can see the change. Magic is in mind. Let it work for you from dawn to dusk. Still you can fill your moments as you like. The matter is with the perception you have carried with yourself. The difficulty is that you are not a fighter to your will. If you decide it where is the problem?

Many times we are deceived by our lengthy analysis. Do you think other men are having so much time to just be behind you to pull down always? Push out the garbage from the mind. Make room for new beginning. There is no delay in starting new things. You are the initiator to the creation of yours. Nothing has been lost till the will has been lost. No time is bad or good. Every moment is the moment of change.

Every moment is the moment of new dawn.

For whom you are waiting? Is it the fortune, miracle, magic, grace or somebody to do for you? Who will ride your dream? Can anyone drive your vehicle of life? Absolutely it is stupidity to live a life with aimlessness. The struggle in you should at least start now also when you are approaching dusk. Still the remaining slices can be well utilized. What is that you will lose now? The point to be understood is that the greatest grace is that we are in existence. What else can be more important to us than this?

Time is the wealthiest wealth of life. It is with everyman on this earth. The time of day has been given to all equally to work with it. Time is a resource for all the activities.

Are you surviving or thriving?

Life unnecessarily is being sandwiched between trials and tribulations of existence. You have been staring as to why some men are struggling and others are on top of world? The answer is as they are creating their own luck from dawn to dusk. They have known the path of winning. They have learnt their lessons. The life has revealed to them the secrets of success.

Now it is your turn. Do not worry success is going to embrace you? You are very likely to embrace a beautiful day? Your spirit in you should realize to dance with the tune of inspiration. Stand ahead in day very early at dawn. You are sure to meet your dreams today in the shinning sun. All glory is yours. Full yourself with clarity of existence and nature is going to be in your laps.

Man has to create his path towards greatness.

It is not a destination to just reach there. The living is a journey of such finite destinations towards infinite. There are some from destiny others by rewriting destinies and some by fate others by rewriting luck. There are some by efforts others by grace and some by self others by society. And again we have some by mistakes others by misfortune. Whatever it may be, overall a wonderful anonymous journey of life by man.

Where is my school of dreams?

Let it be one class after the other to build the dreams of life. Without which my existence shall have no meaning. I have to stroll within from dawn to dusk. The fitness of purpose will surely map one day with your dreams. Every man has something to share. He may have a lesson for all of us. Please start revealing about yourself. There may be hidden real time experiences to move the heart and mind.

Memories are chapters of existence from dawn to dusk. It may have the secret to resolve your present crisis. The point of discussion is that the more you look into bringing out things on surface the more the process of realization becomes beneficial to the individual and equally to the society as whole.

Every moment of life can be peaceful. Man can do it. This is the prime objective of man today. Life is not such a lucid essay. It is not over in a paragraph, page, books, and followed by series of volumes. It requires writing again and again. We all are authors of our own lives.

Life is a painting.

There are infinite combinations of colours. You can colour it as you like it. Get immersed in the colour of life. Share your colour with everybody. The existence has coloured the world for us to experience it through the beauty of green fields, blue sky, red roses, pink lotus, black clouds, yellow flowers, white spring, etc.

Man intrinsically credits all achievements, success, rewards, joy, conquest to himself and at the same time defeats, surrenders, loss, lose, sorrow, unhappiness, misery to fate. The contradiction itself is ridiculous. This is how things are being perceived.

The world had saints and cheaters at any point of its existence.

It is in us to become as we like?

There are many good and bad moments in everyone's life. There is not a single wave which rises in the ocean without falling. Similarly these good and bad waves are the part and parcel in the ocean of life. The waves of ignorance in man have to fall at the feet of existence. We should not allow the impact of these waves to bring disequilibrium in the purity of mind. Trace your weakness as quick as you can to realize the strength of life.

Life is a venture. It is a daring journey of the braves. Who does not want to be at the vertex of life? And it is never late to quit the evils. Why to live with vices when the self is wisely reasoning you? The circle of viciousness is surrounded with cruelty, brutality, nastiness, vengefulness, revengefulness, spiteful, bitterness, wickedness, immorality, flaw, failing, callous, violence and so on to pollute the sphere of humanity.

The World today is breeding warmongers. The practices of witchcraft are victimizing the innocent and ignorant. Vices are dominating the virtues. Cruelty is entering innocent minds. These pollutants of humanity are to be removed from this world. Every man has to operate his own tumor of inhumanity.

People are living in vanity. People are in veils. It has become difficult for the sacred humans to understand the whims the society is facing today. Men are getting tricked and cheated from dawn to dusk. People are envious of one another. Men are suspiciously approaching one another for help. People are literally living in the lurch.

Why judicious living is a mirage today? Do you think we do not have time to see our morals grow? Is the world going to follow the zigzag path now?

More jiggling is bringing in fragile principles of living. The society is day by day falling into the irresolvable jeopardize. Men are equally making women immoral. There are jezebels everywhere polluting the millions and millions of the homes in the world.

Man is shamelessly living like a vagrant. Man has to work towards solidarity. How to demolish the world of criminals? Why this underworld is flourishing? Where to get the solace? Is there any time frame? Are we not losing and wasting the precious time of existence without adding any justifiable value to it? Can human vanquish evil?

Please look at these two words "EVIL" and "VEIL". Either way you arrange it, it always has the negative meaning. Drawing a veil over and over has been the man's evil. Man can disguise to pursuits unidentifiable in the real world. Are we not becoming junk? The demarcation of transition from good to bad is many times untraceable.

Unknowingly knowing the mistake also is wisdom not to intentionally reproduce it again and again. Man needs a sacred mould to be molded for humanity. There is no use of bailing water from a dry well. It is foolishness to remain thirsty when the nature is flooding the existence with ocean of knowledge.

Man keeps thinking he is left with time but the saddest part of the story is he passes away without the fulfillment of his dreams. You may not be a perfectionist to start the things. You may not be an idealist to start the practice of ideals in living. You may not be a saint to start praying god. You may not be a humanist to start loving humans. The importance of time is to move with time. You may not be a naturalist to speak about nature. You may not be a dancer to dance with the rhythm of life.

There is nothing new to the above discussion. What matters is the change we all are trying to make?

Why the life is losing its freshness?

Time is in control of no human. The state of ends is also not the domain of humans. What is with human is the journey between these ends. The game of any sports cannot be owned by any player individually though players play by participating in the game. The life is also more or less similar to such games from dawn to dusk.

If you are in the game you may have even the last second to kick a goal. But if you have not begun to play the game then you are away from the golden opportunity of experiencing the game of existence.

"Still have time" is absolutely situational. It is more of case to case availability for the individual humans. The problem is to what extent the time from dawn to dusk is transforming you to the desired expectations of existence.

Losing time is like losing life. Losing time is like losing opportunity. Losing time is like losing living. Time can be fresh only when you are becoming new and only when you are blooming. It is only when you are opening up life evolves out a fresh from dawn to dusk.

A little Boldness

When William Shakespeare wrote,

"To thine own self be true, and it must follow, as the night the day, that thou canst not then be false to any man", he meant that we could not go wrong if we followed the promptings of our conscience.

A little boldness can make huge difference. Without this the ideals, zeal, zest, inspiration, aim, dedication, vision and mission tend to be weaker and fall down without achieving the desired targets.

Man has to pray and he gets it. Nature gives it when you ask for it. This is the positive heat which runs through the blood. The ideals should vigorously flow through our veins with the blood.

Life is always in front of you. Mind also tells it is in front of you. You see your body activities in front of you. The nature, earth, universe, life, existence and your soul everything is in front of you. What else is required to realize what you are? All your actions, reactions, results, emotions, thoughts, desires, needs, aims, ambitions, satisfaction, sacrifices, are in front of you.

You are witnessing everything happening. You are in all. Then where and why is the search? What else your mind is willing to perceive? This is nothing new of today. It is happening from dawn to dusk since existence.

Will man come to know himself?

A doubt in mind goes this way; is my coming into existence with this bodily form itself is the prime purpose? Later on it is the revealing of the unfolded manifestations of existence. As many minds that many conclusions. It is as good to say that every man is an individual book of learning and realization with his own chapters of life. Finally the real goal of knowledge is liberation.

Learning is to liberate only.

Liberate from what? Why liberation for man? The goal of love is bliss. Once you are through with your book, the purpose intended by the author of life has been met.

Chapters written by destiny are being rewritten by the dreams of humans. Destiny is being supplemented by creation of humans. He again comes up with another idea, concept, philosophy, taste, charm, colour, text, style, through men to meet his intended purpose. Thus his manifestations are continuing to invade the existence.

Man for no reason should blame another man. How can one book harm another book? All these books manifested as unique lives have one or the other lessons for the entire existence.

Life is a goal, career, money, achievement, power, opportunity, play, thrill, experience, journey, expedition, essay, book, gift, existence, whatever it may be, however it may be, wherever it may be, anywhere the universality of its presence, features, characteristics, attributes, inheritances, genesis, philosophies, theories, all are from the same source of boldness of entire existence.

You do anything a little boldness is required. This is the trust, faith and hope in you. The intensity of boldness is great when the principles of life are clear and fair. A fair man is always bolder than the liar. Why senses dictate our mind? What the country, religion, culture, faith, belief has to do when man is reacting to his inner senses?

The summary appears to be clear that throughout dawn to dusk the categorization of the human activities, actions, reactions, broadly can be done into the inner and outside world. When we speak of inner it is synonymous to the spiritual life. On the other hand outside symbolizes the material world. It is the world of bondage. It is the world of chains. It is the world of relativity.

It is trying to understand absolutism. It is experiencing the threat from inner world of humans.

A little boldness can abolish the ego of worldliness. It just needs to go in our veins, brains, mind and soul. The spirit in us is always bold to face the world. Man is very bravely facing the outer world guarding the inner world. We should be proud to say we are humans of the infinite.

One day Man's inner world will dissolve the outer world.

Then there will be only one world.

The Universal World.

WORLD: INNER, OUTSIDE & EXISTENCE

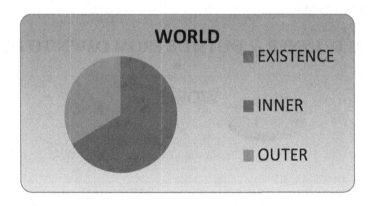

Where do you stand in the above pie-chart showing sample distribution of possible worlds under study? Can you locate yourself completely in one segment? Or your share is a percentage distribution of all the three?

Why cannot we have a single world at a time? Say either aligning ourselves to completely 100% to inner or outer world. I think this is where the major problem of man lies.

Man is unable to decide his world. He is born in one world. He lives in one world. He thinks in world. He struggles in one world. He is happy in one world. He is sad in one world. He learns in one world. He liberates in one world. He is human in one world. He is saint in one world. He is devil in one world. He is god in one world. And finally he owns no world.

Existence makes one world.

&

Man makes his world.

As many man that many worlds. All these generate from the same source and again they dissolve there with experience and purpose of existence.

World, Man, Earth, Universe and Existence all are dynamic in nature. It transforms every moment. You take either the mass balance or the energy balance and it is scientifically as well as spiritually in motion.

There is at the same time exchanges taking place in between the inner and the outer world. All the three the inner world, the outer world and the entire existence is circling the mystery of life. The core is the life. What it is? It is from where? The finite elements of the existence keep questioning the infinite from dawn to dusk.

WORLD: INNER & OUTSIDE FROM DAWN TO DUSK

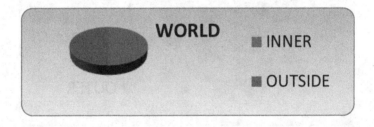

It is for the readers to decide. What type of world man wants? Is it 50% inner and 50% outside? Or is it 100% inner? Or is it 100% outside? What is really feasible? Practically where do we stand. This is the starting point of regeneration, reformation, reinvention, redefining, reconstruction, realignment, of man. Time again is the deciding factor. Time influences the look of man.

Man has to strike balance between self and world. The theory of dominance activates the mind of man. Action is the response of mind. Thoughts are the seeds of man.

How to become heroes and villains? It is always in our hands. You have to reason out your becoming? No one else is responsible for what you are? All the doctrines, philosophies, degrees, education, wisdom, knowledge, realization teach this universal truth to all humans in this world.

HUMAN is HERO and VILLAIN.

Man has both the faces. He has stories of his heroism and terrorism. Humanity needs more and more stories of heroism. It needs humans who can sing the songs of humanity.

Many stage dramas, shows, pictures, articles, documentaries, novels, films, campaigns, have been on man depicting heroism and barbarism. In fact the society two has admired both the tastes of man and is still continuing to quadrant the category of humans.

Anything which is for the material world gets linked to stress, strain, pain, struggle, fear, ego, competition, threat, possession, wealth, grief, criticism, abuses, evils, destruction, delusions, war, mistakes, cruelty, duality, barbarism, power, negativism, confusion, complex city, vices, doubts, insecurity, instability, and so on.

On the contrary which is for the inner world gets linked to ethics, divine, values, purification, spirituality, meditation, concentration, discipline, morale, nobility, sacrifice, liberation, salvation, purity, gratification, thanks, love, hope, trust, faith, saintliness, positivism, cleanliness, simplicity, virtues, stability, peace, bliss, and so on.

Why man fails to distinguish between good and bad? Why man fails to differentiate between the causes of sadness and happiness? More and more such analysis is required to undergo refinement in speech, thoughts, ideas, values, behaviors and living. It is not that the world is new to it. It is diminishing in implementation in society.

Man is born with five senses of hearing, smelling, tasting, seeing and feeling. Now it is up to man to decide, what he wants to hear, smell, taste, see and feel. The gross problem lies with our senses. If the taste is for bad things then good things are not your likes. If there is no feeling of humanity, then you are not concerned for the kindness, mankind and your inclination towards spirituality are not at all a matter of concern.

The human mind is a composite of many qualities and tendencies. It consists of likes, dislikes, optimism, pessimism, hatred, love, constructiveness, destructiveness, cruelty, dominating qualities,

Time is the healer of mistakes, failures, grievances, complains, worries, fears, but man has to work with positivity. There are infinite ways to live. Try to open them with trust, faith, hope and sincere commitments.

Be bold not to be sold in the world for a mere bribe of the gold. Hold your values and ethics as the wealth of life. Pray to nature with open mind for gracious dawn to befall on you. The morality in you is the reflection of boldness.

Boldness is a way of true living. Do not surrender to situational results? Rise to face the race of righteousness.

Every dawn has a solution for every problem. Try resolving them and there are as many ways as many wills. Have a will to do and things will be done. Try to do things for the welfare of the people. Work with people. Never work against people.

Time will turn the wheel of fate. Is it not that like attracts like? Either it is law of attraction, law of retaliation, law of the universe, law of nourishment,

A little boldness can fight all the evils. The seeds of evils germinate in the mind of an individual prior to rooting out in society. It expands its network engulfing the entire society.

Boldness in man can kill the evil in man. Persistence of evil in man makes the human in him devil. The angel in man can kill the devil in man. God and ghost are the two states in the same man.

A godly man is the ideal man for humanity. The man of ghost is bound to destruct the humanity .The courage and cowards are the two states in the same man.

A courageous man can kill the coward man. A deeper insight here brings to the surface that the involvement of man is indispensable in any activity either good or bad. So if we have only good in man, than the question of bad never arises.

Man and mind have been competitors to each other since the existence of life. Man tries to dominate mind, mind equally tries to dominate man. The winner of the two decides the whole matter.

Who is powerful man or mind? Does mind has a physical structure like man? Where is mind seated in man?

We humans have created and learnt so many languages like French, Arabic, German, English, Urdu, Hindi, Chinese, Japanese, to express the feelings of humans to other humans and nature. Man interacts outside and inside with the aid of language. Irrespective of the particular language for communication, the basic purpose of it is same all over the world.

Thus human needs to love, trust, faith, hope, express, feel, hear, care, taste, act, explore, hate, play, ride, think, invent, construct, destruct, dismantle, assemble, encourage, discourage and so on according to the situation from dawn to dusk.

Human's exploration is inside and outside. The outside exploration is always because of the inside exploration. Human has to overcome fear. Kill the fear which weakens you, depresses you, and holds you, so that your freedom of life attains what it actually wants.

Will man perish just as an organism? The biological man is no better than the insect of life. For this existence, the marvelous mind was not needed. What is that makes man different from the animal? Does animal and man's goal are same?

Does man has any divine goal in reality?

Summing Up & Exercise for Readers- Chapter- IX

- Do you believe in realization?
- How it can reform you?
- Have you realized from your life?
- Do you use the tools of realization?
- What you have realized to improve humanity in you?
- Does your realization is lessons for other people?
- Do you analyze your realization?
- Has realization started transforming you into better human?
- Are you reaping the grace of realization?
- Is realization helping you to enrich your maturity in living?
- Be bold to change and practice boldness in life for the right cause.
- According to me, "Resistance to yield for badness is an admirable virtue of man." Cultivate this habit.
- Develop good habits which utilize time effectively and efficiently.

- Time is the greatest wealth of humans. Do not waste it.
- Time calls for responsibility. Take it. Deliver it. Do it.
- Write your autobiographies of realization to further explore the findings and conclusions on humanity.
- These may be lessons for the coming generations. Share your learning with society.
- Give to society as you have got from society. Give to world as you have got from world.
- Give to man as you have got from man.
- Thank the nature and existence for nourishing and nurturing you.
- Think, think, and think to contribute for humanity till the last breath.
- Get the right goal of life.
- Get the right definition of life.
- Get the right idea of life.
- Get the right mission of life.
- Get the man in you to convert into champion of humanity.

Chapter X

REGENERATING HUMANITY

"If Homes are happy Humans are happy"

-Dr Shree Raman Dubey

"My ideal, indeed, can be put into a few words, and that is: to preach unto mankind their divinity and how to make it manifest in every moment of Life", -Swami Vivekananda.

Gautama Buddha, born as prince Siddhartha, 6th century B.C, renounced the world to become one of the greatest spiritual teachers of all time. He had everything, kingdom, palace, family, wealth, happiness, joy, what not, but what made his mind to renounce the world. Why he thought for the world? As an individual he was very prosperous and there was no necessity to quit the worldly things.

A transformation within him broke his shield of mortality in search of immortality. He was searching the eternal truth. What is the nature of the body? It will become old. The body will be subjected to different kinds of illness and disease. Life will go out of you. You will be no more. The body will die. The body perishes to become dead body. Nothing is eternal. I am not going to have eternal youth. I will not be as beautiful as I am today. All these were running in the minds of Gautama before he went on to enlighten himself.

Anybody born in this world cannot avoid growth, development, decay and death. The monk has realized the world is full of sufferings. Now the question is of the physical sufferings or of the sufferings in the mind.

Where exactly humanity is suffering? Is it subject of the mind? Are we so weak to remove the sufferings? Why we cannot convert the sufferings into serenity and calm? Many times the society is perplexed because the good humans are suffering more as per the perception of the people from the community of goodness. The one possible reasoning is that the nature keeps warning them through these temporary sufferings to the good people in order to stop them from becoming bad. A positive fear is introduced through these to uphold the righteousness with sacrificial mode of operation by the good people. To be an ideal a fear of idealness is essential to stop from derailing. Sufferings may be imparting the lessons of humanity this way.

Live for an ideal and that ideal alone. Stand on it to make the world sit. Nothing should rise above the divine values.

Do you have real desire for the ideal?

Who will bring in Renaissance of Humanity? Where do we stand with our activities from dawn to dusk, understanding, living and becoming requires a periodic self performance analyses as input for further correction in making ourselves complete.

To begin with a model, I have attempted to design a questionnaire for your quick feedback, so that you can start evaluating yourself. No external evaluation can be better than your opinion.

Unless you put a question to yourself you are not making yourself accountable. The findings from these can show the trend you are following.

Always remember that the road to heaven is only through the hell. There should be more and more God-Man in the world. What is the aspect of personal god?

Once you dissolve, you become one with the god. The comparison scope has been deceased in oneness. Till you are body the argument with the creator is at peak. Supreme resides in you but man's madness of inheritance begins to doubt all that is his manifestation.

Are you really moving where you were supposed to be? Just as the commercial establishments and industrial organizations maintain accounts and evaluate their performance periodically, similarly every man is an unique organization of human with mission, vision, objectives, goals, resources, skills, talents, cultures, values in operating his life for the benefit of self and society. He has to have his self performance analysis to check the inputs and becoming of the self as output. Say you have no goal then where is the question of beating the bush for accomplishment.

In my perception it goes to say this way,

"When you have never contributed to the society then why to blame society for not accepting you today".

If we smile the day will also smile. If you are cheering the day will also bring cheer. Every day is reflection of your thoughts, ideas, energy, perception, actions, learning, living and realization. If good thoughts are flowing in the mind, definitely your spirits are high and the day looks a shinning one with full potential to work together with you enthusiastically. On the other hand if your mind is full of bad thoughts, the very promising day is made bad by your actions not being good and finally losing from dawn to dusk.

Mind is Day.

The way you think the day is. It is good so you feel good. It is lazy you feel lazy. You feel to play with emotions hence you are emotional. It is inspiring so you are aspiring to excelling. The beginning is with you. So is the final actualization. To rise or fall in the day is your thought. You think the day is lost so as you.

Day has all the answers to man's query.

The way you think the day becomes. This is independent of any land on earth or any place in universe. The outside influence on you is always marginal in impeding your growth philosophically, intellectually, spiritually, and above all as humans. The disturbance and turbulence arises in you. You are the culprit of your state of mind.

Mind radiates what it receives. Man has nothing to blame another man.

A man ruins his own opportunities of goodness because of not big things but small things which start at mind. Before we see things as social conflict, all are bad seeds of the mind.

Mind should be full of life from dawn to dusk. Man is the proprietor of his life. Man is the inventor of his thought. Thought is the creator of man.

Conception is incomplete without experience and realization.

What is the difference in man either he is the son of Ganga, Indus or Nile? What is the difference in man either he is American or Indian? What is the difference in man either he is black or white?

Instability in life is due to the diverse forces of thought in mind. Nothing in the world is to be denied. The world should have more and more professors of philosophy to voice the essentiality of humanity. This world exists as the mind and if the mind changes, the outlook of the world changes. How to define the real world is a challenge to every man?

Knowledge differentiates the appearance of good today, as bad tomorrow. Why man fears to give up his individuality? What are our real ideals?

How to find path to liberty?

And can this be done in a single day? Every day is a part of the whole process. Do not relinquish the day? A day lost weakens the complete bead of the process. The changing of the world can be only through the changing of the individual. Let us carry the message of fraternity to all believers, to all visionaries, to intellectuals, to enfolding of all the gods existing in humanity.

Let us avoid wrong rather than realizing after wrong. Realization makes things anew but may not give you the lost time. Do not lose the time you have. If you are not happy with the world it infers you are not happy with yourself. If you are worried about the wrong in the world it infers you are concerned about the wrong in you. You are trying to send message of humanity to the world, it infers you are becoming human.

Revolution in Mankind

"Learn from the people
Plan with the people
When the task is accomplished

The people all remark
We have done it ourselves"

-Lao Tzu

Whatever the mind of man can conceive
and believe it can achieve.

At this point of time we are blessed that men like us have initially thought for the world, society, nature, earth, universe, existence, life, death, success, failure, happiness, sorrows, good, bad, humility, humanity, realization and have equally worked through imparting teachings, discourses, writing books, by all means have tried to uphold the spirit of living for the future.

Now it is our turn and responsibility to carry forward the desires of the good soul, divinity of thought, power of dream, blessings of grace, and plant the seeds of humanity. By the time you realize there may not be opportunity and time to implement, this itself is curse for the rest of life. The beginning needs more dedication and determination.

Once you are on the right path, next is only a matter of journey
and destination.

Unless you question yourself the agitation to uplift the life does not get activated. The purpose here is to at least let the mind start pondering and wandering in search of perfection.

Below is only a sample pattern to interrogate yourself from dawn to dusk. A set of questionnaire formulated on the basis of man's life from dawn to dusk. Life is not easy as just few paragraphs scribbled on paper is known to one and all.

The point being emphasized here is as to how a new beginning can be brought to man himself, the society he makes, the understanding he has for life, ideal standards of living, the perception of the world, the vision on the emerging human mix, the socializing of the new world, the globalization of existence, and so on from dawn to dusk. We do something throughout the day.

Do we really do which adds value? It enhances better living. It refines you. It revives you. It brings a transformation. It gives us a new wisdom for humanity. In totality are we getting regenerated?

My dear friends with faith and courage I foresee the future of humans, "The sincerity towards reinventing man is surely going to pay universal dividends uninterruptedly in the indelible evolution of continual existence what man has been bitterly experiencing till today".

A new order will be established. This is the rule of the land. This is the law of nature. This is the law of universe. This is the law of man. This is the law of god. This is the law of the world. This is the law of all.

When the time comes the change does not wait for the time. The time is the universal equalizer. Time has the secrets of this creation. The wheel of time is moving from dawn to dusk.

Keep flooding your mind with gusty questions regularly. Let it be troubled in mapping them to the best possibilities of existence.

Learning by questioning is one of the practical ways of redefining life. There were seers and peers of truth in every civilization. As the wind removes the clouds so the name of god destroys the cloud of worldliness.

What is our actual problem? Is it not surrendering to another man? It appears we do not like surrendering ourselves. This is the intrinsic truth of man. Every man knows it. Then why is the unacceptability.

Man's reliability is being questioned by man. Man's humanity is being questioned by man. Man's integrity is being questioned by man. Man's loyalty is being questioned by man. Man is questioning man.

Do you think there should be a man on every man to examine him? Why the system of vigilance on each other? Can we not be true to ourselves?

Man has a tendency to examine the other man more than himself. Let us do this exercise again and again till the corrections near to perfection of existence.

Even the learned, knowledgeable, educated, sacred, noble sometimes tend to lose their values and morals. Who is to be blamed the circumstances or the man? Is it that man acts negatively because of the influence of circumstances? Or is it that man creates the situation worse for himself? All of you should realize by this time either this or that ultimately the sufferer is man irrespective of the cause, affect and effect.

Category of Society

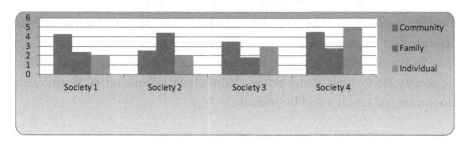

The above table reflects the type of major society mix related to preference in community, family and as an individual it is built up. Wherever it is family or community dominating in the society, the society has a group vision and objective. In contrast to it the society being lead by individual dominance somehow appears to fall behind the group ideologies as per the general observation from dawn to dusk.

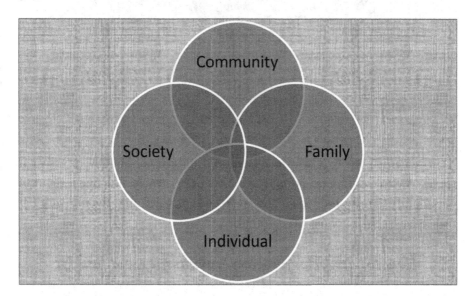

With great regrets the readers may agree to the fact that the world has no recognized school of reforming the self affiliated to the education system authorized and approved by god. Hopefully the almighty thought it right as the nature is designed to impart lessons of life from dawn to dusk.

Look at the spheres of community, family, individual and society to understand the overlapping areas of human's faces and living in the world. You may be a secularist but when you are representing the community you belong your limitations becomes your hindrances in truly implementing your independent ideologies of life.

To further refine our own understanding on humanity in the sphere of society let us look at the below chain which is built up of all different communities, families and individuals.

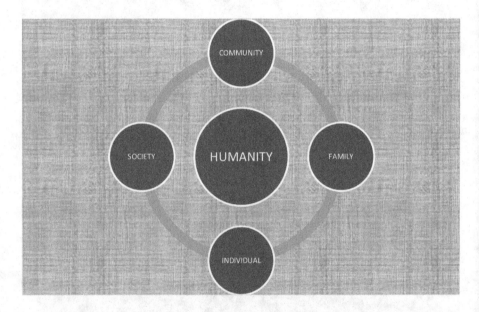

Man remains with this task to relearn and relearn continually to arrive at the excellence of understanding the secrets of existence. The outer chain of community, family, individual and society keeps redefining the humanity at respective levels, autonomy and authority.

How to categories a society, community and family?

The world needs more of Darwin, Newton, Einstein, Socrates, Plato, Aristotle, Buddha, Jesus, Rama, Krishna, Paramahansa, Vivekananda, Mother Teresa,

Abdul Kalam, and so on, to explore its own world beyond the limitations of existence.

Where is the Wheel of Revolution of Humanity?

It is truth that continuous selfless actions gradually cleanse the mind of dross and impurities. It is then that this ignorance ceases and the individual obtains the full blaze of illumination. It is sometimes difficult to decide what works ought to be done and what ought to be shunned. Work and no work are from the same source.

Humanity stands to question every community, family, individual, society and nation. The goodness of an individual is not projected in the shadow of bad community. The goodness of a community may be protecting the evils of an individual from being exposed to society in true sense. The hide and sick among humans and groups is manipulating the reality of humanity. The reality can only be realized if the reformation in the individual takes place from dawn to dusk.

Society Vs Humanity

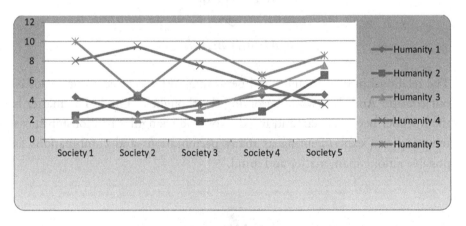

The relationship between society and humanity is a serious concern from dawn to dusk. The type of humanity which develops depends upon the vision and mission of a society. The type of society which develops depends upon the vision and mission of humanity.

How life maps it is a matter differing from man to man?

<u>Dignity of Humanity</u>

"Mind is the temple of man".

-Dr Shree Raman Dubey

Let the god of existence reside in it. Make good thoughts your permanent tenant. Everything starts with the basic thought. Tame it to be good. Then with trust and faith you will see it becomes your culture to be good.

A good thought will take up good path.

If the mind is clear where is the problem of confusion, doubt, turbulence, noise, ego, etc? Children play with toys all over the world. This is universality with oneness of existence.

Mind is Man.
&
Man is mind.

The relationship is of thought and becoming. Why our becoming is not in our control? And then while becoming the thought in mind. The matter is the intruder between man and mind. Now the triangular relationship starts tempting and experimenting as many permutations and combinations as possible among man, matter and mind.

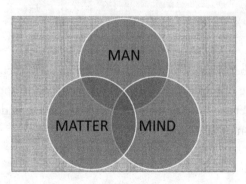

Why matter should be given chance to dictate man and mind? How to rank them in order of dominance? How to rank them in order of essentialities of existence? Do our mind's control man and matter equally? The sphere of matter envelops the true nature of mind sometimes. It again coils back like the spring of existence. Existence is the way through which the mind experiences reality during the living through the instrument of body.

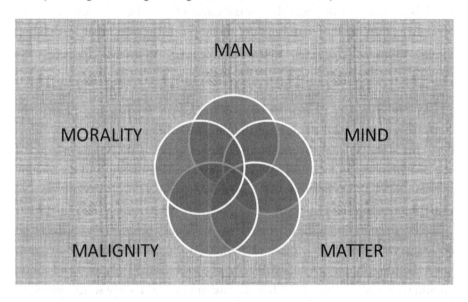

A ripen fruit automatically detaches itself from the tree holding it. Such is the case with cycle of life too. The matured ones have to give way to the offspring's of nature. Malignity is a way to morality. The sphere of man, mind, matter, malignity and morality is very crucial in building the principles of humanity. All cannot dominate at a time. When matter is driving mind morality may have the tendency to be sacrificed. When morality is at the zenith the matter may be concerned to the spirituality of humans. Matter also has the inner and outer world as the man and mind.

The transformation from materialism to idealism in man is a continual process in the cycle of man's life.

Are work and philosophy different? Are we working for god? Are we working for ourselves? The need for the mind to know certain things beyond our routine living does not arise in all. It is where the curiosity is not helping sprouting of inspirations in individuals as well as society.

Humanity is attainable in all provided we undergo the churning process of existence. You have to realize truth through experience. This is a natural filtration and refinement process for humans in existence from dawn to dusk. The concern for dignity of the self is the beginning of humanity in you.

Man is the son of god. Man is the child of god. Man is descendant of almighty. After the lord man is heir of the world. It is evident that in all living beings man is the prime beneficiary of existence. What a legatee man is in this world? He is the whole recipient of the entire existence.

It is enough searching god? God may be wondering on the man's triviality in life. The core purpose has not been addressed yet. It is lagging the thought of the substance which a true man should have inherited.

This is the universal truth despite it is being debated since its origin. All the doctrines are more or less based on it. Realization of god is to be done by every individual. Means and ways are different. The truth is that the goal of every man is same.

Now the question is the divinity of man. All are working towards universal freedom, the final liberty. How to fly away from the bondage? Man's real, survival, moral and social duty will always be in conflict. The moral and action should have realistic union. Milk and curd are from the same source but with different characteristics. Similarly good and bad are not different to the source. They emerge with their respective attributes.

Humans have been wrongly baptizing the concept of duty. Life and death are the same thing, looked at different points, again and again from the same source. Rising from the source and falling back to the source in nutshell is the cycle of life.

Every man has the stomach with him from dawn to dusk. But the hunger strikes only at the point of requirement. It is not that you are hungry around the clock. Thus the energy is generated and consumed at the same source. Whatever you attain, gain, lose, realize, share, help, humiliate, learn, deliver, excel, experience, satisfy, fight, flight, teach, meditate, conceive, deceive, explore, exploit, summarize, during this journey is the in and out from the same source of existence.

Dawn and Dusk are also the points of time,
from the same source of existence.

Every man is an individual wave of life in the ocean of existence. Some rise very high, but to again and again fall back to the bed of existence.

Life is thus an opportunity to rise against this fall forever and ever, the final attainment of freedom. Many people have lived their lives but still are not happy. Is it due to lack of containment? There are many people who will not refrain from doing illegal but great souls do not need laws.

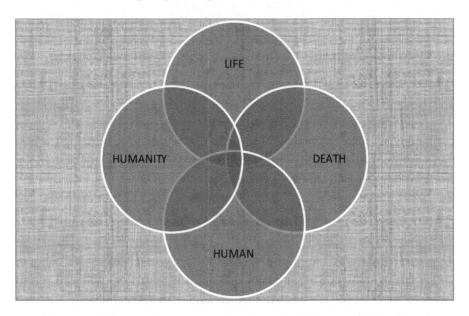

The spheres of life, death, human and humanity mutually overlap to create another world of existence. It is a mixture of emerging thoughts, research findings, civilization cultures, redefined ideologies, and survival strategies, human's intellectual perceptions, individual wisdoms, society's general consensus, and so on from dawn to dusk. This is in struggle with the real world of existence where humanity is to be reestablished and regenerated.

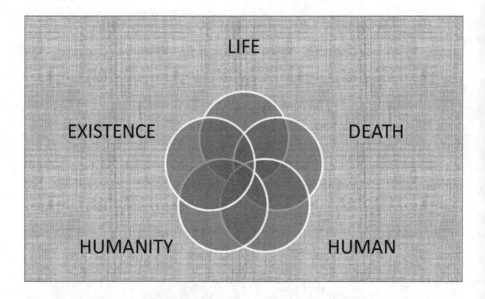

The complexity increases as the conflict between the real existence and evolved or emerged existence increases. This friction is continuously bringing the best face of human in the world. This is the face of ideal human we all are looking for from the very beginning of existence.

Man works for what?

Happiness and sadness are the states of the same source you are searching to attain throughout your life. It is not that quitting your work will lead you to freedom; on the contrary it is work which alone can liberate you.

Man is growing all the time that does not mean a person disowns the stages of childhood, youth and old after growing out of them. The whole summary of understanding is to lead noble soul towards its higher destiny.

The mind evolves through knowledge.

Purposelessness in life often manifests in a strange depression. The tranquility comes after one transcends from the state of man's being.

The perfect man should bear sufferings and pleasures with equanimity. The man has excelled who has no influence of the state of mind. What we want is to see the man who is harmoniously developed great in heart, great in mind, great in the deed, great in thoughts, great in action, great in learning, bold in voice, and so on. Is it impossible to have humans of manly attributes?

Where is the man of the future who can hold the dignity of humanity? How to become dignified? Is this not going to raise competition among us? Yes this is where the perfection in you is being carved out by the existence.

Life without competition in true spirit is sign of death.

The dying man very reluctantly forgoes his breath. It is liberation only which is with freedom of life.

Life unattached is the purest form of existence. Being in the existence you are out of it. There is nothing ridiculous about this truth when you have really understood it.

Even the wise are perplexed. Continuous selfless actions gradually cleanse the mind of dross and impurities. It is then that ignorance ceases and the individual obtains the full blaze of illumination. Learning will continue till living.

Authors, linguists, readers, institutions, publishers, schools, universities, academicians, educationists, reformists, activists, humanists, researchers, communities, societies, homes, nations, continents, have to collectively work towards establishing a complete new order of humanity all over the world. The reality is being diluted at the cost of irreparable damage to humanity.

The problem with us is, we do not realize it even after reaching the graveyard. The modern world is being built on the cloned hypothesis of life which is likely to be rejected in times to come. The responsibility is not being owned by the human of today.

The era of modernization, outsourcing and standardization of living has changed the scenario of survival. The race has derailed the peace of human. The power play brings benefit to the reserved masses only. It is a huge task the civilization is facing today amidst disparities and diversities from dawn to dusk. The solution is within us but lying beneath a load of ignorance.

Who will mine out the man in us? Let one and all ask for it from dawn to dusk. Life is too anxiously looking for a promising change beyond the criticism of humans. It is exploring the same through us. Sometimes you age out holding on to the wrong things rather than experimenting a new thing. It may not be easy to take the risk but it is better than the repentance we harbor throughout our life. Man is butchering man. How to mitigate it? Will man die for another man's survival?

The whole world is within man. Man everywhere, anywhere and at anytime the issue continues to prevail remaining permanently unresolved. We cannot have a world without man. Will the characteristics of man change? Man is fighting man from dawn to dusk. He is stripping out another man in him.

As daily food is required to survive, so daily mentoring of the mind is also required. The daily food for mind is meditation. Daily you have to remind yourself that you are harming yourself by harming another man from dawn to dusk. Man has to reform and restructure himself. His organization should be saved from sinking. Try to float yourselves. Learn to swim through the pollutants of mind. Rise and rise above your own self again and again till you have risen to the infinite end of existence.

Where can I run away from my fellow man?

I have all my beginning with him and have to perish in the community of humans. I have to return to my source of origin. Humans are at work all over the world. Definitely it cannot be without purpose. The food you ate was cultivated by someone. The clothing you wear was knit by someone. I am not aware of my contribution but it has its own connectivity and dimension.

Man of Action

"Will of Man can only become Man of Action"

Man is for action in life. Life cannot be defined without Man's play. The world is the stage for the drama. There are two dramas in man's life going together simultaneously i.e; the inner and outer world. Where is the real man of action from dawn to dusk? Before action is the will.

My readers can further put their thought on this which I am advocating truly for the betterment of mankind in the world, "Will of Man can only become Man of Action".

Have first the will to act. Have the will to do things. Then it is the action which does everything. Make your inner as well as outer world participate into this process of reforming humanity. You may be at Church. Temple or Mosque attending the prayer physically in the outer world but at the same time the prayer has impact inside in your inner world trying to connect with the almighty. Here both your inner and outer world is working towards the spirituality you are trying to seek from the existence.

Let us become

"Will of Man" and "Man of Action".

Both the will and action are equally important for shaping our dreams into reality. The power of will naturally will be seen in the action of existence. It speaks the inner voice of man in all walks of life. It is the inner strength which rules the outer world.

If the will of man is established towards humanity then the will of world gets established towards humanity. If the man of action has decided to work for humanity then the world of action too has decided to work for humanity. A very close microscopic observation of the happenings from dawn to dusk will help you to understand the chain of activities in making humanity.

There are many activities which may simultaneously be undergoing in the inner world of man. This is a true way to transform the self towards humanity. You are trying to become human by your effort directed inside yourself. The biggest change can come to man only from the inner world. All the external actions directly or indirectly are having reactions towards the inside world.

Today the world needs men who can act, act, act without instructions, no prior guidance, terms and conditions are secondary, unconditional contracts, true to their self with ownership of cause and responsibility. Along with them a hoard of humans should follow blindly in the pursuit of humanity. This is the century of action from dawn to dusk.

Enough of the gneisses, theories, evolutions, histories, theologies, philosophies, doctrines, epics, holy books, sacred collections, races, religions, policies, summits, governments, nations, schools, institutions, culture and rituals, we have been with these illusions and delusions and them for long,

long time, only with teachings, preaching, and writings, without actions and only confrontations till date.

Let us now speak only by actions.

The doer is primarily important to the whole process of restructuring in regenerating humanity. Man's childish ideas of doing this and doing that shall not die. Human's desires, dreams, ambitions, urge, thirst, hunger, starvation, restlessness, continues to map with the existence. Why everything in this earth is fraught with fear? World wants fearless man of man to be the humans of change.

What the world wants first, the man or the idea? However a man may conduct himself, there will always be persons who invent the blackest lies about him. Until we are ready to sacrifice everything else to one idea and to one alone, we never will see the light.

How to help mankind?

Where are the right kinds of people? Many things may occur to the mind, but it gradually makes a mountain of a molehill if you try to express them. Bullies are always cowards. Man should bring together a few real men. Man should have politeness and sympathy with people of all sects. Man can work with great energy through cardinal virtues only. Never shall you be able to know anything and you persist in pleading ignorance. Something of a higher order and imperishable value should be done.

Who can save mankind? The man who is pure and who dares does all things. Which is higher, the renunciation of the world or the renunciation of the self? Hundreds of new plans will be created and destroyed from dawn to dusk.

Can worldliness and realization of god go together? Yes, definitely when it is by the worthy man. Yes, surely when it is by the man of integrity. Yes, rightly when it is by the man of character. Yes, undoubtedly when it is by the man of universal existence.

What is man's ideal? Is loyalty free from man's success? Achieving something without integrity is like using soap without water. The bath without foam cannot clean your dirt from the body. Thus your ability to perform with integrity gives you clearer perception of life. Then there is neatness, fairness, cleanliness, in whatever you do and wherever you do.

How many of us have questioned ourselves this? We have been living worst than the insects. A real transformation is required to redefine humanity. We have to create a new order of humanity? Let us become self-reliant in delivering.

Live in harmony with all.

Harmony brings honey to humanity. How to harvest honey in our society? It is only possible by the man of action. Man of action should focus on building more and more honey hives in the world. Let man of harmony flock together to these hives in sharing the nectar of life.

Homes should produce honey. Harmony should breed happiness in society. Happy society is the building block of happy humanity. Taking revenge today for an act of someone executed years ago in history does not justify by any reasoning with the eye of humanity. Fought wars are bad memoirs in the history of humanity. Men of action have to create new fortunes. Imitation of the past inhumanity will not fetch us anything substantial to accelerate our new mission of regenerating humanity.

Olden wars were lessons in humanity.

Do not you think they could have been avoided? Were the men fighting them happy? It was not the loss of men this existence had to bitterly face but it was humanity which was mercilessly murdered.

What did humanity gain?

What success did human write in the history of humanity? What irreparable loss it has brought to mankind on this earth? Man of action has to stop these inhuman wars. They are to be ceased inside the man as well as outside the man.

All the goodness of today lies in the goodness of moment. All the goodness of tomorrow lies in the goodness of today. The invention of the electric bulb lightened the homes thus eliminating the darkness of yesterday forever. Similarly the man of today should be known for humanity by the man of tomorrow.

Let this campaign accelerate to decelerate inhumanity from dawn to dusk.

The future man should never come to know that man had been killing man. Let us work with this spirit as man of action towards removing all such evidences unwanted for the new mankind.

Let the new order of humanity have untainted history and a platform of purity as its fresh benchmark. One idea that I see clearly as daylight is why the world is burning with misery? Let us bless the day's we were born. What else can be greater than this dawn? And another idea which keeps burning in my brain is how to devise a machine or mechanism which could uninterruptedly on automation could go on producing man of action inherited with the seed of humanity.

Every new thought should purify the man. It must add to civilization's progress. The eyes must open to spiritual vision.

Man has to question his god.

The only god you believe in, the sum total of all souls, and above all, your god the, god of action, good, kind, noble, wicked, your god the miserable, unhappy, sorrow, cheers, tears, joy, your god the rich, poor, of all races, of all species, of all evolutions, all being the subject of worship by man. The God, who is in you and is outside of you, who works through you from dawn to dusk needs to be gratified from dawn to dusk.

Man has to save his life. Men are frittering away their energies in doling out unnecessary things from dawn to dusk. People should be taught to help themselves. Man has to rouse the people of the place to start societies to educate the people.

Throughout the world are places of special significance to different religious groups, cultural groups, and traditional groups but with the central theme of love for humans and ultimately it is humanity.

Every human needs holy grace.
&
Every human is cut from the same cloth.

Here's just a sampling of the world's sacred spots humans have worshiped to get the grace in one form or other at different times of the same existence.

The land at Mecca and the Mount at Fuji is in what way different to each other. Consider The Great Himalayas and river Ganga's sacredness for the Hindus in India and World.

A collective name for Israel, Jordan, and Egypt is the Holy Land. Since long this has been a place of pilgrimage for Christians, Muslims and Jews.

Why not the humans of today realize the necessity of collectivism to reach the oneness of existence? This is the only definition of unification for global universality. Why we do not realize the truth in humanity?

How can our roots be different when the land earth is one? We breathe under the one universal infinite roof. We breathe the same air of the universe. How this differentiation has exponentially grown over the centuries?

Where is the difference in existence? People who have been shedding crocodile tears never feel for their actions. It is not the different faiths that should be the cause for worry among humans. Why it is not the other way is incomprehensible till date?

Similarly the Mount Fuji, in Japan, is sacred to the Buddhist and Shinto religions. And The Black Hills of South Dakota are a holy place for some Native American people, who travel there in quest of a vision, a moment of peace and oneness with the universe.

The existence is one and the truth is also one.

The China's sacred mountain is Mount Fai Shan. It is thought to be a center of living energy, a holy place for Taoists and Buddhists. The Sacred Mosque in Mecca, Saudi Arabia, is sacred to Muslims.

Lourdes, France, is the home of a Roman Catholic shrine where the Virgin Mary was said to appear to St. Bernadette.

And Tunisia, became one of Islam's holy cities when, according to legend, a spring opened up at the feet of a holy leader, revealing a golden chalice last seen in Mecca.

Why "Man of Action" is linked to holy lands? Is the land becoming holy due to the divine humans? Or the land is gracing humans to become divine? It is a subject of philosophy with continual research for humans from dawn to dusk.

They are today known by many names. They all were messengers of happiness, peace, bliss, harmony, love, truth, faith, belief, hope and love. Their deeds made them immortal in the annals of history. They were heroes in the chronicles of humanity.

Their preaching's on humanity vibrate from dawn to dusk. They are the guidelines and benchmark to understand the inner world of humans.

Embrace the grace at the earliest if you want to experience the bliss of existence. The flight and fight of time will never end in the life of humans. No information is reveled from the graveyard of the individual.

It is only his deeds that are the holy epics of life. References are made to the sacrifices in life. Memories do rekindle the inspiration provided their seeds are from the background of humans living and dying for humanity.

Will humanity be saved by the bell?

Our focus should be on the humans the existing life in existence rather than faiths he has been exploring. The world is flooded with many faiths like Judaism, Christianity, Islam, Hinduism, Buddhism, Jainism, and many. A witness by one human in this moment can only be a review by other humans in another timeframe. It is only experience that realizes you the truth.

Before you ring the bell in temples it should ring loudly in your minds from dawn to dusk. It has the divine voice of humanity. It roars in the society to alarm humans the importance of humanity. Do not dwell till the left over time is spilled forever. Any step towards action in the right direction is an appreciable effort by human.

Life should not become letters of reminders. If you are soft with yourself then this is unpardonable mistake you are encouraging in your life from dawn to dusk. You are to be evaluated rigorously if you want to reap the benefits of the awareness coming to you in time for your welfare.

The core issue is the ethics of living not the inherited culture, tradition and religion primarily the human is surrounded with from dawn to dusk.

Why the basic insight into the inner self in human is missing right from the first civilizations?

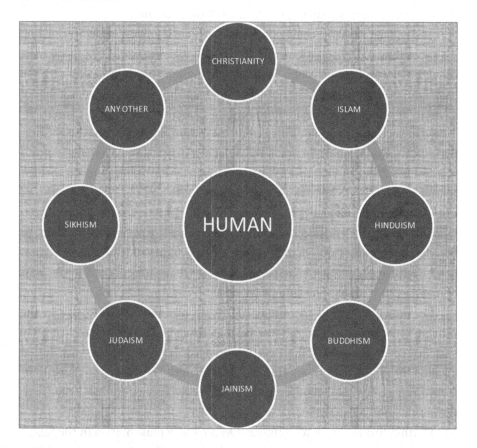

Compassionless does not open the heart .It is only love that floods the society into humanity. Man has to develop the will towards the human in him. He is answerable to the human in him. Man may deceive the whole world but cannot escape without confession to the human in him.

The above circle of human has so many faiths linked to him. All are different paths to the same destination of humans. All are different faiths to the same destination of existence.

The quest for humanity is related to the human in man.

Why man is happy with cruelness in him? How he can get rid of his rudeness? Offensiveness is the man's immediate defense against man. Man is unable to give up immorality with crudeness in him. Will impoliteness become the policy of living by the emerging next generation humans? Without the relevancy of the argument man is losing the reliability of his reasoning.

Today's man is overseeing the world with an inferior perspective of life. The abundance of distractions due to the materialistic world has made man blind to the world of humanity. Scarcity in living was somehow in line with the principles of spirituality. May not be a very inspiring philosophy but a school of thought not to be rejected comparing the present scenario of the world.

Man's action should not kill the human in him. How we can reap the best permanent results out of the small means at our disposal? The narrowness and scarcity is subject of the mind. This negative state of mind is to be thrown away forever. The field is to be made ready and then the seeds of spiritual knowledge can be sown.

Oh, my dear friends, to live even for a day in the full light of freedom, to breathe the free air of simplicity, the refinement, reformation and regeneration can be felt running down your nerves. It is not that we were born in the land of enemies. It is always the land of friends.

Let us try truly and there may not be an unknown man to you in the pursuit of humanity. The saddest part of times is that we never sincerely searched the human in us. It lay getting decayed slowly as the mummy buried awaited for reincarnation one fine day. All strength is in you, have faith in it. It will not go without manifestation. The renaissance of human is must to restore the glory of existence.

Definitely our ideas have a future. Do not buy a mass of pain in the future for a little pleasure in the present. The problem is how to operate the idea? The problem is how to guide the idea? The problem is how to germinate the idea?

A leader must be impersonal.

Filled with madness of love and yet in it no bondages. What is the good of my repentance? There is no salvation for a coward even after millions and millions of years of penance.

Human in man at the level of non-differentiation is to be reaffirmed. How will renunciation come? It is only possible when man should be the fear of fear, terror of terror, ruler of ruler, leader of leader, bolder than the bold, dreamer of dreams, stronger than the energy of energy, finally the ruler of destiny.

I have a resolution for all of us that every man should say, "The human in me is the ruler of destiny and I should under any circumstances only follow the preaching that is good for universal humanity".

Is reincarnation in human form inevitable? Does man's goal changes with peace and time? Why man is sinking lower and lower everyday from dawn to dusk? Is not a man useful member of the society?

Whatever I am trying to reproduce, reedit, reaffirm, relearn, reconsider, rediscover, retrieve, is only to revive, reform, restructure, reorganize, reinstate, reconstruct, reconcile, regain, reestablish, the dignity of humanity through the promising readers also being the seekers of humanity. They are equally the main focus and are the future instruments of measuring the skewness of humanity. I firmly believe every reader of dawn to dusk to rethink again and again on the subject of humanity which the world is losing day by day.

We are learning in the school of misery. Adversity is our teacher. The sorrows and pains are our chapters. Who supplies the man's necessities? Can man fulfill the other man's necessities from dawn to dusk? Why man has been flocking to money, health, power, beauty and long life at the cost of other man?

Man is the child of infinite.

Child has all the potential to expand to the widest end of the existence possible to see the horizon of life. Why man is not caring for the spirit? Is liberty the first condition of growth? Can religion be old and new? Hope that humanity will regain its lost splendor.

Most of the becoming of man is the product of influence and impact of the community in which he dwells. The purity of the body and mind can be sustained only in the purity of community. How can air be pure in dusty environment? To see the air free of dust you have to rise beyond the envelope of cloud polluting it. Unless you build your values no one will value you. No man wishes to be ruled by another. This is an inherent characteristic of all living beings in universe.

Woman in Man

*I am sure none of us can repay the debt
to mother for being our mother.*

Without her how could we come into existence?

Here is the beginning of man? Man is born to give birth. Man is born to die. The creator dissolves in creation. That means the continuity and discontinuity of life is again in the hands of man. Again you are created from the dissolved. The creation is continuous in the man, world, nature, universe and existence.

You go back to the same source from where you come. This is an infinite process as we have come to know so far. The present is understood as is being witnessed. The past prior to coming into existence and the future after existence has remained in the minds as a trance till today.

The dawn is created from the dusk. Both of them are from the same source. Dawn dissolves into day to create the dusk. Woman is the personification of universal creation. Thus woman in man is the spirit of creation. Woman is the source and sink of man. Man comes to the world from the cradle of woman.

Woman is to be worshipped by man. Woman is the earth in man. Everything generates from the woman in man.

Man and Woman are from the same source of existence. It is the creator's infinite possibilities man is embracing. Nothing lasts for finite. It evaporates to condense again merging in the same source. We all are good at philosophies. We have travelled in these faculties for long. Many researchers have been working deeply to explore the basic truths of life. The humanity has no doubt benefited in enriching their mind. Mind in turn has incited the urge for transformation in man and woman. Where we want to go from here? How we perceive our origin presently? These all are trying to address the genesis of woman in man.

All men are marginally womanish. A bit of motherly instinct in male gender cannot be differed .The caring, parenting, loving, affection, are all the natures of mother. Our home's happiness is based upon the mutual understanding of the relationship between man and woman, and boy and girl. The importance of gender cannot be out of discussion. Woman's role is equally important in overall development of humanity. They are the first teachers to their offspring. The infants nurturing phase is the foundation for the future.

Every man is the reflection of his mother.

Every land is the reflection of mother earth. Every planet is the reflection of universe. Every existence is the reflection of universal existence. The point to be picked up is that the origination is from the same source like the rainbow dispersing the different colors. The life too similarly has scattered with different mothers, different children, different looks, different tastes, different minds, different thoughts, and different opinions, to come out of the rainbow to realize its truth as existence. Being in the honey you may not know the honey. Once you have known that you are honey you may not try to be out of your source of honey.

Unknowingly the child starts developing a perception of life after coming to the world from mother's womb. This is how the laws of nature are applicable to grooming the man in the child.

Childhood is time of prime exposure to the concept of life, existence, parents, ancestors, nature, world and universe. Every dawn brings in new thing to be explored by the children of existence. Their curiosity to the new happenings is amazing.

Parenting is an indispensable experience. You have so many faces to share with life. The need is as per the time of life.

Woman is man's second half.

Man is incomplete without woman. It equally holds good for the woman. The girl child after the father's protection tries to look for the husband's love. The needs and requirements change with time. The tuning is to be regularized harmoniously. The present unwanted divorces all over the world speak of the evils of man. These are unappreciable disturbances for both the families. No external world is responsible for this. The relationships are weakly bonded. The social living requires a better insight into the understanding of each individual members of the family. This is beginning of humanity at home.

Society is the mirror of home.

If homes are strong, well built, then the society will be stronger and valued one. The values are to be inculcated at home. Women are the backbone of home. They are life to the whole process of development. They are not to be discriminated on the basis of gender.

Home is the building block of society. Man and woman are the limbs of the block. The relationship between man and woman is beyond the laws of attraction code. This is a natural behavior governed by the life.

Male and female are no two separate quadrants. Without their togetherness the completeness of life cannot be achieved. The better their relation the better is the fragrance of life and the beauty of life is seen from dawn to dusk.

Today's world has given them equal status and platform as men. To be very true they were never unequal to male. By nature they are the manifestation of love, peace, togetherness, kindness, beauty, joy, harmony, cheer, caring, hospitality, nursing, tenderness, representing the man's other face of existence.

"Man and Woman are the wheels of existence.

Just As

Dawn and Dusk are the ends of existence."

The continuation of the human life is through both of them. Only single male gender or female gender existence will have no purpose to the system of reproduction subsequently ceasing the offspring leading to extinct of human race.

This is where man has to look into woman and woman has to look into man towards establishing the humanity again to its glory. The theory of dominance, either man or woman may not be much of choice to the learned society. The truth man should understand is that by no means male is superior to female or female is inferior to male gender. The coin of life has to have these faces of gender. Can a single gender sustain the human life? The war of genders is more because of the ego in man.

Will the human race ever extinct?

A woman is never a liability for man. Neither man is a liability for woman. The relationship between the two is that of the gardener and garden. What will the gardener do without the garden? This is how man and woman are bounded to each other. The problem is our attachment and detachment is subjected exploitation and manipulation of the relationship from dawn to dusk. The purity in association is diluted with the misunderstandings. The misapprehensions are the immature deterrents in splitting the relationship.

The male Man cannot inherit the characteristics of woman. At the same time female Man cannot inherit the characteristics of man. Both of them are unique. The nature has designed us so to understand the beauty, love, affection, admiration, attraction, affinity, caring, creativity, music, dance, to bring some sense to the rhythm of existence.

Man cannot develop without woman.

Woman cannot develop without man. Man and woman need to brainstorm but most of the times it is seen that the storming of the brains spoils the amicable negotiations leading to unrest for the family members.

People have been unnecessarily worrying though the milk is not boiling to spill. Woman has two home's philosophy with them. They have to strike balance between the two ideologies forever. Their role of mother goes beyond acknowledgement.

Woman has been mother to the human life.

This represents the other outlook of man. Mother has an entirely complete different picture from the attributes and responsibilities of the father. She is the care taker of the life. She is the first teacher to child. She is the first to hear the cry of the baby. She is the first to feel the pain of new born life. She is courageous to nurture the life before bringing it to the world. She is herself nature. She is the personification of the universal nature. Her existence is as important as the existence of the universe.

Life in mother's womb is a wonderful experience but once we are out of the prime womb, the recall of that state is hardly with us when we enter the universal womb. Then being here after an experience hopefully another migration takes place and then from there again, this cycle advocates the basic principle of energy.

Who does not know that eggs are hatched not smashed? The selection of the natural process in giving, bringing and taking life is yet the mystery. Human science is trying to probe into it through the recent developments of research and application of advanced mind and brain. Few new concepts, sprouts of hope, and the curiosity to unfold mystery from dawn to dusk is an opportunity to humans to know more and more about the secrets of life.

Man's patience is at test. Without the turbulence violent energy is not created which can unravel the mountains of mysteries. Man is father of man. Man is mother of man. Man's form of woman is stronger and the universal seat of existence. Father with his limitation is the supporter of the mother with her dawn blessing the child of existence.

Does not man exist to bring in existence? The importance of genders of man naturally reflects to the understanding of variability with purpose of life. One has to bear the pain; other has to rear the existence. In the bringing up of life by life from dawn to dusk the parenting is revealed to the world.

Parenting is the personification of universal love in existence. Mother and Child are like the Earth and Man.

An opportunity breeding another opportunity, an existence understanding another existence, one life revealing truth to another life, one life supporting another life, directly or indirectly, the survival, growth, development, exploration are embedded with one another, thus forming a universal link of existence, one nature into another, but ultimately into the oneness of existence. This is the beauty of life.

Life is the greatest gift to experience the existence from dawn to dusk. Women have been striving hard to fulfill their family dreams.

Family is the building block of society. A good society can breed up only with good family. The association of man should be at peace. The difference in the individuals, the differences of the families, the major differences at the societies, the differences at the group of societies, the differences at the states, at the nations and finally at the global family platform. The roots of differences are to be truncated regularly to stop sprouting of the branches of conflicts through the lessons of humanity.

Is there necessary social evils?

Man is a social animal. Does humanity is now a matter of new socializing concepts? The social faculty is at crossroads to these. The trend of globalizing and socializing is different in the developed nations compared to the developing nations. Are the social reformers not concerned about it? What will evolve out of It.? Do we have a foresight for humanity?

Literacy needs a new definition all over the world from dawn to dusk.

The education of humanity is more concerned on the overall development rather than on the academic curriculum. The institute's orientation may help the beginners later during their years of living after school pass out. A complete foundation should constitute all the possible ways and means required to reorganize and restructure the process of learning.

"Will His Own invention become redundant?"

Can there be separation between sex and reproduction? This is one area which disturbs the society at different phases of life? Rather than the cause for existence it has been abused again and again from dawn to dusk. The society faces the problem of a desired child especially very particular about the gender.

Man should look towards eliminating abortion of life. It is painful to understand that we have been killing fetus against the law of nature.

Will mankind, ever learn this to respect the dignity of basic element of existence. It appears sex has become a subject of recreation more than the purpose of reproduction. It will continue to be a prime factor for the healthy relationship between man and woman. This epicenter of cyclone is invariably uprooting the grounds of humanity.

Humanity flows between the banks of man and woman. Man and woman are made so by nature to understand the above subject with their respective minds. In continuation to the above dilemma the school of thought from some section of society for legalizing sex work brings us to cross roads of humanity.

The society itself is getting sampled out with variability's and attributes so rapidly that a general consensus looks to be a mere eye wash now and then among the nations at global platform of humanity.

Remember, it has not developed today. It is the world's oldest profession. Many had their living through it. What makes it continue in society? Who is responsible for breaking homes? Who is responsible for breaking love? Does pleasure at bar and homes have two different meanings? It is a question for the entire reformist in the world. Is lust taking over love? Is sex becoming a matter of trade?

Man is worried with power, money, name, fame. stardom, wealth, materials, and what not. Moreover the factor of sex is becoming critical issue for the emerging societies today. Illegality is penetrating into the legality of morals faster than the time of existence. Anything beyond the line of limitations is invariably going to uproot the basics of humanity.

Undisciplined humans are creating society of inhumanity. Divorce is abuse to love of existence. It is an insult to the relationship between man and woman.

How humanity evaluates it is a matter of concern to all of us? The time is ticking fast from dawn to dusk.

Is woman a commodity to be traded with man?

Survival may have its own limitations but not to the freedom of trading in flesh in any civilization. It is not an exclusive subject of debate but a deeper understanding between the genders of existence. Some news of assaults, embarrassments, teasing, divorces, keeping pouring in all over the world narrating the true story of sufferings of women. Is it not the responsibility of man to bring them the same respect they die for in the existence from dawn to dusk?

Let us be women who love unconditionally. Let us be women willing to lay down our sword words, our sharp looks, our ignorant silence and towering stance and fill the earth with extravagant love.

Let us be women who make sensible home. Let us be divine women who open our arms and invite others into an honest, spacious, glorious embrace. Let us be women who carry each other. Let us be women who give from what we have. Let us be women who leap to do the difficult things, the unexpected things and the necessary things. Let us be angel women who live for peace. Let us be women who breathe hope. Let us be women who create beauty.

Let us be women who are savvy, smart, and wise. Let us be women who shine with the light of God in us. Let us be women who take courage and sing the song in our hearts. Let us be women who say, yes to the beautiful, unique purpose seeded in our souls. Let us be women of boldness who call out the song in another's heart. Let us be women of wisdom who teach our children to do the same from dawn to dusk.

Let us be women of humanity who love, in spite of fear. Let us be women who love, in spite of our sad, bad, good and fair stories. Let us be women of courage who love loudly, beautifully, divinely. Let us be women of spirituality who pray for the well being of the entire existence.

Every man should remember his mother.

She is the goddess of life.

Man's first home is mother's womb. All the preparation goes on to send you to the World's Womb. Right after the pregnancy is confirmed a new life begins in a life. Man's mother takes on all the pain in the world to justify her cause in the existence.

She is the creator of the creature again. This is where the root of life remains. Show me a single human who had any different source of coming to this world? Show me a single human who had any different source of returning away from the world?

We all vanish after a period of life on this earth. We stay, play, do drama with emotions, fight and flight with ego and execute many such activities finally to say goodbye to the existence. Why we come and go from the world could not be deciphered entirely by the humans even till today?

"At times it is all illusion and at times it is all reality". This is probably how life appears to all of us. At times we are glorified and in no time the misfortune swallows us without any notice to the concerned going to suffer. Life is a mix of all these certainties, unpredictability's, mysteries, from time to time.

Human too cannot be blamed for everything. Human limitations are part and parcel of the humanity.

Let us recite -Glory to all the mothers of the world. Great are their lives in the world. Man would not have seen the world if the woman in him was not created by the creator. Woman is the life source for all. She personifies the existence. She is the love of the existence. She is the beauty of the nature. She is the goddess of the universe.

Anyone who disregards her should be ashamed of his own wisdom. The sororities are to be supported to reap overall development of the education system in the world. Both the genders of man need equality in living and understanding the world. No gender was created to suppress each other anywhere in the world. The perception towards woman need not be sophisticated anymore. The burial of this gender inequality will open gateway to humanity. How can mother be oppressed by anyone?

Existence never differentiated to exploit the woman. It is insensibility of man to demoralize the woman. A harmonious relationship can only build happy homes. The dominating theory of genders needs to redefine their laws for the welfare of woman fraternity.

"My mother was the most beautiful woman I ever saw. All I am I owe to my mother. I attribute all my success in life to the moral, intellectual and physical education I received from her", - George Washington.

The source of life is the goddess of life. Any other thing is perhaps next to it. Can any guardian take the place of mother? No doubt however sacrifices he might have done shall always next to the mother of life. Hence let us be true children to this existence in form of earth, nature, world and universe.

Life should not just remain a list of proposals.

Realization is a way of learning. Your valuable finding can be a established postulate for a new beginning towards further betterment leading to levels of perfection and excellence from dawn to dusk.

Human of Happiness

"Man has come to the world to do something right not to see the wrong of others". –Dr Shree Raman Dubey

Where to find humans of happiness? Are we not the humans with cheers? Is it not that the cheers and tears both are our creation? We are exchanging it among ourselves. This is unwontedly fragmenting the society. This is for no human gain bisecting the society. The introduction of terror is trisecting the society.

Will these disintegrated communities and societies bring any value addition to themselves and the world? The formation of groups with negative concepts can only breed negative culture. There are numerous emerging cultures in the world today with their own ideologies and nothing wrong to bank on it but not above the concern of human happiness through humanity.

Each of us has the right to question our dignity of humanity. Why we should compromise with our wanted valuable attributes morals, ideals, virtues, ethics, integrity, loyalty, purity, sincerity, punctuality in building a strong human personality?

Let us become humans who can create cheers, smiles, happiness, jolliness, healthiness, worthiness, truthfulness, for millions and millions of humans. Let us start giving to those humans who have less than you. Share your abundance to be graced more and more. By doing this you will be in network of humans living for humanity.

I have a question to my graceful readers, "Don't you feel life is a workbook?" The more and more you work with the sheets of day from dawn to dusk the refinement in living becomes your part of existence.

Work from dawn to dusk towards building happiness in humans. Work towards making humans smile without a conditional reason. Work towards wiping out the tears of unhappiness from the unfortunate lives. Work towards owning the pains of neighbors. Work, work because without work where is the ray of results.

There is no end to the wrong list. It is infinite in creation by the negative mind. Our focus is to switch on from bad to good things. Off all such plug in connections from where the mind is charged with negativity. You can surely practice and cultivate this as we do to save energy in our homes to avoid the energy crisis.

The crisis of humanity can be addressed in the same fashion. Fundamental to the practice is what to practice so that any default repetition of the commands gives you again and again only the goodness of humanity.

Why to blame god for our sufferings? Human is sailing in dark and gloomy clouds. Human can see himself with clarity when the complete clouds of ignorance have poured down. When will a new dawn of this sunrise befall on the entire existence?

Happiness is for humans. Humans are for happiness. How to obtain this without disparities? Does destiny rules the law of disparities? Why man has the limitations to implement the law of equality?

Let us not be criticizers of the human. Only screaming about others speaks of the inhuman nature of man. Why the world is experiencing different category of humans? When the basic nature and source is divine then why this deviation? Why this degradation? Why this destruction? Why this devastation? Why this chaos? Why this turbulence? Why this panic? Why this inhumanity?

What will bring you joy? Can you list out a statement of it? Will the joy remain with you forever? Joyfulness, cheerfulness, happiness, humbleness, kindness, sacredness, blissfulness, peacefulness, generousness, goodness, healthiness, wellness, and so on man are desperately waiting to embrace.

Man quickly wishes to get rid of all these cruelness, helplessness, sadness, loneliness, badness, untruthfulness, foolishness, unpleasantness, sorrowness, unworthiness, weakness, ego, anger, worry, fear, evilness, narrowness, idleness, creating a negative environment around him. If the surroundings are unhealthy there is every possibility of polluting your own ideals of living.

Humans have to come out with a revolution to check this pollution all over the world. Pollution of humanity is an illness humans would never like to live with. Practice of humanity can only clear our polluting society from dawn to dusk. How to remove the pollutants of humanity? Can education be one of the prime tools?

Humanitarians can only bring happiness. Harmony is the essential rhythm of human. There is no other music of life as humanity which soothes society. Sophism is only sucking society. How to develop champions of humanity?

Every single home should have one champion of humanity. Every single home should have one architect of humanity. Why human is losing his happiness? Will our tears go forever?

Every dawn brings a ray of hope for humanity all over the world. Let this ray make us pure every day.

Equality in life has been a subject of debate since the existence of man. Whatever you have is due to the law of natural giving. It knows best why it is so. But the reasoning is not pacifying the human's outer as well as inner world. Where to seriously know about this universal truth? There are several areas of research alive to understand the happiness of humans.

How to stop this split? Society is breaking down? Man is sectionalizing himself. The nobility of man only for the sake of short temporary goals of ignorance is being lost. This is at huge cost to the existence of humans. Irreparable damage is to be checked from dawn to dusk. Irretrievably we are losing the legacy of humans.

Who will restore the glory of humans? Humans should be like the humming birds. Keep smiling with sweetness of happiness. Humans should be buzzing with happiness throughout the day. Liveliness of humans is ending in soreness. It has to infinitely remain with humans. The issue is as old as humans.

A new process of learning is the demand of the rising dawn to transform the society.

With great love in my heart for the readers,

"If Homes are happy Humans are happy".

How to make our homes happy? Who will do this in the family? How family members can integrate from dawn to dusk to achieve this? Have you been sent to the world to take happiness or create happiness? I am here to give happiness then why I am worrying about acquiring happiness? It is a very good question to all for conducting workshop. Importance of happiness is what we all are dying for. It is through both the means either good or bad.

Why cannot happiness be attained through heavenly means? Why man is not nearing the grace of heavens?

Man has been struggling to get it through both the means. Why both the means are the choices to man? Deprived ones are advocating the path of happiness opposite to the ones in abundance from dawn to dusk.

Life is full of crests and troughs. World should not be seen as a different identity. Will literacy incite humanity? Where are the real roots of reformation? They are within man. It is not sprouting in the mind, body and soul. A comprehensiveness of humanity is to be globally quested. The eagle's view is to be dared by all of us. If there is any element of doubt the main objective is likely to collapse.

How to turn defeat into victory?

All around us there is a negative environment that is trying to tug all of us pulling down to the level of insects in society. How to build the confidence in the self? Unless fear is removed to challenge the good, goodness cannot become a habit. Habit for happiness is to be explored from dawn to dusk. A person is a product of his own thoughts. Mind is a manufacturing unit. It keeps producing countless thoughts from dawn to dusk. Categorically it falls into positive and negative thoughts.

Positive thoughts lead you to victory, success, triumph, joy, happiness, cheers, vision, mission, objectives, aim, goals, path of purpose, mankind, humanity, dignity, lively and more and more towards the core of living with divinity. Negative thoughts lead you to defeat, unhappiness, depression, rejection, sadness, misery, unrest, disquiet, jealousy, proud and so on towards inhumanity.

Every day is a fine day, wonderful day, better day, success day, victory day, dream day, happy day, love day, bliss day, action day, wisdom day, play day, learning day, teaching day, joy day, opportunity day, creativity day, innovative day, inspiring day, excelling day, helping day, energy day, skill day, cheer day, bold day, pray day, run day, jog day, painting day, exploring day, expediting day, mentoring day, project day, as you perceive as many days of existence.

Life has many ways to receive the days.

Exploitation of woman is another prime subject of concern which today's society is facing despite the literacy rate of the world. Is that more awareness of the inner things is causing restlessness? The discipline line between the genders is a point of argument even today. Is it a matter of individual attitudes towards the opposite gender?

How to resolve issues of genders in society? The impact of gender on society towards humanity needs a greater emphasis right from the childhood stages to the right understanding of life as man and woman. The various relationships a man and woman are into as individuals, family, groups, socializing, organizations and nations. It is the purity and transparency of the basic bond between man and woman which builds the ideal society with values of humanity.

The smallest living unit in any organism is a cell. Over and above human is made up of trillions of cells, tissues, organs, organ systems, DNA, genes and the other anatomy of bones, skulls and skeleton. Human body is like a complex machine. The mystery of the reproductive system of all organisms and no doubt the humans without which we cannot grow, maintain life and reproduce.

Is it not surprising and brainstorming to understand that the human is executing different tasks from dawn to dusk as cells differentiate from each other to perform different tasks within the body? The group of cells works to perform a specific task. The nerve tissue carries messages from the brains to the rest of your body by sending electrical impulses. The work within the human body is as if through a control system not within the body. What to say about it?

Conflict between man and woman should convert into understanding between man and woman. Woman and man are like earth and sky which never separate but appear to meet only at horizon. Is not sky equal to earth? The question of equalizing woman and man seems to be ridiculous as they are already equated by god. Nature has made the balance.

The forces of attraction and repulsion between woman and man are governed by the concern of each other in many ways during the whole process of living. A good couple, a cheerful couple, a happy couple, a satisfied couple, a contained couple, a peaceful couple, a well learned couple, a good mannered couple, a spiritual couple, a healthy couple, a smiling couple, an inspiring couple, an excelling couple, a vibrant couple, an energetic couple, a sportive couple, a nice couple are all reflection of the better understanding of woman by man and equally man by woman. If both are living and dying for each other from dawn to dusk, then where is the scope for misunderstandings, inequalities, exploitations, discriminations, criticisms, divorces, separations, breaking up of families, unnecessary chaos in the society. The overall development probably can be done through more education, better awareness, reformation and restructuring, sincere transformation, dedicated welfare, true literacy, understanding spirituality and committed attitude of man. The focus should be to apply all the above to expedite the entire refining process of humanity.

We live in a world in which the monetary value of professionals does not always correlate with the magnitude of value they create for society like nurses, teachers, reformers and spiritual masters, gurus, saints, and many service providers.

Everything cannot be compared with money? Things cannot be evaluated by money. Man is not a share market to rise and fall as index. Money has never been a yardstick for measurement of success, achievement, accomplishments, performance whatsoever you may consider it for analysis.

This is where the role of society, community, man and humanity comes in picture. We are running towards the unnecessary resources of life. The demarcation between requirement and super flux is very essential for the individual to arrive at.

Summing Up & Exercise for Readers Chapter- X

- Are you regularly evaluating yourself from dawn to dusk?
- Are you ranking your priorities, needs, desires, necessities, wishes and aims?
- Are you scientifically interrogating and measuring yourself?
- Are you assessing your living periodically?
- Are you apprising yourself your appraisals sincerely?
- These are the tools to diligently craft your ideal human personality. A habit of these is going to become a permanent culture of humanity in you.
- Look at the table below. Start formulating the assessment tool to evaluate your position in life today.
- Every day develop a new table to review yourself.

Sr .No	Assessment Areas	Yes	No
1	Are you humanity conscious?	Yes	
2	Do you examine yourself?		No
3	Do you manage yourself?		No
4	Do you make others smile?	Yes	
5	Do you make others happy?	Yes	
6	Do you give your time to people?	Yes	
7	Did you help anyone today?		No

- Have a daily, weekly, monthly and annual review of what you are becoming.
- Practice with these realized learnt tools.
- These are reforming tools of fabricating humanity.
- These are reestablishing tools of cleaning inhumanity.
- These are regenerating tools of bringing in the humanity in the world.
- Do you penalize yourself for your bad thoughts, bad deeds, bad ideas, bad behaviors, bad manners, etc?
- If not, have you questioned yourself for this?
- Do you fear monitoring yourself?
- Do you hate yourself becoming good?
- Do you map your actions with reactions?
- Write an essay on "Why you are not happy?"
- Attempt writing more such essays wherever you are in turbulence.
- Develop transparency in opening hearts to your fellow men.
- Feel the importance of relationship.
- Never miss an opportunity to kiss humanity.
- Live for society from dawn to dusk.
- Help without recognitions.

- Never resign from your virtues in struggle of life.
- Ask yourself the reason of turbulence you face daily from dawn to dusk.
- Can you not prepare a daily report on yourself with causes that influence, impact and trouble you?
- Avoid conflicts, arguments, criticisms, abuses, assaults, sins, ill-words, bossism, enmity, etc not conducive to the flourishing of humanity.
- Make at least one person happy every day.
- Learn at least one lesson of humanity every day.
- Teach at least one person every day importance of humanity.
- Plant at least one seed of humanity every day.
- Let the dusk end up to receive a brighter dawn every day.

Summary

"Spirituality is an umbrella to the humanity of the world from dawn to dusk"

I believe that my affectionate readers by this time when you have been nearly through this inspiring essay might have come to know the burning idea of this author. I myself went in ton of tears to understand that humanity is a more serious subject of address rather than a piece of essay.

Human is attitude. Attitude cannot be taught in schools. Attitude is one to one philosophy. On this incomprehensible subject man's attitude is infinite. With all the background of thoughts, ideas, ideals, values, morals man develops the attitude for the onward journey. Any activity undertaken is result of this attitude and above all rules the attitude of man on man making the differences in humanity.

No higher education can promise to bring cheers unless the attitude of man is bent to deliver humanity. With these facts, truths, scenario, turbulence, chaos the world is sailing I find myself difficult to summarize the gist of this book. However, its inclination I feel has been understood by each one of us and all who have sincerely participated in it.

The journey of dawn to dusk is eternal. It is immortal by nature. It is in, out, around, beside, beneath, along, among, and between nature, man, world, mind, body, spirit, soul and universe. It is as you perceive it. It is as you conceive it. It has been the history of the past and is the vision of the future.

Memories are the chapters of lessons from dawn to dusk. Our reminiscences are both beneficial as well as deterrent in forward march.

Your life is your imagination. Imagine being the emperor of humanity and there you see you have been seated on the throne of happiness. The life with concern is a trajectory of its own dynamics. I have to do for the world. I have to die for the world daily. I have to live for myself or for the world from dawn to dusk. This has been squeezed by many civilizations and generations for no pouring of rain to quench the thirst of humanity. There has been even no marginal misting despite deliberations for years and years together.

It is time for the humans of today to bring a new look to humanity and a new look to the world. What is the fun of dying daily? Bold are the ones who live forever dying once. This is the true ideal to live a life of freedom. Nothing can resist truth. We want great spirits. Where are the great spirits? Work consistently in one direction with disciplined focus and you are surely going to embrace humanity.

Organization is power. The secret of it is obedience. Obey the laws of humanity. What can be a better organization than the world? Where can be a bigger organization than this? A factory of humans committed for a universal goal of humanity. It is the heart, the heart that conquers the brain. It is the heart, the heart that conquers the mind. We all are into manufacturing love for humanity? The universal product is love. It is to be marketed all over the world. Let us be the marketing executives and sales man to market humanity as much as we can. Right now there is no other International Trade as important as business of humanity.

Humanity is a global business today. My dear readers a career in it is far fetching than any other careers of the world. It has no retirement. There is no bossism. It is open for all. There is no evaluation and appraisal. You are the examiner as well as the examinee. You all are owners of your entrepreneurship producing humanity. The world needs more and more entrepreneurs of humanity today than ever before. Why do not you become a professional in humanity?

Let us look at it differently. Rather than the spiritual plane directly we move towards it through the concept of individual performance, contribution, exploration, liberation, salvation, before a generalized consensus of society, community, nation and world is arrived on to transform humanity.

The Soul is the index of life. We go on evolving, shifting and changing until we find our fulfillment from dawn to dusk. Where do we completely find it? Going within may mean a change for us, but it does not mean feeling blankness. It gives man a fresh start. Awaken the sense of soul- life.

Misery comes because we do not listen to the voice within. Do not be discouraged by failing and faltering. Do not forget that you are little child. Life to reach the highest fruition must find its expression from within. If we can let our mind dwell even for a moment on infinitude it will revive us.

Who will revive us? Who will restore the humanity? Who will love us? Who will care us? Who will secure us? Who will save us? Who will protect us?

And all these can only be resolved by the guilt of every human of the wrong he is doing. Guiltiness can only bring all the humbleness in you. It is as similar to the importance of home to the human who is homeless.

Because you are associated with a human you have a story of both of you. It may be good or bad but a relationship cannot be without a story. If you escape the relationship then also you will have one with your own self reflecting you. The point to understand is that humans are bound to compare, interact, detract, discuss, react, care, retreat, criticize, invite, detach, attach, love, hate based on the theory of dominance. Any attribute which is predominant that moment, you turn to reflect that attribute in your personality from dawn to dusk. Much of commonsense supplemented with comprehensible wisdom is the requirement for the human to rise above the clutches of survival.

Carelessness injures our lives from dawn to dusk. Negligence is the other disease cancerous to the inner self. Our inner voice is invariably unarguably pleading to redeem us. Who will do our goal refinement? How you respond to the world matters much to your perception of living? The cold war between man and world perhaps is the hypothesis being researched by the humanity.

You are thinking about the world? Is the world equally thinking about you? You are thinking about your neighbor, colleague, mate, family, relatives, and society? Are they equally concerned about you? Does reciprocation makes a difference?

How would you describe yourself? As an upholder, questioner, reformer, follower, leader, preacher, marketer, scavenger, winner, failure, humanist, crusader, and so on as per your own analysis, evaluations and assessments.

What is a simple habit that consistently makes you happier? Do you have any habits that continually get in the way of your happiness? Which habits are important to you?

Habits are the building blocks of Personality. Have you ever managed to gain a challenging healthy habit, or to break an unhealthy habit? If so, how did you do it? Do you embrace habits or resist them? Has another person ever had a high influence on your habits?

> **A fish can swim the whole ocean of the world but cannot climb the smallest plant on the earth. The elephant can ravage jungles together to plain lands but cannot fly to a foot height above the earth.**

Such is the diversity in creation. This is where all the secrets of existence are being revealed. No one is big and no one is small. No one is great and no one is useless. Every one of us is unique. We are the part of the universal creation.

Man is created to create opportunities of understanding the creation from dawn to dusk. The kingdom of animals and plants are doing the same but may be beyond the understanding of sciences explored by human. The definition of humanity is not be limited to the humans only but it broadly is for the entire universe including the flora and fauna of the whole world.

Life has its own limitations. Limitations bring in a greater understanding of the existence. It reveals lessons in phases. Neither you nor I truly can make difference to the universal limitations. Man has the potential creativity to work with these limitations in shaping yourself to be the ideal human.

The earth rotates on its axis and revolves around the sun. This is the geometry of existence. The arrangement of galaxies cannot be altered. Man can keep questioning that is why we are here on this planet earth. Nothing is mystery if perceived as a laboratory for experiments. The search is eternal.

"Eternity is the universal law of existence".

Will man be free from the gravitational pull of destiny? Will humanity rise above the man's desire of individuality? Every existence of man will have new dimensions to these philosophies.

Man will have dawns of ideologies to unfold at the bank of existence. The perception of today may not always be an accepted hypothesis in times to come in existence. The avenues from nature to man is in the hands of existence.

Man has been crying for liberation bowing at the feet of existence. Can we not be liberated in minds to universally live with the existence? Misery is caused by ignorance and nothing else. What the world wants is character. The world is in need of those kind men who are burning within with the fire of love. Their selfless march into reestablishing humanity will eventually bring in appreciable changes in the attitude of millions and millions. Admirably we should gratify the efforts of volunteers living and dying for humanity from dawn to dusk.

Liberation from materialism to idealism is where human is being questioned from dawn to dusk. Is there any limit to abundance in life? Is there any limit to healthiness of humans? Is there any limit to happiness of humans? Creativities are the novelties in humans. The homes should not compete to undo the sharing of love.

Life itself is an experiment from dawn to dusk.

It starts at dawn to end with some findings at dusk. The cycle of action and reactions continue from dawn to dusk. Every man is executing his role to stabilize the process of reaction under the set of some governing laws of life.

Do you know what the tax on life is? The tax on life is humanity. Every man should pay this to society. Society is the collector of this tax. It is everybody's responsibility to religiously remit it to the existence of humans. It enriches us by adding value of faith, trust, love, hope, kindness and compassion. It brings passion to all living humans from dawn to dusk.

This can be done in all walks of life. It is right from farming to global business. Readers are aware that the migration of humans started with the curiosity of trading between lands. That is to fulfill the gaps between surplus and scarce. The trading of commodities and exchange of products through the sea and land route flourished among many nations in Europe, Asia, Africa, North America, Central Area, Asia Pacific regions many centuries ago. Thus humans started to have global culture.

The impact of Global Culture on Global Humanity is a very new subject for all the nations in the world today. All our past experiences, barriers of migration, rituals, traditions, beliefs, faiths, perceptions, need to redefined. It is moving towards a universality which we speak through the various doctrines of humanity.

"Human needs Global Homes of Happiness".

Universality is aiming oneness. There should be only one definition of humanity in world. There should be only one definition of man in world. There should be only one definition of human in world. How human can differ from another human? How man can truly differ from another man? How can neutrality in creation fail? There should be only one education in the world. It is the wisdom of humanity. There should be only one way of worshiping in the world. It is the worship of humans.

The tiger in Asia is the tiger in Africa. This specie is universal in natural characteristics. It has no specific race, no specific religion, no specific culture, no specific doctrines, no specific discrimination, completely unique than the elephant. The elephant all over the world are again revealing their uniqueness.

Every living organism is blessed with uniqueness despite its land of living. The specie cannot of its own outcast its natural characteristics. Similarly the human is specie of unique characteristics. How it can be different at different places? The diversities in physical appearance, the texture and the outlook cannot be the reason of the inner differences in human all over the world.

Human is same throughout the world.

Time is witnessing all the play. All homes can unite to form a universal home. All families can unite to form a universal family. All nations can unite to form a universal nation. All ideologies can be put together to define a universal ideology. All philosophies can be integrated into a new universal postulate. Why these are not happening? All humans can join together to reestablish universal humanity.

Why the world has been dramatizing shameful conditions? Why man is failing to obey the promissory notes of humanity? The world must not allow our creative protest to degenerate humanity. Has anyone won the world by physical violence? People might have won wars but not humans. People should win humans. Nations might have won nations but not humans.

A Victory without human hearts is worse than defeat. A man living without the spirit of love is worse than dead. A man hunger of another man's flesh is worse than beast. When will the monster in us die? Why the sword of literacy is unable to pierce the shields of demons? What has gone wrong in homes to fuel the brothels with love? Why we are brutalizing the humanity in the world?

The world was to be populated with humanists rather than brutalists. How humans can stop brutalism? Can we eliminate the earthly desires? How can we be enlightened? Will brutality, cruelty, enmity, inferiority, illiteracy, impunity, hooliganism, terrorism, barbarism, insanity be removed from the dictionary of humans?

Inanition in us is the prime reason for inhumanity. We have to incite our life. Man should aim indiscriminating living now onwards. Nevertheless the knowledge gap remains a barrier forever from dawn to dusk.

Can all the humans become knowledgeable at the stroke of midnight? Can the dawn of miracle transform humans?

Why Man is drowning himself in inhumanity from dawn to dusk? Is there any treatment of this mental illness to ruin humanity? Is killing lives only the way left with humans to resolve the difference within them? Is it really difficult to address the behavioral attitudes of a person? The science interrogating human's psychology is at cross roads of humanity. The scope for newer subjects and theories is at the dawn of every human.

Every dawn has the immense power to fight the negativism of the mind. The half of our lives is lost in unnecessarily trying to poke nose with the existing ridiculousness of life. There is no end to man's righties.

Where are the rightists? Rowdyism is protecting the baseless principles of loafers in the world and invariably such people loaf away their precious time for nothing at the end. Aggressiveness is leading to arrogance rather than any value addition in overall personality of humans.

Why we are making an angry world? Why we are drifting away from happiness? Why a good world cannot be established? Do you think that the world pollutes the mind? Or It is the mind which makes the world bad? The question that human is being made bad by human only is under continual debate from dawn to dusk.

Loafers need to be guided by the literates.

They are to be brought in the main stream of humanity. Awareness is the prime step towards the journey of transformation. Let the world not lose any opportunity to spread the message of humanity from dawn to dusk.

A gap in perception, literacy, ideas, thoughts, wisdom is to be bridged by man for another man. Man should learn by teaching fellow men. Man should help himself by helping fellow men. These are as old as the civilizations of humans. It is not that these were not practiced earlier but the need is more today. Today man has to evaluate himself. Today man has to reform himself. Today man has to make himself aware of the shortcomings of humanity. Man has to become ideal to lead with humanity.

The role of good society is to build more and more better societies from dawn to dusk. The role of educated communities is to literate more and more communities all over the world. The world needs to live purely in today dissolving all the differences of the past and worries of the future. Then only a new bright dawn is likely to embrace the emerging world.

Live in toady.

Today is the day of action. Tomorrow is only to speak about history. Before you are a hero you have to be the doer. Before you are liberated you have to pass through the trials of liberation. Before you have invented you have to be innocent child playing with innovations. Before you have discovered you have to struggle with your quest of search and survival. Before you are ashes you have to win over the death of reality. Before you are no more you have to become one with the existence.

Let reality triumph for ever. If you have done the best you have passed the test. Why we should be loathing to humanity? The loather in all of us should leave our mind for ever and forever.

Man has been receiving sudden bouts of gloominess or sullenness now and then at the stroke of dawn and dusk. Is resentment in us is the impact of moodiness? Why man's rhythm is like the swing of moods?

Is life literally becoming a moon walking? No doubt the material worlds always have been mouth-watering for humans. This unassisted vision needs the mentoring towards humanity under the umbrella of spirituality as umbrella may not avoid the rain but is a tool to protect yourself wetting from the rain.

I greet existence with the learning that,

"Spirituality is an umbrella to the humanity of the world".

Moods are like dooms. They are dooming our opportunistic mind into pessimistic recreations. Unpleasant words are like sword. Let it not cut the strong magnetic forces of attraction converting it into the forces of repulsion. We should judiciously repel all such repellent forces in the world.

Create centers of humanity all over the world. Oxygenate the humans suffering from respiration of humanity. Fill them with the air of inspiration to freshly breathe the freedom of humanity. Live to create living for other fellowmen. Utilize opportunities to create opportunities for other men in the world. The hope lies in you. Do not lie the truth to make the dawn dusk for the world.

> Man learns as he lives.
> Man realizes as he acquires wisdom.
> Man teaches as he matures.
> Man preaches as he becomes divine.
> Man flirts as he is not out of lust.
> Man loves when his heart opens up.
> Man helps as he understands alms.

The world needs more number of altruists. Altruism is the principle any ideal man should never give up for priceless dishonesty.

Humans should win humans. It is not that humans are not uniting? We are uniting for the undesired missions? All visionless humans are uniting to bring chaos in the world. The results of this type of such unifications are not in the interest of universal humanity. All wrong ideas united can only bring untidy to the world humanity.

All intellectuals should not unite to breed unethical living in the world. No doubt there are groups, communities, cooperation's, teams, institutions, organizations working for humanity in the world. In addition to it there are national and global summits a world forum to voice the regeneration of universal humanity.

I salute all of them slicing and dicing from dawn to dusk in restoring universal humanity. Let us all look within to understand the human in front of you. It is only by knowing and understanding your pain that you can bring some gain to the human who seeks happiness from you. You need not be cursing yourself till you are attempting to work for the truths of humanity.

Great convictions are the mothers of great deeds.

Can we not raise the masses?

Man should not lose his innate spiritual nature.

I pray to my readers to keep the motto before you,

"Elevation of humanity without harming the values of human".

Let us lift and shift ourselves from the racial injustice, discriminations, disparities, diversities, inequalities, restlessness, greediness, jealousy, enmity, unfaithfulness, negativism, pessimism, aristocratism, brutalism, mercilessness towards a newer better plane of healthiness, happiness, idealism, cheerfulness, opportunism, volunteerism, humanism, kindness, humbleness, spiritualism and humanity from dawn to dusk.

Let us not seek to satisfy our thirst for freedom by drinking from the cup of bitterness and hatred. There are many areas where truths are yet to be realized by humans. It has no sense if we are not doing the right things. An unwanted thing rightly done is not a noteworthy achievement to be credited by truthful humans. The human basics of life are the prime essentialities the world should immediately look into redefining, developing and implementing it for living from dawn to dusk without sacrificing the objective of humanity.

In conclusion I appeal my readers, "Let us make a free society in which all persons live together in harmony and with equal opportunities of life from dawn to dusk. We are the heirs of a great civilization and its rebirth into a new, modern and dignified life now depends on one and all". Cherish positive thoughts to see the positive results. The road to good is the roughest and steepest in the universe.

"World is suffering because of practice in peace".

Human has drained billions of years in transforming himself into an ideal human. And not even near to the expectations of basics of humanity. It had more of the blows of preaching but less of the impacts in practicing. There are millions and millions of books and doctrines already occupying the places of the world. They are worthy of being declared nonperforming assets.

What use is of the huge inventory of literature on humanity when an ounce of it is not practiced even by the one percent of the entire population wearing the cap of humanity? We hardly see positive events organized to honor the Oscars of the Invention in Humanity.

Mind has an in built affinity to associate with negativism more rather than positivism. Why it happens in humans? Are there equally dominating quadrants of love and hatred in the mind of humans? The brains all with its magical power also seems to avoid the cruel thinking in humans. How to put checks on these? We have to guard our own roots and branches of existence.

The University of Humanity is within all of us. We are maintaining very unappreciable attendance. We yet prefer to be the students of back benches. Why the strength to face and lead from the front is not coming to the man in us? We are timid in our approach towards living the life of ideals.

Where are the Champions of Humanity? Who will lead with humility? Who will counsel the terrorists? Who will rehabilitate the sufferers? Why the humanists are failing to close the deals of humanity? Are we looking for better human negotiators to ultimately negotiate humanity?

Let us stop selling humanity. Let us stop crucifying humanity. Let us stop negotiating humanity. Let us stop criminalizing humanity. Let us stop murdering humanity. Let us stop Can humanity be priced? Can humanity be sold? Are not we the victims of trap of collective folly? It appears that the power of collective wisdom has lost its sanctity.

I am happy to join with you today in what will go down in history as one of the learning on humanity. Life is not a leisurely walk. Do not simply stroll it away. Ambling may not help us to convert our ambitions of humanity into reality.

Cheerless lives are useless lives in the world of humanity. Man has to develop pills for the contraception of inhumanity. A continuous assessment of the self cannot be neglected or forgone in transforming ourselves into humans of humanity.

In my opinion the external world of man orbiting around the inner centre of humanity is much similar to the theory proposed by the Polish Astronomer Nicolaus Copernicus that the sun is the centre of the solar system; with the planets (including the earth) orbiting round it. In fact the human system is governed by the laws of cosmic which can be probably inferred to the destiny we have been saying again and again.

Does the humankind have the same destiny as that of the individual human? It may be humorous to mankind but the mystery is yet unwilling to decipher the existence. Who will explore the substantialism of the human truths? Who will wipe the widow's tears? Who will bring a piece of bread to the orphan's mouth? Who will give vision to the blinds? How will poverty of the world feed all? How will inhumanity perish in the world? How the economies of the world will bridge the gap between supply and demand of humanity?

We need not wonder over our assurances and promises we make from dawn to dusk. We do little against our deeper commitments. This is the man presently dwelling in us. Where is time to be ideal in the race of madness? Where is time to experience the bliss of peace in this restlessness? Fairly speaking there is no betrayal by the laws of nature. The law of union and the law of separation are both to be implemented within the governing principles and limitlessness of existence from dawn to dusk.

Man wishes to remain in the world forever. Do you feel the same? Why most of us are not prepared to gracefully migrate from the world? The purpose of the individual might have been realized by the world. The world cannot break the laws of the creator.

Man is the media between the world and the creator without any authority on both of ends. Man truly neither possesses the world nor the creator. Man neither owns the world nor the creator.

"Man is a journey not a destination from dawn to dusk".

Give humanity a chance to change the man in you.

As this ideal human can only change the world.

Thanks Giving

The Philosophy which I have analyzed is,

"Dawn rises to set in Dusk and Dusk sets in to rise in Dawn".

What man can give to another man? It is only by grace man can do something for man. Man can only serve man in all walks of life. Man can love man. Man can know man. Man is for man. Man is by man.

I will be very glad indeed to know that my readers are adding to the ideas, thoughts, views, opinions on dawn to dusk. I shall be extremely happy to hear that the readers are practicing the values they have built to become humans.

All you need is his grace. How many times you have seen him inside you? How many times you have sincerely asked god in you to come out? Have you ever voiced it with strength of purity in you?

How many human's goal is god?

Call him with sanity and he shall reveal himself to you?

Are there different wills of man and god? Man in physical form is unable to realize the god in him. He is himself distancing Him. This is the darkness in which humanity is sailing.

Man despite the enlightened soul in him is searching for the light in the world. People accomplish the most when their objectives are clear.

Let us remind ourselves over and over again that everyone can be an

"Architect of Humanity."

We are right, but most people still think they're too small or insignificant to make a difference. Most of us feel that something is holding us back; that circumstances are preventing us from living the life we want to live.

In the search for what matters most, life as teacher teaches all that what was holding us back wasn't something "out there." Instead, it was our own fear that we were not feeling important enough to matter. It was the fear itself that was holding us back. So we should develop a strong mind with believe, hope, trust, faith and love.

"Prayers never betray our believes"

Man is the betrayer of his believes. My way of describing the belief that we each have a sacred purpose and we should stop at nothing to fulfill it, must make some way into my readers mind for development of confidence from dawn to dusk. Without confidence in yourself you cannot justify thyself. Without faith in yourself you cannot justify thyself. Without love in yourself you cannot justify humanity in thyself.

We all have been thinking about this thing called life since it came into existence. We have to lead it with humility. We have to make our own path of existence.

The truth is, when we are in our twenties we think a lot about planning a life. We look for someone to plan it with; we look to build a career to make our life, friends to complete it, kids to enhance it. Though life has a natural way of upending your carefully made plans it is you again to recreate your destiny. Lead yourself beyond your destiny.

All of a sudden you can find yourself having to plan this thing called life all over again. There is no structured format applicable to one and all. The choice of change is the only option with you.

Every dawn is a new definition.
Every dawn is a new outlook.
Every dawn is a new way.
Every dawn is a new dream.
Every dawn is a new idea.
Every dawn is a new thought.
Every dawn is a new opportunity.
Every dawn is a new face of existence.

This Life, or whatever way we are told about it, whatever we have understood it so far, can either be thrilling, excelling, thriving, achieving, soaring, flying, dancing, merrymaking, expanding, limiting, safe, secure or wide open, creative and sometimes scary, has many forms, faces, it is infinite.

Life is infinite.

It's ours to color as we like, to live as we think, to chase as we dream, to hold as we believe, to understand as we learn, to paint as we perceive, to draw as we visualize, to decide as we realize, like that so many ways, wills, desires, moods, hopes, trust and finally to create ourselves as humans.

Many times we all have been thinking about this, listening about the boring nature of living. Why do we feel this frustration? Why do we irritate for no reason at times? Why can't it be more creative? Why should it be the same way as when you were little?

Is life so limiting? Why we are not expanding? We live in air tight compartments despite the open world of happiness. The beautiful landscapes are captured on the walls of homes in frames imprisoning the beauty of nature.

The history of great leaders hangs on the walls of parliament to abuse their sacrifices for humanity. The streets are beautified with the centers having monumental statues of the martyrs. We have failed to learn from the lessons of martyrology. We merely bow to these heritages unconditionally.

We are living in the world of presentation rather than the substance of living. Man is escaping the responsibility of humanity with the diplomacy of innocence. Hardly have we seen governance at any level obeying the principles of incorruptibility. Negotiations lack ingenuousness from dawn to dusk.

Man's power of discretion has failed to administer the human in the man. Virtuousness comes with the dreams and goes with the dreams.

Littleness is in the mind. Smallness is in the mind. Narrowness is in the mind. It is stopping the vastness of existence. A little creativeness can bring tremendous new look to the entire concept of humanity from dawn to dusk.

It takes courage to push up, push back and be creative with the gift of life. But that's exactly what building a life of your own requires. It requires you to be creative, to think outside of the ignorance box. Be innovative. Be man of will. Be man of action. Be man of words. Be man of virtues. We all have to become the guardian of hope, trust, faith and love.

Your life is yours to create and then recreate. Once you realize this, your life never is the same again. You finally achieve becoming ideal, moral, divine, valuable, and respectable and a complete human.

Learning to love yourself is the greatest love of all? This is the beginning to know the man, woman, champion, and leader in you.

That's what I've been thinking, what do you think my dear friends? Tell me, I'd love to know.

I pay tribute to the endless heroism of youth. Let us energize our entire struggle of reestablishing humanity.

I thank the World Community for their great contribution from time to time in diagnosing the epidemics in humanity.

I greet, before I go any further,

"Life is irrevocably irreversible".

Before it becomes irreparable, unattainable, irremediable, it should sincerely be directed towards humanity.

God has sent us to this beautiful garden of life to learn his creation gratifying it but never to possess it degrading the humanity of existence.

When I say this, I mean that more or less this is the universal concern we all should have to reestablish humanity.

My sincere love and good wishes will always remain with all of you. I will be happy to hear from you now and then. Our good deeds have the same frequency in the world. The vibration of humanity is felt by every human of the world wherever he is having his home in the universe.

I pray from the bottom of my heart for well being of one and all.

Finally to say,

"Man is a journey not a destination from dawn to dusk".

If I have made a single human happy today from dawn to dusk then I have lived up to my ideals.

Dr Shree Raman Dubey

Professor of Happiness

University of Humanity

Appendix A

TOOL 1:

13 T's Principle to be at TOP, is an effective tool designed by the author to resolve the issue troubling you. It is a technique of mapping the variables to arrive at a final score summarizing the scores of individual columns.

This helps you to rank your variables affecting the solution of the problem you are trying to resolve.

13 T's	Target	Task	Tools	Time	Trend	Trouble	Tackle	Team	Talent	Training	Teaching	Testing	Taming
Target	5	4	3										
Task	5	5	4										
Tools	5	5	5										
Time	5	5	5										
Trend	5	5	5										
Trouble	5	5	5										
Tackle	5	5	5										
Team	5	5	5										
Talent	5	5	5										
Training	5	5	5										
Teaching	5	5	5										
Testing	5	5	5										
Taming	5	5	5										
Score	65	64	62										

- How to work with this tool?
- Let us select the variable "Target" and it is to be matched with all the other thirteen variables target, task, tools, time, trend, trouble, tackle, team, talent, teaching, testing and training.
- Do you have a perfect target set for yourself?
- If you feel yes, then you can give the maximum rating of 5.
- Say you have targets but not specifically set then the evaluated rating may be 4.
- If more inferior then say you conclude with 3.
- If it is manageable but not satisfactory say 2.
- And finally the least 1 for whatever you have.
- This way if a variable is successfully matched with the other thirteen variables with maximum rating in all then a score of 65 is achieved under that variable.
- The highest score is ranked 1 signifying the descending order of criticality.
- The critical variable is the one with highest rank and least score.
- The next possible highest score is 64.
- This will be given 2nd rank.
- It is critical than rank 1 variable.
- Rank 3rd is more critical in nature than rank 2nd and rank 1st.
- This way the matrix is completed and a final summary of ranks is tabulated with the variables with corresponding correction actions for improvement and solutions.
- This analysis helps you to regenerate your position of solving problems in life from dawn to dusk.

13 T's	Rank	Corrective Actions	Results/Improvement
Target	13	Specific targets setting	Clear Goals
Task	10	Formulate Right Task	Vision Clear
Tools	5	Search for new tools	Increase in performance
Time	3	To find time	Good Association
Trend	1	Not critical	acceptable
Trouble	2	Not critical	No trouble
Tackle	6	Improve strategy	Confusion reduced
Team	4	Togetherness required	End results gain
Talent	9	More Learning	Skills enhancement
Training	12	Critical	Knowledge on skills
Teaching	7	Joined Institutions	Certification helped
Testing	11	Critical / Implementation phase	Success
Taming	8	Regular Practice	Part of living

- It is a very quick way of accessing the criticality of variables without complex mathematical calculations.
- It is very useful for people specifically not from the mathematical background to understand the importance of mapping.
- The above is a model based on increasing the performance of an individual with resources.
- Look at this sphere of 13 T's Principle.
- This is a template model which can be utilized to elaborate study and analyze your environment for findings, suggestions, reasoning and conclusions to improve your aspects of humanity in living from dawn to dusk.

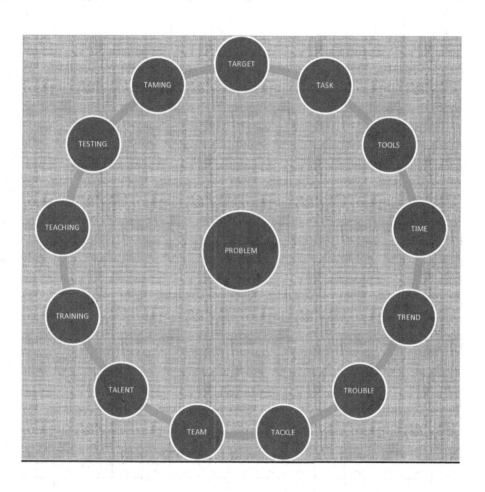

TOOL 2:

Variables	Personality	Virtues	Ethics	Integrity	Loyalty	Divinity	Purity	Faith	Trust	Hope	Love	Morality	Humanity
Personality	5	4	3										
Virtues	5	5	4										
Ethics	5	5	5										
Integrity	5	5	5										
Loyalty	5	5	5										
Divinity	5	5	5										
Purity	5	5	5										
Faith	5	5	5										
Trust	5	5	5										
Hope	5	5	5										
Love	5	5	5										
Morality	5	5	5										
Humanity	5	5	5										
Score	65	64	62										

- The tool-2 can be used to access the ranking of variables or attributes of humans.
- A man can do his own analysis.
- This is a self-analysis tool which can very easily be implemented to rank the man in you.
- The above is model with limited attributes.
- The man can examine himself and rank the levels of humanity where he stands.
- A practical approach in correcting yourself is the basis for ranking your attributes of humanity.
- Attributes which are critical in your analysis should be attended on top priority.
- This way the effectiveness of the tool can be achieved in shaping yourself as an ideal human.

Let us see 13 T's Principle applied in a different form where the problem is with central ""HUMAN", influenced and under impact with various essential and major variables to become IDEAL HUMAN.

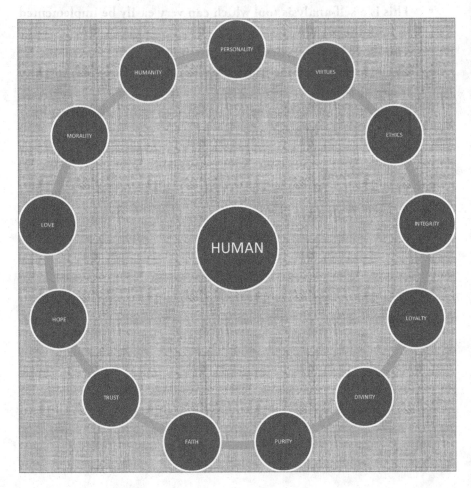

Tool 3:

You can list out points and work with it for improving yourself.

You can make a list which ponders you very frequently from dawn to dusk daily. You can start with immediate ones and later add them to work for improvement in those areas. This is a technique based on your own art of living. In fact it is words of wisdom which impacts, influences and incites your daily actions in reestablishing humanity.

Art of Living	Words of Wisdom	Improvement in Humanity
Perception	Always have yours	
Thoughts	Do not borrow it	
Confrontation	Do not try to win it	
Assumptions	Ask for it do not assume it	
Listening	Witness the orator	
Self Examine	Analyze Yourself	
Self-Managing	Measure Yourself	
Connecting People	Say to those who hear you	
Family	Nothing above this	
Friends	When time comes to help	
Work Place/Offices	Your goal	
Self-Energy/Inspiration	Your Idea	
Caring	Your hospitality	
Winning	Your Attitude	
Uncertainty	Your Approach	
Personality	Your Values	
Longevity	Your Dream	
Tenacity	Your Perseverance	
Giving	Your Gratefulness	
Ego	Cultivate positive ego	
Competition	To bring out excellence in you	
Sacrifice	Your Understanding	
Happiness	Your Bliss	
Failure	Your Attempts	
Learning	Your Lessons	

The column "Improvement in Humanity", will differ from person to person. Once the art of living is tuned and aligned with the words of wisdom a new dimension is established to your entire outlook of life.

This Tool 3 is beneficial in shaping your living from dawn to dusk. You may change the variables in art of living as you are progressing in life. All may not need attention at the same time. A good result is outcome of a practice trying to seek perfection with the tool day by day.

Tool 4:

A Case Study

Let us try to understand the basic application of 13 T's Principle with a case study. The beginning point of any chaos is the uncontrollable feature of it. The root is not known till the damage is irreparable.

Every human faces it from dawn to dusk in different intensities and impacts. The problem in all walks of life starts with a query. The art of questioning itself has all the answers to the problems.

Identifying your problem properly itself gives you invariably 75% of the solution. Then the worry is about the ranking of the attributes and how it affects your decision making.

Human Resource Management is gaining importance in developing better Human Capital all over the world. This reflects an elegant blend of art, science and culture. Humans are being groomed scientifically with a spiritual base.

The Human Outlook is changing. Humans are experiencing an era of transition. More of mathematics in the human accounting is being introduced through the performance appraisal systems. It is not that you are to be only professional efficient in material gains and productivity but equally in the morals and humanity.

With the above background let us see how this tool can help individuals to improve their problem tackling skills. Humans need to have feasible solutions to experience the peace of existence.

Recurrence of the same problem is just like straightening the dog's tail. Take help of the prevention technique rather than the maintenance concept of management. Human should at the very instant try not to err to escape correcting himself again and again.

13 T's Principle

Flow Chart

- What is the target to be achieved?
- How it is to be achieved?
- Within what time it is to be achieved?
- What is the trouble in achieving the target?
- How to tackle the trouble in achieving the target?
- Who will tackle the trouble?
- Where is the team?
- How big is the team?
- How should be the team members?
- How to form a good team?
- What type of talent is required to form a good team?
- Do the acquired talents need training?
- What type of training can be provided?
- Will the post training talent make any difference?
- Where to get the training?
- Who will teach the team to develop into a good effective talent?
- After all the homework, how to test the team?
- Where to test the team?
- Does the shortcoming in training still exist?
- If yes, then how to tame the talent for the required desired skills competency level?
- Thus a regular cycle of this flow chart keeps reviving and refining your process of problem resolving.
- The number of iterations will vary from person to person depending upon his interpretation, perception and comprehension of the findings from this principle.

Sample Problem: To get 100 marks by writing all ten questions in the exam.

Analysis: The problem can be analyzed step by step in line with the 13 T's Principle.

1. Target   : To get 100 marks.
2. Task   : To write all ten questions in exam.
3. Tools   : Pen is being used, pencil, geometry box, calculator.
4. Time   : Completion time of task is 3 hours.
5. Trend   : Moderate Writing Speed
6. Trouble : My problem is that I could not attend ten questions in the exam.
7. Tackle   : How to tackle attempting writing all the questions completely.
8. Team   : Self has to do it. Exam is not a group task. I am the team.
9. Talent   : My preparation for exam is good. My knowledge strength on the subject is good.
10. Training : Do I require any special training in writing exams.
11. Teaching : Who will teach me? From where to develop additional skills.
12. Testing : How to test my acquired abilities?
13. Taming: I practiced but could not pass the exam. Why I was not successful? What are the reasons for my failure?

A Big Goal can be broken down into small goals as individual targets say T1, T2, T3…..Tn, for macro analysis and again breaking down of T1 into T11, T12, T13….T1n, for micro analysis. Then a composite integrated analysis is studied for decision making.

Once the target and task is identified, then the technique, policy, strategy, laws and ideas as tools are to be implemented within the time frame to control the trend by steering it with your synergy of team knowhow and talent with additional training into the exercise from consultants or expertise to map the end results. Thus a proper sequence of application takes us nearer to the desired goal.

With the help of a table it can be organized to visualize the relationship matrix. The users are at liberty to represent in as many styles as they want till it is meeting the purpose of resolving the problem.

Like this model as discussed here, similar models suiting to one's need may be worked out, analyzed, tabulated and concluded with action plan for betterment of the case being studied.

We live in theory of the world more rather than by practice from dawn to dusk. Human has to practice before he can raise himself to be a true preacher.

Humans are lacking in application. This is an area the World's Education System should look into it seriously for the new world.

Keep applying yourself for changing, refining, reforming, restructuring the human in you. Then finally a dawn will be at your feet having transformed you into the ideal human.

Thus the dusk will merge with the dawn of existence forever.

Tabulation:

13 T's/ Variables	Goals/Desired	Achieved/Actual	Shortfall/ Variance	Action Plan
Target	100 Marks	60	40	To attempt all questions.
Task	10 questions	6 questions	4 questions	To attempt 100%
Tools	Pen	pen	Nil	
Time	3 hours	3hours	nil	Extra time
Trend	Moderate speed	Wrote with slow speed	Attempted less number of questions	To increase writing speed along with recalling answers
Trouble	100% Potential	50% Potential	50% Potential	To improve writing skills
Tackle	100% Ability	70% Ability	30% Ability	To increase by increasing writing skill
Team	100% Confident	70% Confident	30% Confidence	It is to be improved by honing writing skills
Talent	100% Skills	50% Skills	50% Skills	To make up the shortfall, I have to join training for improving writing skills.
Training	50%	25% by self	25% by coaching	Professional training required.
Teaching	25%	nil	100%	Critical for me.
Testing	100%	70%	30%	Training and Teaching incomplete. To undergo till variance is nil.
Taming	100%	100%	nil	Successful in my goal.

Printed in the United States
By Bookmasters